**Praise for *12 Angry Men: Reginald Rose
and the Making of an American Classic***

"Reginald Rose was one of the architects of an exciting era of powerful, socially conscious dramas using the new medium of television. Phil Rosenzweig's compelling book recounts the struggles and successes of a time that brought issues like human rights, urban poverty, abortion, and racial justice into our living rooms and daily conversations." —Glenn Frankel, author of *Shooting Midnight Cowboy: Art, Sex, Loneliness, Liberation, and the Making of a Dark Classic*

"Phil Rosenzweig's excellent book tells the story of Reginald Rose, the chief creator of two of American pop culture's most enduring law-related works—the film *12 Angry Men* and the television series *The Defenders*. More so than any other works of the mid–twentieth century, *12 Angry Men* and *The Defenders* capture both the inspiring promise and the endangered status of the proverbial rule of law." —David Ray Papke, Marquette University

"A very smart look at the influence of one particular television show and its movie version on many different, and surprising, parts of society, not only in America, but around the world." —Tom Stempel, Professor Emeritus in Film at Los Angeles City College; author of *Storytellers to the Nation: A History of American Television Writing*

"Drawing on his extensive research and years of teaching management courses, the author traces the evolution of one of the most celebrated dramas of the twentieth century in this first biography of NYC's Reginald Rose (a lead writer in the midcentury's Golden Age of Television) and study of his courtroom masterpiece championing socially conscious themes of legal justice and civil rights, . . . [T]he book is filled with fascinating information, photos, and insights into the man and his work's socio-historical context."—*DC Metro Theater Arts*

12 Angry Men

12 ANGRY MEN

Reginald Rose and the Making of an American Classic

Phil Rosenzweig

EMPIRE STATE EDITIONS

AN IMPRINT OF FORDHAM UNIVERSITY PRESS

NEW YORK   2021

The Library of Congress has cataloged the hardcover edition as follows:

Names: Rosenzweig, Phil, author.
Title: Reginald Rose and the journey of 12 angry men / Phil Rosenzweig.
Description: New York : Empire State Editions, an imprint of Fordham
    University Press, 2021. | Includes bibliographical references and index.
Identifiers: LCCN 2021027354 | ISBN 9780823297740 (hardcover) | ISBN
    9780823297757 (epub)
Subjects: LCSH: Rose, Reginald. Twelve angry men. | Rose, Reginald—Film
    adaptations. | 12 angry men (Motion picture)
Classification: LCC PS3535.O666 T9376 2021 | DDC 812/.54—dc23
LC record available at https://lccn.loc.gov/2021027354

Printed in the United States of America

23 22 21   5 4 3 2 1

First edition

To our next generation:
Lauren, David, Greg,
Elise, Tom, Caroline

CONTENTS

Reginald Rose and the Journey
of *12 Angry Men*

INTRODUCTION

THE WEEK BEFORE EASTER 1957, eight feature films opened in New York City, a typical week in an era when Hollywood turned out more than three hundred movies a year.

They would have to compete for attention with several dozen showing at scores of theaters across the city. The box office leaders were Cecil B. DeMille's *The Ten Commandments* and Mike Todd's *Around the World in 80 Days*, big-budget extravaganzas, filmed in vivid color and projected in widescreen, and still drawing large crowds since their release in late 1956.[1] The most popular movie of the new year was *Funny Face*, with Fred Astaire and Audrey Hepburn dancing in elegant costumes on lavish sets. The eight new releases would enjoy only a brief moment of attention before a next wave arrived for the Easter weekend, led by *The Spirit of St. Louis* with James Stewart as aviator Charles Lindbergh, plus *Boy on a Dolphin*, the English-language debut of a dazzling new actress, Sophia Loren.[2]

The new movies were a mix of adventure and westerns and romance, from major studios and second-tier producers. They would reach the cinemas a few at a time, one on Monday, two on Wednesday, and four on Friday. The last one would open on Saturday, the worst possible day, since newspaper reviews would come too late to boost weekend attendance. It was called *12 Angry Men*.

The star of *12 Angry Men* was Henry Fonda, one of America's most admired actors, but otherwise the movie didn't have much going for it. The story, about a jury's deliberation in a murder case, was downbeat. The

1

director, Sidney Lumet, was a thirty-two-year-old making his feature debut. Shot in black and white, the action consisted of a dozen men arguing in a single, dingy room. There was little to excite an audience: no romance, no comedy, no fancy costumes, and no exotic locations.

The movie had been produced by Fonda and the screenwriter, Reginald Rose, with financing from United Artists. Wary about its commercial prospects, the studio limited the cash outlay to just four hundred thousand dollars, forcing Fonda to defer his entire fee. Filming took place over four weeks in the summer of 1956 on a soundstage at Fox Movietone Studios, on Tenth Avenue at the edge of Hell's Kitchen in Manhattan. When they were done, the cast and crew quickly moved on to other projects. No one imagined they had created anything special.

Leading up to the April 1957 release, United Artists tried to drum up interest by getting articles into newspapers and magazines. Still photographs from the movie elicited little interest. The studio's publicity firm was blunt: "THE BIG VISUAL PROBLEM is how many layouts you can get from 12 men in one room."[3]

When 12 Angry Men opened at the Capitol, an opulent movie palace just off Times Square, results were disappointing, Fonda recalling that the audience "barely filled the first four or five rows."[4] After three weeks of modest attendance it was replaced by a movie with greater appeal: The Little Hut, a comedy love triangle with Ava Gardner, Stewart Granger, and David Niven as castaways on a tropical isle. Posters showed a scantily clad Miss Gardner leaning against a palm tree with the caption: "MGM presents a saucy comedy in BLUSHING COLOR."[5]

In city after city, the story was the same: 12 Angry Men played to small audiences and was soon pushed aside. By the middle of May it had all but disappeared from first-run theaters, and at year end, revenues were barely enough to crack the top one hundred. By any commercial measure, the movie was a flop.

Even so, critics had taken note. The New York Times praised 12 Angry Men as a "taut, absorbing, and compelling drama," and Variety called the acting "the best seen recently in any single film."[6] In December, it was named one of 1957's ten best movies by more than a dozen publications, including the New York Times, New York Journal-American, Daily Mirror, and Saturday Review.[7] More good news arrived in February 1958 with Academy Award nominations for Best Picture, Best Director, and Best Adapted Screenplay. For a few weeks, the producers hoped that success at the Oscars might lead to a second release and better revenues. Alas, it was not to be. When the envelopes were opened, 12 Angry Men lost in all three categories to the year's biggest hit, *The Bridge on the River Kwai*, another big-budget spectacle, shot on location in the jungles of Asia with a cast of hundreds, in brilliant Technicolor, and filmed and projected in CinemaScope.

From there, *12 Angry Men* dropped out of sight. Three years would pass before a trickle of domestic revenues, boosted by foreign receipts, covered its costs. Henry Fonda found the experience so unpleasant that he never produced another movie.

TODAY THE STORY IS entirely different. *12 Angry Men* is revered as one of America's greatest motion pictures. It is admired by critics, recognized by the American Film Institute as one of the one hundred best American movies, a list headed by *Citizen Kane*, *The Godfather*, and *Casablanca*. It is also beloved by the public, ranked by IMDb, the Internet Movie Database, as the fifth highest rated movie of all time, ahead of *Schindler's List*, *Lord of the Rings*, and *Pulp Fiction*.[8]

It is also an important movie, used to teach civics in high schools, to illustrate points of criminal justice in law schools, and to shed light on group dynamics and interpersonal behavior in management courses. The image of Henry Fonda as Juror 8, the lone dissenter standing courageously against prejudice, has become iconic, instantly recognizable and found in everything from serious tributes to humorous parodies.

12 ANGRY MEN IS SOMETIMES described as a Henry Fonda movie directed by Sidney Lumet, and other times as a Sidney Lumet movie starring Henry Fonda. That's not surprising, as directors and actors usually receive the most attention, but it's unfortunate. Above all, *12 Angry Men* reflects the vision and values of its author.

Reginald Rose was a leading writer in what would come to be known as the Golden Age of Television, that brief span in the early 1950s when a new medium was bursting with creative energy, before commercial forces led to the raft of game shows, insipid comedies, and cookie-cutter westerns that caused FCC chairman Newton Minow in 1961 to describe network television as a "vast wasteland."

In those early years, when established playwrights and Hollywood screenwriters had little interest in television, the doors were flung open for a new generation, eager to seize an opportunity. Of the many good young writers, the very best of them—the "Mount Rushmore of live television writing" according to Ron Simon, curator of the Paley Center for Media—were Paddy Chayefsky, Rod Serling, and Reginald Rose.[9]

Paddy Chayefsky was the first television writer to achieve widespread acclaim. He wrote about the lives of everyday people, displaying a fine ear for dialogue and an innate understanding of the power of the small screen in teleplays like "Holiday Song," "Printer's Measure," and most famously, "Marty." After great success as a television dramatist in the 1950s, he returned to prominence in the 1970s as a screenwriter, winning Academy Awards for *The Hospital* and for his greatest achievement, *Network*. Brilliant and original, Chayefsky was also notoriously temperamental, known for quarreling with producers and ready to take offense at perceived slights.

Rod Serling was a prolific writer whose stories ranged from combat and corruption to tales of the supernatural. After his breakthrough with "Patterns," a story about ambition and power, Serling wrote for the last great live anthology, *Playhouse 90*, winning Emmys for "Requiem for a Heavyweight" and "The Comedian," two of the finest television dramas ever made. Visionary, intense, and proud, he frequently clashed with censors. In the late 1950s he moved to Hollywood and created *The Twilight Zone*, an imaginative program that has been endlessly syndicated, making Serling, who introduced each episode in his precise diction and clipped cadence, as famous as the series.

Next to these outsize characters, Reginald Rose is much less known. In part, that's because he stayed longer in live television, where performances were captured, if at all, on a kinescope, a crude device that filmed the cathode ray screen but was not suitable for rebroadcast. (A complete kinescope of the original performance of "Twelve Angry Men" was located only in 2003; for years the Paley Center had only the first half, referred to by staff members as "Six Angry Men.") Moreover, fewer of Rose's plays were made into motion pictures, and his later television work has not been widely syndicated. Ironically, the writer who stayed longest in television left behind less material to be watched by future generations.

Rose is less known, too, because he did so little to attract attention to himself. He presented himself as a reasonable and even-tempered man, generally pleasant and affable, and not prone to histrionics or displays of temper. What secures Rose's status as a top television writer is not only his skill as a dramatist but his willingness to explore themes of social importance. For a dozen years, from 1953 to 1965, he consistently took up vital issues of the day and made them accessible to a wide audience. While the networks were pushing for mass entertainment, Rose refused to appeal to the lowest common denominator, explaining that "the blithe assertion that 'entertainment' is incompatible with high and valuable purpose is incomprehensible to me."[10] He wanted to write plays that "might cause people to sit around their living rooms and talk and think."[11]

Rose's concern with social justice was apparent from his first original drama for CBS's *Westinghouse Studio One*, when he broached an ambitious theme: collective responsibility and man's inhumanity to man. For the next four years, he addressed topics ranging from prejudice to civil liberties to mob violence in a series of superb teleplays. As the age of live television wound down, Rose wrote "The Cruel Day," about the use of torture in French Algeria, and "Black Monday," about school desegregation. He also wrote "The Sacco-Vanzetti Story," a two-part teleplay about the trial and execution of two Italian Americans in the 1920s, a *cause célèbre* and miscarriage of justice.

As the days of anthology television ended, Rose took on the most demanding project of his career, collaborating with Herb Brodkin on *The Defenders*, a weekly dramatic series about a father-and-son legal team. For most of the four-year run, from 1961 to 1965, Rose was the story supervisor, writing many episodes of *The Defenders* himself and overseeing a team of writers and editors for the rest, delivering a one-hour drama every week, 132 in all, on topics from mercy killings to free speech, from censorship to civil disobedience, from the insanity defense to the blacklist. The top drama of its era, *The Defenders* won thirteen Emmys, including three in a row for Best Dramatic Series. Bob Markell, a close collaborator on the series, said that it stood for "emotional truth and a sense of fighting injustice. There was really a caring about justice and injustice. Sometimes it was almost a cry."[12]

After *The Defenders*, Rose spent the next decades writing stage plays, movie screenplays, and television miniseries. Some were successful and others less so, but none could match the growing fame of *12 Angry Men*. By the time he died in 2002, at age eighty-one, Reginald Rose's jury room drama overshadowed the rest of his achievements. In its obituary, the *New York Times* described Rose simply as a "TV Writer noted for *12 Angry Men*," devoting most of the article to that single work, and with barely two paragraphs to the rest of his long and productive career.[13]

THIS BOOK TELLS TWO STORIES: the life of a great television writer and the journey of his most famous work.

The first is long overdue. While his more famous contemporaries have been the subject of full-length biographies, which dwell as much on their personalities as on their work—Paddy Chayefsky described as "the angriest man in television" and "the man who was mad as hell," and Rod Serling as "TV's last angry man"—Reginald Rose has remained less well known to the general public. It's time to bring Rose's long and successful career, its origins and its accomplishments, into view.

Sidney Lumet once said of Rose: "He tended toward a bit of sentimentality because his belief was so intense. He so believed that people were good."[14] It would be more accurate to say that he believed people *can* be good when a society's institutions function effectively. Rose was less a believer in the innate goodness of people than in the need to create the circumstances that bring out their best. He agreed with James Madison that because men are not angels, laws are needed to ensure that rights are observed and liberties protected.[15] He was a liberal in the true sense of the word who embraced its core tenets: "free speech, rule of law, scientific inquiry and individual conscience."[16]

What led this man to become so committed to topics of justice and civil liberties? Part of the answer lies in the political climate of the 1950s. Rose would later remark: "In a way, almost everything I wrote in the fifties was about McCarthy." That's true enough, if "McCarthy" is taken to mean not just political inquisitions but a broader concern about justice, but it invites a larger question. Every television writer in the early 1950s grew up in the same political climate, and many of them shared Rose's liberal sentiments. What made *this* man, more than any other writer of that era, so acutely concerned with questions of justice? Why did Reginald Rose, rather than another writer, become a champion of the powerless and marginalized, once saying that "Issues that bother me are issues concerning people who want to impose their beliefs on others"?[17]

The story of Rose's career has not been told before, and some of the elements that *have* been told, including by Rose himself, are of questionable accuracy. A good dramatist knows how to eliminate the unnecessary, how to excise characters and scenes that are extraneous, and at times Rose did just that, describing important events of his life with lines that are straighter and simpler than might be the whole truth. This book aims to tell the full story for the first time, to map the course of his career and reveal the man behind it.

THIS IS ALSO THE STORY of Rose's most famous work, set in the context of its time. It traces the journey of *12 Angry Men* from the chance experience that served as his inspiration, to early drafts in which characters and dialogue took shape, to its performance on *Studio One* in 1954. While Rose focused on writing original dramas for CBS, discussions between Henry Fonda and United Artists led to a movie deal. We follow Rose through various drafts of the movie screenplay, with scenes added and deleted, to Sidney Lumet's casting, which overcame the sudden death of one actor, and his collaboration with cinematographer Boris Kaufman, culminating in filming over four weeks in June and July 1956. We see, as well, how a movie that fared poorly on its release has gone on to become so respected and beloved around the world.

Some misconceptions are corrected along the way. Rose often said that *12 Angry Men* was inspired by his jury duty in 1954, but research conducted at the New York City Courts and drawing on the Manhattan district attorney homicide files suggests that the true story about Rose's jury experience differs in an important way from the one he usually told. It has often been stated that Henry Fonda had the idea to make a movie of *12 Angry Men*, but unable to get studio support, he put up his own money to finance the picture. That turns out not to be true. Or that Sidney Lumet got his chance because, as a first-time director, he was an inexpensive option, a plausible claim but not correct. I will also shed light on how the script developed, with much of the final screenplay present from the very first outline, but many other important elements taking shape over the course of several revisions: names dropped, motivations expanded, scenes added, dialogue extended, and perhaps most significantly, the ending changed several times, with Rose settling on the shattering climax only days before filming began.

My aim is not, however, to set the record straight or to uncover details for their own sake. Above all, it is to tell the story of a remarkable writer and courageous man, working in a new medium and in turbulent times, and about the great drama he created.

PART I

ORIGINS

1

░░░

Dreams of a Writer

THE WAY FROM NORFOLK STREET in Manhattan's Lower East Side to 113th Street in Harlem can be measured in distance, about seven miles or 120 city blocks. It can also be measured in the time taken by immigrants to move from crowded tenements downtown to the relative comfort of uptown.

For the ancestors of Reginald Rose, that journey took forty-five years and two generations. It began in 1865, with the arrival of William and Berthe Rosenthal and their five young children, one family among countless others from Central and Eastern Europe who passed through Governors Island at the end of the Civil War. Three more children were born in the next few years, so that the census of 1870 shows a family of ten, living in two bedrooms at 5 Norfolk Street, at the corner of Grand Street. Their neighbors were also Jews from Germany and Poland, with names like Hellman, Obermyer, Stern, Cohen, Rosenberg, Gerechter, and Schick; the heads of household were working in the needle trade as tailors and milliners, or making a living as peddlers and grocers, clerks and barbers, or tin smiths and brass finishers.

The 1870s were a decade of massive immigration, transforming the Lower East Side into the most densely populated area of New York City, with dire living conditions and poor sanitation leading to frequent outbreaks of infectious disease.[1] Like many families, the Rosenthals supplemented their income by taking in boarders, often single men saving money to bring their relatives from the old country. By 1880, the family had moved two blocks south to a tenement at 179 East Broadway, on the other side of what is now Seward Park. The oldest children had left home but there was a new arrival, a ninth child named Hannah. The 1880 census lists William as employed at a wine and liquor store. The oldest child still at home, Isaac, age sixteen, worked as a cigar maker; next was Alexander, age fifteen, listed as a student and destined for a better lot in life.

As families saved money they began to move from the Lower East Side, aided by bridges and subways that opened in the last decades of the nineteenth century. Soon there were Jewish neighborhoods in the Williamsburg and Brownsville sections of Brooklyn, followed by a "colony" of Eastern European Jews along Lexington Avenue between Seventy-Second Street and One Hundredth Street in the Upper East Side.[2]

Alexander Rosenthal, the middle child of William and Berthe's nine, completed his studies and became a lawyer. He did well socially, too, marrying Regina Hast, the daughter of a rabbi who gave birth to two sons: William, in 1892, and Sidney, in 1899. The 1900 census shows the young family living with Regina's parents and her four younger brothers at 405 East Fifty-Seventh Street, near First Avenue. A cantor lodged with the family, bringing to eleven the number of people in a single unit, but for Alexander Rosenthal, a lawyer married to a rabbi's daughter and no longer in the Lower East Side, it was a big step up.

Another community developed farther uptown, in Harlem north of 100th Street, an area described by the newspaper *Forward* as "a Jewish city, inhabited by tens of thousands of Jews."[3] Soon the area east of Lenox Avenue, toward the Harlem River, rivaled the bleak conditions of the Lower East Side. West of Lenox Avenue, however, toward 7th Avenue and beyond, was a much more prosperous enclave with spacious private dwellings.[4] Here, at 237 West 113th Street, Alexander and Regina Rosenthal made their home. (Harry Houdini, one of the most famous showmen in the land, lived a few doors away, at 278 West 113th Street.) The 1910 census lists Alexander, forty-four, as head of a household that included nine people: Regina, her parents, sons William, now seventeen, and Sidney, ten, plus two servants and a lodger. In a single generation, Alexander had gone from one of nine children in a Lower East Side tenement to the head of a family with two children, living in what Irving Howe described as an "aristocratic Jewish neighborhood."[5] His father had been a merchant who took in boarders; Alexander was a lawyer who could afford servants.

By 1920, the family still lived at 237 West 113th Street but now their name was Rose. Surnames were shortened for a variety of reasons: to avoid the stigma of German ancestry after World War I, to remove a Jewish association and assimilate in broader society, or for simplicity. Six family members lived together: Alexander and Regina, now fifty-three and fifty, her elderly parents, and sons William and Sidney, plus a servant girl. William, a graduate of Columbia Law School, and his father were general practice lawyers.[6]

On March 8, 1920, William Rose, twenty-seven, married Alice Oberdorfer, twenty-four. Alice's family had followed a similar path, beginning with the arrival of a Jewish merchant named Isaac Oberdorfer in the 1860s. (Over the years, the family name was variously spelled as Oberdorfer, Obendorfer, or Oberndorfer.) One of his sons, Adolph, married Regina Jonas, called Jennie, in 1894; within a year Jennie Oberdorfer gave birth to a daughter, Alice, and then a second one, Edith. The marriage did not last, and by 1900, Jennie was raising two daughters on her own, at first on East 74th Street and later at 317 West 112th Street, where she made ends meet by taking in seven boarders. The address suggests the better neighborhood of Harlem, but with ten people in the unit, living conditions were very crowded. After her marriage to William, Alice moved in with his family on West 113th Street. Nine months and two days later, on December 10, 1920, Alice gave birth to a son. With two grandmothers named Regina, what name was possible other than Reginald?

IN 2000, AS HE APPROACHED his eightieth birthday, Reginald Rose published a volume of memoirs, *Undelivered Mail*, written as a series of letters to long-lost friends from his last year of high school. Included among the letters are various clues about his early years.

As Rose tells it, he went to kindergarten three blocks from the family home, at PS 10 at 116th Street and St. Nicholas Ave.[7] In 1927, his parents' marriage broke up. "Father divorced her when I was six," he wrote. "After the divorce he went and hid in a bottle of rye until he died, some thirty-odd years later. I remember him only as a small, whining man in an immaculate pearl grey fedora and matching spats."[8] Rose's memoirs make no further mention of his father, the lack of any meaningful contact confirmed by his son, Jonathan, who said: "He really had no relationship with his father." There was some contact with relatives, mostly aunts and uncles on his mother's side, but for the most part he was raised by his single mother.

After the divorce, Alice Oberdorfer Rose found work as a stenographer, and for the next eight years, her son recalled: "My mother struggled like hell to raise me, working in dreary thankless jobs, and living a generally lousy lonely life, aided not in the least by my father."[9] By 1930, Alice and nine-year-old Reggie lived in a boarding house at 308 West Ninety-Third

Street, between West End and Riverside Drive. (The 1930 census also shows William Rose, thirty-seven, living with his father, Alexander, sixty-four, and younger brother Sidney, at 50 West Seventy-Seventh Street, the father and son listed as self-employed lawyers.)

For middle school, Reggie Rose attended PS 166, an imposing structure on West Eighty-Ninth Street, built in the Collegiate Gothic style with tall gables and cathedral windows. A sculptured façade led into a spacious entrance hall with soaring ceilings and an impressive staircase. Rose's eighth-grade class reflected the ethnic mix of the Upper West Side, described as half Irish and half Jewish. "In our cozy, racially mixed neighborhood," he recalled, "there was no place for religious hatred."[10]

Rose was a voracious reader from an early age. He loved Ernest Hemingway, admiring Hemingway's meticulous style and economical phrasing, and was especially inspired by the Nick Adams stories.[11] Another favorite was James T. Farrell's *Studs Lonigan* trilogy—*Young Lonigan* (1932), *The Young Manhood of Studs Lonigan* (1934), and *Judgment Day* (1935)—set in Irish Catholic neighborhoods on Chicago's South Side from 1916 to the Great Depression. *Studs Lonigan* described in searing detail the life of a young man, torn between the expectations of his immigrant Catholic parents and the temptations of pool rooms, drinking and gambling, and illicit sex. It was written in what Rose would later describe as "languages and images forbidden in the novels of the early thirties" that "set new standards for realism in literature as did [Eugene] O'Neill's early work in theatre."[12] Many of the themes that Rose explored in later years, from tough street kids to conflicts between parents and children, can be found in *Studs Lonigan*.

He also took an interest in writing, recalling years later: "I started seriously when I was 10. I mean really seriously."[13] Soon he was crafting his own stories, sometimes under the covers at night, writing by flashlight.

By his recollection, Reggie was a good student but not among the best. Toward the end of eighth grade, he was one of a handful invited to take the entrance exam for Townsend Harris High School, a "special school for bright boys" that offered an accelerated program for high achievers. Every year, 140 boys from across New York City were admitted into a rigorous curriculum that let them graduate in three years rather than four, the aim to get "bright boys into college a year earlier."[14] Rose writes that he agreed to take the test because it let him skip regular lessons for a day. But pass he did, and in the autumn of 1934, not yet fourteen years old, Reggie Rose began the ninth grade at Townsend Harris.

For the next three years he attended school on the top three floors of a massive structure at Lexington Avenue and Twenty-Third Street.[15] Rose described his days at Townsend Harris as "six hours of daily death endured," surrounded by "infant prodigies" with whom he had little in common.[16] History was taught as "a collection of dates without flesh or color, to be stored in my memory and left unattached to the humanity which made them memorable."[17] The place had all the joys of a Dickensian factory: "Suck them in, cram them full of the essential facts at an accelerated pace and fling them out, still children, stunned with knowledge, never once exposed to ideas. There was no time for ideas. No time for questioning. No time for the beauty of discovery."[18]

Not long after Reggie turned fourteen, his mother remarried. Alice's new husband was Leonard David Engel, born in 1888 in Baltimore, and by 1915 living with his parents at 610 West 150th Street in Manhattan, working as a cigar salesman. After the United States entered World War I, he was inducted into military service and sailed for Europe in January 1918 with the American Expeditionary Force. By 1930, at age forty-one, Engel lived with his widowed father at 324 West 107th Street. He enjoyed music, and at a concert he met Alice Oberdorfer Rose. It was a good match, a bachelor of forty-six and a single mother of thirty-eight. They were married on January 26, 1935, and after a brief honeymoon, the family of three took up residence at 41 West 86th Street.

Engel sold Dictaphone equipment and was paid mostly on commissions, and although the family was never well off, their combined income allowed them to move into Franklin Towers, a twenty-story building at 333 West Eighty-Sixth Street, between Riverside Drive and West End Drive. Opened with great fanfare in 1927, Franklin Towers was an apartment hotel, with an elegant lobby and two ballrooms, that offered residents once-a-week maid service. The family apartment had two bedrooms and two baths; the separate baths were a special source of pride for Alice. Life was incomparably better than in the crowded homes of her youth or in the boarding house where she had raised her son. Still, life during the Depression was precarious, and Rose recalled his mother exhaling with satisfaction each month when the rent could be paid.

In *Undelivered Mail*, Rose writes respectfully but not intimately about his stepfather. He knew only the broad outlines of Leonard Engel's life— that he hailed from Maryland and had served in World War I—but did not know his stepfather's exact age, only that he was quite a bit older than Alice. Reggie describes Engel as sober, earnest, and reliable. He was no fan of Franklin D. Roosevelt, but aside from occasional grumbling about the New Deal there was little talk about politics.[19] Engel was a practicing Christian Scientist, and Alice was a member of the Ethical Culture Society, but otherwise religion was largely absent from the household.[20] At one point his mother asked if Reggie wanted a bar mitzvah, but he said no; religion held little interest.[21]

Other than weekly bridge nights, the couple stayed close to home. Rose would recall: "From 1935, when my mother and stepfather were married and sailed to Bermuda on a seven-day honeymoon, until 1959 when my stepfather died, my parents never travelled anywhere which required an overnight stay except for one weekend, September 1937, when my step-father won the New York Salesman of the month award at the Dictaphone Corp., and the all-expenses paid weekend at the Hotel Traymore in Atlantic City that went with it. They were never able, in twenty-four years of marriage, to afford a trip on their own."[22]

After years of struggling as a single mother, Alice was satisfied with a reliable husband who provided financial stability and companionship. Much later, Rose remembered Leonard Engel with appreciation, describing him as a "hard-working, honest man who was willing until I was able to manage on my own, to be responsible for me. And that was one hell of a gift, eternally unrepayable, given without complaint and received, I find myself ashamed to say, oft-times grudgingly."[23]

WHILE REGGIE ROSE WENT to high school at Lexington Avenue and 23rd Street, the center of his life remained the Upper West Side, that large rectangle bounded by Riverside Drive to the west and Central Park West to the east, and from 72nd Street to 110th Street. Farther south were the tenements later cleared for Lincoln Center, and beyond that the rough neighborhoods of Hell's Kitchen. North of 100th Street was Harlem, by the 1930s home to a growing Black population arriving in the Great Migration.

The main commercial district ran along Broadway between Eighty-Fifth Street and Eighty-Ninth Street and included Reggie's favorite delicatessen, the Tip Toe Inn, at the corner of Broadway and Eighty-Sixth Street, next to Schulte's cigar store and Perla's pharmacy. One flight up was Hon Young's, the only Chinese restaurant in the neighborhood. The closest movie houses were Loew's at Broadway and Eighty-Third Street, a converted vaudeville house called the Riverside at Broadway and Ninety-Sixth Street, and Loew's Lincoln Square at Broadway and Sixty-Sixth Street. High school held less interest than card games with his pals, getting to know neighborhood girls in varying degrees of intimacy, and following the New York Giants and their star players, Mel Ott, Carl Hubbell, and Jo-Jo Moore. On a few occasions Reggie went with friends to jazz joints on Fifty-Second Street, the Hickory House and Kelly's Stables, where they listened to Charlie Christian on guitar and Chick Webb on drums.

Through it all, writing was a constant interest. Levy's Stationery store held a magical spell: "I could buy a ream of yellow paper there, 500 virgin sheets for fifty cents."[24] Blank paper held endless possibilities: "Five hundred sheets of yellow paper 8½ by 11, unwrapped as soon as I arrived home, and dreamed over, and I remembered the thrill, the joy of anticipation, the hopes I had for those five hundred blank, canary-yellow pages. Surely they would see great work, brilliant short stories, triumphant plays, the definitive American novel; the Pulitzer Prize was waiting to be won in those pages, perhaps even the Nobel Prize for literature."[25] One day, Rose dreamed, he might "sell a short story to *Collier's* magazine or to *Esquire* or to, miraculously, *The New Yorker*, and rocket myself into a dazzling literary career."[26] In more sober moments he expected to share the fate of most adults he knew: "A job in an office, naturally. That was as far as my plans for my future went."[27]

IN THE 1950S, ROSE WOULD become known for television dramas about social justice, but his memoirs reveal little concern about current affairs, whether unemployment during the Depression or the rise of Fascism in Europe. Rose may have enjoyed listening to jazz on Fifty-Second Street but did not recall any reflections about race relations. Nor does he describe traveling anywhere outside New York City. There is no mention of hitchhiking to New England, riding the rails to Washington, DC, or lighting out West, nor, like some of his peers, of dreams of joining the Abraham Lincoln Battalion to fight Fascists in Spain.

On May 30, 1937, Reggie and some friends watched a Memorial Day parade. A few very elderly Civil War veterans rode at the front in open cars, followed by combatants of the 1898 Spanish-American War, and finally veterans of World War I, just entering middle age. A few of the more prescient youths might have sensed that they, too, would soon be swept up in a war, but Rose, at sixteen, did not record any such feelings.[28]

A month later, on June 22, Rose graduated from Townsend Harris High School. After three indifferent years, the ceremony held little interest. "I wasn't sure what was more important," he recalled, "getting to graduation on time or getting home to listen to the heavyweight title fight." Joe Louis was about to take on the champion, James J. Braddock, with the action to be broadcast live on the radio. Reggie's heart as well as his money were for Louis: he had offered five-to-three odds to a friend, betting a quarter against fifteen cents.[29] "If I was going to lose a quarter," he recalled, "I wanted to hear it blow by bloody blow."[30]

The ceremony featured an address by a former principal of Townsend Harris who lectured the boys about "the responsibility of the extra-bright

to a depression-dazed America." "That was me he meant," Rose later reflected. "I sat there hoping depression-dazed America wouldn't expect
miracles of me right way. I couldn't even begin to oblige until after the
fight. Joe Louis was getting his hands taped by now and I was nervous as
hell."[31] Racing home, Reggie turned on the family Philco, a large console
with push-button controls ("No stoop, no squat, no strain") to hear Louis
win in the eighth round, marking the happy conclusion of his high school
career.[32] By then he was ready to move on: "I felt no sense of accom-
plishment anyway, merely relief that the dreary corridors and stagnant
classrooms and sad dying teachers were behind me for all time. Thus high
school disappeared from my life with neither fanfare nor regrets."[33]

GRADUATES OF TOWNSEND HARRIS were automatically granted entry to
the City College of New York (CCNY), most of them enrolling at the main
campus in Upper Manhattan. Some of Reggie's mother's relatives owned
a company that manufactured ribbons and notions, and thinking that Reggie would make a good manager, agreed to pay the tuition fee for him to
attend CCNY's School of Business and Civic Administration, located in the
same building as his high school at Lexington and Twenty-Third Street.

For two semesters, fall 1937 and spring 1938, he took courses in economics and mathematics.[34] After that single year, he dropped out.[35] One
reason was financial. In a 1967 interview he put it bluntly: "The money ran
out. It was the head of the depression."[36] His son suggests another reason:
"He just wasn't interested in going to school to become a businessman. It
wasn't for him."[37] Instead, he went to work.

Rose's memoirs describe a first job, paying ten dollars a week, at the
company where his mother worked as a stenographer, S. Leibovitz & Sons,
a manufacturer of shirts and pajamas located on Leonard Street between
Broadway and Hudson in Lower Manhattan.[38] Every morning, mother and
son boarded the Seventh Avenue subway at Broadway and Eighty-Sixth
and headed to the factory in a grimy industrial area, where they worked
in a cluttered space on the second floor, barely thirty feet apart but with
no contact throughout the day.[39] As an inventory clerk, Rose kept track
of each completed order—this many shirts of one size and color, and that
many shirts of another size and color—to maintain a list of stock on hand.[40]
"Do I have to explain how vastly boring the work became after the first
few hours of the first day?" he recalled. "Subtracting twelfths of dozens for
eight-and-a-half hours every day, five days a week. I couldn't bear that job,
but I couldn't leave it. The ten dollars a week was just too important."[41]
Four dollars went to his stepfather, who no longer had to dole out a weekly

allowance of three dollars, the net difference of seven dollars a week "a considerable dividend to a family living treacherously close to the edge." Reggie kept the other six dollars, twice his previous allowance: "For the time being that was sheer luxury."[42]

As Rose tells it, he spent the next couple of years at a series of low-paid jobs, mostly involving clerical duties of one kind or another. All the while, he continued to write: "I wanted, yearned to be a writer, and had taken the first, tottering steps. I was working on a short story which, when finished, would be submitted to *Collier's* magazine, and if rejected to the *Saturday Evening Post* and *The New Yorker* and *Esquire*."[43] Mailing out stories was not a trivial expense, each submission calling for two nine-by-twelve-inch manila envelopes that cost three cents apiece, plus sixteen cents for stamps. Adding the cost of paper, typing ribbon, and carbon paper, Rose estimated the cost at twenty-five cents per story, "almost the price of two lunches." Sometimes he would forgo lunch to send out his stories.[44]

Returning each day to Franklin Towers, Rose would ask the front-desk clerk, Mr. Fitzgibbons, to check mailbox 910. "The mail was a monumentally important element in my life then," he recalled. "It might contain, and I would be treacherously close to embracing God if it did, a check from one of the magazines to which I'd sent my short stories."[45] No acceptance letter ever came: "There was no check, ever, only a depressing, endless stream of rejection slips." One high school friend, Barney Clayton, read the draft of a radio play and offered encouragement: "I could never do this, write like this, invent people and stories. But you can do it, you are doing it, and you should keep on doing it, because I'll bet you ten bucks right now that some smart son of a bitch will notice you sooner or later and you'll wind up doing it for the rest of your life. Don't let the bastards wear you down."[46]

As he reached his twentieth birthday, Rose still lived with his parents at Franklin Towers, the 1940 census listing Leonard Engel, fifty-one, salesman of office appliances; Alice, forty-four, stenographer; and Reginald, nineteen, a "ribbon clerk," the general term for office help. Annual income was $4,745: Mr. Engel earning $2,542, Mrs. Engel $1,428, and Reginald contributing $775, or about $15 per week.

The following year, now four years out of high school, Rose moved into his own lodgings, a furnished room with a shared bath at Broadway and Eighty-Eighth Street.[47] He had a better job, joining the New York City publicity department of Warner Bros., working out of their offices on West Eighteenth Street. He was also becoming interested in a girl he had met at a local youth group. Barbara Langbart, two years younger than Reggie, lived with her mother and grandmother. She had graduated from Walton

High School in the Bronx, an all-girls school known for its strong academic program, and was accepted at Cornell but her mother would not let her enroll, so she got a job instead. Jonathan Rose describes a picture in a family album of the young couple courting in Central Park: Reggie with his fair hair swept up and Barbara with bobbed hair and dark features, "like a Mediterranean princess, she was glorious looking."[48]

THE ATTACK ON PEARL HARBOR, December 7, 1941, took place three days before Reginald Rose turned twenty-one. He enlisted in the armed forces and spent the next four years in the military, rising to first lieutenant. Military service was a broadening experience, as Rose went to several regions of the country and met a wide range of people. It also provided inspiration for his later work. In a 1962 interview with the *New York Herald Tribune*, Rose said: "I spent a total of a year in Alabama, Mississippi, Georgia, and northern Florida during the last war. I can't tell you which was worse. I also spent some time in Virginia at an Officer Candidate School. I spent a year in southern Indiana, which is like being in the south, and at Fort Devens in Massachusetts I trained a company of Negro troops from South Carolina. They were youngsters, eighteen and nineteen. They told me the terrible story of what it is like to be a Negro in the South."[49] The *Herald Tribune* reporter described how Rose, normally even-tempered, became visibly bitter as he recalled the day his officer class traveled by train from Richmond, Virginia: "Thirty-two of the new second lieutenants were white and one was a Negro. The Negro could not sit with his white comrades as they waited for the train. He had to go to a separate waiting room."[50] These experiences moved him deeply and found expression a decade later in television plays about racial prejudice and injustice.

In September 1943, Rose, not yet twenty-three but a commissioned officer, was granted a furlough to return to New York and marry Barbara Langbart, who had just turned twenty-one. She lived with him briefly on an Army base until he was billeted to the Pacific, where he spent a year in the Philippines and Japan.[51]

After his discharge from the Army, Rose returned to New York and resumed work at Warner Bros. With housing scarce, the young couple initially lived with Barbara's mother and grandmother in their one-bedroom apartment at 175 West Ninety-Third Street. Soon they found lodgings on the Upper East Side and moved into a small apartment at 134 East Eighty-Second Street, on the corner of Lexington Avenue, above a veterinarian. In October 1949, they welcomed a son, Jonathan.

After three years at Warner Bros., and very likely thanks to a reference from one of Barbara's relatives, Rose joined a small advertising company that specialized in men's and women's wear.[52] The Ray Austrian Advertising Agency, with offices on East Thirty-Fourth Street, was one of countless small agencies near Madison Avenue. Years later, after he was established as a television writer, Rose could look back with bemusement at the concerns that occupied copywriters. One story summed up his experience: "I remember with great clarity three sterile days spent trying to name a new brassiere developed by one of our clients. Toward the close of the third day I leaped to my feet with what I felt to be divine inspiration. I had the name! Into the office of the agency president I raced (this is possible in small agencies) and stood proudly before him. 'The name of the brassiere is . . . Upsa-Daisy,' I said. He looked at me for a moment. Then he spoke: 'By God, boy, you have got a flair for this business.'"[53]

By 1951, the family of three moved back to their familiar neighborhood in the Upper West Side, renting a small apartment at 147 West Seventy-Ninth Street. Rose worked at the ad agency by day, but still harbored dreams of writing fiction. By this time, he estimated that he had penned more than one hundred short stories, several plays, and the first half of three novels. He had not sold any. Frequently he was discouraged: "I'd question my talent. And as soon as I'd finish that, I'd get to work on another story."[54] Adding to the pressure, in fall 1951, Barbara was expecting a second child. Rose recalled: "I had a kid and my wife was pregnant, and we didn't have money for the obstetrician."[55]

Fortunately, a new opportunity was about to present itself. Like many Americans, Rose had bought a television set and tuned in to watch the evening fare. He was not impressed by what he saw: "I watched all this stuff, and I said, 'God I can do that,' me who had been doing this for fourteen years and never sold a thing."[56] In what he described as an act of "sheer desperation as a protest against the nightly agonies television had to offer," Rose took one of his short stories and fashioned it into a television script.[57] Sending stories to magazines had never met with success; perhaps television would lead to a better outcome.

OVER THE YEARS, ROSE TOLD the story of his first sale a few different ways. In one version, Rose contacted Phil Minoff, television critic of *Cue*, the leading entertainment magazine in New York, for advice about selling a script. Minoff referred him to a young director named Sidney Lumet, who invited him to CBS offices at Madison Avenue and East Fifty-Second Street. Rose left the script with Lumet, who called back that afternoon with good news. "We're buying the script," he said. "How's six hundred fifty dollars?"[58] Rose was thrilled: "The show was *Danger*, the network was CBS, the script was called 'The Bus to Nowhere,' and it was the first I had ever written. Three weeks later it went on the air, starring Kim Stanley and Whit Bissell, and was actually not bad at all."[59] Rose couldn't believe his good fortune: "My experience in writing television scripts was absolutely nil, my talent questionable. The script was read immediately and bought because Sidney Lumet and his producer Charles Russell liked it and needed it."[60]

In another version, some years later, Rose told roughly the same story with a few different details: this time the phone call came from Russell on the following day. As for pay: "I didn't even ask how much. It didn't matter."[61]

One element of these accounts is clearly wrong: "The Bus to Nowhere," a tale about alien abduction in the California desert, was not performed on *Danger*, a crime melodrama, but a CBS science fiction program, *Out There*. Other points may be correct, but it's also possible that Rose simplified things, and perhaps by quite a bit.

The December 8, 1951, issue of *Cue* included a three-page article by Minoff titled "For No Earthly Reason," describing an imaginative new science fiction program, *Out There*, that CBS had launched in September.[62] Produced by John Haggott, the program had episodes by top science fiction writers like Robert Heinlein and Ray Bradbury. If Rose contacted Minoff in early December about a science fiction story, it's likely he was inspired by this article. And given that Minoff had recently interviewed John Haggott at length, it's probable that he referred Rose to Haggott, the producer of *Out There*, rather than to someone at *Danger*, and certainly not to a young director whose duties did not include script approval. This alternative version agrees with a 1954 CBS press release, which explained that Rose sold his first television script "when he turned to TV producer John Haggott, who engaged Rose to write a script for the CBS program, 'Out There.'"[63] It also tallies with the recollection of *Danger* producer Charlie Russell, who said that he met Rose in late December 1951, *after* Rose made his initial sale. The most likely sequence is therefore from Rose to Minoff to Haggott, and a meeting with Lumet and Russell coming a bit later.

With the passage of time, Rose may have forgotten about John Haggott, who left television in the mid-1950s and died in 1964 at age fifty; or perhaps he streamlined the story, excising a less important figure and making his link to Lumet seem stronger. The details don't really matter. Whatever the exact sequence, "The Bus to Nowhere" was the break that he needed. The script was quickly put into production and aired on December 30, 1951.

As Rose said, it was not bad at all. "I was thirty years old, and I finally sold something," he later said. "I went home a hero."[64]

2

***

Getting Started
(1952 to Summer 1953)

FOR A YOUNG WRITER, NEW YORK in the early 1950s was the right place and the right time. For a brief time, as Reginald Rose discovered, it was possible to submit a script one day, sell it the next day, and see it performed on television a few weeks later.

These fortunate circumstances were the result of events that had been In progress for some years. Throughout the 1930s, even as radio was the wonder medium for news and entertainment, engineers were at work on the next innovation, which promised to "add radio sight to sound."[1] At the 1939 World's Fair in New York, NBC's David Sarnoff proclaimed the age of television and demonstrated his company's new products. NBC's main rival, CBS, was also at work on the new technology. America's entry into World War II put the brakes on advances in commercial television, and for the next four years NBC and CBS made their technology available to the military. Their truce would last until the end of the war. "Peace will find the world on the threshold of television," said Sarnoff.[2] As CBS boss William S. Paley put it: "There we stood at the end of 1945 poised for action."[3]

At the beginning of 1946, there were forty-four thousand television sets in the United States, many of them in greater New York, the only region with any commercial broadcasting. The first televisions had tiny screens, just seven inches diagonally, and grainy images. Not that there was much to see. NBC broadcast a few hours just four nights a week, mostly live sports and Broadway previews. CBS's station, WCBS, broadcast ten hours per week, much of it boxing and wrestling from Madison Square Garden, shown via a single, stationary camera. The first television news program was a fifteen-minute segment on Saturday evening delivered by Douglas Edwards, the only CBS reporter willing to take the assignment.[4] Serious reporters wanted to stay in radio, where they could reach an audience of millions. Few imagined there was any upside to looking into a camera and speaking to a tiny number of viewers.

All of this would change with astonishing speed. Major electronics companies—Magnavox, Philco, Sylvania, Motorola, and Westinghouse—threw themselves into television production and soon offered ten-inch, twelve-inch, and even fifteen-inch sets. The larger sets were expensive, priced at several hundred dollars, but proved to be enormously popular. (They were also all made in the United States.) In a single year, the number of television sets jumped by a factor of five, to 222,000. Also in 1947, CBS extended its coaxial cable from New York to Philadelphia, Washington, DC, and Richmond, as well as north to Boston. Next, it set up a microwave link that reached west to Ohio, Kentucky, and Indiana, allowing broadcasts from New York to reach the Mississippi River.

In 1948, television sets again grew by a factor of five, now reaching 1.2 million homes. The networks began to offer a full lineup every night of the week. Among the most popular shows was NBC's *Texaco Star Theatre*, with its host, Milton Berle, hailed as the first "Mr. Television." CBS began the year with just twenty hours of programming each week, but by September had doubled its offerings, adding *Arthur Godfrey's Talent Scouts* and *Toast of the Town*, which later took the name of its host and ran for twenty-three years as *The Ed Sullivan Show*.

The networks also invested in broadcasting and production facilities. NBC set up studios at 30 Rockefeller Plaza and beamed its programs from atop the Empire State Building, the highest point in Manhattan. CBS responded with an antenna on New York's second tallest structure, the Chrysler Building, on Forty-Second Street. It built a studio one block away, converting loft space above the main concourse at Grand Central Station. While commuters dashed to make their trains, actors and stagehands one floor up turned out some of the finest programs of early television. Advertising agencies like J. Walter Thompson and Young & Rubicam connected sponsors with producers and directors and sold the programs to the networks.

The following years, roughly 1950 to 1957, have come to be known as the Golden Age of Television. Evenings were filled with excellent dramatic performances, beamed live from New York to a growing audience around the country. For a new generation of actors, directors, and writers, it was an era of wonderful opportunity. Jack Klugman, at the time a young stage actor, recalled: "We were hungry. There wasn't enough work in the theater, and here was an outlet, live television."[5] For directors, live television called for a new set of skills that went beyond anything needed for stage or screen, as they had to select camera shots while the performance took place. Set designers were recruited from the theater and learned how to create sets in tight spaces, accommodating the movement of cameras in a live show.

For writers, too, the rapid growth of television opened new possibilities. With established writers focusing on Broadway or Hollywood, the field was wide open to newcomers. One young man who got his start in those days, Tad Mosel, later recalled: "No 'self-respecting writer' would deign to write for television. Even drunken screenwriters wouldn't write for television."[6] The result was a golden opportunity for young writers, who suddenly found themselves in demand.

OF ALL THE PROGRAMS on evening television, the greatest prestige was attached to dramatic anthologies, one-hour live broadcasts that brought quality entertainment into homes across the country.

NBC was the fastest out of the gate, taking to the air in May 1947 with *Kraft Television Theater*, a weekly anthology packaged by J. Walter Thompson. In October 1948, NBC added *The Philco Television Playhouse*, produced by Fred Coe, broadcast every Sunday evening. *Philco* was packaged by the Hutchins Agency, which engaged Talent Associates to produce the program; this involved everything from securing rights to material, to hiring the cast and crew, to creating the final product.[7] As sponsor, Philco paid twenty-five thousand dollars per week, a share of which was kept by the agencies with the rest going to pay for production, cast and crew. With little money for original work, and since the best writers were not interested in television anyway, Coe relied largely on existing materials. *Philco* opened with *Dinner at Eight*, a play by Edna Ferber and George S. Kaufman, and followed up with programs such as Jane Austen's *Pride and Prejudice*, William Shakespeare's *Twelfth Night*, and Charles Dickens's *A Christmas Carol*.

To direct the weekly programs, Coe assembled a small team that included Delbert Mann. Still in his twenties, Mann had worked with Coe at the Nashville Community Playhouse, and recently graduated from the Yale School of Drama.[8] *Philco* ran on a two-week cycle with alternating directors; after performing a show on Sunday night, Mann would arrive at NBC the following day and receive his next script, leading to two busy weeks of reading, casting, and rehearsal, followed by another live performance. Live television, said Mann, "provided an unprecedented and never-to-be-repeated opportunity for young actors, writers, directors to learn and practice their craft in professional but pressured circumstances."[9]

At rival CBS, the leading anthology was *Studio One*, produced by Worthington Miner, who was also CBS's director of programming. A Broadway producer and director in the 1930s, Miner had become disenchanted with the theater, believing it to be elitist and narrow—a luxury for the rich, he called it, in the richest city of the country.[10] Television offered a way to reach a national audience with programs of high artistic standards, a medium that could educate as well as entertain. Miner joined CBS television in 1939, and when World War II ended took charge of all programming. In 1947, he hired Hubbell Robinson from Young & Rubicam to serve as executive vice president in charge of programs. Miner and Robinson shared the goal of creating high-quality programs, which they called "mass with class."[11]

Studio One premiered on November 7, 1948, and for its first season was broadcast every other week, twenty-two performances in all. Many early programs were current Broadway plays or adaptations of literary classics, such as the plays of Shakespeare, Nathaniel Hawthorne's *The Scarlet Letter*, and the Yiddish tale, *The Dybbuk*. For its second season, *Studio One* landed a major sponsor: Westinghouse Electric Corporation, one of America's leading industrial companies with a product line that ranged from heavy equipment to kitchen appliances. CBS's flagship anthology was rechristened *Westinghouse Studio One*, and for a weekly fee of twenty thousand dollars, Westinghouse got national visibility for one hour every Monday night.

With Worthington Miner in charge, and supported by two excellent directors, Paul Nickell and Franklin Schaffner, *Westinghouse Studio One* became a widely admired program, described by William S. Paley as "one of the most literate, adult, well-done dramatic series on television."[12] The two best dramatic anthologies were broadcast on successive nights, NBC's *The Philco Television Playhouse* on Sunday and *Studio One* on Monday. Delbert Mann recalled: "The rivalry was hearty but the respect was great."[13] There were a few notable differences: Coe relied on a stationary camera, finding it difficult to move heavy cameras while changing focus or panning, whereas Miner created a new style of visual storytelling, using multiple cameras and moving them about the set, then cutting between long shots and close-ups to create a sense of energy.[14] In *Watching TV: Six Decades of American Television*, Harry Castleman and Walter J. Podrazik describe a 1949 performance of "Julius Caesar": "In one very effective sequence, Miner moved the camera into a tight closeup on the eyes of one of the Roman conspirators and played the actor's prerecorded voice to reveal his inner thoughts. Viewers experienced the unnerving but exciting sensation that they had jumped inside the man's mind as he thought about the assassination of Caesar. That was something even Broadway couldn't do!"[15] *Studio One*'s pioneering techniques were widely emulated, with the BBC sending a team to New York to absorb the latest innovations.[16]

The most visible face of *Studio One* was its hostess, Betty Furness. A svelte blond, thirty-three years old, Furness had acted in several forgettable movies before she tried her hand at live television commercials. She turned out to be a natural, gracious and unflappable, and presented Westinghouse products with charm and style. Furness became, as David Halberstam wrote in *The Fifties*, "the queen of American appliances, standing between a great faceless industrial company and American housewives. She knew little about the machines themselves except that they seemed well made and that the people who made them seemed like solid Americans from Ohio."[17] Initially paid $150 a week, in 1952 she signed a three-year contract for $100,000 a year, more than $2,000 per program, making her one of the top earners in television.

IN EARLY 1952, AFTER FOUR years in charge of *Studio One*, Worthington Miner left following a salary dispute.[18] For the rest of the season the anthology relied on several interim producers, with Donald Davis as overall supervisor. One of the interim producers was John Haggott, whose science fiction program *Out There* had not been kept on after its first season.[19] It is possible that Haggott was instrumental in bringing Reginald Rose to *Studio One*, or perhaps the idea came from Miner while he was still in charge; whatever the exact sequence, Davis asked Rose to adapt a western novel for his program.[20] When he asked why they had chosen him, Rose was told there was "a western *feeling* to your writing." He noted with amusement: "I'd never been to the West! I stuck the bus [in "A Bus to Nowhere"] in the Mojave Desert because it was the only place I could think of suitable for Martian research."[21]

Rose adapted three plays for *Studio One* in 1952, all of which would be performed in the second half of the year. Adapting a novel for a one-hour program—which really meant forty-eight minutes of airtime after credits and commercial breaks—was no easy task. It meant reading a full novel, choosing key elements, identifying important scenes and dropping others, distilling key characters, and writing sharp dialogue. As a self-taught writer, Rose had to learn by doing.

The first of Rose's teleplays for *Studio One* was the opening episode of the autumn 1952 season, "The Kill," based on a novel by Cameron Owen about a woman wrongly accused of murder. It was directed by Franklin Schaffner and starred Grace Kelly, only twenty-two but well known thanks to her role opposite Gary Cooper in *High Noon*. Next, in October, was "Little Man, Big World," directed by Paul Nickell, about political power and corruption in a large Midwestern city, based on a novel by W. R. Burnett; and six weeks later, in November, "The Formula," directed by Schaffner, a tale of intrigue and espionage based on a novel by Gordon Sager.

The following year, Rose adapted two more novels for *Studio One's* 1953 summer season. On August 3, it performed "The Roman Kid," based on a story by Paul Gallico about a New York sportswriter who falls in love with a young Italian woman during a visit to Rome.[22] Four weeks later, it broadcast "Letter from Cairo," about the mysterious disappearance of an intelligence agent, based on the thriller by James Robbins Miller. In all, Rose wrote five teleplays for *Studio One* in 1952 and 1953. After he was established as a writer of original plays, Rose would dismiss those early efforts as mediocre, but they were essential in helping him to learn his craft. Just as important, they let him demonstrate a talent and a work ethic that showed the bosses of *Studio One* that he was capable of more.

Working for CBS, and supplementing the income from his day job, was increasingly vital. In April 1952, Barbara Rose had given birth to a second son, Richard. The family lived at 147 West Seventy-Ninth Street in a cramped apartment, one bedroom for the parents and one for the boys. After a full day at the Ray Austrian Advertising Agency, Rose would come home and spend evenings working on adaptations for CBS, demonstrating, as his son put it, "substantial personal discipline." The small living room had a desk not large enough to work at, leaving Rose to write on a foam card table, sitting on his bed. "That's where I remember my father writing," Jonathan Rose recalled.[23]

WHILE WRITING FOR STUDIO ONE, Rose also contributed original scripts for *Danger*, the half-hour crime melodrama. *Danger* proved to be a valuable experience for two reasons: it gave Rose a chance to write original stories rather than adaptations, and it brought him into contact with Sidney Lumet.

Danger took a hard-boiled look at the world of gangsters and grifters, small-time hoods and cynical detectives, and con men and crooks. It was produced by Martin Ritt, who had studied at the Actors Studio with two of the great names in theater, Elia Kazan and Lee Strasberg, and was then

recruited to CBS by Hubbell Robinson.[24] To direct, Ritt chose his frier
a young Russian recently arrived in New York named Yul Brynner. Anoth
of Robinson's young hires, Charlie Russell, joined as associate producer.[25]

Each episode of *Danger* had a different story and different cast, although a few actors, notably Ed Binns, appeared regularly. It was produced
at CBS's studio at Grand Central Station and broadcast on Tuesday nights
at ten o'clock. *Danger* was notable for its distinctive music, with jazz gui-
tarist Tony Mottola playing dissonant chords and syncopated rhythms to
create an edgy mood. The opening episode, on September 19, 1950, called
"The Black Door," was lauded as "a gem."[26]

Danger was packaged by Cecil & Presbrey, which lined up a sponsor,
the Block Drug Company, a Brooklyn-based firm whose brands included
Polident dental powder, Poli-Grip denture adhesive, and Ammident toothpaste. Block paid a weekly fee of $5,000 to Cecil & Presbrey, which kept
$1,500 and used $3,500 to pay for the cast, staff, and all production costs.
For that sum, CBS would begin each program with the words: "Now for a
tale of *Danger*. Presented by Ammident, the toothpaste that reduces tooth
decay." The simple tag line led to a boom in Ammident sales, prompting
one of Block's marketing managers to marvel that all he needed to do was
"push a button and TV would sell the product."[27]

Developing scripts for a weekly series was a constant challenge. Some
came from Ritt's friend, Walter Bernstein, an Army veteran who had written for the armed forces newspaper, *Yank*, during World War II, and then
briefly tried his hand in Hollywood before coming to New York. Ritt doubted
that Bernstein would be interested in earning three hundred dollars for a
half-hour crime show, but the writer was happy to have steady work.[28]

Partway through *Danger*'s first season, Brynner wanted to hire an assistant director and thought of a young actor named Sidney Lumet.[29] The son
of Baruch Lumet, a prominent actor and producer in the Yiddish theater,
Sidney had been involved with his father's productions from an early age.
By the 1930s, with the Yiddish theater in decline, Sidney began to act on
stage and radio, and became one of the leading child actors on Broadway.[30] After military service during World War II, Lumet returned to New
York where he studied acting with Sanford Meisner at the Neighborhood
Playhouse and then organized a theater workshop in Greenwich Village
called the Actors Workshop.[31] He supported himself with small acting roles
and by teaching at the High School of Performing Arts. In 1948, Lumet
married the actress Rita Gam.

One day in late 1950, Gam was shooting a commercial at CBS when
Brynner stopped by and asked if Sidney would be interested in directing

television.[32] Lumet was initially cool to the idea, sharing the common skepticism of theater actors toward television, but Brynner persisted.[33] The next day, Lumet stopped by the studio at Grand Central Station and was enthralled. "He just fell in love with it," recalled Gam.[34] "The intensity of the control room was just his tempo. The whole complication of having to direct the cameras and the actors all at the same time appealed to him. He was very quick, very bright, very immediate, very tactile. He loved running between the control room and the floor and the actors."[35] Years later, long after he had become a famous movie director, Lumet still recalled the exhilaration of directing live television.[36]

Also joining *Danger* was a twenty-five-year-old set designer, Bob Markell. Live television posed a special challenge for set designers, as large cameras and microphones on small sets left little room for actors to move around. "You had to leave enough room for the bulky camera, so the actors wouldn't hit them," said Markell.[37] Originally assigned to a CBS detective show, *Charlie Wild, Private Detective*, when Markell heard that Martin Ritt was going to produce *Danger*, he put in for a transfer and soon came aboard.

The team of producer Martin Ritt and director Yul Brynner, assisted by Charlie Russell and Sidney Lumet, would stay intact for just a few months. The first to leave was Brynner, who won the lead role of a new Rodgers and Hammerstein musical, *The King and I*, which opened on Broadway on March 29, 1951. (By now the part of the King of Siam is so indelibly associated with Brynner—with his shaved head, exotic features, and stern visage—that we strain to imagine him as a director of live television.) With Brynner gone, Lumet was asked to direct *Danger*.

The next change came a few weeks later, and for an entirely different reason. When the House Un-American Activities Committee (HUAC) opened hearings in 1947 about alleged Communist influence in the entertainment industry, its focus was on Hollywood. Television was in its infancy and hardly seemed worthy of attention. As the new medium grew in popularity, however, it began to attract scrutiny. In 1950, a group called American Business Consultants published a pamphlet, *Red Channels*, which listed 151 people in show business with alleged links to so-called Communist front activities, many of them active in television.[38]

The effect of the Hollywood blacklist on movie studios has been well documented, with many writers, directors, and actors unable to find work for several years. In some respects, the impact on television was even greater. Whereas movie studios earned their revenues directly from box office receipts, television networks depended entirely on corporate sponsors. As CBS president Frank Stanton later put it: "When the chairman of the board of General Foods and the chairman of the biggest agency in the business says, 'We're gonna wipe you out,' that's pretty powerful talk. General Foods was the biggest advertiser we had."[39] The effect was chilling.

In spring 1951, as *Danger* reached the end of its first season, Martin Ritt was summoned to the fourteenth floor of CBS headquarters at 485 Madison Avenue and informed he would be replaced.[40] Ritt could guess why: He had joined various liberal organizations in his youth and was involved with a 1944 benefit for Russian war relief at Madison Square Garden. That Russia had been a wartime ally mattered little; the Soviet Union was now an enemy, and past associations were taken as evidence of Communist sympathy. For Ritt, dismissal from CBS was the start of a five-year stretch of unemployment.

An executive at Cecil & Presbrey soon invited Charlie Russell for lunch: "He told me Marty was resigning, and since I had been a part of the show from the beginning, would I take over as producer of *Danger*?"[41] He agreed, and *Danger* began its second season in September 1951 with a new team in charge: Charlie Russell, thirty-three, as producer, and Sidney Lumet, twenty-six, as director. They were a study in contrasts, Russell quiet and conservative in manner, described by Walter Bernstein as "elegant, buttoned-down Brooks Brothers," while Lumet was in constant motion, "a hyperkinetic Jew."[42] Over the next years, they would develop a very close working relationship.

Russell soon found himself embroiled in problems stemming from the blacklist. The owner of a supermarket in Syracuse, Laurence Johnson, warned Mel Block of Block Drug Company that *Danger* relied on actors and writers with Communist sympathies. Block assured Johnson that *Danger* would get rid of any suspected Reds, and soon Russell began to receive unmistakable signals from CBS executives.[43] Before one program, he was told not to cast John Randolph, an actor associated with leftist political causes. Russell held his ground and insisted that Randolph was the best actor for the part, but after that program Randolph did not act in television or movies for several years.[44] Next, Russell was told by another CBS executive that he was using too many scripts from Walter Bernstein. The message was unmistakable: "Walter was not acceptable to CBS."[45]

Russell went to see Bernstein and with great regret gave him the news. "I knew it would happen," said Bernstein. "I've been expecting it."[46] Like Ritt, he had been active in leftist causes during the Spanish Civil War and had written for the leftist publication *New Masses*. No one accused Bernstein of being a member of the Communist Party or suggested that his modest earnings were finding their way to Party coffers, nor did anyone find anything objectionable about the stories he wrote for *Danger*. It didn't matter. Given the climate of the times, Bernstein couldn't be hired.

In his 1982 memoirs, *In the Worst of Times It Was the Best of Times*, Russell recalled that the blacklist posed two very different problems. One was a matter of principle: "I considered myself apolitical, but I did have strong feelings about personal freedom, and I reacted emotionally to these witch hunts."[47] The other was practical, since a weekly program demanded a steady supply of scripts and good writers were scarce. Rather than lose Bernstein, Russell suggested that he submit scripts under a different name. Bernstein opened the telephone book and picked a name at random, and for the next months submitted scripts as Paul Bauman. When no one noticed that he was using a front, Bernstein put Russell in touch with two other blacklisted writers, Arnold Manoff and Abraham Polonsky. Over the next two years the trio became mainstays of *Danger*, contributing a total of twenty-nine scripts credited to names including Paul Bauman, Joel Carpenter, George Marrow, and Kate Nickerson.

For a while, Russell kept the source of scripts to himself. Sidney Lumet was busy with casting, set design, rehearsal, and camera work but was not involved in script development. One day over lunch, as Lumet complained about the unfairness of the blacklist, Russell could no longer contain himself. "I'm using blacklisted writers on the program, Sidney," he said, adding quietly: "If it is revealed, it will come as a complete surprise to you. Understand?" "I understand," Lumet replied, adding after a pause: "You got Walter working, haven't you?" Russell nodded. "Great," said Lumet.[48] Russell recalled: "I don't think this revelation came as a surprise to Sidney, since he hadn't seen a writer in the office, rehearsal hall, or studio in months."[49]

DANGER'S NEED FOR SCRIPTS also provided opportunities for Reginald Rose. Although his first sale probably came from a referral from Phil Minoff to John Haggott, not Sidney Lumet, the confusion is understandable. Minoff liked *Danger*, calling it one of "the finest half-hour dramatic series in television," and may have suggested that while at CBS, Rose also stop by to meet Lumet and Russell. (The links between Minoff and Lumet are numerous: the following summer, when Minoff took his annual summer holiday, Lumet penned one of his weekly columns.[50] Also, during *Danger*'s third season, Minoff contributed a script, "Words Fail Me," which aired on March 17, 1953.)

In his memoirs, Charlie Russell recalled that one day, "a soft-spoken, unassuming man came to my office and introduced himself. He was

Reginald Rose, an advertising agency copywriter, who had written a script for *Danger* that he would like me to read."[51] Russell places the meeting very soon after the episode "The Lady on the Rock," which aired December 18, 1951, and before the next one, "Passage for Christmas," performed on December 25.[52] If Russell is correct, he met Rose almost immediately after "The Bus to Nowhere" was bought by *Out There*. Once Reginald Rose had his foot in the door at CBS, he wasted no time expanding his contacts.

Russell liked "You're Wanted on the Phone, Al," calling it a "a well-written script, one of those tightly confined character pieces."[53] It was perfect for *Danger*, the story of a couple whose apartment is invaded by two hitmen with orders to rub out "Al Clark." (It also bore notable similarities to one of Ernest Hemingway's Nick Adams short stories, "The Killers," in which a pair of menacing hitmen drop in at a restaurant, looking for their victim.) After much pleading, the couple persuades the intruders to call their boss and verify the address. The hitmen discover they've come to the wrong Clark residence and depart, leaving the couple shaken but unharmed. Aired on February 26, 1952, it marked Rose's second sale.[54]

Over the next months, Rose contributed several more scripts to *Danger*, some original and some adapted from other sources. Several had suitably ominous titles: "Operation Nightmare," "The Missing Night," "A Name for Baby," and "A Night of Reckoning." All were directed by Sidney Lumet, marking the start of a close relationship between writer and director.

Between original works for *Danger* and adaptations for *Studio One*, Rose stayed busy throughout 1952 and 1953. "I wrote thirteen television plays while I was still working at the agency," he recalled.[55] "It was hard to come home and work at night and on weekends, but I did it. Whatever they paid, I said yes." With a growing family, there was no way to quit a day job that paid two hundred dollars per week. But at last, he was writing steadily and selling his work.

3

⁞⁞⁞

Two Programs, Two Movies
(1952 to 1954)

WHILE REGINALD ROSE WAS WRITING for *Danger* and *Westinghouse Studio One*, other events were taking place that would prove crucial for the eventual production of *12 Angry Men*.

During its first years, NBC's leading anthology, *The Philco Television Playhouse*, had performed classic plays and adaptations of novels and short stories. In 1952, producer Fred Coe began to develop original teleplays.[1] In part, he could afford to invest in new material thanks to a larger budget, made possible by a second sponsor, Goodyear Tires, which alternated weeks with Philco. There was another reason, too: Hollywood studios, at last taking the threat of television seriously after several years of declining box office revenue, began to make movies in brilliant color and widescreen projection. "Movies are better than ever" was their tagline. Now television would have to raise its game, too.

Coe began to cultivate a group of young writers that included Horton Foote, Robert Alan Aurthur, David Shaw, and the most famous of all, Sidney Aaron Chayefsky, better known as Paddy. A Jew from the Bronx, Chayefsky had served in the Army during World War II, returning with a Purple Heart and a nickname—bestowed, so the story goes, after begging off kitchen duty by claiming he had to go to Mass. "Okay, Paddy," said his officer. After a brief and unsatisfying stint in Hollywood, he returned to New York and looked for work as a television writer. One program he approached was *Danger*, with Charlie Russell later recalling that in early 1952: "A stocky, rather assertive man came to the office and advanced to my desk. 'Hey, you're Charlie Russell. I'm Paddy Chayefsky. I hear you're looking for good writers with good stories. Is that true?'"[2] With a great deal of finger pointing and hand waving, Chayefsky told the story of a man who calls in sick for work, goes to a bookie to place a bet, and is witness to a murder. Russell bought the story, and "Hello, Mr. Lutz" was aired in April 1952 to strong reviews. Despite this promising start, Chayefsky decided that he preferred the broader canvas of a one-hour drama, and soon was enlisted by Fred Coe.

Chayefsky's first drama for *The Goodyear-Philco Playhouse* was "Holiday Song," the story of Holocaust survivors who meet again on the New York subway.[3] Performed on September 14, 1952, it was well received and Coe asked for more. Chayefsky's next plays explored the stuff of daily life, what he called "this marvelous world of the ordinary." As he put it, "The function of the writer is to give the audience some shred of meaning to the otherwise meaningless patterns of their lives. Our lives are filled with endless moments of stimulation and depression. We relate to one another in an incredibly complicated manner. Every fiber of relationship is worth dramatic study."[4] These close-ups of everyday life, sometimes called kitchen sink dramas or slice-of-life dramas, found a receptive audience in living rooms across the country.

In the first months of 1953, Chayefsky wrote several acclaimed dramas for *The Goodyear-Philco Playhouse*. "The Reluctant Citizen," broadcast on February 8, told the story of a Russian immigrant so frightened of the government that he is afraid to take steps toward naturalization. "Printer's Measure," on April 26, was about an aging printer, an Irish immigrant, who is worried about mechanization and the loss of his livelihood, and who mentors a young man and conveys the values of his craft. Both were skillfully directed by Delbert Mann. They seemed like an odd couple, a writer from the Bronx and a director from Tennessee, yet they complemented each other well. Mann explained: "Paddy wrote insightfully of a life, people and vernacular that were largely foreign to me. I understood the human relationships, the pains and sorrows and frustrations of which he wrote."[5] The partnership was effective: "I never felt threatened by Paddy's strong presence. I was the director and he never overstepped the bounds, for he instinctively knew the best moment to speak and when to fall back and to let me work out a problem with the actors. We made a good team."[6]

In February 1953, during rehearsals for "The Reluctant Citizen" at a hotel ballroom, Chayefsky noticed a hand-lettered sign: "Girls, please dance with the man who asks you. Remember, men have feelings too." Sensing the makings of a story, Chayefsky began work on a script about a man who goes to a dance club seeking companionship. The working title was "Love Story."[7]

One Monday morning in early May, after directing a comedy on Sunday night, Mann arrived at NBC and learned that his next script wasn't ready. In need of a replacement, Coe contacted Chayefsky: "How are you coming with the script?" The writer said it would need another couple of weeks. "How about *this* week?" said Coe. "We've got to have it *this* week."[8] With that, Chayefsky hurried to finish "Love Story," along the way giving it a new name: "Marty."

"Marty" told the story of a shy thirty-six-year-old butcher who is painfully aware of his lack of appeal to the opposite sex. At a dance hall he meets his female counterpart, who has been ditched by her blind date. Chayefsky commented: "I set out in 'Marty' to write a love story, the most ordinary love story in the world. I didn't want my hero to be handsome, and I didn't want my girl to be pretty. I wanted to write a love story the way it would literally have happened to the kind of people I know. I was, in fact, determined to shatter the shallow and destructive illusions—prospered by cheap fiction and bad movies—that love is simply a matter of physical attraction."[9] The main character, Marty Piletti, was said to be Italian American, but his appeal was universal. (According to Martin Ritt, Chayefsky had written the part for him to play, but as Ritt was blacklisted the part went to Rod Steiger.)

On May 24, 1953, *The Goodyear-Philco Playhouse* broadcast "Marty." Delbert Mann had thought the performance went well but was astonished at the overwhelming response: "The phones were ringing even before we went off the air, strangers as well as friends calling, some in tears, people saying 'That's the story of my life. Thank you.' It is safe to say we got more letters from viewers on 'Marty' than from all the [other] shows of that season together."[10] Phil Minoff of *Cue* wrote that the "relationship between these two forlorn souls became, for us, the most touching play we have watched in five years of televiewing. Gosh, how we cried!"[11]

The broadcast of "Marty" was a watershed moment in television history, an experience shared by millions from coast to coast. It also signaled a change in the author's fortunes. Before "Marty," Chayefsky made ends meet by writing sketches for nightclub comedians.[12] Now he was the most acclaimed dramatist in television. He followed up with a string of successful plays: "The Big Deal" in July, "Holiday Song" in September, and "The Bachelor Party" in October. Audiences across the country tuned in to watch the next play by Paddy Chayefsky.

With a team of writers turning out excellent dramas, Fred Coe and *The*

Goodyear-Philco Playhouse were at the top of their game. *Variety* gave the show a special citation, praising it as "the most consistent of the medium's dramatic showcases" and "the first program to develop a stable of writers."[13] Minoff praised Coe's team for "the finest writing in the entire medium," telling *Cue*'s readers that no other program "can boast a crew of playwrights so dedicated to the very specialized art of creating real people on a small screen for the benefit of two or three real people in a living room."[14]

Within a few years, the success of "Marty" and other top-flight dramas would, paradoxically, lead to the demise of the serious dramatic anthology. Mann would later comment: "Although we certainly had no knowledge of the future, the warning signs were pointed out in an editorial in weekly *Variety*," which noted that Goodyear Tires was "distressed over the Coe-inspired format whereby a great majority of the TV Playhouse original vehicles mirror the joys and heartaches, the foibles and the frustrations of the people big and little who make up America today."[15] Goodyear was paying large sums of money to sponsor the show, and expected ever-larger audiences. The relentless search for commercial success would be the undoing of artistic vision.

IN LATE 1952, AS *DANGER* entered its third season, CBS asked Charlie Russell and Sidney Lumet to take on an additional assignment. *You Are There* had been a radio show that recreated momentous events with leading figures from history—Napoleon and Catherine the Great, Galileo and Sigmund Freud—"interviewed" by CBS reporters as the events unfolded. It was a fun way to make history come alive and the format had worked well as a radio show, relying on listeners to use their imaginations. Now CBS wanted to make *You Are There* into a television program, and asked Russell to produce and Lumet to direct. They agreed and were now responsible for two live programs: *Danger* on Tuesday night and *You Are There* on Sunday evening.

In need of scripts, Russell thought of his trio of blacklisted writers. Over lunch at the Sea Food Grotto at the Gotham Hotel on Fifth Avenue at Fifty-Fifth Street,[16] Russell asked Walter Bernstein, Arnold Manoff, and Abraham Polonsky if they were familiar with the radio program *You Are There*. Yes, they said. "What would you think about making a TV series out of that program?" Russell asked. "Do you think it could work?" The response was immediate. "Absolutely not," said Polonsky. "There are too many problems," Manoff added. Bernstein made it unanimous: "I think it's a terrible idea."

"Well," Russell said, "that's my next assignment. Are any of you interested in doing some work?" At that, he recalled, "a smile of joy went around the table, followed by exclamations such as 'What a great idea for a TV show,' 'What problems, there aren't any problems that can't be solved.' 'That's a wonderful idea.'" Of course, they were interested: "They were all blacklisted and they were all broke."[17]

After some reflection, the trio advanced an audacious idea: rather than contribute some of the scripts, why not let them handle *all* the writing? Since *You Are There* dealt with historical themes, they could write episodes that would—at times subtly and at other times overtly—shed light on current events. Bernstein recalled in *Inside Out: A Memoir of the Blacklist*: "The idea had the arrogance of genius. Why should we work piecemeal when we could take over the whole show? What did it matter that we had been blacklisted? The best defense is a good offense."[18]

For Charlie Russell, relying on Bernstein, Manoff, and Polonsky ensured a steady flow of strong material. It was also a dangerous gamble that could threaten Russell's career if the word got out.[19] Russell took the risk, partly as a matter of principle, believing that one's political views were a private matter. Only once did Russell feel the need to broach the subject with his writers: "Listen, I don't want to know what your private political beliefs are. All I want to know is, do you want to overthrow the government?" No, they replied in jest, "We just want to overthrow CBS." (They were not the only writers to bristle at such requests. When Warner Bros. instructed employees to complete a loyalty survey, Julius and Philip Epstein took the opportunity to tweak their employer. Asked if they had belonged to any subversive organization, they listed one: "Warner Bros."[20])

You Are There premiered on February 1, 1953, with "The Landing of the Hindenburg," a story suggested by CBS executive William Dozier, and written by Polonsky but credited to a front, Jeremy Daniel. Dozier proposed a few other topics, including the capture of famous criminals like Jesse James and John Dillinger, which Russell accepted but mixed with scripts that had relevance to the issues of the day: "The Witch Trial at Salem" by Manoff, "The Crisis of Galileo" by Polonsky, and "The Dreyfus Case" by Bernstein, all about courage in the face of injustice.[21]

You Are There was shown at six o'clock on Sunday evenings, a perfect time slot for family viewing, and soon became a hit. To keep the premise from seeming too corny, the producers wanted an authoritative figure to serve as host, and picked Walter Cronkite, a rising star in the news department, to play the role of news anchor while reporters in the field described historical events. Cronkite read the lead-in and closing tag line in his sonorous baritone: "What sort of day was it? A day like all days, filled with those events that alter and illuminate our times. And *you were there!*"

As with *Danger*, Russell was the sole point of contact with his writers, meeting them occasionally at locations safely removed from CBS offices. (For the most part they kept their own company, having regular lunches at Steinberg's Dairy Restaurant on Broadway and Eighty-First Street.[22] Bernstein's 1976 movie about the blacklist, *The Front*, directed by Martin Ritt, included scenes of blacklisted writers meeting at a delicatessen resembling Steinberg's.)

For several months, Lumet did not know the source of the scripts. When Russell hinted that some came from blacklisted writers, Lumet assumed he meant Bernstein. "At the time, I didn't know of the triumvirate of Bernstein, Polonsky and Manoff," Lumet would later say. "But when the amount of scripts reached the level it did, I asked Charlie how Walter could keep up with such a schedule. It was then he told me about the other two."[23] Later in his life, Lumet expressed regret that he could not meet the writers: "I had known Walter Bernstein and of course saw him socially during this period, but I had never met Polonsky. The level of sheer writing was so high that to some degree the shows almost directed themselves. Good words were not to be found easily in television scripts."[24] Unfortunately, it was imperative to keep the secret. If the source of scripts became known, the sponsors—one of which was an industry group representing "America's Electric Light and Power Companies"—would likely have pulled the plug.[25]

Directing *Danger* and *You Are There* turned Sidney Lumet into something of a television wunderkind. A June 1953 feature in *Life* magazine described his frenzied schedule: *You Are There* rehearsed five mornings each week leading to a live broadcast on Sunday evening, and *Danger* rehearsed five afternoons each week leading to a live performance on Tuesday night.[26] The *Life* reporter watched as Lumet directed an episode of *You Are There*, "The Defense of the Alamo," broadcast from CBS studios at Grand Central Station: "Lumet devised a 90-second battle in which three cameras alternated between 23 different shots of terrible violence. Directing the performance from the control room, Sidney shouted and waved his arms and seemed to die 20 times over . . . Sidney gives all his time to each show, and ends up exhausted but exhilarated." Lumet commented: "In this rat race I ought to be having a nervous breakdown every week, but I feel just great."[27] (By coincidence, "The Defense of the Alamo" was performed on Sunday, May 24, 1953, just hours before "Marty" was broadcast on *The Goodyear-Philco Playhouse*.)

Directing live television taught Lumet how to choose shots in advance, a skill he used to great effect when he began to direct movies. Also, since both programs had a different cast every week, Lumet developed a wealth of personal contacts. He said: "If you take, let's say six actors a show, six times 70 is 420 different actors to work with in a year's time, God knows how many different writers, production people, video engineers, audio men. The exposure was brilliant."[28] The value of Lumet's personal network would become clear a few years later, when he chose the cast for his first feature film. Of the jurors in 12 *Angry Men*, six were known to Lumet from *Danger* or *You Are There:* Martin Balsam, Ed Begley, Ed Binns, E. G. Marshall, George Voskovec, and Jack Warden.[29] A single episode of *You Are There*, "Washington's Farewell to His Officers," featured no fewer than three: Binns, Marshall, and Voskovec.

WHILE TELEVISION CONTINUED TO GROW in popularity and in quality, important developments were also taking place in the motion picture industry.

America's first movie producers started on the East Coast, at the Edison Laboratories in New Jersey and at studios with names like Biograph, Kalem, and Vitascope.[30] By 1920, most had packed up for the sunshine of Southern California, and soon an entire industry was based in Hollywood, with backlots and sound stages, plus all the supporting industries from cameras to catering. A movie might be set in New York City, but aside from a few location shots, it was likely filmed in Burbank, West Hollywood, or Culver City.

In the 1950s, a small group of filmmakers were eager to bring movie production back to New York. Some had made instructional films for the Army Signal Corps during World War II and now worked in theater or television. Although the major studios were reluctant to shoot in New York, a breakthrough came in late 1953 with the announcement that a motion picture would be filmed on the docklands in Hoboken, New Jersey, across the Hudson River from Manhattan.

The movie's director would be Elia Kazan, whose early successes on Broadway led to excellent motion pictures including *A Tree Grows in Brooklyn* (1945) and *Gentleman's Agreement* (1947). Back in New York, he directed Arthur Miller's first play, *All My Sons*, and then won great acclaim for Tennessee Williams's *A Streetcar Named Desire*, which opened in December 1947 with Marlon Brando as Stanley Kowalski. His next play was an even greater triumph: Miller's *Death of a Salesman* opened in February 1949 with Lee J. Cobb giving an unforgettable performance as Willy Loman. Kazan followed up with the movie version of *A Streetcar Named Desire* (1951).

For their next project, Kazan and Miller wanted to make a movie about labor abuses on the Brooklyn waterfront. They developed a script, *The Hook*, but got a cool reception from Hollywood studios. With the Korean War raging, studio bosses were reluctant to make a movie about corruption and crime at home. At 20th Century Fox, Darryl F. Zanuck said he might be interested if the labor bosses were revealed to be Communists. Miller and Kazan said no, as there was no hint that mobsters who controlled the docks had any Communist connections. They returned to New York empty-handed.

In summer 1952, Kazan was called to testify before the House Un-American Activities Committee. Pressured to admit his earlier links to the Communist Party, which he had joined briefly in the 1930s, Kazan provided the names of former party members—in the parlance of the times, he "named names." His actions, although far from unique, led to a falling out with Arthur Miller, and their project about union corruption was shelved.

Now estranged from Miller, Kazan teamed up with Budd Schulberg, a writer who had also cooperated with HUAC, and who had developed a series of investigative stories by Pulitzer Prize–winning journalist Malcolm Johnson, called "Crime on the Waterfront," into a script. They pitched the idea to major studios in Hollywood but again found no interest. A gritty urban tale, said Zanuck, was not "adaptable to the widescreen CinemaScope technique to which Fox has committed its entire output."[31]

Kazan was ready to give up when producer Sam Spiegel offered to make the movie with backing from Columbia Pictures. Kazan agreed, and on November 6, 1953, Columbia announced that Marlon Brando would star in the movie, now called *On the Waterfront*. The cast included several actors from Kazan's earlier works, including Karl Malden and Rudy Bond from *A Streetcar Named Desire*, and Lee J. Cobb from *Death of a Salesman*. Rod Steiger, recently seen on television as "Marty," would also have a leading role. Most exciting was the news that it would be filmed on location, along the Hudson, and not in Hollywood.[32]

To give the movie a realistic look, Kazan made an unusual choice for cinematographer. Boris Kaufman, born in 1897, had been raised in Moscow, in a family of filmmakers. In 1927, he moved to Paris and began to collaborate with a young French director, Jean Vigo. Their first movie, *A Propos de Nice* (1930) was a short documentary with images of life on the busy promenade in Nice. It featured imaginative camera work, including aerial views and time-lapse shots, as well as close-ups using a 35-millimeter Kinamo handheld camera, which let Kaufman capture people from all strata of society, from restaurant workers to society types, at close range. A second collaboration with Vigo, *Zero de Conduit* (1933), was a short fictional film about the antics of boys at a boarding school. Their third collaboration, *L'Atalante* (1934), told the story of a couple living on a river barge in France. Filmed in winter, it had a documentary feel, mixing open-air images of the river with close-ups of its occupants, the camera so close that it conveyed the claustrophobia of living in a confined space.[33]

After Vigo's death from tuberculosis, Kaufman continued to work in Paris with filmmakers Abel Gance and Dimitri Kirsanoff. The fall of France in 1940 forced Kaufman to flee to Canada, where he worked briefly as a cameraman for the National Film Board of Canada. He moved to the United States in 1942 and shot documentaries for the Office of War Information but was barred from working on feature films because he was not a member of the cinematographers' guild. After the war ended, with his options limited and possibly under suspicion because his brothers were Soviet filmmakers, Kaufman turned to short subjects and documentaries. In 1947, he made a thirty-eight-minute black-and-white docudrama produced by the US Information Service, *Journey into Medicine*, that followed a fictional young doctor on his path through medical school and residency. There was no dialogue, only a narrator describing the lives of doctors and their patients as the images told the story. The movie received an Academy Award nomination for Best Documentary and brought Boris Kaufman to wider attention.

Elia Kazan had been impressed by *Journey into Medicine*, with its blend of documentary reality and effective lighting, and wanted Boris Kaufman for *On the Waterfront*.[34] Ironically, Kazan's appearance as a friendly witness before HUAC may have allowed him to select Kaufman, as only a man with strong anti-Communist credentials would have been allowed to hire someone with family in the USSR.[35]

Filming *On the Waterfront* began in December 1953. Interior scenes were shot at the Fox Movietone Studios in Manhattan, but much of the action was filmed in Hoboken, either on the docklands or at Our Lady of Grace Church. Kaufman's cinematography made the waterfront come alive, although the bitterly cold weather and shifting light proved difficult. The challenges of weather were compounded by the idiosyncrasies of Spiegel, a notoriously meddlesome producer.

Day-to-day management on the set was the responsibility of the production supervisor, George Justin. (His wife, Valerie, said that Justin's unofficial task was to keep Spiegel away from Kazan.[36]) Born Isadore Josowitz in 1916, he grew up on the Lower East Side and developed his love of movies at a cinema on Cannon Street. After earning a bachelor's degree from City College of New York, he changed his name in 1941. Justin spent World

War II in the Army Signal Corps making training films. After returning to civilian life in 1946, he worked on documentary and industrial films and taught at the New Institute for Film in Brooklyn but was itching to work on feature films. *On the Waterfront* was a chance to show that New York could be a viable site for movie production.[37] Completed in February 1954, it was slated for release the next summer.

THROUGH THE 1940S, the movie industry had been dominated by five studios: 20th Century Fox, Metro-Goldwyn-Mayer, Paramount Pictures, RKO, and Warner Bros. They were vertically integrated, handling everything from production to distribution, running their own studios and networks of cinemas. They also had the power to sign actors to exclusive contracts of up to seven years. Just below the five major studios were three second-tier studios—Columbia Pictures, United Artists, and Universal Pictures—and below them, lesser players like Allied Artists and Republic Pictures.

Many actors were unhappy with exclusive contracts, and some, including James Cagney, mounted challenges in the courts. Cinema owners, too, objected to the practice of block booking, which forced them to exhibit movies as dictated by the studios. A series of lawsuits charged that the movie industry violated antitrust law, and in 1948, the US Supreme Court issued a set of rulings in *United States v. Paramount Pictures* that broke the power of the studios. Some of the weaker ones fell into financial difficulty, and by 1951, United Artists—founded in 1919 by Mary Pickford, Charlie Chaplin, D. W. Griffith, and Douglas Fairbanks—was losing one hundred thousand dollars a week and headed for bankruptcy.[38] Sensing an opportunity, Arthur Krim, a forty-year-old lawyer, and Robert Benjamin, a forty-one-year-old executive at Universal, approached United Artists' two remaining founders, Pickford and Chaplin, with an offer: Let us take a controlling interest and manage the company. If we can turn a profit, we'll split the returns but keep the stock. Seeing little alternative, Pickford and Chaplin agreed.

Once in charge at United Artists, Krim and Benjamin shifted the company's focus. Although the Paramount rulings gave independent producers the right to compete with major studios, they lacked financial resources and access to distribution. Moviemaking was a highly risky venture, with most projects losing money or barely breaking even, and banks were reluctant to lend money. Independent producers faced a catch-22: banks seemed to be willing to finance only those producers who were wealthy enough not to borrow. ("Who had assets?" Robert Benjamin asked rhetorically. "Only Sam Goldwyn, and he backed himself."[39])

Stepping into this mix, United Artists became the first virtual studio, providing funds to back the production of movies and then arranging distribution, without owning any piece of the process. As Krim observed: "Unless you're a creator yourself, the best approach to making films is to invest prudently in those who do."[40]

Krim and Benjamin got off to a good start with *The African Queen* (1951), produced by Sam Spiegel and directed by John Huston, starring Humphrey Bogart and Katharine Hepburn; and followed up with *High Noon* (1952), produced by Stanley Kramer and directed by Fred Zinnemann, with Gary Cooper and Grace Kelly. Both were critical and financial successes.

No longer bound by long-term contracts, several actors began to try their hand at movie production. One of the first was Burt Lancaster, who formed Norma Productions with his agent, Harold Hecht, in 1948, and turned out a series of movies, all backed by major studios: *Kiss the Blood off My Hands* (1948), a crime drama starring Lancaster and distributed by Universal; *The Flame and the Arrow* (1950), distributed by Warner Bros.; and *Ten Tall Men* (1951), a French Foreign Legion adventure distributed by Columbia. Three movies, with three different distributors, all financed independently.

For their next projects, Lancaster and Hecht moved away from major studios and looked to United Artists for financing and distribution. First, they made *Apache* (1954), followed by *Vera Cruz* (1954) an adventure set in Mexico with Lancaster and Gary Cooper. (*Vera Cruz* was a major inspiration for the Westerns of Sergio Leone. The parallels to *The Good, the Bad, and the Ugly* [1966] are striking: fortune hunters scheming over a stash of gold, against the backdrop of a civil war, and a final duel with rapid close-ups of hands reaching for holsters.)

Increasingly confident in their ability to make movies, Lancaster and Hecht began to look for new sources of material. The success of "Marty" on *The Goodyear-Philco Playhouse* gave them an idea: Why not turn a television program into a feature film? In September 1953, the *New York Times* reported that Norma Productions had acquired screen rights to "Marty," with Paddy Chayefsky to write the screenplay.[41] In fact, the report was premature, as Chayefsky had rebuffed Hecht's first offer, possibly because Fred Coe had ideas of his own to make "Marty" into a film.[42]

Discussions went on for several months, during which time "Marty" received two Sylvania Awards, the top television award of the day, with Rod Steiger named Outstanding Actor and Paddy Chayefsky winning for Best Original Script. Finally, in April 1954, a deal was struck. *Variety* reported:

"In what's believed to be the first such deal of its kind, a tv-eed dramatic program along with its director and writer are going to Hollywood for a theatrical filmization."[43]

The contract called for Lancaster and Hecht to produce the movie with financing and distribution by United Artists. Chayefsky would receive $15,000 for the movie rights and screenplay, more than twelve times the $1,200 he earned for the television script, plus 5 percent of any profits.[44] It was a lot of money, but Chayefsky would not say yes unless Delbert Mann was named as director. Harold Hecht agreed, but still the writer was not satisfied. Worried that Hecht might fire Mann and bring in a different director, Chayefsky insisted on being named associate producer, which would let him veto any directorial change. Again, Hecht agreed.

Offered eight thousand dollars to direct his first feature film, Mann at first said no. "I turned it down," he explained in his 1998 memoirs, "but not just because of the money. I had no great desire to do it, and had never even thought about Hollywood and a film career."[45] But Chayefsky was adamantine, insisting he would not make the movie without his favorite director.[46] Mann believed that Chayefsky "felt a desperate need for help and protection from those whom he feared would cheapen and distort his work. He insisted that I go along to help him protect his baby from the Philistines of Hollywood."[47] To sweeten the pot, Chayefsky gave up two thousand dollars of his fee, so that Mann would get ten thousand dollars while Chayefsky earned thirteen thousand dollars plus 5 percent of profits.[48] For both writer and director, the movie version of "Marty" would turn out to be a financial windfall.

With the deal to make *Marty*, the wall separating movies and television had been breached. For movie studios, television was no longer just a competitor but also a source of material. The combined effect of *On the Waterfront* and *Marty* was immense: the first showed that a movie made in New York could be commercially successful, and the second proved that a television program could be the basis for a feature film.

These many factors would come together two years later for the movie version of *12 Angry Men*, a motion picture based on a television program, filmed in New York, directed by Sidney Lumet, with cinematography by Boris Kaufman, and a cast drawn from *Danger* and *You Are There*.

4

###

Original Dramas for *Studio One* (Summer 1953 to Spring 1954)

WHILE THE *GOODYEAR-PHILCO PLAYHOUSE* was thriving under the leadership of Fred Coe, CBS's flagship anthology was stuck in neutral. Only in May 1953, a full year after Worthington Miner's departure from *Westinghouse Studio One*, did CBS finally name a permanent producer: Felix Jackson.[1]

Felix Joachimson was born in Hamburg in 1902 and spent his early years as a playwright in Vienna and Budapest. In 1937, he fled the Nazis, shed his German name, and made his way to Hollywood. There he wrote the screenplay for *Destry Rides Again* (1939) with James Stewart and Marlene Dietrich, and produced movies with one of the leading starlets of the day, Deanna Durbin. Despite an age difference of nineteen years, they wed in 1945, a marriage that lasted four years. In 1946, Jackson moved to New York and joined Young & Rubicam, the advertising agency and television packaging house.[2] Two years later he was hired by CBS to produce the *Schlitz Playhouse of Stars*, a thirty-minute anthology, and from there was tapped for *Studio One*.[3]

Now in charge of *Studio One*, Jackson promised to broaden its range of programs.[4] He made a daring choice for the 1953 season premiere: an adaptation of George Orwell's *1984*.[5] Directed by Paul Nickell, *Studio One's* "1984" used a stark set with dramatic lighting to depict life in a totalitarian state. (The commercial breaks, with Betty Furness cheerfully presenting modern consumer appliances, offered an ironic counterpoint to images of tyranny and oppression.) Jack Gould, television critic of the *New York Times*, applauded "1984" as "a masterly adaptation that depicted with power, poignancy, and terrifying beauty the end result of thought control—the disintegration of the human mind and soul. The new TV season has come alive."[6]

Taking a cue from Fred Coe, Jackson decided to develop original material. His first step was to hire a story editor. Florence Britton, age forty-four, had been one of the Goldwyn Girls in her early twenties, a leggy young woman who appeared in a handful of movies with names like *Confessions of a Coed* (1931), *Compromised* (1931), and *Lady with a Past* (1932). She stopped acting after wedding the owner of a coffee company, Chock Full o'Nuts, but when the marriage unraveled, Britton returned to work, taking a job at Young & Rubicam. There she met Jackson, who brought her to *Studio One* in June 1953.

As story editor, Britton became the first point of contact with writers, responding to their submissions and guiding their efforts.[7] Writers would first develop an outline, often three to six pages long, describing the story and its main characters. If Britton liked the outline, she would pass it on to Felix Jackson, and if he concurred, the writer would be asked to develop a full script. More reviews awaited, not only from Britton and Jackson but also from CBS executives in charge of programming. Sometimes they said no—a script might be too controversial, too close to something that had been produced elsewhere, or otherwise unsuitable. Finally, Westinghouse would have to give its approval.

"Florence was a great character, right out of the twenties," recalled Chiz Schultz, at the time a young production assistant for *Studio One*. "She was a blonde and had a Dutch boy haircut. She always, at her desk, wore this incredibly large, wide-brimmed hat, and had a cigarette holder. I was just in awe."[8] More importantly, Britton "had a terrific story sense." Her standards were exacting, but writers came to see her as an ally. Many of the outlines she rejected came back with a witty note encouraging the writer to try again, signed with a large and flowing initial, F.

As Jackson and Britton sought to develop original scripts, they had their eyes on three writers: Gore Vidal, Rod Serling, and Reginald Rose.

Gore Vidal, twenty-eight, was the son of a prominent political family whose debut novel, *The City and the Pillar*, had created a stir for its open depiction of homosexuality. From there he tried his hand at detective novels and wrote a few television scripts, one of them for *Danger*. In time Vidal would shift to Hollywood, contributing to the script of *Ben-Hur*, and would eventually become one of America's best-known novelists, but in the early 1950s, he was seen as a promising writer for *Studio One*.

Rod Serling, twenty-nine, was a native of Binghamton, New York. He had served as a paratrooper in World War II and at age twenty-one traded his combat fatigues for a typewriter. "In the beginning," Serling recalled, "there was a period of about eight months when nothing happened. My diet consisted chiefly of black coffee and fingernails. I collected forty rejection slips in a row."[9] In 1950, Serling signed with a New York agent, Blanche Gaines, who became a source of support and counsel. From his home in Cincinnati, where he worked for WKRC-TV, Serling turned out dozens of scripts which Gaines pitched to various programs.[10] "Blanche kept me on a year before I made my first sale," he recalled.[11] By 1952, Serling was beginning to make a name for himself with scripts for *Lux Video Theater*, *Suspense*, *Medallion Theater*, and *The Motorola Television Hour*. A year later, he moved to New York and continued to turn out scripts, many of which Gaines first offered to *Studio One*.

At thirty-two, Rose was the oldest of the three but had only recently proven his value to CBS. By summer 1953, he had written five adaptations for *Studio One* and several melodramas for *Danger*. Although still working full time at the Ray Austrian Advertising Agency, he had shown enough promise for *Studio One* to suggest he take the next step.

And so, after "considerable urging on the part of Florence Britton," Rose set to work on a one-hour-long drama.[12] He approached the challenge with what he called "something less than absolute confidence."[13] Original dramas required much more than adaptations or half-hour melodramas: the writer needed to devise a source of conflict and develop a longer story line, with more interesting characters and incisive scenes, and considerably more dialogue.

To those challenges, Rose gave himself one more: rather than portray the lives of ordinary people, he wanted to address issues of social importance. For his first teleplay, Rose wanted to dramatize "man's indifference to the needs of his fellow man." He recalled: "I sat down to write this script with an intense personal feeling of indignation at mankind's sometimes terrifying irresponsibility and disregard for the basic needs and rights of people. Vaguely I thought of genocide, pogroms, lynchings, wars—the conglomerate tragedies of the ages allowed by human beings to fall upon other human beings through neglect, stupidity, indifference, and just sheer laziness."[14] Each time he tried to devise a story, he ran into obstacles and went back to what he knew best: "half-hour cops-and-robbers dramas, which I knew were easily done and eminently salable."[15]

AFTER A FEW FAILED EFFORTS, Rose completed a ten-page outline which he titled "The Remarkable Incident at Carson Corners."[16] It told the story of elementary school children in a typical American town who invite their parents to school for an evening performance. The mothers and fathers arrive in a light-hearted mood, expecting to see a play or a pageant, one of them musing: "What have those cute and clever kids cooked up?" They are surprised to find the class arranged as a courtroom and shocked when the children declare that court is in session. A boy, Billy McGinnis, has gone missing, last seen playing with a toy boat in a rain-filled excavation site near the school. The boat and his cap have been found, but Billy is presumed drowned, and the children charge Mayor Woodbridge, present in class, with his death. The mayor is furious, but the children proceed with the trial. A first witness overheard the mayor accept a kickback from the building contractor in exchange for approving a poorly conceived excavation. Another witness says that he offered to fill in the hole but was turned down because the mayor didn't want to bear the costs. Just as the mayor's greed and dishonesty are laid bare, there is a commotion outside the classroom. A state trooper arrives with Billy, who had gotten lost, took shelter in the back of a truck, and was found several miles away. Tired but safe, he is reunited with his family. The townspeople file out, relieved at the happy ending, while Mayor Woodbridge sits alone, disgraced and humiliated.

Florence Britton liked the premise of Rose's play, but felt that after a strong opening act, the story went off the tracks.[17] She encouraged him to keep the main idea—schoolchildren turning their class into a courtroom and putting adults on trial—but to make several changes. In the revised version, Billy McGinness is not missing but dead, having fallen through a fire escape railing. The children accuse the elderly janitor, Mr. Kovaleski, of pushing the boy, presumably because Billy had discovered a few collection boxes stashed away in the school basement. At first the evidence seems persuasive, and a few quick-tempered fathers are ready to mete out punishment. Yet as various witnesses are called to testify, a series of flashbacks reveals a very different story. The school principal, first on the scene after the accident, unwisely moved the boy, possibly aggravating his injury. The town doctor, father of a child in class, failed to respond to the urgent call for help because he was on his lunch break and didn't want to be disturbed. The head of the chamber of commerce, also a father in class, used funds to spruce up Main Street rather than pay for school repairs. The town building inspector, also present, failed to report the faulty railing during a routine inspection some years earlier. All these men, through negligence rather than malice, contributed to the boy's death. The final flashback is the most stunning: the contractor who originally installed the fire escape was none other than the father of the dead boy. His sin was to do a slipshod job so he could go home early, never imagining that one day his son would die as the result.

Amid these revelations, the children's teacher arrives at school. Miss Frank is shocked to find Mr. Kovaleski on trial and reveals that she had given him the collection boxes for safe keeping, only to forget about them until their accidental discovery. The janitor had nothing to do with the boy's death, unlike several adults present, who must atone for their deeds and acknowledge their rush to judge an innocent man. Mr. McGinness, overcome with remorse, delivers the climactic speech: "We can't let it happen again. We're human beings. We live together . . . all of us . . . right next door! We've got to live for each other . . . or we're nothing!" As the other parents file out, he says in a low voice: "I forgive you . . . Someone forgive me."

Compared to Rose's original outline, the final script was much more satisfying. Instead of one culprit there were several, most of them guilty of errors of omission. There would also be no happy ending. A boy really had died, and many seemingly upstanding citizens had contributed to the tragedy.

"The Remarkable Incident at Carson Corners" was directed by Paul Nickell and broadcast on January 11, 1954. Viewed today, it seems preachy and its many flashbacks repetitive, yet at the time it was bold and unconventional. Rose had challenged the veneer of small-town tranquility and raised questions about individual responsibility and collective guilt. As he later wrote: "I hoped that I made clear that the Carson Corners schoolroom was, in effect, our earth, and that the events which transpired in Carson Corners were miniatures of the events which somehow diminish mankind."[18]

The program received high praise, with Phil Minoff making special mention of the writer whose career he had helped launch: "For the drama's author, young Reginald Rose, this was a first attempt at an hour-long original for TV, and it was a masterful job. It must have been a difficult one, too, for there were nearly two dozen speaking roles and several intricate flashbacks to contend with."[19]

Rose's first teleplay prompted requests from parent-teacher groups and civic organizations for kinescopes, which they hoped to use to spark discussions. "The public response to *Carson Corners* was quite remarkable," he later wrote. "This kind of thing is immensely gratifying to the writer, and I remain quite impressed at the effect which a single showing on television can have upon a staggering number of people."[20]

FOR HIS SECOND TELEPLAY, Rose addressed an issue that was beginning to gain national attention: racial prejudice.

In the years after World War II, advances in civil rights were taking place on several fronts. Major league baseball broke the color barrier in

April 1947, when Jackie Robinson joined the Brooklyn Dodgers. In 1948, the Democratic Party adopted a strong position on civil rights at its national convention, prompting South Carolina governor Strom Thurmond to lead a walkout of Southern Democrats. Two weeks later, President Harry S. Truman issued Executive Order 9981, abolishing racial discrimination in the United States Armed Forces.

Even so, in late 1953, when Rose decided to write about racial prejudice, the civil rights movement was still at an early stage. Only the following year, in May 1954, would the US Supreme Court issue its landmark ruling about school desegregation, *Brown v. Board of Education*. Other watershed events were more than a year away: the brutal killing of Emmett Till in August 1955 and Rosa Parks's refusal to give up her seat in December 1955, which triggered the Montgomery bus boycott and brought the Reverend Martin Luther King Jr. onto the national stage.

How did a young white man, raised in relative comfort on New York's Upper West Side, become so passionate about race relations? Part of the answer came from his experience in the military, listening to the experiences of young Black soldiers and witnessing the humiliation of a second lieutenant in Richmond, Virginia. Although Jim Crow laws were in force in the South, Rose had no illusions that racism was confined to one region of the land. There were many recent examples in the North, including the violent reaction when a twenty-eight-year-old Black man, Howard E. Clark Jr.—a graduate of Fisk University and an Air Force veteran, now employed by the Chicago Transit Authority—moved his wife and their two small children into the all-white Chicago suburb of Cicero in July 1951. Large crowds converged on the building and demanded that the family leave, as police stood by but did not intervene. While the Clark family was away, a mob broke into their third-floor apartment, smashed windows, and threw their furniture onto the street where it was set on fire. Illinois Governor Adlai E. Stevenson eventually called in the National Guard to restore order. The apartment building was cordoned off with barbed wire while the crowd, estimated at upwards of four thousand, tried to break through. Close to one hundred whites were arrested. After two days of tense confrontation, the crowds dispersed. Eventually the Clark family moved elsewhere.

Rose watched newsreels of the Cicero riots and was appalled by what he saw: "fearsome, hate-twisted faces of women in the mob, some of them actually holding small children by the hand as they hurled rocks at their neighbors."[21] He was horrified by images of "mothers and little children with hatred on their faces outside the homes where blacks were moving in."22 Here was the stuff of powerful drama: "The inhuman, medieval attitudes of these free, white Americans had so disturbed me that I had decided to do a play about them in an attempt to explore the causes behind this mass sickness."23

Rose wanted to tell the story of a Black family moving into an all-white neighborhood. At first unsure how to structure it, he eventually had a moment of inspiration: "I woke up one morning and had the entire idea in front of my eyes. It was complete."24 From there: "I sat down then and within a very few minutes had worked out the basic story of 'Thunder on Sycamore Street.'"25

He sent the outline to Florence Britton, who told him over lunch: "Everything is perfect except we can't do a Negro, and that's the end of it."26 Westinghouse sold its products nationwide and worried that any sympathetic portrayal of Black Americans would be unacceptable to a large section of the country. A program about racial prejudice was out of the question. "This was 1954," Rose would later comment. "Blacks were still your maid or your local tap dancer."27

When Britton suggested they find a different reason why neighbors would object to a new arrival, Rose proposed a Jewish or Catholic family, but again the answer was no. Eventually he suggested an ex-convict, reasoning that "An ex-convict as the protagonist was the obvious choice since this could offend no known organized pressure groups."28 This time the story editor said yes.

Rose's nine-page outline for "Thunder on Sycamore Street" began: "In the quiet town of Eastmont, on a quiet shaded street there is a long row of homes. These homes, from the outside, are exactly alike, conservative, solid, respectable upper middle-class homes owned by the people who manage the groceries, the real estate firms, the railroad yards of America."29 He structured the play as three stories that take place in parallel, each one revealing the thoughts and worries in a different household. Act 1 begins as three men return home from work at 6:40 PM. The father in the first household, Frank Morrison, looks forward to 7 o'clock when he will join other neighbors outside the home of the new arrivals. He is a narrowminded and aggressive man, determined to force them to leave. Act 2 takes us into the second house where once again it's 6:40 PM, and Arthur Hayes has just returned home. He is troubled by the plan to confront the new arrivals, but his wife is worried about the neighborhood's reputation and insists that he join the others.

Act 3 takes place in the house of Joseph Blake, who recently served a prison sentence for killing an old man through reckless driving. Mrs. Blake is worried about a confrontation and pleads with her husband to agree to move, but Joseph Blake is adamant that they will not be hounded out of town. The three stories merge into one at seven o'clock as the crowd gathers and the Blakes hear "the tramping of feet and a growing chorus of angry voices." When a rock shatters a window, Joseph Blake opens the front door to confront the mob. One of the leaders demands they leave town, to which Blake "flings his convictions on personal freedom, and then his defiance, into the teeth of the waiting crowd. When he finishes, there is only stunned silence." When another rock strikes Joseph Blake, drawing blood, Arthur Hayes breaks ranks and comes forward to help. Rose described: "He begins to stride forward, fiercely aware now for the first time in his life that injustice must be acted against and not merely mourned." Some of the crowd begin to lose their resolve, and Frank Morrison exhorts them to remain: "What will become of Sycamore Street if these people are allowed to stay? . . . I don't have to tell you! . . . Listen to me, people." But by now his neighbors have no appetite for further violence and begin to disperse. Morrison calls after them—"Come back here"—but to no avail. The last word belongs to Arthur Hayes, who implores his wife: "What are you standing there for? My neighbor's head is bleeding!"

"Thunder on Sycamore Street" was directed by Franklin Schaffner and broadcast on Monday, March 15, 1954, barely two months after "The Remarkable Incident at Carson Corners." So that viewers might identify more closely with Joseph Blake, Felix Jackson decided not to cast a well-known actor, choosing instead Kenneth Utt, a floor producer for *Studio One*, in his first acting role.[30] Rose watched the live performance from the control room and was moved by the power of the drama: "I don't think I'll ever forget hearing and seeing Kenny Utt thunder out the lines, 'I own this house and God gave me the right to live in it. The man who tries to take it away from me is going to have to climb over a pile of my bones to do it!' and then watching him walk off the studio floor minutes later as the play ended, tears flowing down his cheeks, trying to work his way out of a role which he had really lived as he played it."[31]

Rose had hoped that the public would recognize the story as an allegory about prejudice in general, and his intuition was justified: "It was variously felt by viewers with whom I discussed the show that Joseph Blake was meant to symbolize a Negro, a Jew, a Catholic, a Puerto Rican, an ex-Communist or fellow traveler, a Japanese or Chinese, a Russian, an anarchist or an avowed atheist. Not one single person I spoke to felt that he was actually meant to be an ex-convict. This was extremely gratifying to me and made me feel that perhaps 'Thunder on Sycamore Street' had more value in its various interpretations than it would have had had it simply presented the Negro problem."[32] A generic story about prejudice made the message *more* powerful, not less so. Jack Gould of the *New York Times* agreed: "While 'Thunder on Sycamore Street' happened to deal with discrimination against a man who had been in jail, it could have dealt just as easily with any of the prejudices, political and religious, that can grip a community. Seldom has the Golden Rule been reaffirmed with such power and suspense in a television play."[33] He singled out the author: "Reginald Rose is a television writer to be watched" for having created "a drama of uncommon sensitivity, craftsmanship, and valor. Next to George Orwell's '1984,' it was as fine a work as *Studio One* has done this season."[34]

The broadcast of "Thunder on Sycamore Street" prompted many enthusiastic letters, one from the National Conference of Christians and Jews, which thanked Rose for taking up the topic of prejudice. Subsequent discussions with the National Conference of Christians and Jews would lead Rose to write about another topic in the news, juvenile delinquency.

WITH TWO SUCCESSFUL TELEPLAYS in three months, Rose was gaining a reputation for taking on important social issues. Best of all, CBS put him on salary, the exact terms not revealed, but likely about ten thousand dollars for ten original outlines, with more to be paid for each one that was produced.[35]

At last, Rose could afford to write full time, although his son recalls that he remained with the Ray Austrian Advertising Agency at least through the summer. As a recognition of his status as a professional writer, Rose signed on with the Ashley-Steiner Agency, which represented many leading television writers and directors and packaged programs for network broadcast. With offices at 579 Fifth Avenue, at the corner of Forty-Seventh Street, Ashley-Steiner was at the center of a booming industry.

The first months of 1954 found Rose at work on several projects. He had completed a third original teleplay for *Studio One*, "The Death and Life of Larry Benson," about a returning Korean War veteran and the family that waits for him, addressing themes of grief and loss. It was scheduled for broadcast in late May, to coincide with Memorial Day. Rose was also preparing to adapt *An Almanac of Liberty*, a book by Supreme Court Justice William O. Douglas, due to be published in November. *Studio One* had agreed to broadcast a drama to coincide with the book's release, and Felix Jackson asked Rose to write the script.

Reginald Rose had plenty to keep him busy, but a random event was about to change his life.

Part II

THE TELEVISION PROGRAM

5

A Visit to Foley Square (Spring 1954)

OVER THE DECADES, Reginald Rose consistently said that his most famous work was inspired by a summons for jury duty in early 1954. "The receipt of my jury notice activated many grumblings and mutterings," he once recalled, "most of which began with lines like 'My God, eight million people in New York and they have to call me!'"[1]

On the appointed date, Rose arrived at the General Sessions courthouse on Foley Square in Lower Manhattan where he joined dozens of other New Yorkers, most of them wearing "the same grim, horribly persecuted attitude."[2] What happened next came as a revelation. Many years later, Rose could still recall the powerful emotions of his first time in a courtroom: "It was such an impressive, solemn setting in a great big wood-paneled courtroom, with a silver-haired judge. It knocked me out. I was overwhelmed."[3] And then the epiphany: "I was writing one-hour dramas for *Studio One* then, and I thought, 'Wow, what a setting for a drama.'"[4]

Rose never named the case, but at times he offered clues. In 1956 he wrote: "A month or so before I began the play I sat on the jury of a manslaughter case in New York's General Sessions Court."[5] Years later Rose was more specific about the date, saying he had been "called for jury duty to the Foley Square courthouse in the spring of 1954."[6] Since the play was complete by late May, it's likely the trial took place in March or early April.

On another occasion, Rose said more: "The case involved a Bowery bum who inflicted wounds which then caused somebody to die. There were several counts, from manslaughter in the first degree down to assault."[7]

He added: "Everybody had him guilty, but on what count? The side I was on battled for assault because the guy he injured didn't take care of his injuries. It seemed to us his responsibility was to go to a doctor, but he didn't. He went to his bed and stayed there. His wounds became infected, and he died three days later. We prevailed, and the judge said we were absolutely right."[8] A few years later, Rose said roughly the same thing: "I was on a jury for a manslaughter case, and we got into this terrific, furious eight-hour argument in the jury room."[9]

By comparing these clues to the Manhattan district attorney's records, we can identify the trial that best fits: *The People v. William Viragh*, held at the General Sessions on Foley Square in late March 1954.

The Manhattan district attorney's homicide docket for 1950 to 1953 lists 713 homicides, of which 323 led to criminal charges. Most charges were for first-degree or second-degree murder, with roughly one quarter— eighty in all—leading to a charge of manslaughter. Of those eighty, most resulted in plea bargains, often to a lesser charge, while twenty went to trial. Of those twenty manslaughter trials, only one led to a conviction on the lesser charge of assault: the trial of William Viragh.[10]

Other facts about *The People v. William Viragh* closely match Rose's descriptions. The trial began on March 18 and ended on March 24, fitting the date of "spring 1954." The crime scene, on East Ninth Street in the East Village, and the victim, who was known as a local drunk, agree with Rose's account of the deceased as a "Bowery bum." The cause of death, recorded in the homicide docket as "Punched," fits Rose's description of the injuries, a relatively uncommon cause of homicide in 1950s New York, far less frequent than stabbing, shooting, or strangulation. As for the "silver-haired judge," Edward McCullen was sixty-five years old and can be seen in photographs with an authoritative presence and thinning gray hair, although many General Sessions judges of that era, all of them white men, could probably have fit that image.

There are two small differences: the victim did not sustain injuries one day and die a few days later, nor was the initial charge first-degree manslaughter. But on the main points—date, location, participants, cause of death, and eventual conviction—*The People v. William Viragh* closely agrees with Rose's account. Significantly, no other homicide matches even a few.

THE CHARGES AGAINST WILLIAM VIRAGH stemmed from a brief altercation on the afternoon of Thursday, November 5, 1953. Patrolman Albert O'Leary was called to 425 East Ninth Street, one block from Tompkins

Square, where he found a man "lying on his back in the street, unconscious, feet to curb." The victim was taken to Bellevue Hospital at First Avenue and East Twenty-Eighth Street where he died the next morning without regaining consciousness. An autopsy revealed a fractured skull and brain trauma.

The dead man was Dimitri Mateichik, age sixty, a laborer who lived nearby at 614 East Ninth Street. Born Deomid Matwejozuk in Poland, he came to the United States in 1913 and was naturalized in 1935. Married with three grown sons, Mateichik was known as a heavy drinker, not uncommon in the neighborhood close to the Bowery.

Police investigators pieced together what had happened. Witnesses said that Mateichik had spent the afternoon in a bar at 432 East Ninth Street. Around five o'clock, for reasons that may have had to do with money, Mateichik had a dispute with the bar owner and a few patrons, and pulled a knife, cutting the owner's hand, although not seriously. A few of the men ejected Mateichik from the bar, where he stood on the sidewalk, shouting profanities through the window and cursing passers-by before staggering away.

A pair of customers had watched the scuffle from their seats at the back of the bar. One of them, known locally as Lefty, was overheard to say, "I'm going to get him," and got up to walk toward the front of the bar, leaving his cigarettes and loose change on the counter as if he intended to return. By the time Lefty reached the front door, Mateichik had stumbled several yards down the street, but now he had turned and was heading back toward the bar. Witnesses saw Lefty approach the older man and strike him. Mateichik fell and hit his head on the curb, where he lay motionless.

Police at the Ninth Precinct station soon identified Lefty as William Viragh, age forty, a regular customer who lived nearby. At first Viragh denied any involvement, but after police told him that he had been positively identified by several witnesses, he admitted his role. The District Attorney tried to ascertain if a crime had been committed. Had Viragh deliberately walked over to Mateichik? Yes, said witnesses. Had anyone else struck Mateichik, perhaps when he was bundled out of the bar? No, the only blows were struck by Viragh. Had Mateichik thrown the first punch at Viragh? No, he had not. Based on this testimony, the District Attorney ruled that Mateichik's death was a homicide, the manner of death listed as *Punched*.

In December 1953 the Grand Jury indicted William Viragh for manslaughter in the second degree. Coming before a judge on December 16, Viragh entered a plea of not guilty. Such cases often lead to a guilty plea on a lesser charge, but in this instance no deal was struck, although case files do not indicate whether the DA declined to offer a plea bargain or whether Viragh turned one down.

The trial began on Thursday, March 18, with Bellevue Hospital's medical examiner telling the court that Dimitri Mateichik had died from a fractured skull. Patrolman O'Leary described finding the victim in the gutter of East Ninth Street. Six other witnesses testified on the first day, including John Mateichik, who had identified his father's body at the morgue. The following day, witnesses talked about the fatal encounter. The bar owner and another customer described the scuffle in the bar. A neighbor, Anna Husinko, provided eyewitness testimony, explaining that she had watched from her fourth-floor window across the street as a thin man in a jacket walked up to a larger man in an overcoat and punched him twice. She could not identify their faces but maintained that she had seen the events clearly.

When the trial resumed on Monday, March 22, the prosecution called its final witness, the arresting officer, Seymour Gall, and then rested its case. After a short recess, defense attorney Harold Frankel called William Viragh to the stand. The defendant gave his version of events, explaining that he had gone outside with the intention of guiding the drunken man away from the bar, but that Mateichik had raised a fist and threatened him. Knowing that the older man had a knife, Viragh struck him in self-defense. He had meant to assist Mateichik, he said, not to harm him. Once his testimony was finished, the defense rested.

On Tuesday, March 23, Judge McCullen instructed the jury to determine whether Viragh was guilty of manslaughter, or the lesser crime of assault, or not guilty of any crime. Deliberations began on Wednesday, March 24. After some time, the foreman sent a note to the judge: "This jury would like to have you clarify 'Assault in the second degree' for information of the Jury. Respectfully, Murray R. Moll, Foreman." After receiving the judge's clarification, the jury continued its deliberations before sending word that it had reached a verdict. Back in court, it found William Viragh guilty of second-degree assault. At that, Judge McCullen dismissed the jury. The following month, he sentenced the defendant to two and a half years in state prison, with the sentence suspended. Viragh was a free man.

THE TRIAL OF WILLIAM VIRAGH matches the descriptions that Reginald Rose gave of his jury service on almost every point, but it also presents a puzzle.

The case file, pulled from the New York City Department of Records, includes a mix of typed documents and handwritten notes about the police investigation, various witness statements, and a few sections of the official court transcript. Although case files don't always list the jurors, this one contains a handwritten sheet, in a clear cursive script, with the names of the jurors, ten men and two women, plus two alternates. Reginald Rose is not among them.

What could explain this discrepancy?

Could Rose have been referring to a trial other than *The People v. William Viragh*? The chances of that are exceedingly remote. No other homicide matches even a few of the parameters—date, location, description of victim, cause of death, and verdict. It's scarcely possible that a different case could match all these details *and* somehow be omitted from the homicide docket. (We can hear an echo of Rose's eventual script: "You're asking us to believe there was a different case that was almost identical? The odds are a million to one!")

Could the list of jurors refer to a different trial? No. Two jurors are mentioned in the court transcripts—the foreman, Murray R. Moll, and a juror who posed a question during the trial, Irving Auerback—and both appear on the handwritten list. It's clear that Rose was not a member of the jury of *The People v. William Viragh*.

Could Rose have served under a different name? Again, no. Reginald Rose was not a *nom de plume* but his legal name, the only one he used throughout his life.

A more likely explanation is that Rose was summoned for jury duty in March 1954 and went to the Foley Square courthouse, just as he said. Once there, as he later explained: "You reported to an enormous Central Jury Room where you sat and waited with hundreds of others. . . . A huge lottery wheel was spun and some 30 or 40 names were picked from it. These people, 98 percent of them white males, were taken to a court room. There another lottery wheel was spun and twelve of these men were selected to sit in the jury box. The first name picked became the Foreman."[11]

It's likely that Rose was one of the "30 or 40" people considered for *The People v. William Viragh*—indeed, he *must* have been among them to know about the case at all, as it involved the death of an obscure man and was not reported in major newspapers. Since Rose was *not* chosen to serve, it stands to reason that he was one of the many prospective jurors in the courtroom, but not one of the fourteen chosen to serve as jurors or alternates. That would not be surprising, since more were turned away than were empaneled.

At that point, Rose would have been sent back to the Central Jury Room where, depending on the number of cases to be tried, he might have been selected for different trial, or he might have been dismissed. If he was selected for a different trial, Rose may indeed have served on a jury in the spring of 1954, just not the manslaughter case he described. (In the movie screenplay, Juror 12 remarks: "I'd say we were lucky to get a murder case. I figured we'd get an assault or burglary. Boy, they can be the dullest." Could Rose have been talking from experience, having sat on the jury of a dull case, but recalling a more exciting one?)

It's also possible that, his interest piqued, Rose stayed on to observe at least part of the trial, which would have been open to the public. It's even conceivable that he attended more than one day of the trial, including the reading of the verdict on March 24. More than sixty years later, with the principals no longer alive and court records incomplete, it's impossible to know for sure. Nor does it really matter. Whatever the exact details of his service, Reginald Rose's summons for jury duty in early 1954 *was* a transformative experience.

IMMEDIATELY AFTER HIS VISIT to Foley Square, with his impressions fresh in mind, Rose set to work on a new play. There had already been many courtroom dramas, of course, both on stage and on screen. The conflict between prosecutors and defense attorneys, arguing before judge and jury with the defendant's fate in the balance, offers a naturally dramatic setting. Rose had used it in his first play, "The Remarkable Incident at Carson Corners," when school children turn their classroom into a makeshift courtroom.

This time, Rose would turn convention on its head. He later explained: "No one anywhere ever knows what goes on inside a jury room but the jurors, and I thought then that a play taking place entirely within a jury room might be an exciting and possibly moving experience for an audience."[12] Rose's drama would begin *after* the trial had ended and would follow the jury over the course of its deliberations.

What he needed was a source of dramatic tension. Members of the jury would have to disagree, but about what? Rose later recalled: "Within a week, I had an idea for a play about a jury with evidence that needed to be more thoroughly examined and the idea of one man holding out against the others and beginning to convince them."[13] That was the crucial idea: A single juror would stand alone, and over the course of the play bring the others around to his point of view.

Rose imagined a play that unfolded in real time, taking the form of classical Greek drama, beginning when the jurors received instructions, then following them into the jury room and staying with them until a verdict was reached.[14] There would be no breaks, no flashbacks as in "The Remarkable Incident at Carson Corners," and no parallel stories as in "Thunder on Sycamore Street."

Although by the 1950s women served on juries in the State of New York, Rose decided on an all-male jury. A jury composed entirely of men, he believed, would allow for expressions of strong emotion and moments of direct confrontation, and perhaps even threats of violence, which would be less likely in a mixed jury. Also, the jurors would all be white men, allowing them to express openly any racial prejudices, a theme Rose had tried to take up in "Thunder on Sycamore Street."

With these parameters in mind, Rose moved on to the most demanding task: to devise a case against the defendant that was strong enough for almost all jurors initially to vote guilty, and then to chip away at the evidence so that jurors would shift their votes, at different times and for different reasons. That task, he later said, called for "the most intricate plot of anything I've ever written."[15] Rose worked on the outline for a solid week and was stunned to find that it ran to twenty-four pages, more than twice the length of his previous ones.[16]

The outline that Rose submitted to Florence Britton began with an unusual disclaimer: "It is necessary to handle this synopsis a bit differently than the ordinary synopsis in order to explain clearly a set of facts which actually have been fully established *before* the story begins and which come out gradually during the story." Following this disclaimer, Rose wrote: "It is alleged that Jack Davis, a nineteen-year-old boy, has murdered his father, Harry Davis, by stabbing him with a switchblade knife." As for the details of the murder: "The time of Harry Davis' death was fixed at 12:10 A.M., and the cause was a switch-blade knife wound which entered the chest and plunged down into the heart."[17]

Rose provided a brief description of each juror, but sensing there would be no way to keep twelve names straight, added: "They will be referred to by number rather than name."[18] He offered a quick sketch of each man, creating a group whose diversity in temperament, age, and background would contain the seeds of conflict. With very minor changes, these descriptions would never change—either for the *Studio One* television production in 1954, or the United Artists movie released in 1957. Rose's *dramatis personae* were set from the start:[19]

THE CHARACTERISTICS OF MEMBERS of the jury which will be pertinent to this story are briefly described in these thumbnail sketches:

THE FOREMAN

50 years old. A petty man, not overly bright, but overly pompous. A man who never in his life enjoyed any authority and who intends to make the most of this one opportunity.

JUROR #2

38 years old. A small, meek, mild, hesitant man who finds it difficult to maintain any opinions of his own. A man who is easily swayed and usually adopts the opinions of the last person to whom he has spoken.

JUROR #3

40 years old. A very strong, very forceful, extremely opinionated man within whom can be detected a streak of sadism. A humorless man who is intolerant of opinions other than his own, and accustomed to forcing his wishes and views upon others.

JUROR #4

45 years old. An aesthete. A man who is above and beyond all of this, and is a great deal more concerned with his own intellectual accomplishments than he is with the humanities involved in a murder case. To him the entire affair is in the abstract.

JUROR #5

27 years old. An extremely naive, very frightened young man who takes his obligations in this case very seriously, but who finds it difficult to speak up when his elders have the floor.

JUROR #6

33 years old. An honest, but dull-witted man who comes upon his decisions slowly and carefully. A man who has all his life been the butt of jokes, and accepts this doggedly. A man who cannot be forced into anything against his will.

JUROR #7

42 years old. A loud, flashy, gladhanding salesman type who has more important things to do than sit on a jury. He has to go to theatre that night, for instance. He is quick to show temper, quick to form

opinions on things he knows nothing about, and worries more about the N.Y. Yankees than about this responsibility.

JUROR #8

35 years old. A quiet, thoughtful, gentle man. A man who sees all sides of every question and constantly seeks the truth. A man of strength, tempered with compassion. Above all, a man looking to see that justice is done.

JUROR #9

70 years old. A mild, gentle old man, long since defeated by life, and now merely waiting to die. A man who recognizes himself for what he is, and mourns the days when it would have been possible to be courageous.

JUROR #10

32 years old. An angry, bitter man. A man who antagonizes almost at sight. A virulent bigot who places no values on any human life save his own. A man who has been nowhere and is going nowhere and knows it.

JUROR #11

48 years old. A refugee from Europe who has come to this country in 1938. A man who speaks with an accent, and who is ashamed, humble, almost subservient to the people around him, but a man who will honestly seek justice.

JUROR #12

30 years old. A slick bright advertising man who thinks of human beings in terms of percentages, graphs and polls, and has no real understanding of people. A superficial snob, but trying to be a good fellow.

ROSE'S OUTLINE DESCRIBED the flow of events: "As the story begins, we fade in on a jury room in a New York City courthouse. It is 11:00 A.M. The room is empty. In it is a large table and twelve chairs. A washroom opens off the jury room. The door opens and 12 jurors, all men, file in."[20] After a brief conversation, the jurors take an initial vote: "Juror #8 votes not guilty. The other eleven jurors vote guilty." As they begin to discuss the case, a few points of evidence are mentioned, including a positive identification made by a man who lives downstairs and the eyewitness account of a woman who lives across the street. Various personalities begin to emerge: Juror 7 is impatient, Juror 3 is aggressive, and Juror 10 dislikes the defendant's ethnic group and won't believe what "they" say. Rose added: "We do not know what racial or religious group #10 refers to when he says 'they,' nor do we ever find out."[21] He had taken the lesson from "Thunder on Sycamore Street" to heart: leaving the ethnic group unstated would make the message more broadly relevant, not less so.

Over the next minutes, the jurors argue about various points, but no one changes his vote. When Juror 4 reminds the others that Jack's switchblade knife, an unusual knife purchased several hours earlier, was found in his father's chest, Juror 8 asks that it be brought in for inspection.

Rose's outline reads:

> He asks the foreman to have the guard bring in the knife for the jury to examine. It is brought in, and one by one they look it over at the request of #8. He points out that the odd design of the knife was an important factor in the prosecution's case, that this was what made it so easily identifiable. He sticks it in the table now, and swiftly reaches into his pocket, whips out a knife, flicks the blade open and sticks that one into the table next to the first one. They are identical.

> He explains that he had bought this knife the day before at a pawnshop. There could have been two such knives, he contends. Jack could have given the knife he bought to his friend, the youth who has since disappeared, and someone else could have killed Harry Davis with the same kind of knife. It would have been a remarkable coincidence if this had happened, but the possibility is there. That's all he wants to establish, the possibility—the reasonable doubt. Let it not be so that the knife Jack bought was the death knife simply because the prosecution says it is so, begs #8.[22]

With the jurors at an impasse, Juror 8 proposes another vote, this one by secret ballot. There is a pause for the first commercial break as they vote.

When ballots are counted, Juror 9, the old man, has changed his vote to not guilty, saying he wants to hear more. Over the next minutes, Juror 8 raises several doubts regarding the prosecution's case. He reasons that the noise of a passing elevated train would have made it unlikely for neighbors to hear Jack shout "I'm going to kill you." He questions whether Jack would have come back to the scene of the crime. When Juror 8 says that the defendant was "much too bright" to return to the apartment, Rose included an exchange that remained intact through every revision and was used verbatim in the movie:

> "Bright?" shouts #10. "What do you mean, bright? He's a common ignorant slob. He don't even speak good English!"
>
> "He *doesn't* even speak good English," quietly says #11, the refugee.
>
> #10 stares angrily at #11.[23]

Juror 8 also wonders whether the neighbor below, an old man who had suffered a stroke and walks slowly, could have reached the front door of his apartment in time to identify Jack as he ran out of the building. A reenactment casts doubt on this key testimony. Gradually, a few more votes change to not guilty.

After the second commercial break, the vote stands at six to six. The jurors discuss the angle of the knife wound, and Juror 8 doubts that Jack Davis, an experienced knife fighter, would have used a switchblade to make a downward wound. More votes shift, leaving only three for guilty. When Juror 8 calls into question the testimony of the eyewitness across the street, Jurors 4 and 10 change their votes, leaving only Juror 3. Surrounded and alone, he finally shouts, "All right!" and surrenders.

Having reached a unanimous verdict, the jurors begin to file out. Rose describes the final image:

> There is no dialogue from this point to the final curtain. Jurors #3 and #8 are the last to leave the room. As they begin to leave, #3 stops, turns and goes to the cigarette-littered table. The knife is still sticking in it. He yanks it out of the table, looks at it for a long time, then flicks the blade back into it. He walks over to #8, and silently he gives him the knife, and walks out. #8 looks around the room for a moment and then slowly follows. The door closes and then we cut to a close shot of one of the ballots the jurors had used. Although it is crumpled we can clearly see the two words written on it, "not guilty." Fade out.[24]

READERS FAMILIAR WITH THE 1957 movie will note how many elements were already present in Rose's outline. The arc of the drama, from the initial vote to the final climax, was set from the start. As well, the twelve jurors and their basic characters, the points of evidence that initially seemed strong but are revealed to have flaws, and the sequence in which jurors change their votes—all of these too were clear from the outset. Many important changes were still to be made—scenes added, dialogue expanded, and lines shifted among characters—but much was in place from the beginning.

Rose sent the outline to Florence Britton, who liked it immediately.[25] She had made substantial changes to his first play, "The Remarkable Incident at Carson Corners," and had insisted on major revisions to his second play, "Thunder on Sycamore Street." This one, she could tell, was right from the start.

With a green light, Rose expanded his outline into a full teleplay. Having written such a detailed outline, the task did not take long. Writing a play usually took several weeks, but this one was completed in just five days.[26]

The script differed from the outline in a few respects. The names of the defendant and the victim were dropped; no longer would they be Jack Davis and Harry Davis. From now on, no one—neither the jurors nor the defendant nor the victim—would have a name. Rose also made an important change regarding Juror 10. In the outline, Juror 4 and Juror 10 change their minds when Juror 8 casts doubt on the testimony of the eyewitness. On reflection, it didn't seem credible that Juror 10, described as "a bitter, angry man" and "a virulent bigot," would abandon a position he had held so tenaciously due to a single point of logic. Now, in Rose's full script, only Juror 4—the "intellectual"—would change his vote based on revelations about the eyewitness's vision. Juror 10 would change for a different reason: frustrated with the other jurors, he would unleash a torrent of hateful words that reveal the depth of his prejudice and destroy his credibility. For inspiration, Rose drew upon the final scene of "Thunder on Sycamore Street," when Frank Morrison urged his neighbors to run the Blake family out of town. Rose put many of the same words in the mouth of Juror 10: "Say, what's going on here? . . . Don't you know about them? Where are you going? Listen, I'm trying to tell you something here." Frank Morrison and Juror 10 are essentially the same character: a bigot who appeals to prejudice and fear, and who is eventually rejected by decent people.

As Rose expanded his outline into a full teleplay, he tried to blend four elements. First was "the evidence as remembered and interpreted by each individual member," meaning that the audience learns about the case only as it is described by the jurors. Second, he would try to capture interpersonal dynamics, "the relationship of juror to juror in a life-and-death situation." Third, he would try to explain "the emotional pattern of each individual juror," not an easy task with so many jurors in such a short amount of time. Finally, Rose would try to convey the pressure felt by each juror through the use of "physical problems such as the weather, the time, the uncomfortable room, etc."[27] With twelve jurors present in a single room for the entire play, Rose also had to create reasons for them to get up and move around, to "prevent a normally static situation from becoming too static."

Rose also added a title, the words 12 ANGRY MEN written by hand across the top of the outline. He offered no clues about the origin of the title but may have been inspired by a recent movie called *Eight Iron Men* (1952). (A 1955 movie, *Seven Angry Men*, about abolitionist John Brown and his six sons, had an even closer title, but was released a year after Rose wrote his play. In fact, as of July 1954 it was to be called *John Brown's Raiders*, with the name change coming months later, making it more likely that *Seven Angry Men* was inspired by Rose's play rather than the reverse.[28]) However it came about, the title was well-chosen, as it suggested an ensemble piece about all twelve jurors, and not a play about the heroic efforts of just one man.[29]

It has sometimes been suggested that Rose's teleplay was directly influenced by the momentous Army-McCarthy hearings, which were televised to the nation beginning on April 22.[30] It seems almost irresistible to imagine Rose, a pad of paper on his knee and pencil in hand, fashioning a parable about civil liberties while watching the hearings on television. It makes for a good story but has no basis in fact. "Twelve Angry Men" can be fully understood as the next step in Rose's evolution, extending the themes he had taken up in his first two plays, and inspired by his visit to Foley Square. No additional influences are needed.

AT THE END OF MAY, Rose was the subject of a profile by Steven Scheuer, a nationally syndicated columnist for Key Features. The article had a flattering title: "Meet Mr. Reginald Rose—Outstanding TV Author." Of the many good writers who had emerged in the current television season, said Scheuer, one stood out: "Reginald Rose is the most distinguished of the new writers, and one whose contribution is of more than passing significance." Described as "singularly unassuming" in manner, Rose had an admirable ability: "to tackle challenging themes and, by handling them with truth and understanding, create a theatrical experience of enormous emotional impact."[31] Scheuer spoke glowingly of Rose's first two original plays and made brief mention of the third, "The Death and Life of Larry Benson," to be broadcast the following day, Memorial Day. Rose described how he worked in his small apartment on West Seventy-Ninth Street, writing in cursive longhand on sheets of yellow paper. His wife typed his work: "I pay her a dollar a page—considerably above the prevailing rate, I might add—and I'm in hock to her up to my neck."[32]

Toward the end of Scheuer's column, Rose made the first public mention of his latest work: "I'm also doing the first story I ever took from 'real life.' It's called 'Twelve Angry Men,' and it's the result of my jury duty this year."[33] Barely two months after his visit to Foley Square, Rose had created the most important drama of his life.

6

***

"Twelve Angry Men"
(Summer 1954)

WHEN REGINALD ROSE FINISHED his script for "Twelve Angry Men" in late May 1954, only three weeks remained in *Westinghouse Studio One*'s season. Each week would feature one of the anthology's best young writers. On May 24, *Studio One* performed Gore Vidal's "A Man and Two Gods," followed by Rose's "The Death and Life of Larry Benson" and Rod Serling's "The Strike."

With that, Felix Jackson's first season as producer of *Studio One* came to an end. Franklin Schaffner and Paul Nickell had taken turns directing thirty-eight programs, beginning with Orwell's "1984" and closing with "The Strike." For the next three months, *Westinghouse Studio One Summer Theater* would be produced by Alex March, with a variety of young directors given an opportunity.

THE SAME MONTH THAT ROSE finished "Twelve Angry Men," he submitted a ten-page outline called "The Unborn," about an unmarried schoolteacher who becomes pregnant and the controversy that ensues. How could a woman be pregnant and unmarried while also morally upright, and therefore acceptable for television in 1954? Rose concocted a complex tale: A single woman—shy and inexperienced—goes on holiday, where she meets a man and falls in love. They marry after a brief romance and very soon she becomes pregnant. He confesses that he already has a wife, and the marriage is annulled. A few months later, as her pregnancy cannot be hidden, scandal erupts. Parents are outraged and convene a meeting of the parent teachers association, at which she is accused of being unfit to teach and threatened with dismissal. Eventually she stands to speak and courageously faces her accusers. Rose's outline explained:

> She wants to have this child and wants to bring it up to be good, and decent and useful. She wants to bring up this child herself, in her own home, in her own community . . . In order to do this she needs her job. She is not going to stand there and beg for her job, and she is not going to make excuses for her conduct or explain the circumstances surrounding it. These are not things that human beings should have to do in public upon command. These are personal things and it is her right to keep them personal until she decides otherwise.[1]

The teacher goes on to say that she will explain to her students the circumstances of her pregnancy in a way they can understand. Rose was clear: "She has done no evil, she says strongly. The evil is all in the minds of adults." After a moment of silence, the principal voices his support, the teacher smiles quietly, and the play ends.

Florence Britton and Felix Jackson read the outline but turned it down, perhaps finding it too daring for the times. A Black man could be changed into an ex-convict in "Thunder on Sycamore Street," but there was no way to make an unwed pregnancy acceptable for national television. Although never produced, "The Unborn" is a companion piece to "Twelve Angry Men," written at almost the same time, and both exploring how an individual, initially condemned by a majority, may deserve exoneration. Moreover, both stories relied on elaborate plots, with Rose devising in "Twelve Angry Men" a way for an apparently guilty person to be acquitted and in "The Unborn" for an unmarried woman to be pregnant without sullying her character.

The summer of 1954 was a notable time for the Rose family. Rather than endure another stifling New York summer in the small apartment on West Seventy-Ninth Street, it decamped to Fire Island, the largest of the barrier islands off the southern edge of Long Island. Rose rented a small house, scarcely more than a shack according to son Jonathan, where Barbara Rose and her two young sons spent the summer while Reginald traveled back to the city, still working for the Ray Austrian Advertising Agency. It would be the first of many summers the family spent on Fire Island.

Rose's next outline, dated July 20, was "The Silent City," a story about the fear and worry that accompany the loss of jobs. Set in the fictional town of Fulton, the story opens with John Stark, foreman at the Fulton Radiator Company, announcing to workers that "the factory is to be closed and set up somewhere down south."[2] Much of the workers' anger is unjustly directed at Stark, the bearer of bad news, and a mob descends on his home, chanting and carrying sticks. Stark boldly walks out to meet them and defuses their anger by inviting some to come inside. They are all on the same side, he tells them, and should find a way to work together. Rose described: "Now, slowly, the idea begins to take hold. There is a plant. There are men. There is knowledge. The men know how to construct radiators . . ." If each man contributes one hundred dollars, they can buy the plant and run it themselves. The story ends on a note of hope, with workers taking control of their future.

Studio One passed on this one, too, perhaps sensing that Westinghouse would not be pleased with a teleplay whose villain was a profit-seeking corporate giant. Workers uniting to take control of the means of production had a whiff of Marxism and was not likely to be well received in an age of Red scares and blacklists.

Although neither "The Unborn" nor "The Silent City" went past the outline stage, both stories demonstrated Rose's willingness to address unpopular themes on network television. They were also testimony to Rose's faith that well-meaning people can reason together and find solutions. His skills as a dramatist were improving, but he tended to rely on familiar devices such as the public meeting ("The Remarkable Incident at Carson Corners" and "The Unborn") and the climactic confrontation ("Thunder on Sycamore Street" and "The Silent City").

ON JULY 28, 1954, FIVE MONTHS after filming was complete, *On the Waterfront* opened at the Astor Theater, a fabled Times Square movie house.[3] The long lines that stretched around the block felt like a form of redemption to Elia Kazan after the difficult years that followed his appearance before HUAC. "With that first morning's line at the Astor Theater," he later wrote, "I was back on top of the world."[4]

The movie was a triumph, with Marlon Brando's portrayal of Terry Malloy described as a "brilliant and moving glimpse into the soul of a poor enslaved pier worker."[5] Equally admired were Rod Steiger as Terry's older brother, Charlie, and Lee J. Cobb as the crooked union boss, Johnny Friendly. A. H. Weiler of the *New York Times* called *On the Waterfront* the most "technically brilliant job of movie-making to be unveiled this year" and lauded its depiction of Hoboken's tenements and docklands in "the vivid tones of a documentary."[6] The movie went on to win eight Academy Awards, including Best Picture, with Boris Kaufman receiving the Oscar for Best Cinematography. A commercial and artistic success, *On the Waterfront* proved that great movies could be made in New York.

While *On the Waterfront* was drawing large crowds, the movie version of *Marty* was gearing up for production. Paddy Chayefsky and Delbert Mann had wanted Rod Steiger to reprise his role as the gentle butcher, but producer Harold Hecht felt that the public would not pay to see the same actors it had watched on television. For the lead role he chose Ernest Borgnine, best known for his role as a tough Army sergeant in *From Here to Eternity*. Betsy Blair was cast as the object of his affections. United Artists insisted on keeping costs low and approved a budget of only $350,000.[7]

In early September, filming began with exterior shots in the Bronx on White Plains Road, the Grand Concourse, and Gun Hill Road. Once those location shots were complete, production moved to California. *Marty* may have been set in New York, written by a New Yorker, and first performed for live television in New York, but Hecht-Lancaster Productions wanted to film at the Samuel Goldwyn Studios in West Hollywood.

BY EARLY SUMMER, FELIX JACKSON and Florence Britton turned their attention to the upcoming season of *Studio One*. Impressed with Rose's latest drama, they chose it for the season opener.[8]

The first official mention of "Twelve Angry Men" came from Murray Martin, the publicity agent for *Studio One*. On August 13, he announced the program lineup for September. After the final two programs of the summer season, the 1954 season would open on September 20 with an "original teleplay by Reginald Rose, directed by Franklin Schaffner." Martin offered a synopsis:

> The judge gives the jury his charge . . . and the twelve men—strangers to each other, all from diverse backgrounds with differing outlooks and mores—retire to the jury room to render their verdict. Their decision means life or death for a slum boy accused of killing his brute father. Is the boy guilty? A vote is taken . . . and only one juror votes "Not guilty." He readily admits his humanness: "It's not so easy for me to raise my hand and send a boy off to die without talking about it first." The "talk" that follows is heated and revealing—and until their final decision is reached, the drama is intense and emotional in this play written especially for STUDIO ONE by Reginald Rose, author of "The Remarkable Incident at Carson Corners" and "Thunder on Sycamore Street."

A few weeks later, the cast of "Twelve Angry Men" was announced. The lead role of Juror 8 would be played by Robert Cummings. Handsome and still youthful at forty-four, he had appeared in *King's Row* (1942) with Ann

Sheridan and Ronald Reagan, in Alfred Hitchcock's *Saboteur* (1942), and most recently in Hitchcock's *Dial M for Murder* (1954) with Grace Kelly and Ray Milland. Cummings had also worked in television, starring in a comedy, *My Hero*, during the 1952–53 season.

Perhaps the best-known cast member was Edward Arnold. At sixty-four, his breakthrough role had come as a corpulent financier in *Diamond Jim* (1935). Six feet tall and weighing more than two hundred pounds, and with a booming baritone voice, Arnold credited his success to his size: "The bigger I got, the better character roles I received."[9] He became Frank Capra's favorite bad guy, playing a ruthless tycoon in *You Can't Take It with You* (1938), and a corrupt political boss in *Mr. Smith Goes to Washington* (1939), both starring James Stewart. Two years later, with Europe at war, he played a Fascist who tries to crush free speech in Capra's *Meet John Doe* (1941). In *The Hollywood Studios*, Ethan Mordden summed up Hollywood's idealized view of the American character: "Edward Arnold is bad, James Stewart is good."[10] In "Twelve Angry Men," Arnold would be perfect for the aggressive bigot, Juror 10.

Other cast members included veteran stage and movie actor Franchot Tone as Juror 3, the strongest proponent for conviction; Walter Abel as the intellectual Juror 4; Lee Philips as Juror 5, the young man raised in the slums; Paul Hartman, a comedian and vaudevillian, as Juror 7, the wisecracking salesman; Joseph Sweeney as the elderly Juror 9; and George Voskovec, a native of Czechoslovakia, as Juror 11, the European refugee.

Of course, the real star of *Studio One* was Betty Furness, and Murray Martin's press release paid her special tribute: "When Betty steps before the television camera on September 20, she will begin another season with WESTINGHOUSE STUDIO ONE and mark up another milestone in her unique career. Since June 1949—when STUDIO ONE was in its infancy and when she first took over her role as demonstrator—Betty has created a scintillating new career for women: the woman announcer."

By now, Furness had "appeared on the home TV screens almost 1,000 different times, speaking more than 250,000 words about almost every electrical appliance made by Westinghouse, including an atomic engine for submarines, and a new reactor-generator to harness atoms for peace."[11] Before, during, and after Rose's jurors considered matters of life and death, Betty Furness would sell home appliances to the American public.

AS "TWELVE ANGRY MEN" WAS READIED for production, Rose had to make significant changes to the script.[12] At 8,500 words, his teleplay was far too long to fit into the forty-eight minutes available for an hour-long drama.

He recalled "a struggle to cram all of the detail, action and character I had devised into the less than fifty minutes of air-time available."[13]

To meet the time limit, Rose condensed several passages and deleted a few sections entirely to create a final version of 5,800 words. What remained, he lamented, was only "the bare frame of the plot and the skeletons of the people."[14] Several jurors had only a few lines and were not developed in any depth. It was not ideal, but would have to do.

While editing his play, Rose also fixed a problem concerning Juror 3, the last juror to hold out for guilty. In the climactic scene, surrounded by eleven votes for not guilty, Juror 3 shouts "All right" and gives up. Yet it was not clear why he had been so adamant in the first place. To describe Juror 3 as a "very forceful, extremely opinionated man within whom can be detected a streak of sadism" didn't seem sufficient. *Why* had he wanted so much to send the boy off to die?

To provide better motivation, Rose inserted a brief passage where Juror 3 would mention that he had a son, now a young man, from whom he was estranged. It could be inferred that Juror 3 was transferring anger toward his son onto the defendant. Rose chose a moment in act 1, long before tensions among jurors rise to a boiling point. After Juror 4 says that "children who come out of slum backgrounds are potential menaces to society," Rose added, in pencil, these words for Juror 3: "You're right. It's the kids. The way they are, y'know? (Bitter) I've got a kid. When he was 8 years old he ran away from a fight. I saw him. I was so ashamed I almost threw up. So I told him right out: I'm gonna make a man out of you or I'm gonna bust you up into little pieces. When he was 16 he hit me in the face. He's big, y'know. I haven't seen him in three years. Rotten kid. You work your heart out . . . All right. Let's get on with it. (He looks embarrassed.)"

Rose also shifted a few lines among his characters. In the outline and the first script, Juror 8 had been the source of almost all insights about flaws in the prosecutor's case. Now, Rose trimmed Juror 8's role and let others speak up. When Juror 7 changes his vote to not guilty, he is no longer challenged by Juror 8; Juror 11, the refugee from Europe, would insist that Juror 7 vote with his conscience. Calling into doubt the vision of an eyewitness had originally come from Juror 8; now Rose gave this vital insight to Juror 6. Not only did more jurors offer useful ideas, but Juror 8 became a more nuanced character, no longer providing all the insights himself, but enabling others to contribute.

THE 1954 TELEVISION SEASON OPENED on Sunday, September 19, with the three major networks showcasing some of their best material. NBC's

The Goodyear-Philco Playhouse opened with Paddy Chayefsky's latest drama, "Middle of the Night," about a widower and a young divorcee who find love despite their own insecurities and the disapproval of their families. It starred E. G. Marshall and Eva Marie Saint, now in the public eye for the captivating performance opposite Brando in *On the Waterfront* that would earn her an Academy Award.

The following night, two leading anthologies went head-to-head. At 9 PM, NBC's *Robert Montgomery Presents* featured "Diary," starring Janice Rule and a charismatic young actor, John Cassavetes. Thirty minutes later, CBS's *Westinghouse Studio One* unveiled its season premiere, "Twelve Angry Men."

Studio One was broadcast from Chelsea Studios, a television sound stage at 221 West Twenty-Sixth Street, between Seventh Avenue and Eighth Avenue. At the prescribed hour, the *Studio One* title card appeared and the announcer spoke: "*Westinghouse, Westinghouse Studio One.*" The opening shot revealed the jurors seated in the courtroom box as the judge read instructions from offstage. The guard, played by Vincent Gardenia, intoned: "The Jury will retire." The twelve men stood and filed out while the credits appeared:

TWELVE ANGRY MEN

WRITTEN ESPECIALLY FOR STUDIO ONE BY REGINALD ROSE

When the credits ended, the twelve jurors were in a small room with a single long table and twelve identical chairs, plus a fan, a water cooler, and a coat rack. A door at the far end led to a washroom. Tall buildings could be seen through the windows, with the frequent sound of automobile horns suggesting an urban setting.

To navigate around the small set, Franklin Schaffner placed one camera on either side of the table, able to move on a dolly and pivot to look across the table. Every shot was selected in advance, so that as one camera broadcast the live performance, the other was moved to its next position. There could be no reverse shots from the far end of the table, since that would expose the director and crew. The set provided general lighting, but there was no way to adjust the light for a specific shot.

The actors performed briskly, following the signals of the floor producer who kept one eye on the action and another on the clock. After a few comments—"This had better be fast," says Juror 7 (Paul Hartman), who has tickets to see a Broadway show, *The Seven Year Itch*—the jurors agree to take a first vote. The initial vote shows eleven for guilty, with some hands raised immediately, others after a moment's hesitation, and a few only when it is clear how the others have voted. When the foreman asks for those voting not guilty, Juror 8 (Robert Cummings) raises his hand slowly, visibly self-conscious. "You think he's not guilty?," asks Juror 3 (Franchot Tone). "I don't know," replies Juror 8. "It's not easy to send a boy off to die without talking first."

Over the next minutes, Juror 10 (Edward Arnold), a menacing figure in a dark shirt, strides around the small set, while Juror 4 (Walter Abel), with a neatly trimmed moustache and bow tie, dismisses the boy's alibi in precise tones. Juror 3 speaks the new lines about his estranged son. The murder weapon is brought in and Juror 4 holds it up for all to see, then jams it point down on the table; suddenly Juror 8 slams down a second knife to the astonishment of all present. With matters at an impasse, Juror 8 suggests that the others take a second vote, this time a secret vote, and stands to the side as ballots are distributed. At that point, the screen goes to commercial break. Act 1 takes sixteen and a half minutes. The prospect of a secret ballot offers a moment of suspense, designed to keep viewers from switching channels.

Act 2 begins with a shot of Juror 8 still standing by himself, suggesting no time has elapsed during the break. The ballots are read out loud: guilty, nine times, before a vote of not guilty. Juror 9 (Joseph Sweeney), the old man, says that the boy is probably guilty, but he respects Juror 8's motives and wants to hear more. Over the next minutes, jurors challenge various points of evidence. Juror 5 (Lee Philips) shifts his vote to not guilty, making the vote nine to three. When Juror 8's reenactment suggests the man downstairs could not have gotten to the door in time to see the boy, Juror 3 accuses him of dishonesty. Juror 8 retorts that Juror 3 is less interested in finding the truth than in putting the boy to death, provoking Juror 3 to charge at him, shouting "I'll kill him." Juror 8 responds calmly: "You don't really mean you'll kill me, do you?" The scene fades out. Act 2 takes only thirteen minutes.

As act 3 begins, the jury votes by a show of hands, and is deadlocked at six to six. Now, with minutes remaining, the tempo picks up. When Juror 2 (John Beal) wonders about the downward angle of the stab wound, Juror 5, who grew up in a slum, says that switchblades are typically used with an upward thrust, suggesting the defendant was not the aggressor. Juror 7 is impatient: "I'm a little sick of this whole thing already. We're getting nowhere fast. Let's break it up and go home. I'm changing my vote to not guilty." He is challenged by Juror 11 (George Voskovec) who reminds the jurors that they have a solemn duty and must take their deliberations seriously. Juror 8 calls for another vote, which reveals only three still in favor of conviction. Stunned by this turn of events, Juror 10 unleashes his tirade, leading the others to reject him. Juror 6 (Bart Burns) remembers that the eyewitness wore glasses in court, but would not have been wearing them when she raised her head from her pillow to look out the window, causing Juror 4 to change his vote.

The last holdout, Juror 3, is alone and surrounded. After a short pause—perhaps hurried along by the floor manager, waving his arms to keep the action moving—he shouts "All right" and capitulates. As the jurors gather their belongings and file out, Juror 3 picks up the switchblade and extends it toward Juror 8, perhaps leading to a final confrontation. After a moment's hesitation, he closes the knife and gives it to Juror 8 in a time-honored expression of surrender. Juror 8 watches silently as Juror 3 leaves, and the play ends. Only the most astute viewer would have remembered Juror 3's comment, in act 1, about his estranged son.

As with many live productions, a few things went amiss. Juror 9 muffed a line, pointing to Juror 8 and saying "this gentleman chose not to stand alone against us"—adding the word "not" and reversing the meaning of the sentence. Some minutes later, one of the cameras was visible, protruding from the right. The very last scene, too, had a glitch: as Juror 3 tried to flip open the switchblade, it caught and stopped part way, forcing him to flick it a few more times before the knife opened fully.

Those minor errors aside, *Studio One*'s live production of "Twelve Angry Men" was brisk and riveting. Despite the tight confines of the set, Schaffner had managed, according to Rose, "to capture the speaker of each line on camera at precisely the right moment and composed starkly realistic, tension-filled pictures of the reactions to these lines."[15]

Reviews of the broadcast were excellent, with *Variety* writing: "'Twelve Angry Men' was a wallop on all main counts—script and performances, direction. Seldom in television history has a story been able to achieve so many high points with such frequency and maintain the absorbing, tense pace. . . . The play scored impact after impact as the plain and not so plain joes struggled with their consciences and with each other to arrive at a just verdict. . . . The play was whammo."[16]

For Val Adams of the *New York Times*, the broadcast had posed a quandary. There was no way to watch *Robert Montgomery Presents* on NBC from 9:30 to 10:30 as well as *Studio One* on CBS from 10:00 to 11:00, so he watched the first program in its entirety but only the second half of *Studio One*. In his column the next day, Adams could write only that "Twelve

Angry Men" *"appears to be* an unusually powerful drama" (my emphasis). He saluted the writer: "The play was an original by Reginald Rose, who is known for writing drama with a punch."[17]

The broadcast of "Twelve Angry Men" had the immediacy and power so characteristic of live television, but also had some of its drawbacks. With no way to light specific shots or to frame close-ups, the broadcast had what film scholar David Bordwell called a tendency for "flatly staged mid-range shots, goosed up with close-ups, fast cutting, and meaningless camera movements."[18] The strict time limit also meant that the action often felt hurried, with little time for nuance or dramatic pauses. Moreover, the costumes were undistinguished, the actors mostly middle-aged men dressed in grey suits, looking all of a type. Although the program drew strong reviews, there was plenty of room for improvement.

"Twelve Angry Men" was broadcast from coast to coast, but some people missed it entirely. As the jurors argued in a Manhattan studio, the cast and crew of a Warner Bros. movie, *Mister Roberts*, was aboard a Navy cargo vessel, the *USS Hewell*, sailing from Hawaii to Midway Island. After several days of filming in the middle of the Pacific Ocean, the *USS Hewell* would return to Hawaii, arriving September 29, for additional scenes in Kaneohe Bay.[19] The cast of *Mister Roberts* included William Powell and James Cagney, with the title role played by Henry Fonda.

7

⋮⋮

Gaining Momentum
(Fall 1954 to Spring 1955)

AFTER "TWELVE ANGRY MEN" opened the new season, *Westinghouse Studio One* settled into its normal rhythm. The next weeks featured a mystery, a psychological thriller, and a biography of Thomas Edison, very much in keeping with the anthology's usual fare. Reginald Rose's jury room drama had made a strong impression, but so had his other teleplays.[1]

Rose focused his attention on upcoming projects. In early November, *Studio One* performed "An Almanac of Liberty," timed to coincide with the release of Justice William O. Douglas's book of the same name. A deeply committed civil libertarian, Douglas wanted to teach Americans about the legal foundations of a free society, and prepared an almanac with an entry for each day of the year, often about a famous case or historical event. Rather than dramatize one or another entry, Rose created an original tale that distilled some of the book's themes. His story was set in a fictional town called Ridgeville, where a group of citizens has assembled at the town hall on a sunny morning. In their midst is a stranger named Carter, who was attacked the night before by a group of Ridgeville men simply because he was an outsider. Unsure who called the meeting or what they are meant to do, the townspeople become agitated. Some of them blame Carter. As they do, a clock on the wall begins to move backward, as the worst impulses of suspicion and hatred cause time to reverse. Other citizens stand up for the stranger and eventually put matters right. The better angels of human nature prevail, and time advances again. "An Almanac of Liberty" took up themes of prejudice and mob behavior that Rose had already explored and added free speech, due process, and civil rights.

Although the great majority of viewers were strongly supportive of "An Almanac of Liberty," a loud minority made its feelings known. Present for the live broadcast, Rose answered one of the three studio phones that had been ringing constantly. He later said: "A man who refused to give his name shouted: 'I'm a college graduate so you can't fool me with that stuff. Why don't you 'Studio One' Commies go back to Russia?' This for a play which had a few kind words to say about a basic American heritage, the Bill of Rights!" Fortunately, one viewer had been pleased: Justice Douglas wrote to say he had "loved" the adaptation.[2]

Rose's next drama was performed in early December. Press agent Murray Martin made a strong claim: "Only three or four times in the past five years have I called special attention in advance to an upcoming *Westinghouse Studio One* program . . . and then only because of a special occasion such as an anniversary. . . . But every once in a while along comes a script that deserves, almost demands, special attention. . . . Such a program, I think, will be the *Westinghouse Studio One* presentation of '12:30 A.M.'"[3]

The teleplay marked Rose's first effort to address the problems of troubled youths, a theme he had touched upon in "Twelve Angry Men" when he described the defendant as raised in a slum, his mother dead and his father abusive. Now he delved more deeply into the topic. The teleplay, wrote Murray Martin, "is an eloquent plea for parents and adults to understand children—on their own level, and in terms of their experiences and feelings."[4] All too often, Rose said, children are expected to behave like adults: "They want kids to be grown-ups and they're not. Kids go through so much. It's a hard thing . . . growing up, and nobody seems to remember."[5] "12:30 A.M." was more than a "message play," said Martin: "Reginald Rose, as few other young writers today, has the ability to present ideas in terms of exciting drama."[6]

The program was aired on December 8 to generally good reviews. The *New York Times* found that it "never quite fulfilled its promise," but offered good words for the writer, calling Rose "one of TV's more stimulating playwrights" and credited him with trying to "tackle varying themes instead of essentially writing the same one over and over."[7] *Variety* was even more positive: "Reginald Rose, whose name popped up as a television writer of distinction with his *Studio One* season opener, '12 Angry Men,' and who reinforced his growing reputation with 'An Almanac of Liberty' a few weeks back, can now claim a permanent seat among television's consistently outstanding dramatics."[8]

FALL 1954 WAS A PIVOTAL TIME for *You Are There*, CBS's historical program produced by Charlie Russell and directed by Sidney Lumet, who was down to one weekly program after relinquishing *Danger*. The season began with "The Emergence of Jazz," starring Louis Armstrong as King Oliver, leader of the legendary Creole Jazz Band. Credited to Jeremy Daniel, it was written by Abraham Polonsky, one of the show's blacklisted writers.

Since its premiere in early 1953, *You Are There* had become a very popular program, appealing to young and old alike. School teachers frequently contacted CBS for copies to show in class, but the network had little to offer since kinescopes were not good enough to distribute. Executive producer William Dozier lamented: "We kill ourselves every Sunday from 6:30 to 7. We go through the back-breaking routine of recreating all this history but at 7 o'clock it's all down the drain. Doesn't make sense."[9] An obvious solution was to film *You Are There* rather than broadcast it live. Not only would prints be available for distribution, but CBS would be able to syndicate the program and reap income for years to come. With Hollywood studios actively wooing New York television producers, a solution presented itself: Why not move *You Are There* to the West Coast, taking advantage of studios that were better equipped and less costly, and shift from live performance to film at the same time?

And so, in fall 1954, CBS announced that *You Are There* would cease New York production as of December and resume as a filmed program in Los Angeles in April 1955. To cover the three-month gap, *You Are There* began to work a double schedule, producing its usual weekly live program from Grand Central Station and filming thirteen episodes to be broadcast from January to March 1955. Since Lumet wouldn't be able to handle both, he chose the filmed programs, and let his assistant, John Frankenheimer, age twenty-four, take over the live broadcasts.

Starting in November 1954, Lumet began to direct filmed episodes of *You Are There* at the Edison Studios in the Bronx. Coming with him was set designer Bob Markell, joined by George Justin as production supervisor. For Lumet, working in film was an exciting new experience, entirely different from live television. Rather than alternating between two cameras in real time, he could compose each shot with the best angle and best lighting. Live television had been a rush of activity and energy, but film allowed a director far greater artistic expression. The thirteen filmed episodes of *You Are There* proved to be very important, as they gave Lumet the experience that paved the way for his feature film debut.

Another factor led CBS to move *You Are There* to the West Coast. By late 1954 there were persistent rumors that Charlie Russell was relying on blacklisted writers, and some CBS executives were growing suspicious. Moving from New York would provide a chance, as Abraham Polonsky later put it, for William Dozier to "expunge Russell and his creative unit."[10]

In December 1954, Russell was at the CBS offices, waiting for an elevator, when Dozier turned to him: "*You Are There* is going to be done in Holly-wood from now on and I will be producing it. Also your services are no longer required by CBS." The elevator doors opened and Dozier got on, leaving Russell momentarily stunned.[11] For three and a half years, since taking over as producer of *Danger*, Charlie Russell had supported black-listed writers, providing them with a living and protecting their identities. Now he was out of a job. Bob Markell said: "Charlie defended those writers like you wouldn't believe. And that got Charlie fired."[12]

Sidney Lumet parted with CBS on more pleasant terms. At year end, once the thirteen episodes for *You Are There* were complete, Lumet let his contract expire. After four years directing *Danger* and *You Are There*, he was ready to branch out into new directions. There would be no short-age of projects. Already Lumet had agreed to direct two episodes of *The Best of Broadway* for CBS in early 1955, as a freelancer rather than a salaried employee, and he was also scheduled to direct a stage production of George Bernard Shaw's *Doctor's Dilemma*.[13] He was also keen to direct a motion picture. Delbert Mann had made the jump from television to the movies with *Marty*. Perhaps, in the coming year, Sidney Lumet could direct one, too.

FOR REGINALD ROSE, 1954 had proved to be a breakthrough year, with six one-hour dramas for *Studio One* to his credit. Now it would be the turn of another young writer. Over the last three years, Rod Serling had made steady progress, his earnings rising from five thousand dollars in 1952 to ten thousand in 1953 and then to twenty thousand in 1954, bolstered by two scripts for *Studio One*.[14]

In late 1954, Serling prepared a four-page outline titled "The Pattern," which his agent, Blanche Gaines, sent to *Studio One*. Florence Britton and Felix Jackson liked it, but CBS programming executives said no. Gaines sent it to NBC, where it was immediately picked up for *Kraft Television Theatre*. Now called "Patterns," it told the story of Fred Staples, a clean-cut young man promoted from a regional office to the New York head-quarters of the Ramsey Company, run by a domineering boss, Mr. Ramsey. Serling described "Patterns" as "a story of power, ambition, and the price tag that hangs on success."[15] Like Rose, he wanted to comment on broader social issues: "I was writing about a society that places such stock in suc-cess, and has so little preoccupation with morality once success is attained. This is not the morality of good and evil, this is morality's shady side of the street."[16]

The cast featured Richard Kiley as Fred Staples, Everett Sloane as Mr. Ramsey, and Ed Begley in the role of Andy Sloane. Begley was a versatile actor who had starred on Broadway in Arthur Miller's *All My Sons* in 1947. In 1953, he played the lead role in a *Philco Television Playhouse* production, "Ernie Barger is Fifty," as a well-meaning and affable man who realizes, at age fifty, that he is no longer needed—not by his son, his colleagues at work, or even his elderly father, played by Joseph Sweeney. As Ernie Barger, Begley had conveyed the same mix of amiability and vulnerability that made him effective as Andy Sloane in "Patterns."

The *Kraft* broadcast of "Patterns" on January 12, 1955, was a triumph that almost matched "Marty" for its impact. The *New York Times* effused: "In one of those inspired moments that make the theatre the wonder that it is, 'Patterns' was an evening that belonged to the many, not only Mr. Serling." It was too good to be shown just once: "A repeat performance at an early date should be mandatory."[17] A second live performance took place on February 9 and was as well received as the first. The major anthologies had not yet moved to film, but moments like this were a further push in that direction.

With the success of "Patterns," Rod Serling became an overnight sensation, besieged with letters of congratulations (as well as letters from people who suspected that their boss must be the model for Mr. Ramsey). Movie studios, too, were quick to see the potential of "Patterns," and within a few weeks, independent producers Michael Myerberg and Jed Harris paid twelve thousand dollars for the movie rights and thirteen thousand to adapt the screenplay, giving Serling a total of twenty-five thousand dollars, or ten times what he had earned for the two *Kraft* showings. In a single stroke, he had topped his entire earnings for 1954. Serling wrote to his lawyer: "We hit the jackpot with 'Patterns.'"[18]

Serling was now a hot property, with studios eager to buy the movie rights to his other scripts. "All of a sudden," he recalled, "with no preparation and no expectations, I had a velvet mantle draped over my shoulder."[19] In short order, Serling pocketed $9,000 from 20th Century Fox for *The Day the Century Ended* and $15,000 from MGM for *52 Miles to Terror*. By year end, his income reached $83,658, four times the previous year.[20] The effect was not entirely positive: "I found I could sell everything I had, and I did. Like the hungry kid left alone in the candy store, I just grabbed. A lot of what I sold should have stayed in the trunk."[21]

Regret and perspective came later. For now, after many lean years, the chance to cash in was too good to miss. The lesson was not lost on other television writers. First, Paddy Chayefsky had scored with "Marty"; now

Rod Serling struck gold with "Patterns." Television could provide a good living, but the real money was in Hollywood.

IN EARLY 1955, REGINALD ROSE continued to develop new outlines, some of which *Studio One* accepted while many more were rejected. In January, he submitted "The Endless Night," about a man tormented by guilt and fear, reliving the events of his life during a long sleepless night. Felix Jackson said no but added encouraging words: "Do not give up. There's always hope."[22]

Rose's next outline, "The Alley," told the story of Frankie Dane, leader of a gang called the Hornets, who lives with his mother and little brother in a run-down apartment. A social worker tries to befriend Frankie and steer him away from crime, but Frankie wants the Hornets to murder a man by luring him into an alley and stabbing him. The social worker hears of the plan from Frankie's brother and intervenes at the last moment. The play ends with the hope that Frankie might change his ways.

When *Studio One* was not interested, Ashley-Steiner shopped "The Alley" to other programs, at first without success. "It dealt sympathetically with juvenile delinquency at a time when juvenile delinquents were considered to be eminently unpopular," Rose later commented. "I couldn't for the life of me see what was controversial to begin with, and still don't."[23] In his view, the public should not be deprived of a thoughtful treatment of an important issue: "This kind of predetermination of what an audience's reaction to 'controversial' material might be is obviously infuriating to an author."[24]

The script was picked up by ABC's *The Elgin Hour*, earning two thousand dollars for Rose.[25] It proved to be a lucky break as the program was produced by Herb Brodkin, marking the first time Rose would work with a man who, over the next decade, would become a very close collaborator. To direct, Brodkin hired Sidney Lumet, now able to take on projects for ABC, and giving Lumet his first chance to direct an original drama by Reginald Rose. *The Elgin Hour* changed the title to "Crime in the Streets." Rose noted the irony: "'The Alley' was not an exciting enough title and would not be inclined to titillate an action-hungry viewer into tuning in. Go figure these fellows!"[26]

"Crime in the Streets" was broadcast on March 8, 1955. "Chalk up another major hit," wrote Jack Gould of the *New York Times*.[27] In the role of Frankie Dane, John Cassavetes delivered an "immensely compelling performance," thanks to Lumet's "top flight" direction.[28] The writer was praised for a script of "detail, maturity, and vividness" that provided "an uncannily lifelike re-creation of a city street. . . . Reginald Rose wrote a social drama of enormous power and human insight."[29]

Rose was very pleased with the two lead actors, Cassavetes and Mark Rydell: "Those two roles came alive beyond my most hopeful expectations, but I really didn't realize how authentic and gripping both portrayals were until a month later when I attended a kinescope showing of 'Crime in the Streets' at a New York settlement house."[30] Ordinary citizens, who lived in tough urban neighborhoods, found the portrayals to be very realistic. Most importantly, he was delighted with the director: "Sidney Lumet's direction was absolutely electric and lent a relentless drive to the script which never let up for a moment."[31]

THE NIGHT BEFORE "Crime in the Streets" was performed on *The Elgin Hour*, the Seventh Annual Emmy Awards ceremony was televised from the Moulin Rouge in Hollywood. "Twelve Angry Men" came away with three Emmys: Robert Cummings was named Best Actor in a Single Performance for his role as Juror 8, and Franklin Schaffner took the prize for Best Direction, a fitting reward for what Rose called "perhaps the best-directed show I've ever seen on television."[32] Not least, Rose won for Best Written Dramatic Material, taking the award over a group of nominees that included Paddy Chayefsky. For Rose, who began writing original dramas just a year earlier, it was a moment of great satisfaction.

With three Emmys for "Twelve Angry Men" on March 7 and a highly lauded broadcast of "Crime in the Streets" on March 8, the press was soon alive with reports of potential movie deals for Reginald Rose. A week later, Ashley-Steiner reported that negotiations were underway to sell the rights to both plays.[33]

Of the two, "Crime in the Streets" was considered the better prospect for the big screen. The story line seemed more compelling, the cast was larger and the characters more varied, and a romantic subplot could be added. Barely a month after its broadcast on *The Elgin Hour*, movie rights for "Crime in the Streets" were purchased by Allied Artists, a second-tier Hollywood studio run by Walter Mirisch. Rose received twenty-five thousand dollars plus 10 percent of profits, about the same as Serling's deal for "Patterns."[34] It was his first big payday, more than he earned in an entire year of television writing.

Given his fine work on the television program, Sidney Lumet was an obvious candidate to direct the movie. Rose tried to lobby for Lumet, commenting that successful television dramas come about when a writer finds a director "who understands your type of writing and has an empathy for the characters."[35] He noted that Delbert Mann had handled the television and movie versions of *Marty*, and Fielder Cook, who had directed the television version of "Patterns," had just been chosen to do the movie. In April, it was reported that Lumet was in negotiations for the job and a deal seemed imminent.[36] Yet Hollywood studios tended to prefer directors with experience in motion pictures, and Allied Artists chose Don Siegel, a veteran who had just directed its latest hit, *Invasion of the Body Snatchers*.

Many years later, Lumet said he would have been content to remain in television: "I had no hint whatsoever that I wanted to do movies. I would have been completely happy to spend the rest of my life in television."[37] Perhaps there were times he felt that way, but for any young director, feature films were the place to be. Movies offered a much broader canvas, and the great directors of the day—among them William Wyler, John Ford, Frank Capra, and Alfred Hitchcock—were known for their work on the big screen. For Sidney Lumet, who had toiled in television for five years, breaking into movies was the obvious move. The challenge was to get his first assignment.

Having bought the rights to *Crime in the Streets*, Allied Artists could not only pick the director—it could also revise the story. A romantic angle was developed, reflected in a movie poster that featured a shapely young lady. (The tagline: "How can you tell them to be good when their girlfriends like them better when they're bad!") Don Siegel recalled: "I made many changes in the script, which Reggie Rose didn't like, so my relationship with him was not the best."[38] Filming took place in Hollywood, with Allied attempting to recreate a gritty urban location on a sound stage. Siegel thought the finished product was good but the movie fared poorly at the box office. The public didn't care for a story about gang members plotting to kill an innocent man.[39]

For Rose, *Crime in the Streets* offered a generous payday but taught an important lesson: once a writer sold the story rights, he lost all influence.

BY APRIL 1955, THE MOVIE version of *Marty* was ready for release. Rather than book it into large theaters, which wouldn't keep a movie that wasn't an immediate hit, United Artists placed *Marty* into smaller cinemas, where it might have a chance to grow. In New York City, it opened at the Sutton, an art house with five hundred seats at East Fifty-Seventh Street and Second Avenue, far from the large movie palaces on Times Square. Initial reviews were very good. The *New York Daily News* called *Marty* a "Bronx Style Romance," describing it as "a sentimental, heart-warming, simple story of a couple of ugly ducklings who find compensation for their lack of good looks in each other's love."[40]

Helped by strong reviews and favorable word of mouth, *Marty* took in $20,500 for its second week at the Sutton, then edged higher to $20,800 in its third week.[41] In May, it got an unexpected boost. Entered as one of the American films at the Cannes Film Festival, *Marty* earned "top bravos" from the European audience, which loved its naturalistic acting and sensitive portrayals, so different from the usual Hollywood fare. On the final day, it was awarded the Festival's top prize, the *Palme d'Or*, prevailing over thirty-two other movies from around the world.

With a prestigious European award added to a good initial response at home, *Marty* was turning into a major hit. Instead of shifting to a larger theater in New York, United Artists kept *Marty* at the Sutton, where it played to packed houses and pulled in upwards of $20,000 every week for months on end. By September, it had played at the Sutton for six months, leaving the cinema's managers "more than a little awed."[42] With strong box office results across the country, domestic revenues for the year exceeded $2 million, and foreign revenues added another $1.5 million.[43]

The phenomenal success of *Marty* was a watershed event. For years, Hollywood had looked down on television. Now, as one review put it, the industry was having a change of heart: "Instead of ignoring TV, as movie producers did for years, they are now turning to television as a source of screen material."[44] *Marty* did more than prove that television programs could be adapted for the big screen. It also showed they could become hits.

AFTER WORTHINGTON MINER LEFT *Studio One* in 1952, he signed on with NBC and produced programs including *The Medic*.[45] In early 1955, he embarked on a new project, backed by the Fund for the Republic, a nonprofit organization endowed by the Ford Foundation, and the American Civil Liberties Union (ACLU). Titled *The Challenge*, the program would "expose the widespread misconceptions respecting the intentions of the Constitution."[46]

Miner approached two writers who shared an interest in social issues, Reginald Rose and Rod Serling. "We came out to the Bel-Air Hotel and stayed in our rooms for four days dreaming up outlines for the proposed series," Rose recalled. "We ended up with 39 subjects and many script outlines where we presented two sides of an issue."[47]

The pilot episode of *The Challenge* would examine a controversial issue very much in the news: the loyalty oath. It told the story of Bill Whitman, a friendly school bus driver. After he leaves the children at school one morning, Bill is called to the principal's office and reminded that he has not yet signed the loyalty oath required of all district employees. Bill is a simple man and hardly a political firebrand, but he's troubled by the demand. Having to declare one's loyalty does not seem right. He declines to sign and is fired on the spot. When Bill returns home and sadly tells his wife that he has lost his job, she implores him to go back and sign, saying the family needs his income to survive. Whitman won't compromise his principles; he has never been suspected of subversion and cannot understand why he must declare his loyalty.

The following day, a new driver takes over the school run, but the children chant "We want Bill" and refuse to go to school. Their spontaneous strike—which gave the episode its title, "The Smallest Revolution"—leads to a gathering of the PTA that evening. The principal and staff meet parents in a classroom, now a makeshift town hall cum courtroom. A spirited debate follows. One man states a fundamental principle: a person is presumed to be innocent and should not be forced to declare loyalty. Another counters that if Bill has nothing to hide, he should sign. Still others point out that a loyalty oath is bound to be ineffective, since subversives wouldn't hesitate to lie, while those who refuse to sign may be honest citizens who object as a matter of conscience.

Eventually Whitman is called upon to speak, and in heartfelt words expresses his view that citizens should be presumed to be loyal unless proven otherwise. A law professor sums up the issues: Yes, there are times when individual liberty may have to be curtailed if there is a clear and present danger, and Communism *is* such a danger; but whether a bus driver, a solid citizen and respected by all, presents such a danger is the question at hand. Finally, Bill Whitman and his family are asked to step out of the classroom. The principal calls the motion to a vote: Should Bill be reinstated as driver, yes or no? The story ends there, the decision resting with the viewer—and by implication with all citizens.

Miner asked Rose to write the sections about Bill Whitman and his family, and Serling to write about the PTA meeting and the pros and cons of loyalty oaths.[48] Rose completed his parts on time but Serling, in high demand after the success of "Patterns," did not. "Rod was loaded down with commitments and did not have the time he needed to do his homework," Miner later wrote, forcing the producer to spend a week at the law library of the University of California, Los Angeles (UCLA) to learn about the history of loyalty oaths in English common law and in the United States, and then to write the script himself.[49] The final teleplay was credited to Reginald Rose and Rod Serling as coauthors, marking the only official collaboration between the two men, although in fact they did not write it together.[50]

Sidney Lumet was chosen to direct, and Lumet reached out to art director Bob Markell and production supervisor George Justin, his colleagues from *You Are There*. Jack Warden was cast as Bill Whitman. In September 1955, the pilot was screened before network executives in New York. If successful, *The Challenge* could have become a regular series, with each program highlighting a different issue of civil liberty.[51] Although Miner thought it was one of the best programs he had ever produced, no sponsors stepped forward. "They were petrified," he recalled.[52] Eventually the program was distributed privately, made available by the Educational Television and Radio Center to public organizations, and presented by the ACLU on local television as a public service.

Little noted today, *The Challenge* marked the first collaboration among Reginald Rose, Sidney Lumet, Bob Markell, and George Justin. When the chance arose to work together on a feature film, they would be ready.

PART III

THE MOVIE

8

⠿

Henry Fonda and the Deal for *12 Angry Men* (Spring and Summer 1955)

IN THE FIRST MONTHS OF 1955, one of America's leading actors was at a career crossroads.

Henry Fonda had started in the movies twenty years earlier with roles that emphasized his youth and good looks—he was once described as "the most likable of the new crop of romantic juveniles"[1] and often paired with Hollywood's top starlets. Moving on to more substantial roles, he starred in *Jesse James* (1939) and *Young Mr. Lincoln* (1939), both for 20th Century Fox. One review of his performance as Abe Lincoln summed up his appeal: "Mr. Fonda supplies the warmth and kindliness, the pleasant modesty, the courage, resolution, tenderness, shrewdness and wit that kindles the film."[2] Perhaps his most memorable performance was in *The Grapes of Wrath* (1940), directed by John Ford, based on John Steinbeck's epic novel about a family of Okies traveling from the Dust Bowl to California. The role of Tom Joad, an honest man trying to hold his family together in the face of injustice, allowed Fonda to personify solid American virtues of decency and integrity. It came at a price: Fonda had to agree to a contract that bound him to Fox for seven years.

In early 1942, after the United States entered World War II, Fonda narrated a short documentary called *It's Everyone's War*. Set in the fictional town of Jefferson—an "all-American" town with white picket fences and white faces—Fonda described in a casual but earnest voice how the townspeople contributed to the war effort by working extra hours to produce arms and ammunition. The tone was just right, blending serious purpose with easy confidence. If Henry Fonda said it was everyone's war, well, it must be so.

Although thirty-seven years old and well past the age of compulsory service, Fonda decided to enlist in the Navy. He appeared in one last movie, *The Ox Bow Incident* (1943), as Gil Carter, a cowhand who defends three innocent men against a group of vigilantes, and then reported to naval headquarters in Los Angeles. Fonda spent the next three years as an intelligence officer in the Pacific, taking part in naval operations at Kwajalein, Saipan, and Guam.

After the war, Fonda returned to Los Angeles and fulfilled the last years of his contract with 20th Century Fox. By 1948, he was thoroughly tired of the movies, which he felt were often little more than a series of disjointed scenes. It was, he said, "as if an artist were to paint different parts of a picture on separate pieces of canvas and then have someone else fit them together."[3] Once free from the Fox contract, Fonda was not eager to make another movie. "I'm so tired of audiences made up of studio grips and gaffers," he said. "Isn't there any place left for a working actor?"[4] That place, of course, was on stage, where he had started his career: "In the theater, the actor does a complete job at each performance, inspired by the audience, whose response prevents his job from becoming tiresome."[5]

For his next role, Fonda accepted the lead in *Mister Roberts*, a play about a frustrated naval officer in the calm backwaters of the Pacific Ocean during World War II. The role of Lt. j.g. Doug Roberts, a gentle man who stands up for the sailors as they bristle against the captain's petty orders, was a natural for Fonda. *Mister Roberts* opened at the Alvin Theater on February 18, 1948, getting outstanding reviews and earning Fonda a Tony Award for Best Actor in a Play.[6] The Broadway run lasted for 1,157 performances, through early 1951, and then toured nationally for another nine months, ending on the West Coast.[7] In Los Angeles, Fonda again turned down several movies to act in another play, *Point of No Return*, and then agreed to star in the stage production of *The Caine Mutiny Court Martial* as Lt. Barney Greenwald, the prosecuting attorney who does an unpleasant job with consummate professionalism.

By 1954, Fonda had been away from the big screen for six years. The role that brought him back was the movie version of *Mister Roberts*, produced by Warner Bros. At first he declined the role, saying that at forty-nine he was far too old to play a junior naval officer, but after director John Ford made a personal appeal, Fonda agreed. Filming took place in Hawaii and on Midway Island in September and October 1954, much of it aboard the *USS Hewell*.[8] A big-budget color picture, shot and projected in CinemaScope, *Mister Roberts* was scheduled for release the following summer.

AFTER FILMING *MISTER ROBERTS*, living in his townhouse on East Seventy-Fourth Street, Fonda pondered his next move. In addition to stage and screen there was also television, by now an attractive medium to established actors. He had already performed in one television drama—"Decision at Arrowsmith," a Sinclair Lewis story adapted by Tad Mosel for CBS's *Chrysler Medallion Theater* in July 1953—and was open to more.

Another option intrigued him, too. Following the 1948 Paramount rulings, several actors had formed independent production companies, with Burt Lancaster the first in a growing list that now included Kirk Douglas, Frank Sinatra, Gregory Peck, Yul Brynner, and Robert Mitchum.[9] In February 1955, Fonda formed Orion Productions and agreed to a deal with United Artists to finance and distribute six movies over three years.[10] The following month, he appeared in "The Clown," based on the life of Emmett Kelly, on *General Electric Theater*, a thirty-minute program hosted by Ronald Reagan, and a few days later it was announced that "The Clown" would become the first movie produced by Orion Productions.

Fonda's next role would be for NBC's new hit program, *Producers' Showcase*. Launched in October 1954, *Producers' Showcase* was a prestige program, ninety minutes long, and broadcast monthly, sometimes live from New York and sometimes live from Hollywood. Notably, it was blessed with a big budget that let it attract top stars. Produced by Fred Coe, who had moved from *The Goodyear-Philco Playhouse*, it quickly became recognized as one of television's top shows.

Coe hired Delbert Mann to direct two programs for *Producers' Showcase*. First was Arthur Koestler's "Darkness at Noon," about the 1937 Moscow Purge Trials, an adaptation of the play which had won the New York Critics Circle Award. Produced on May 5 in New York, it starred Lee J. Cobb as Rubashov, a Communist Party member destroyed by the state he had helped to create. Cobb gave an excellent performance although Mann thought he seemed weak and at times acting oddly.[11] The reason became clear a few days later when Cobb was hospitalized with a heart attack, perhaps suffered while on the set of "Darkness at Noon."[12] He would spend the next several months convalescing.

Immediately after "Darkness at Noon," Mann flew to California to direct "The Petrified Forest," with Humphrey Bogart reprising his breakthrough role as the gangster Duke Mantee, this time opposite his wife, Lauren Bacall. Henry Fonda was cast as Alan Squier, the role played by

Leslie Howard in the 1936 movie version. (The supporting cast included two actors who had appeared in "Twelve Angry Men" on *Studio One*— Paul Hartman as the diner owner married to Bacall's character and Joseph Sweeney as his father, Gramp, and two others would go on to play jurors in the movie of *12 Angry Men*—Jack Warden as Boze, the college boy working at the diner, and Jack Klugman as a member of Duke Mantee's gang.)

Rehearsals for "The Petrified Forest" began two weeks before the live performance on May 30. Mann was grateful that Bogart, one of the most famous Hollywood stars and with a reputation for being difficult, was willing to rehearse extensively for a role he knew so well. (The fact that his wife was the costar may have helped.) Mann also enjoyed working with Fonda: "Hank was a sweetheart, a truly great actor and very high on my list of the most special favorites." The broadcast of "The Petrified Forest" was a critical success, described as "flawless in every department."[13] Fonda enjoyed the experience immensely, finding that live television was similar to the stage in terms of energy and excitement.

WHILE IN LOS ANGELES FOR *Producers' Showcase*, Fonda had two meetings that would prove highly consequential. The week before the performance of "The Petrified Forest," Bogart and Bacall hosted a party, described by Delbert Mann as a "real Hollywood party" with a guest list that included Judy Garland, Spencer Tracy, and Frank Sinatra. Several accounts recall a night of heavy drinking, with Fonda escorted back to the Beverly Hills Hotel by Bogart and Sinatra. The next day, still woozy and nursing a hangover, Fonda was contacted by two of Italy's leading film makers, Carlo Ponti and Dino De Laurentiis, who were producing a big-budget movie of Tolstoy's *War and Peace* and wanted Fonda for the lead role of Pierre Bezukhov.[14] A straight-talking Nebraskan was not an obvious choice for an introspective Russian nobleman, but the part was offered and Fonda accepted. (In his memoirs, Fonda suggested that his judgment might have been impaired after a night of drinking, one way to explain a performance that turned out to be disappointing). Filming would take place in Italy, to begin in the late summer and last through fall.[15]

Fonda also met with United Artists executives to discuss possible movies for Orion. Among the properties that United Artists brought to Fonda's attention was a *Studio One* drama from the previous September that had recently won three Emmys, including one for Robert Cummings in the role of Juror 8. Perhaps, United Artists suggested, "Twelve Angry Men" might be suitable for the big screen with Fonda in the main role. Fonda watched a kinescope of the *Studio One* program in a Hollywood projection room and was impressed.[16] The role of Juror 8 was ideal for an actor who personified courage and decency. A straight line seemed to run from young Abe Lincoln to Tom Joad, Gil Carter, Doug Roberts, and now Juror 8. Some accounts have suggested that it was Fonda's idea to make a movie of "Twelve Angry Men," and that, unable to get support from a major studio, he approached United Artists for backing. More likely, based on Fonda's memoirs as well as the fact he had not seen the live *Studio One* broadcast, is the reverse: United Artists suggested "Twelve Angry Men" to Henry Fonda.[17]

On his return to New York, Fonda got in touch with Reginald Rose to inquire if he would be interested in bringing his teleplay to the big screen. Of course, he would. Fonda asked about the script, which would need to be about twice as long as the television program. That wouldn't be a problem, Rose assured him. He had removed large sections to meet the time constraints of *Studio One*. It would be easy enough to restore them and add a bit more.

Going from a live television program to a feature film opened several dramatic possibilities. The teleplay had been set in a single room, but the movie could bring in scenes from other locations. Also, the teleplay had moved forward in real time, but the movie could easily show parts of the trial, or perhaps the crime itself, or even depict the defendant and his father in earlier times.

Fonda considered these possibilities but decided against them: "The more I thought about flashbacks to the trial, or even beyond, before the trial, to what they talked about on the witness stand, the more I thought, no, this is a mistake, we've got to keep it the way it was."[18] Rose went through the same thought process and came to the same conclusion: "I hope Fonda isn't going to want to go anyplace because I think we've got to stay."[19]

Writer and actor were aligned: *12 Angry Men* would be a single continuous piece, moving forward in real time from start to finish. Fonda explained: "So, once having agreed, he wrote it, and it never went anyplace except the little introduction, the instruction to the jury, and a little epilogue at the end which I felt was a brilliant touch."[20]

IN JULY 1955, SIX WEEKS after viewing the kinescope in a United Artists projection room, Fonda and Rose agreed to coproduce a movie version of *12 Angry Men*. The *New York Times* reported: "Mr. Fonda will appear in the role of the high-minded juror who is the only one to hold out for acquittal on the basis of the evidence."[21] Fonda's company, Orion

Productions, would partner with a new company to be set up by Rose, called Nova. 12 *Angry Men* would be an Orion-Nova joint venture, with financing and distribution from United Artists.

Over the next weeks, representatives of Fonda and Rose worked with United Artists to hammer out the details. Rose's agent, Ashley-Steiner, hired Leon Kaplan, a lawyer with offices in the Equitable Building at the legendary corner of Hollywood and Vine. On August 17, Kaplan wrote to Rose with an outline of the deal.[22] The first draft of the screenplay would be due by December 15, 1955. Production would begin after Fonda completed his "current assignments," specifically *War and Peace* but eventually also a movie for Warner Bros.[23] The choice of director rested with the producers: Fonda would propose a candidate and Rose would have right of approval. Principal photography would begin "as soon as mutually agreeable," but not later than July 1, 1956.

Most of the contract was given over to United Artists' financial terms, known as the financing and distribution agreement. United Artists would raise all the money. Neither Fonda nor Rose would contribute any funds, but both would agree to defer most of their fees. Revenues would be split according to a carefully defined formula. First, cinema operators would keep a share of box office receipts, often between 20 percent and 30 percent, with the rest going to United Artists as gross revenue. Of this sum, United Artists would take a "standard distribution fee" of 30 percent, and then recover all direct costs associated with marketing the movie, which often amounted to another 10 percent. Next, United Artists would recover its actual production costs. Only then would deferred fees be paid, including all of Fonda's fee ($175,000) and three-quarters of Rose's fee ($45,000 out of $60,000). If any profits remained after deferred fees were paid, they would be shared among the three parties: 50 percent to Fonda, 25 percent to Rose, and 25 percent to United Artists.

The financial terms heavily favored United Artists, which got three cracks at revenues before the star and screenwriter were fully paid. How could Arthur Krim and Robert Benjamin get such a favorable deal? Simply put, they held all the cards. Since taking over United Artists in 1951, they had established a unique position in the industry, able to secure funds from banks and to arrange distribution through major cinema chains. Independent filmmakers might grumble, but they had few alternatives.

Krim was fond of a baseball metaphor: his aim was to hit many singles, a few doubles, and the occasional home run. United Artists' financing and distribution agreement ensured that it could only lose money if the movie was such a flop that gross revenues were abysmally low, or if production costs exceeded the budget. The name of the game was to choose properties with decent commercial potential and promote them well, while ensuring that production costs stayed within budget.

What could *12 Angry Men* expect to earn? No one could say for sure. William Goldman's 1983 observation about Hollywood was already valid in 1955: "Nobody knows anything. . . . Not one person in the entire motion picture field knows for a certainty what's going to work. Every time out it's a guess and, if you're lucky, an educated one."[24] On the plus side, Henry Fonda was considered a bankable star. *Mister Roberts* was expected to earn several million dollars at the box office, but that was an entirely different kind of movie. A better precedent might be *Marty*, a surprise hit that was on its way to earning more than $3 million, quite remarkable for a movie without a big-name star. Of course, *Marty* was a love story, albeit an unconventional one. There was no telling if a legal drama, with a dozen men arguing in a dingy room, could do anywhere near as well, with or without Henry Fonda. All things considered, a reasonable estimate of box office revenues for *12 Angry Men* might have been in the range of $1.5 million to $2 million.

Based on such an estimate, United Artists calculated what it could afford to spend. In his August 17 letter to Rose, Kaplan wrote: "UA is of the opinion that if this picture is made in black and white small screen with Fonda's entire salary and yours deferred except for $15,000, the cash costs should not exceed $350,000."[25] Fonda and Rose pushed for $400,000, but knew better than to ask for more, since higher costs would delay their receipt of deferred fees and reduce eventual profits. It was a standard dilemma: Save money while making the movie and the quality could suffer, but splash out for a higher budget and there would be less chance of making a profit.

The final budget called for a cash outlay of just under $400,000. To make sure that costs would be tightly controlled, United Artists added a clause to the financing and distribution agreement stipulating that if the budget was exceeded, the company would get a higher share of any profits. Everyone understood: Sticking to the budget was crucial.

For United Artists, the Orion-Nova production of *12 Angry Men* was a routine project, one of about fifty movies that it planned to back that year. Its expectations were modest. If box office revenues reached two million dollars and costs stayed on budget, United Artists would earn a satisfactory return.[26] If revenues fell short, it was still protected. Hitting a single would be just fine. In the unlikely event the movie turned out to be a hit, United Artists could gain handsomely.

The two coproducers had quite different prospects. If the movie did well, Henry Fonda would earn his $175,000 fee and claim 50 percent of net profits, potentially a lucrative outcome; but if it did poorly, he might receive nothing at all. As an established star venturing for the first time into movie production, Fonda was willing to take the risk.

As for Reginald Rose, even if the movie was a commercial failure, he would still earn fifteen thousand dollars, about ten times what he had been paid for the television program. If it did well, he would receive an additional forty-five thousand dollars in deferred fees, plus one quarter of net profits. These sums paled compared to what Fonda stood to earn, but were a huge step beyond what Rose had made as a television writer, and far more than he got for *Crime in the Streets*. Eager to tell the world about the deal it had secured for its client, Ashley-Steiner announced that Rose had "tapped the Hollywood jackpot."[27]

The contract between United Artists and Orion-Nova was signed in August 1955. With that, Henry Fonda left for Italy to film *War and Peace*.

Charlie Russell, producer, and Sidney Lumet, director, of CBS programs *Danger* and *You Are There*.

Felix Jackson became producer of CBS's *Westinghouse Studio One* in May 1953 and encouraged Reginald Rose to write original dramas. (Getty Images)

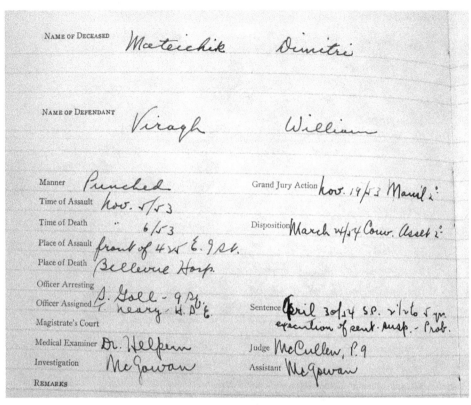

NAME OF DECEASED	*Mateichik*	*Dimitri*	
NAME OF DEFENDANT	*Viragh*	*William*	

Manner	*Punched*	Grand Jury Action	*nov. 19/53 Man'l ?*
Time of Assault	*nov. 5/53*		
Time of Death	*" 6/53*	Disposition	*March 4/54 Conv. Asset ?*
Place of Assault	*front of 425 E. 9 St.*		
Place of Death	*Bellevue Hosp.*		
Officer Arresting			
Officer Assigned	*S. Goll - 9 Sq.* *T. Neary - H.D.E.*	Sentence	*April 30/54 S.P. 3 1/2 to 5 yr.*
Magistrate's Court			*execution of sent. susp. - Prob.*
Medical Examiner	*Dr. Helpern*	Judge	*McCullen, P.9*
Investigation	*McGowan*	Assistant	*McGowan*
REMARKS			

Reginald Rose was very likely inspired by the trial of William Viragh, charged with manslaughter in the death of Dimitri Mateichik. Called for jury duty in March 1954, Rose was deeply moved: "I was writing one-hour dramas for *Studio One* then, and I thought, Wow, what a setting for a drama." (Manhattan District Attorney's Office Homicide Docket)

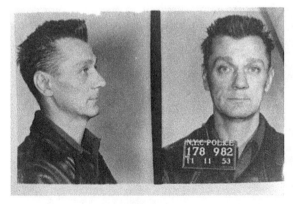

Booking photos of William Viragh, charged with manslaughter in the death of Dimitri Mateichik, November 11, 1953. (NYDA Case # 3504/William Viragh District Attorney's Office, County of New York, Criminal Record of William Viragh, B178982)

#7 (CTD)

Look at the kid's record. At fifteen
he was in reform school. He stole a
car. He's been arrested for mugging.
He was picked up for knife-fighting.
I think they said he stabbed somebody
in the arm. This is a very fine boy.

#8

Ever since he was five years old his
father beat him up regularly. He
used his fists.

#7

So would I! A kid like that.

#4

All right. Let's say he's a product
of a filthy neighborhood, and a
~~rotten~~ broken home. We can't help that.
We're not here to go into the reasons
why slums are breeding grounds for
criminals. They are. I know it. So
do you. The children who come out
of slum backgrounds are potential
menaces to society.

Top left: Reginald Rose in a November 1954 publicity photo, after he signed with a leading agency, Ashley-Steiner. (Publicity photo, PR collection).

Rose's first script did not explain why Juror 3 was so adamant about convicting the defendant. To provide stronger motivation, he inserted a comment about Juror 3's estranged son: "I haven't seen him in three years. Rotten kid. You work your heart out . . ." (Reginald Rose Papers, Wisconsin Center for Film and Theater Research)

"Twelve Angry Men" was broadcast live on September 20, 1954. Directed by Franklin Schaffner, it starred Robert Cummings as Juror 8 and Franchot Tone as Juror 3. (Photofest)

"I'll kill you!" Franchot Tone, as Juror 3, threatens Robert Cummings, Juror 8, at far right.

Left: Henry Fonda as a young actor, 1930s. (University of Wisconsin)

Right: In Los Angeles, May 1955, for a live television broadcast of "The Petrified Forest" with Humphrey Bogart and Lauren Bacall, Henry Fonda was shown a kinescope of *Studio One*'s "Twelve Angry Men." (Photofest)

Reginald Rose and Henry Fonda in New York City, after agreeing to co-produce *12 Angry Men* with financing and distribution by United Artists. (University of Wisconsin)

Fox Movietone Studios, Tenth Avenue between Fifty-Third Street and Fifty-Fourth Street, New York City. (Marc Wanamaker / Bison Archives)

George Justin, production supervisor, and Sidney Lumet, director. (George Justin Collection, Museum of Modern Art)

Sidney Lumet with his book of diagrams, showing each shot. (Courtesy of MGM Media Licensing, 12 ANGRY MEN © 1957 The Estate of Henry Fonda and Defender Productions, Inc. All Rights Reserved.)

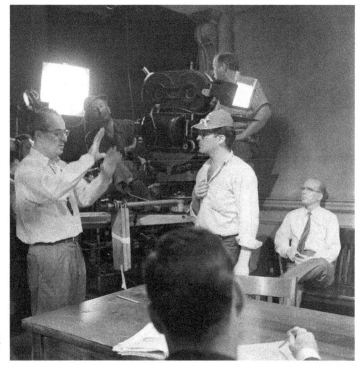

Director of photography Boris Kaufman with Sidney Lumet, John Fiedler seated. (Courtesy of MGM Media Licensing, 12 ANGRY MEN © 1957 The Estate of Henry Fonda and Defender Productions, Inc. All Rights Reserved.)

The rain sequence: A crew member holds the sprinkler as transluscent backdrops show the city at night. (Courtesy of MGM Media Licensing, 12 ANGRY MEN © 1957 The Estate of Henry Fonda and Defender Productions, Inc. All Rights Reserved.)

On the set of *12 Angry Men*, Fox Movietone Studios, July 1956. (*Left to right*): Henry Fonda, Sidney Lumet, Lee J. Cobb, Boris Kaufman, and Reginald Rose. Cameraman Saul Midwall at rear. (Courtesy of MGM Media Licensing, 12 ANGRY MEN © 1957 The Estate of Henry Fonda and Defender Productions, Inc. All Rights Reserved.)

9

***

Developing the Screenplay (Fall 1955 to Spring 1956)

THE SCREENPLAY OF *12 ANGRY MEN* was just one of many things occupying Reginald Rose in fall 1955.

In early 1955, Barbara Rose became pregnant with twins. That spring, the family moved from their small apartment on 147 West Seventy-Ninth Street to a larger one at 151 West Eighty-Sixth Street, between Amsterdam Avenue and Columbus Avenue. The new home had several rooms off a long hallway, with views of the busy thoroughfare.

Rose was working for CBS under a contract that called for him to submit twelve original outlines. During the summer months, while the family stayed in a rental home on Fire Island, Rose sent several outlines to Florence Britton and Felix Jackson. "The Joiner" was about a working-class family that moves into an upscale neighborhood thanks to the father's successful construction business, only to be spurned by members of the nearby country club, who subject family members to a variety of humiliations. Rose demonstrated his sympathy for the disadvantaged, this time a white family from a different social class. Jackson wrote back: "Florence and I love your outline of 'The Joiner' and are submitting it as it is." Someone higher in the approval hierarchy said no, and "The Joiner" went no further.

In July, Rose turned in "The Son of a Respectable Man," about the conflict between a demanding father and a son who has not lived up to his expectations. It was not accepted. In August, the same month that the movie contract with United Artists was finalized, Rose submitted "The

Courtroom," a story about the trial of a youth who is charged with the death of his younger brother, the favored son. Jackson answered with a detailed letter mailed to Fire Island. After a few personal niceties, he went to the point:

> Reggie, I cannot summon up any enthusiasm for this outline, and in as much as we have been working together for quite some time, I'd like to give you my reaction today more in general terms than in specific ones, and I want to be one-hundred percent honest with you. . . .
>
> It seems to me as if you were almost obsessed with the father and son problem, and as if this obsession had a hold on you and was intruding into all of your creative ideas (let's say almost all of them.) I wish you could free yourself from this problem long enough to sit back and analyse your own creative ability.
>
> I have no doubts that you are in a position today to dictate your own terms and to have everything you write performed or published. But I'll be damned if I'll recommend a play or an idea of yours just because it is Reginald Rose. I value our professional and personal relationship much too highly for that.[1]

Rose appears to have taken these comments to heart, and over the next months turned in five very different outlines in rapid succession. "And on the Seventh Night We Hate" told the story of a young woman whose boyfriend joins a right-wing hate group. "The Gathering" was about a family dinner where various arguments and tensions are brought to a halt by an air raid siren; after it turns out to be a false alarm, family members are able to put their problems in a more sensible perspective. "Dino" was the story of an adolescent, released from reform school, who struggles to fit back into society. "The Indestructible Man" was described as an "off-beat comedy," a rare attempt at humor. "Tragedy in a Temporary Town" was a tale about vigilante justice at a work site. Of these, only "Dino" was accepted by *Studio One*, and scheduled for broadcast in January.

Despite the many rejected outlines, 1955 was shaping up to be another successful year. *Studio One* had performed three of Rose's teleplays: "The Broken Spur," a western drama, in February; "The Incredible World of Horace Ford," about a man with a vivid imagination, in June; and "Three Empty Rooms," about unhappy newlyweds, in September. Two outlines that had been rejected by CBS were performed elsewhere, thanks to Herb Brodkin. In February, Brodkin had produced "Crime in the Streets" on ABC's *The Elgin Hour*. Later that year, after Brodkin moved to NBC's *The Goodyear-Philco Playhouse* (after Fred Coe left for *Producers' Showcase*), he bought "The Expendable House," a tale about soldiers at an atomic bomb test site—the title refers to a house at ground zero. Rose also had big paydays from sales of the movie rights to "Crime in the Streets" and "Twelve Angry Men," earning twenty-five thousand and fifteen thousand dollars, respectively. All told, it had been a very good year.

IN NOVEMBER, BARBARA ROSE gave birth to twin boys, Andrew and Steven, who joined Jonathan, now six and starting the first grade, and Richard, age three. The family of six settled into the larger apartment on West Eighty-Sixth Street.

While caring for his family and writing new outlines, Reginald Rose completed the screenplay for 12 Angry Men. Writing forty-eight-minute scripts had forced Rose to choose between plot and character. If the plot was complex, he would be able to offer "only brief fragments of people"; if characters were developed fully, there could be only "the barest sketch of a plot."[2] With so many jurors shifting their votes, "Twelve Angry Men" had necessarily emphasized plot. Now that he no longer had a rigid time limit, Rose could develop characters more fully, while also adding to the plot.

Rose began by restoring material he had trimmed from his original script. He then added dialogue to flesh out the characters and their motivations. The jurors still did not have names, but at least they were given occupations that suggested something about their personalities: Juror 2 was a bank clerk, Juror 4 a stockbroker, Juror 6 a house painter, Juror 7 a salesman, Juror 11 a watchmaker, Juror 12 an advertising man, and so forth. As for Juror 8? Rose's protagonist, logical and precise, would be an architect.

Rose's screenplay made substantial changes to the first scenes. The Studio One play had opened with the jurors in view but the judge's voice off-camera; the movie would begin in the courtroom with the judge and defendant present. The first scene in the jury room was expanded so that almost every juror would be introduced briefly through words and actions. By the time they are seated, the audience is acquainted with them all, other than Juror 9, the old man, who makes a beeline for the men's room and is not seen again until the jurors take their seats.

As he extended the script, Rose added a scene with Juror 7 and Juror 8 speaking briefly in the adjoining washroom, a useful way to provide a change of location and to vary the pace. Rose also added an important section, with Juror 11 asking whether the defendant would have returned to the scene of the crime if he really had killed his father, a question that provokes a sharp debate and helps to establish the character of the immigrant watchmaker.

Rose also added a few scenes that he would later remove. After the side conversation with Juror 7 in the washroom, Juror 8 returns to his seat and turns to Juror 9, who had joined him in voting not guilty, and says "Thanks." The old man says softly: "I don't have arguments to make for you," and Juror 8 replies: "I don't know if there are any more to make. I just have a feeling . . . ." It's a remarkable comment that, for the first and only time, provides an insight into Juror 8's mind. Rose later deleted this comment, forcing viewers—along with the other jurors— to guess what Juror 8 is thinking.

He also added a telling exchange early in the deliberations. As jurors wonder if the boy had a motive to kill his father, Juror 6 raises a broader question: "So if he didn't do it, who did? Who else had the motive?" Juror 8 explains that the jury is tasked with passing judgment on the defendant, not solving the crime, which prompts Juror 4 to say: "We can't help asking ourselves who else might have had a motive. And so we ask, if the boy didn't kill his father who might have?" Juror 8 observes that the victim "was a tough, cruel, primitive man who never held a job for more than six months." Plenty of people might have wanted to kill him: "He could have been murdered by any one of the many men he served time with in prison. By a bookmaker. By a man he'd beaten up. By a woman he picked up. By one of the asocial characters he was known to hang out with."

A jury might very well have such a discussion, but in the context of the play it carried risks. At best, it's a distraction. If the jurors start down this road, how do they come back to the case against the defendant? More crucially, if jurors begin to ponder who else could have committed the crime, they may well conclude the most likely answer is *nobody*. The evidence against the boy may have its faults but at least there's plenty of it, with witnesses who swear they heard him threaten to kill his father, or saw him run away from the scene, or watched the killing as it happened. That said, not a shred of evidence is presented to implicate anyone else—no one else who threatened the victim, or was seen entering or exiting the apartment, or did anything that suggests involvement in the murder. In the absence of *any* such clues, simple logic suggests that the defendant is probably guilty. Rose may have realized the danger of this line of questioning and eventually scrapped it.

The third passage that Rose added for his first draft, but later removed, concerned testimony from a psychiatrist. When Juror 1 reminds the others about a doctor's testimony, Juror 10 blusters that he "wouldn't give a nickel" for such tests. Juror 1 is undeterred: "The psychiatrist definitely stated that the boy had strong homicidal tendencies. . . . He described all those tests, inkblots and all the stuff, and he said the kid is definitely a killer-type." Juror 11, a voice of reason, notes that "many of us are capable of committing murder. But few of us do. We impose controls upon ourselves to prevent it." Psychiatric tests by themselves prove nothing: "To say that a man is capable of murder does not mean that he has committed it." When Juror 10 tries to rebut this point by asserting that psychiatric tests *can* be useful, Juror 8 springs his trap: "You're the one who said, and I quote, I wouldn't give a nickel for a psychiatrist's testimony." Caught trying to have it both ways, Juror 10 responds angrily. This passage was dropped, too, perhaps because director Sidney Lumet cast as the defendant a youth who seemed timid and frightened, hardly someone who appeared prone to violence.

Most importantly, Rose changed the climactic scene. In the *Studio One* version, the last holdout, Juror 3, resists briefly before shouting "All right," then hands over his knife to Juror 8 as the others file out. It was not a very strong ending, but the best that Rose could muster to bring a forty-eight-minute program to a rapid conclusion. Now Rose devised a more satisfying confrontation. Alone against the eleven and unable to present any valid arguments that justify conviction, Juror 3 explodes in rage and rushes toward Juror 8, his fists clenched and ready to strike. Rose's script reads: "It seems as though #3 must inevitably hit #8. #8 waits for it, hands down. #3 half-raises both fists, stands there tensely, his face contorted with silent rage." Just in time, Juror 3 turns aside and slams his fists on the table. Violence has been averted. As the other jurors file out, the camera lingers on their faces while Juror 3 stands alone. The guard says quietly: "Let's go, mister." Juror 3 takes his coat and returns to the table where the knife is sticking upright. He picks it up and rams it on the tabletop, where it stands quivering. After a moment's pause, he walks out, slamming the door behind him.

The ending was better, but still not quite right.

THE FIRST MONTHS OF 1956 saw the broadcast of two Reginald Rose teleplays. In January, *Studio One* performed "Dino," with sixteen-year-old Sal Mineo as the troubled teenager. Again, Rose returned to topics of juvenile delinquency and dysfunctional families, with a concerned adult in the role of helper—not a social worker, as in "Crime in the Streets," but a psychologist.

In February, NBC broadcast what would be one of Rose's most celebrated teleplays. "Tragedy in a Temporary Town" took up subjects close to Rose's heart: justice versus prejudice, rule of law versus the mob, and human beings at their best and their worst. Rose had submitted the outline in November 1955, with a cover note to Felix Jackson:

> I searched for a location in which a small community is relatively unsupervised by law and, should the temper of the community be right, and the proper situation unfold, the people of the community might feasibly try to make their own laws, and be their own judge, jury and punishment agency. I finally decided that just about the only type of community which might fit these conditions in our time is that phenomenon of unrest, war, economic turmoil . . . . . the trailer camp. So that is the setting of this play, a trailer camp near a Pacific coast aircraft manufacturing city.

With "Tragedy in a Temporary Town," Rose was trying to go beyond anything he had attempted to date. "Thunder on Sycamore Street" had been set in a tidy residential neighborhood; this story took place in a construction camp. "Twelve Angry Men" was set in the jury room of a courthouse with a guard standing by; this story would unfold in the absence of law. Two years earlier, Florence Britton had insisted on changing the unwelcome neighbor in "Thunder on Sycamore Street" from an ethnic minority to an ex-convict. Now, perhaps because the times had changed, or because of his growing confidence and larger reputation, Rose upped the ante. Ethnic groups were now explicit: the mob was white, and the accused was Puerto Rican, his family referred to as "Spics" and "greaseballs." Perhaps that was why *Studio One* said no.

Undaunted, Rose's agent sent the outline to Herb Brodkin, who agreed to buy it for *The Alcoa Hour*, which had taken over from Philco and alternated weeks with *The Goodyear Playhouse*. The financial reward was sweet, with Rose earning four thousand dollars for the script.[3] NBC didn't flinch from the strong language but raised a different objection. Rose's script had been set at a construction camp with barracks made of aluminum. At the insistence of Alcoa—the Aluminum Company of America—the barracks would be made of wood. There could be no unpleasant associations with the sponsor's product.

"Tragedy in a Temporary Town" was the third collaboration between Brodkin and Rose, and when NBC hired Sidney Lumet to direct, marked the third time (after "Crime in the Streets" and *The Challenge*) that Lumet would direct one of Rose's original dramas. It was broadcast live on February 19, 1956.

In the opening scene of "Tragedy in a Temporary Town," a teenage girl runs into the center of the camp, crying that someone grabbed her in the dark and tried to kiss her. She had shouted for help and the assailant fled, but she remains terrified. A group of white men, led by Frank Doran, played by Jack Warden, is intent on finding the culprit: "We seal off the camp, then gather up each man over 15." Alex Beggs, played by Lloyd Bridges, objects: "We should call the police. You can't just become the law."

The men go through the camp, trailer by trailer, with Doran leading the questioning. Beggs, meanwhile, learns that it was his own teenage son who tried to kiss the girl, meaning no harm but acting too forcefully, but is too afraid to say so. Eventually suspicion eventually falls on a Puerto Rican boy, and Doran wrenches him from his family. As the men prepare to lynch the boy in a clearing illuminated by automobile headlights, Beggs is finally spurred to act. He confronts the mob, shouting and brandishing a club: "You pack 'a pigs! You dirty stinkin' pigs! . . . Just look at yourselves! Don't it make you creep with shame? Twenty dirty thick-skulled pigs, and all of a sudden, you're the law! Well let me tell you something! Every time pigs like you mob together to become your own law you crawl one step closer to the cliff."[4]

"Tragedy in a Temporary Town" was a powerful drama that earned critical praise and two Emmy nominations, for Rose as the writer and for Bridges for Best Single Performance by an Actor.[5] The episode also earned an award from the Ford Foundation's Fund for the Republic for its depiction of "mob violence and race prejudice," as well as the 1956 Television Award of the Anti-Defamation League of B'nai B'rith, which called it "the most dramatic and forthright television program of the year bringing the message of democracy to the American people."[6] Having received the same award for "An Almanac of Liberty," Rose cemented his reputation for writing about issues of social justice.[7]

AS TELEVISION GAINED RESPECT as a dramatic medium, Simon and Schuster began to publish collections of plays by leading writers. First was Paddy Chayefsky, whose *Television Plays*, published in 1955, included "Marty" and five others from *The Goodyear-Philco Playhouse*, each with commentary from the author. Chayefsky expressed pride at the quality of television dramas, mentioning not just his plays but those of contemporaries: "There were four or five hour shows last year that were far and away superior to anything on the current Broadway stage or anything issued by the movie industry." He could not resist a dig at the networks: "Perhaps they might even start paying the television writer a decent wage for his work."[8]

Simon and Schuster next approached Rose for a similar collection, which was published in early 1956. *Six Television Plays* included several of Rose's best works in the order they were performed: "The Remarkable Incident at Carson Corners," "Thunder on Sycamore Street," "Twelve Angry Men," "An Almanac of Liberty," "Crime in the Streets," and "The Incredible World of Horace Ford." ("Tragedy in a Temporary Town" had been performed too recently to be included.)

In the foreword, Rose described his journey as a television writer, starting with his first half-hour play at the end of 1951: "That play shall remain nameless, as shall the next dozen plays I turned out, all of which were written between January 1952 and November 1953, and all of which were uniformly mediocre."[9] His two years at CBS, writing for *Danger* and adapting novels for *Studio One*, were treated merely as an apprenticeship for his subsequent works. Rose expressed appreciation to the medium that rescued him from the drudgery of the advertising agency: "Writing for television has been, for me, an exciting and rewarding experience . . . I am sincerely grateful to the medium which has presented my work to huge audiences and paid me well for it."[10]

Reflecting on the six teleplays, Rose said that "The Remarkable Incident at Carson Corners" was his "favorite of all the television dramas I've written." No doubt it held a special place in his heart as his first original drama, but he also liked its structure and theme. "Whatever it was," he noted, "I've been trying to top it ever since."[11] The first one to catch the eye of filmmakers was "Crime in the Streets," which had seemed most suitable for the big screen. As for "Twelve Angry Men"? It was listed first on the cover, a nod to its status as an Emmy winner, but otherwise it received no special attention. There was no inkling, in the spring of 1956, that it would become the defining work of Reginald Rose's career.

AS PRODUCTION OF *12 ANGRY MEN* drew nearer, Rose completed a second draft of the screenplay, expanding several sections and adding a few scenes that proved to be important. After Juror 8's exchange in the washroom with Juror 7, Juror 6 enters and tells Juror 8 that the defendant is "guilty for sure. Not a doubt in the whole world." The housepainter makes another comment that forces Juror 8 to think anew: "Supposing you talk us all out of this and the kid really did knife his father?" Rose also added the memorable scene in which Juror 8 challenges Juror 4 to recall the names of actors in a movie he had recently seen, rebutting a seemingly damning point of evidence—that the defendant could not remember the actors in the movies he claimed to have seen—and putting a dent in Juror 4's aura of infallibility.

Rose's second draft also gave much more importance to the weather. The television play had made no mention of the weather, and the first draft had only a few comments about the heat. Now Rose repeatedly mentioned the oppressive heat, leading up to a dramatic thunderstorm and, after the clouds have cleared in the movie's closing scene, a sense of release. The deafening downpour also forces the jurors to take a brief pause, which allowed for an exchange between Juror 8 and Juror 1 that gave depth to a relatively undistinguished character.

As Rose fine-tuned the script, he made subtle changes in phrasing. In the first scene in the jury room, Juror 12 describes the trial as if it had been entertainment: "It had a lot of interest for me. No real dead spots, if you know what I mean." In the washroom scene, Juror 6 talks about the weather: "What a murderous day. You think we'll be much longer?" During the thunderstorm, Juror 1 recalls a deluge that interrupted a high school football game: "And it starts to come down, cats and dogs, just like this. Just whoosh, you know, right down. Well, it was murder, you know?" These terms—*no real dead spots*, *a murderous day*, *it was murder*—are used casually, without a trace of irony, the jurors making no connection to the case before them and exhibiting no understanding that they are tasked with a decision that is, quite literally, a matter of life and death. Small touches, perhaps, but testimony to Reginald Rose's growing skill as a writer.

ON SATURDAY NIGHT, MARCH 17, 1956, the Eighth Annual Emmy Awards honored the best in television for 1955. Rod Serling won for Best Original Teleplay Writing for "Patterns." Four days later, the Academy Awards ceremony was held at the Pantages Theater. *Marty* had received eight nominations, including Best Screenplay, Best Actor, Best Director, and Best Picture. Those nominations felt like reward enough for producer Harold Hecht, who hadn't imagined that the Academy's top prize would go to his modest picture. He was several drinks into his private celebration when the major awards started to go for *Marty*. Best Screenplay went to Paddy Chayefsky, a popular choice and not surprising, but then Delbert Mann won for Best Director, often an indicator of the final award. By the time the Best Actor award went to Ernest Borgnine, Hecht was hardly able to stand upright.[12] And then the grand prize: the Oscar for Best Picture to *Marty*. Hecht maintained sufficient composure to express his thanks for a magnificent ten months, beginning with the *Palme d'Or* at Cannes in May

1955, continuing through the fall with packed cinemas across the country, and now culminating in the biggest Oscar of all.

With revenues that topped three million dollars, *Marty* had become a major money-maker. Even after United Artists took its 30 percent cut, recouped its marketing expenses, and covered all production costs, there were still generous profits to distribute. Paddy Chayefsky's share came to seventy-five thousand dollars on top of the thirteen thousand he had received for screen rights and script adaptation. *Marty* brought him, Chayefsky remarked, "far more than I thought I'd receive originally."[13]

For television writers, the success of *Marty* was immensely gratifying. "Paddy and I both lived on West Eighty-Sixth Street," Rose later said. "I went over to Paddy's house when he won the Oscar for *Marty*, just to look at it, and he let me hold it."[14] Thanks to *Marty*, television programs were now seen as an incubator for feature films.[15] In the next two years, movie studios bought the rights to thirty-seven teleplays, many from *Studio One*, *The Goodyear-Philco Playhouse*, and *Climax!* Rod Serling led the list with five sales—"Patterns" and four more—followed by Paddy Chayefsky and Robert Alan Aurthur at four each. Rose had three: "Crime in the Streets," "Twelve Angry Men," and most recently "Dino," whose movie rights were bought by Allied Artists, perhaps to capitalize on Sal Mineo's fame following his role opposite James Dean in *Rebel Without a Cause* (1955).[16]

Shortly after *Marty* won for Best Picture came the announcement that another Chayefsky teleplay would be made into a movie. "The Bachelor Party," broadcast on *The Goodyear-Philco Playhouse* in October 1953, was bought by Hecht-Lancaster, who again hired Delbert Mann to direct, with financing and distribution again by United Artists. Chayefsky insisted that his latest deal was not just an attempt to recreate the winning formula of *Marty*, but the similarities were unmistakable. Both were modest black-and-white features about the lives and loves of ordinary people set in New York City. *The Bachelor Party* would go into production soon, with filming to take place in summer 1956, and was expected to arrive in cinemas in April 1957—the very same week, it would turn out, as *12 Angry Men*.[17]

10

Assembling the Team (Spring 1956)

MOVIES, IT IS SAID, are a director's medium. Writers craft the words, actors strut and fret across the set, but what appears on the screen reflects the artistic vision of the director.

For the Orion-Nova production of *12 Angry Men*, the choice of director was especially important. Both coproducers were novices. Henry Fonda, actor, had spent the last months in Europe shooting *War and Peace*, and would soon begin another movie, *The Wrong Man*, for Alfred Hitchcock. Reginald Rose, writer, was primarily occupied with scripting original television dramas. Neither had assembled a cast, hired a crew, built a set, rented equipment, or managed a budget. Whomever they selected to direct *12 Angry Men* would have to take on many of these responsibilities.

Correspondence between Orion-Nova and United Artists in August 1955 noted that Fonda and Rose had identified three suitable directors: Franklin Schaffner, Delbert Mann, and Sidney Lumet. Of the three, Schaffner was the logical pick. He was the most experienced, with more than one hundred episodes of *Studio One* to his credit; but more importantly, he had directed the live broadcast of "Twelve Angry Men," winning an Emmy for his efforts. No one was surprised when it was reported in November 1955 that negotiations were underway for Schaffner to direct *12 Angry Men*.

Yet the August 1955 letter had listed three candidates. Of course, it was prudent to mention more than one, since any of the three might be unavailable or unwilling to agree to terms, but it's also possible that Rose knew he wanted Lumet and included multiple names to avoid settling too quickly on Schaffner.

The second name, Delbert Mann, was best known for his work with Paddy Chayefsky at *The Goodyear-Philco Playhouse* and by now had directed the movie version of *Marty*, which was earning strong reviews. (His Academy Award for Best Director was still a few months in the future.) Mann had never directed a Rose teleplay, but he had recently worked with Fonda on "The Petrified Forest." Without question he was a very credible option.

Sidney Lumet was the youngest of the three but also very experienced, having directed hundreds of live episodes of *Danger* and *You Are There*, as well as the thirteen filmed episodes of *You Are There*. By mid-1955, he had already directed two of Rose's teleplays, "Crime in the Streets" and *The Challenge*, and would soon direct "Tragedy in a Temporary Town." Rose admired Lumet's work and enjoyed working with him, commenting some years later: "Sidney Lumet was wonderful. He does his homework like no other director, and he is the warmest guy. Everybody was 'my love,' and 'you gorgeous wonderful thing,' and rehearsals were filled with kissing and hugging and wild exclamations of joy. Actors have never been more loved than when they were loved by Sidney Lumet."[1]

A year earlier, Rose had said that the director of a television program was best qualified to direct the movie version, a comment intended to help Lumet become director of *Crime in the Streets*. That appeal had been unsuccessful when Allied Artists went with Don Siegel. Facing the identical situation one year later, Rose no longer found the logic so compelling, choosing Lumet over Schaffner. His preference may have gone beyond Lumet's skills as a director. Rose regretted that his friend had missed out on *Crime in the Streets* and wanted to make sure that he would get the nod this time.

For his part, Henry Fonda likely did not have a strong preference. Although he had not worked with either Schaffner or Lumet, he was at least familiar with Lumet. While starring in *Mister Roberts*, Fonda had been invited by a cast member to attend an off-Broadway play, *Ward Six*, directed by Lumet, and came away impressed. Still, it's doubtful that Fonda would have pushed for Lumet based on a single brief encounter several years earlier. More likely it was Rose who wanted Lumet, and Fonda agreed. As Lumet once said: "I didn't have to go get that big job. Reggie came to me."[2]

And so, in February 1956, shortly after "Tragedy in a Temporary Town," Sidney Lumet was named director of *12 Angry Men*.[3] He was ready to make the most of it. In a 2008 interview, Lumet was asked if he had wanted to direct *12 Angry Men* because of an interest in themes of justice. He waved off the suggestion with a laugh: "Absolutely not! I was interested in doing my first movie!"[4] On another occasion he said: "Nothing about the material has to appeal to you on your first feature—you just say 'yes'!"[5]

Franklin Schaffner was unhappy at being passed over, his disappointment especially acute given the acclaim for his *Studio One* production. In the 1960s, he would make his mark directing outstanding movies including *Planet of the Apes* (1968) and *Patton* (1970), the latter earning him the Academy Award. But all that came much later. In early 1956, Schaffner felt that the job of directing *12 Angry Men* had been taken from him.[6]

According to Charlie Russell, it's possible that Schaffner never really had a chance. In his 1982 memoirs, Russell recalled that in the spring of 1955, Lumet was in an especially ebullient mood: "Ma'darlin' it looks like I'm going to direct a feature." He went on: "They're going to make Reggie Rose's *Twelve Angry Men* as a film and if all the details are worked out I'll direct it." "What details?," asked Russell. Lumet answered: "They haven't got all the money yet, but they'll know in two or three weeks."[7] Russell came back: "I thought you said you wouldn't work in Hollywood." Lumet replied: "No, they're trying to get it made in New York. That's one of the details."[8] If Russell's account is correct, Lumet may have had the inside track even before Fonda and Rose agreed to terms with United Artists.

WITH JUST THREE MONTHS until filming was to begin, Lumet assembled his team. First, he brought on board two of his most trusted colleagues, George Justin as associate producer, responsible for day-to-day operations, and Bob Markell as art director, in charge of set design. Justin had supervised *On the Waterfront*, but so far Markell had only worked in television. Crucially, they had a good working relationship. "George, Sidney, and I had done so many shows together," said Markell. Now they would work together on a feature film.

When it came to choosing a cinematographer, Lumet believed that Boris Kaufman's realist style would be perfect. After *On the Waterfront*, Kaufman had filmed the movie version of *Patterns* in 1955 and Elia Kazan's *Baby Doll* at the end of 1955. "Boris was one of the great black and white cameramen," Lumet later commented. "He was a great, great artist."[9] The two would work together six more times in the 1950s and 1960s, on some of Lumet's best movies: *The Fugitive Kind*, *Long Day's Journey into Night*, and *The Pawnbroker*.

As for the cast, there was only one given: Henry Fonda would play Juror 8. The rest of the cast was selected by Lumet. As Bob Markell confirmed: "It was the director who chose the twelve angry men."[10]

Three jurors from the *Studio One* production were asked to stay on: Joseph Sweeney as Juror 9, the old man; Edward Arnold as Juror 10, the unpleasant bigot; and George Voskovec as Juror 11, the immigrant watch-maker. Voskovec, who had worked with Lumet on *You Are There*, was an especially appropriate choice. He had led an avant-garde theater group in Prague in the 1930s but fled the Nazis in 1939 and came to the United States. When World War II ended, he went back to Prague and tried to relaunch his theater group, only to find himself out of favor with the Communist regime. Once again forced to leave, he returned to New York in May 1950, but upon arrival at LaGuardia Field was taken into custody. Someone had raised suspicions about alleged links to leftist organizations, a bitter irony given that he was disliked by the Communists. For the next ten months, Voskovec was detained on Ellis Island, with no charges filed and no way to refute allegations.[11] After his release, he complained about his lengthy incarceration in a letter to the *New York Times*: "The current procedure of immigration hearings places the alien in an extremely weak legal position. The burden of proof rests with him and he is not faced with specific charges. It seems to me that the introduction of fairer practices would in no way jeopardize national security, while unquestionably making immigration procedures more consistent with the basic principles of democracy and human rights."[12] Voskovec later wrote a teleplay based on his experience, "I Was Accused," broadcast on NBC's *Armstrong Circle Theater* on December 13, 1955. For the role of Juror 11, the immigrant who speaks movingly about the responsibilities of citizens in a democracy, no one was better qualified than George Voskovec.

For several parts, Lumet looked to actors he knew from *Danger* and *You Are There*. Ed Binns, a regular on *Danger* who also appeared in "Tragedy in a Temporary Town," was cast as Juror 6, the plain-speaking house painter. E. G. Marshall, a mainstay of *You Are There*, took the role of Juror 4, the hyperrational stockbroker. For Juror 1, Lumet chose Martin Balsam, a member of Elia Kazan's Actors Studio. These men exemplified what Lumet found so remarkable about television's early days: "The burst of talent in acting, directing, writing was just so unbelievable. Perfectly non-descript, normal looking actors—E. G. Marshall, Eddie Binns, Marty Balsam—suddenly finding themselves having wonderful acting careers, and that's all because of TV."[13]

Lumet also reached out to Jack Warden, whom he had directed in two very different roles: the friendly bus driver who loses his job because of the loyalty oath in *The Challenge* and the leader of the vigilantes in "Tragedy in a Temporary Town." Warden was cast as Juror 7, the wise-cracking salesman.

Jack Klugman was chosen to play Juror 5, the young man raised in the slums, very likely on the recommendation of Fonda. They had worked together in "The Petrified Forest," but their connection went back to Klugman's first professional role as chief petty officer Dowdy in *Mister Roberts*, when they toured together and got along well.[14] Late in his life, Klugman said: "I think Hank got me the job on *12 Angry Men*, because I was really too old for the part, but he never mentioned it, he never told me he got me the job."[15]

The most crucial role to cast was Juror 3, the principal adversary and dramatic counterpoint to Juror 8. The television role had been played by Franchot Tone, who had a precise and controlled manner but was not an imposing presence, either physically or emotionally. Lumet wanted an actor of greater power and passion, one who could hold his own with Henry Fonda. Lee J. Cobb was a perfect choice, perhaps suggested by Marion Dougherty, a well-known independent casting director.[16] After several months convalescing from his heart attack in May 1955, Cobb had recently returned to the screen, playing the wise Judge Bernstein in *The Man in the Gray Flannel Suit*. On March 8, he signed to play Juror 3, for which he would get second billing, testimony to his reputation.[17]

To round out the cast, Lumet picked two young actors with stage experience. Robert Webber, thirty-one, had served in the Marine Corps in World War II, then hitchhiked to New York to try his hand at acting. His Broadway debut came in 1948, and over the next years he worked steadily, leading to his current role in *No Time for Sergeants*, a comedy at the Alvin Theater. Webber was cast as Juror 12, the advertising executive.[18] John Fiedler, also thirty-one, was a stage actor from Wisconsin who had recently made his off-Broadway debut in Chekhov's *The Sea Gull* thanks to a reference from Montgomery Clift.[19] Fiedler would play Juror 2, the meek bank clerk. For both Webber and Fiedler, *12 Angry Men* would be their first movie.

A final role, important but uncredited, was played by Rudy Bond, a member of Actors Studio. Elia Kazan had directed him twice: as Steve, Stanley Kowalski's neighbor and pal in *A Streetcar Named Desire* (1951), and as a sympathetic longshoreman in *On the Waterfront*.[20] Cast as the judge, Bond appears in the opening scene of *12 Angry Men*, reading the instructions in a bored tone while playing distractedly with a pencil. He tells the jurors they have "a grave responsibility," but his droning voice suggests that he considers the defendant's guilt a foregone conclusion, an important element that sets the context for the jury's deliberations.

AS LUMET PREPARED to direct his first movie, two other movies were in production in New York City, both with consequences for *12 Angry Men*.

First was *Edge of the City*, based on Robert Alan Aurthur's "A Man Is

Ten Feet Tall," broadcast live on *The Goodyear-Philco Playhouse* in October 1955. It told the story of Alex Nordman, a troubled young white man AWOL from the Army, who joins a warehouse crew and is befriended by Tommy Tyler, a Black longshoreman. The crew boss, Charlie Malick, is a bully who demands kickbacks from Nordman and aims racial taunts at Tyler, but a code of silence prevents the longshoreman from complaining about his abusive behavior. Eventually Malick provokes Tyler into a fight. When Tyler is killed, Nordman breaks his silence and takes a stand for his fallen friend. The role of Alex Nordman was played by Don Murray and the crew boss by Martin Balsam; Tommy Tyler, a rare leading role for a Black man, was played by a bright young talent, Sidney Poitier. The depiction of interracial friendship was a first on television and network affiliates in the South howled in protest, but NBC held firm and the program was aired to strong reviews.[21]

To turn the teleplay into a feature film, Aurthur teamed up with David Susskind and Alfred Levy, partners at Talent Associates, and secured financing from MGM.[22] To direct, Aurthur wanted Martin Ritt, hardly seen since his dismissal from *Danger* in 1951. His road back began in 1955, when Arthur Miller asked Ritt to direct a pair of one-act plays, *A Memory of Two Mondays* and *A View from the Bridge*, the latter a story about dock workers with Van Heflin and Jack Warden.[23]

When *A View from the Bridge* closed in February 1956 and Ritt became available, Aurthur asked him to direct his movie. Sidney Poitier would reprise the role of Tommy Tyler, with Alex Nordman to be played by John Cassavetes. For Charlie Malick, Ritt recommended Jack Warden: "This actor did an outstanding job in *A View from the Bridge*, and we think he is absolutely right for the role in this film." His powerful performance as a vigilante in "Tragedy in a Temporary Town" may have been a factor, as well.[24] With a budget from MGM of $515,000, filming took place from late March through early May, much of it at the dockyards along the Hudson River at Twelfth Avenue and Thirty-Third Street.[25] The principal photographer was Joseph Brun, but Boris Kaufman was brought in for some of the exterior shots in Central Park, the West Side Highway, Riverside Drive, and Harlem. The finished picture was released in January 1957.

BEFORE *12 ANGRY MEN* could go into production, Henry Fonda had one more project to complete: Alfred Hitchcock's *The Wrong Man*.

By 1956, Hitchcock was in the prime of his career, having recently made some of his greatest movies—*Rear Window* (1954), *To Catch a Thief* (1955), and *The Man Who Knew Too Much* (1956)—and soon to make others—*Vertigo* (1958) and *North by Northwest* (1959). Amid these big-budget movies came *The Wrong Man*, a somber black-and-white picture that combined Hitchcock's taste for suspense and paranoia with the realism of a documentary. Film historian Robert Osborne said: "Hitchcock loved to investigate an ordinary guy trapped in a situation beyond his doing—[a situation] that he didn't *cause* to have happen, but that *happened to him*."[26] *The Wrong Man* was that sort of story, with Fonda cast as a jazz musician mistakenly accused of a crime.

The Wrong Man was the only movie Hitchcock made based on a true story, and he tried to stay faithful to actual events.[27] Filming began in New York in late March 1956, with location shots outside the Stork Club at 3 East Fifty-Third Street and in the Jackson Heights neighborhood of Queens. Many scenes were filmed at night, giving the movie a dark and moody tone. (The New York Police Department, not happy with how it was portrayed, hounding an innocent man, offered little help.)

The entire movie was to be filmed in New York, but after several freezing days on location, Hitchcock decided he had enough. Cast and crew were told that production was moving to California, and after a brief pause, filming resumed on a Warner Bros. sound stage, with Queens houses and offices recreated with the clever use of backdrops.[28] One set provided a highly realistic view of tall buildings through the windows of an insurance office. Another backdrop—of which Hitchcock was particularly proud, according to art director Paul Sylbert—created an elevated train line just outside the window of a lawyer's office, with flashing lights and train sounds to make it seem as if an elevated train was passing by.

Although not among Hitchcock's most famous films, *The Wrong Man* was notable in many respects. Director Peter Bogdanovich called it "one of the most emotional of Hitchcock's pictures, told with extraordinary restraint and sense of reality, just the opposite of the kind of artifice Hitchcock is famous for."[29] Bernard Herrmann's minimal score added to the mood, its muted horns and insistent bass line creating a sense of mounting pressure, a motif Herrmann used again in his final score, for another movie of urban paranoia, Martin Scorsese's *Taxi Driver* (1976).[30]

Filmed immediately before *12 Angry Men* and employing some of the same documentary feel, *The Wrong Man* is something of a companion piece, although Fonda's roles contrast sharply. In Hitchcock's movie, Fonda plays a decent man who is wrongly accused and struggling to keep up with events beyond his control; in Lumet's film, Fonda's character takes control of events to see that justice is done for someone else. *12 Angry Men* is remembered as a high point in Fonda's career while *The Wrong*

Man is largely overlooked, but both are testimony to his acting brilliance. Bogdanovich described Fonda's performance in *The Wrong Man* as an example of understated and intense characterization: "It's a tribute to Henry Fonda, as an actor, that he's able to so completely enter into this Italian Stork Club musician that you really do lose the thought that this is Henry Fonda."[31] Robert Osborne commented: "Nobody played the ordinary man better than Henry Fonda, who was anything but an ordinary guy. He had that ability to *be* every man."[32]

WHILE FONDA WAS MAKING *The Wrong Man*, Lee J. Cobb and Edward Arnold were about to make a Columbia Pictures movie about organized crime. Called *Shakedown on Biscayne Drive* (but later released as *Miami Exposé*), Cobb played a Miami police lieutenant pursuing racketeers who are trying to bring gambling into Florida, with Arnold in the role of a mobster. After location shots in Miami and Cuba, production moved to Los Angeles for studio work. There, on April 26, Arnold died from a massive cerebral hemorrhage.[33]

Suddenly in need of a replacement for Juror 10, Lumet and Fonda immediately thought of Ed Begley. After his performance in the television version of "Patterns," Begley landed a stage role that he considered the crowning achievement of his career. *Inherit the Wind* was a courtroom drama based on the Scopes Monkey Trial of 1925, with Paul Muni playing defense attorney Henry Drummond, based on Clarence Darrow, and Begley as prosecuting attorney Matthew Harrison Brady, based on William Jennings Bryan.[34] The play opened on April 21, 1955, at the National Theatre to critical and popular acclaim. While Begley appeared nightly in *Inherit the Wind*, he also found time for other roles, including in the movie version of *Patterns*. Most recently, he had appeared in "Man on Fire" on *The Alcoa Hour*, directed by Sidney Lumet. When Edward Arnold died suddenly, Lumet got in touch, and on May 29, barely three weeks before rehearsals were to begin, Begley agreed to play Juror 10.[35]

ONE MONTH BEFORE REHEARSALS were to start, United Artists approved the final budget for *12 Angry Men*. It called for a cash outlay of just under four hundred thousand dollars, financed with a loan from Bankers Trust. The movie was inexpensive but hardly rock-bottom, costing about as much as *Marty* and *Edge of the City*.

The greatest share of costs, totaling $109,000, went for the cast. Aside from Fonda, whose fee was entirely deferred, the highest paid actor was

Lee J. Cobb, who earned $5,500 for each of six weeks—two weeks of rehearsal and four of filming—plus air travel from California and expenses in New York, for a total of $34,832. Next was to be Edward Arnold at $3,000 a week; the May 10 budget removed the late actor's name but still showed that figure. Other cast members got less: E. G. Marshall earned $2,000 per week, Jack Warden $1,500, Jack Klugman $900, Joseph Sweeney $850, Martin Balsam $750, George Voskovec $750, Robert Webber $700, Edward Binns $600, and John Fiedler $450. Although the lowest paid of the twelve jurors, Fiedler would earn $2,700 over the six weeks, not bad in 1956 for a young stage actor making his first movie. The rest of the cast—the judge, guard, clerk, and alternate jurors, plus extras and stand-ins—earned much less.

Sidney Lumet later quipped that he had been asked to direct because he came cheap, but his salary of fifteen thousand dollars, plus five thousand dollars in deferred fees, was more than the ten thousand dollars that Delbert Mann had earned for *Marty* in 1954, and more than the ten thousand dollars that Martin Ritt was paid for *Edge of the City*. Much of the remaining budget went for a crew of more than thirty that included associate producer and production supervisor George Justin, cinematographer Boris Kaufman, art director Bob Markell, and assistant director Don Kranze, as well as the usual complement of cameramen and lighting operators, technicians for grips, props, and booms, a sound mixer, a script clerk, make-up, and wardrobe. Other costs included rental of the main sound stage at Fox Movietone Studios, one week to build the set and four weeks to film, with charges for cameras, lights, and cranes, plus two days on location at Foley Square in Lower Manhattan. Postproduction costs would cover editing, mixing, titles, prints, and scoring.

Provided that *12 Angry Men* stayed within its budget, a reasonable performance at the box office would allow for repayment of the Bankers Trust loan as well as payment of deferred fees to Henry Fonda of $175,000, to Reginald Rose of $45,000, and to Sidney Lumet of $5,000. With any luck, there might even be something left over.

11

⋯

Six Weeks of Work
(Summer 1956)

AS A MOVIE ACTOR, Henry Fonda had often felt frustrated by the lack of rehearsal time. "I've made 50-odd movies and only once did I rehearse," he said in 1955. "I'm convinced that better films would result from careful rehearsal."[1] As coproducer he could do as he pleased, and in early June 1956, the cast of *12 Angry Men* arrived for two weeks of rehearsal at Steinway Hall, 113 West Fifty-Seventh Street, in Midtown Manhattan.[2]

Sidney Lumet, too, was glad to have time to rehearse. *Danger* and *You Are There* had gone from script to production in just a few days, allowing no chance to explore dramatic possibilities. Rehearsals would let actors understand what Lumet called the "entire arc of the role," feeling its evolution from beginning to end.[3] By acting a scene over and over, and trying slightly different tone and cadence, actors might find a "magical accident"—an insight that brings a novel interpretation.

Convening his actors for the first time, Lumet explained what he hoped to achieve: "There's going to be no artificiality in this. You are going to be the whole picture. This is not a tract. This is not a pro-jury or anti-jury thing. It's just a thing about human behavior. No glass tabletops. No basement room. Just you and the fullness of your behavior. It's right in your laps."[4]

At first the actors read their parts aloud, and then began to block the movements. After one week, the actors felt they were ready. "We could have left at the end of the first week and put this on a stage and played it to an audience," said Fonda. "The second week was spent performing the play, from beginning to end, twice a day."[5] Jack Klugman concurred: "We rehearsed it like a play. We rehearsed it right through."[6] Klugman remarked that rehearsals could be a waste of time if directors didn't have a clear sense of what they wanted to achieve. Not with Lumet: "Sidney knew what to tell you."

In his 1995 book *Making Movies*, Lumet described a movie as a mosaic of tiles, each setup with a distinct camera position and lighting. The director and cinematographer shaped and polished each of these tiles, and then "you literally paste them together and hope it's what you set out to do."[7] As the actors rehearsed, Lumet and Boris Kaufman moved through the room to envision each shot. Bob Markell recalled: "Sidney *became* the camera. He would go around, while they were rehearsing, and that's when he would conceive the shots."[8] Kaufman would take Lumet's directorial concepts and determine the best lighting. In a 1960 interview, Lumet said: "I don't know of another cameraman who has the sense of dramatic interpretation that Boris has."[9]

Lumet and Kaufman included a few setups of long duration, with the camera moving on a dolly for a shot that included multiple actors, but most setups were brief, either a close-up of a single actor or a medium shot of one actor looking over the shoulder of one or more juror. As the movie progressed the pace picked up. Lumet explained: "The cutting tempo was accelerating steadily during the movie but would break into a gallop in the last thirty-five minutes or so. This increasing tempo helped enormously both in making the story more exciting and in raising the audience's awareness that the picture was compressing further in space and time."[10]

Lumet and Kaufman also devised a lens strategy. "As the picture unfolded," Lumet recalled, "I wanted the room to seem smaller and smaller. That meant that I would slowly shift to longer lenses as the picture continued. Starting with the normal range (28 mm to 40 mm) we progressed to 50 mm, 75mm, and 100 mm lenses."[11] The angle of the camera changed, too. The first setup in the jury room began at a high vantage point, well above eye level. After that, the camera was lowered to be even with the actors, and by the end of the movie was looking up. "In that way, the ceiling began to appear. Not only were the walls closing in, the ceiling was as well."[12] The combined effect was powerful: "We created a claustrophobic tension by gradually changing the camera lenses to narrow the room and crowd up the table."[13]

AS THE ACTORS REHEARSED, Reginald Rose revised the script one last time, deleting some lines and streamlining the dialogue, perhaps based on suggestions from Lumet and the cast. He also reimagined the final scene. In the *Studio One* teleplay, Juror 3 had simply shouted "All right" when he gave up. Rose's first screenplay ended with Juror 3 rushing at Juror 8 and almost coming to blows, but it was still not clear why Juror 3 had argued so forcefully for conviction, nor was there any sense of resolution.

At last, Rose hit upon a solution. The last man holding out for conviction, Juror 3, insists that the facts support him: "They're all here," he says, gesturing to his wallet and inadvertently dislodging a photo. The shooting script describes shot 369: INSERT—PICTURE FALLS OUT OF WALLET. Next we see a close-up of the photograph, father and son, arm in arm and smiling, some years earlier. Juror 3 remains defiant for a moment—"You lousy bunch of bleeding hearts! You're not going to intimidate me!"—until the sight of his son overwhelms him, causing him to tear the photo into small pieces while shouting: "Rotten kid! You work your heart out!" At last confronted with the source of his pain, he collapses in grief and sobs: "No. Not guilty." The other jurors file out, leaving only Juror 3 and Juror 8. No longer adversaries, Juror 8 walks to the coat rack, takes Juror 3's coat and, in a final act of compassion, helps him put it on. Reginald Rose had transformed the final scene from one of anger and confrontation to one of empathy and transcendence.

The shooting script totaled 387 setups, including two added at the beginning and two at the end. The first image would be an establishing shot, a wide-angle exterior view that looked up at the massive courthouse, a symbol of authority and strength, very much like Boris Kaufman's opening shot from *Patterns*, of the American Stock Exchange. The second shot takes the viewer inside the courthouse, starting with a view of the rotunda and moving down a corridor to show ordinary citizens going about their lives, arriving at the door of the courtroom. Two setups were added at the end, when the jurors emerge from their cramped deliberations, one just outside the courthouse doors as Jurors 8 and 9 briefly exchange pleasantries, and a final wide-angle shot of the jurors walking down the courthouse steps and returning to their lives.

At about the same time, Rose wrote a short script for a "TV Featurette" to be filmed at the same time as the movie and intended to be shown as an advertisement or a movie preview. Henry Fonda was to speak directly at the camera from the movie set: "If you've ever served on a jury, this room will probably look familiar to you. But if you've never been called for jury duty before, take a good long look at it, because one day your turn will come, and in a room like this one, you'll spend what may be the most exciting and dramatic hours of your life—and the most important hours in the life of someone you've never met." Fonda's words were to be interspersed with a few clips, designed to promote the upcoming movie: "That's how it happens in our picture, '12 ANGRY MEN.'" (See the appendix for the full script.)

WHILE THE ACTORS REHEARSED at Steinway Hall, Bob Markell designed the set at Fox Movietone Studios, a large structure built in the 1910s that occupied the entire block along Tenth Avenue between West Fifty-Third Street and West Fifty-Fourth Street. Orion-Nova rented the Large Sound Stage, a single open area with a high ceiling that was spacious enough to accommodate all three sets: the jury room, the courtroom, and the washroom.

For the jury room, Markell used the same layout as the *Studio One* production: a rectangular room with a table and chairs, a watercooler and coat rack, and an overhead fan. Markell designed the set in American institutional style, with wood paneling, heavy trim, and ornate corbels. Instead of a single long table, he took two tables of slightly different width and placed them end to end. The twelve chairs included some with rounded backs and others with straight backs, a few with arms but most without. The effect was to make the room appear haphazard and shabby. Markell commented: "I went to great lengths with the radiators, the dirty walls in some places, and stuff like that. It was very real."[14]

At one end of the set, behind Juror 7, an overhead fan was affixed to the wall, with two washrooms marked Men and Women. "We wanted to give a real period feeling of authenticity," said Markell. "I had my scenic artist paint frosted glass." At the other end, behind Juror 1, was a coat rack with a few hangers. Markell built the rack with a removable back. "I knew the way Sidney shot," Markell said. "When we were doing live television I always left him room to get through fireplaces, through windows, and things like that. I always left a way for Sidney to get the shot."[15] Sure enough, the final shot in the jury room, when Juror 8 collects Juror 3's coat, is seen from a vantage point behind the coat rack, possible only by shooting through the removable back.

Markell put the main walls on rollers so that stagehands could move them for each shot. "There was one problem, though. I decided to make each wall ten feet high. Boris's lights were only nine feet up, so every time I wanted to move the sets it became impossible without moving the lights. That did slow our production a little bit."[16] Since Lee J. Cobb was not yet back to full health after his heart attack, Markell built a small room in a corner of the sound stage and furnished it with a bed so that Cobb could occasionally take a rest.

The *Studio One* set had windows with simple backdrops of a generic cityscape. A feature film called for something more, so Markell created detailed backdrops by taking photographs of the buildings across from the courthouse and made them into large panels to be placed several feet beyond the jury room windows, creating an illusion of depth. The panels were made of a translucent material so that building lights could appear to go on when the skies darkened.

The backdrops soon became a point of contention. "Fonda came into the project a little uptight," said Lumet. "I knew rehearsals were going very well, but two or three days before shooting, I could feel his tension building."[17] The day before filming began, Lumet and Fonda visited the set. As Lumet recalled: "Fonda went pale. I said, 'Hank, what's the matter?' And he said, 'That backing looks like shit.'"[18] Remembering the superb sets for *The Wrong Man*, Fonda complained: "When I worked with Hitchcock the backings were so real you'd walk into them because you thought they were three dimensional."

Lumet assured Fonda that the backdrops would be fine, but in fact they were never quite right. One problem had to do with lighting, which needed to be toned down for the backdrops to look realistic; another problem had to do with perspective, as one building appeared at an odd angle. When the backdrops were flooded with light, the problem of perspective was accentuated. Bob Markell, thirty-two years old and working on his first motion picture, found it difficult to speak with Kaufman, an eminent European cinematographer and Academy Award winner with a formal manner. Rather than raise the matter directly, Markell and his crew quietly worked after hours. "That night after we were closing shop, we scotch-taped on the back some translucent plastic, so it diffused these hot spots."[19] The backdrops looked somewhat better, but not many viewers would be convinced. It would always be obvious that the performance was taking place on a soundstage.[20]

ON FRIDAY, JUNE 22, 1956, the cast and crew of *12 Angry Men* arrived at Fox Movietone Studios for the first day of filming. It was a pleasant day in New York with temperatures in the high seventies. That evening, a few miles to the north, at the Polo Grounds on 8th Avenue and 157th Street, the New York Giants would play the Milwaukee Braves, with a pair of young stars, Willie Mays and Hank Aaron, twenty-five and twenty-two years old, patrolling the outfield in front of seventeen thousand fans.

The day began like every day for the next four weeks, with associate producer George Justin's memo to the crew. This one was brief: "We will fly thru these few scenes and finish early, so that everybody can have a nice, long relaxed week-end."[21]

The first scenes took place in the courtroom as the judge instructs the jury. Markell had built a courtroom set in one corner of the large sound stage. He recalled: "We see the jury box and the kid at the table, and we see the judge, so it did not take up much room."[22] The defendant is seen only briefly, but long enough to make him a real person with feelings and frailties. Played by John Savoca, he has dark eyes and dark hair that suggest he may be Puerto Rican, although his ethnic group is never stated.

Production resumed on Monday, June 25, with the most demanding scene of the entire movie. The twelve men enter the jury room and begin to interact, some outspoken and impatient to get going, others reticent and cautious. Fonda's Juror 8 is polite but distant, standing apart from the others and gazing out the window. For several minutes the camera snakes its way through the small room, as every juror other than Juror 9 speaks at least a few lines, giving some clue about his character. Kaufman shot the scene using a crane with thirteen different positions to move in and around the set, with lighting shifting as the camera moved. "Boris Kaufman needed seven hours to light the shot, from 8:30 until 4," Lumet recalled. "We got it on Take 4."[23]

With that scene complete, filming proceeded according to Lumet's elaborate diagrams, each one indicating what actors would be in the shot and which way they would be looking. "I spent nights puzzling the problem and my script became a maze of diagrams," he said.[24]

Every setup was categorized by one of three kinds of light: broad daylight for roughly the first half of the movie; transition lighting when the storm gathered and light faded; and finally, after darkness fell, when the overhead lights were turned on. Lumet remarked: "Those three moods, essentially, were a guide to the shooting."[25] For each kind of light, all setups were classified by the background wall, called A, B, C, and D. Lumet explained: "Starting with my widest shot of wall A, I keep shooting every shot in which wall A is the background. I keep moving in against wall A until the last close-up against that wall has been shot. Then we shift to wall B and go through the same process. Then wall C, and then wall D."[26] Filming proceeded in a methodical fashion. "The camera went around the table, shooting chair by chair," said Lumet. "Once lights and camera were pointed at a chair, then every speech, no matter its order in the movie, was shot."[27] What would eventually look like an exchange between two actors, the camera going back and forth between them, might be the edited result of setups from different days: "Lee Cobb arguing with Henry Fonda would naturally have shots of Fonda (against wall C) and Cobb (against wall A)."[28] Since the movie would not be shot in sequence, the director and the actors had to recall the emotions of each moment. "That's where rehearsals were invaluable," said Lumet. "After two weeks of rehearsal, I had a complete graph in my head of where I wanted each level of emotion in the movie to be."[29]

The difference between a feature film and a live television broadcast was best illustrated in the scene where Juror 8 produces the second knife. The *Studio One* broadcast could shift between two cameras but had no way of setting up an individual shot, much less use rapid editing to heighten the tempo. Franklin Schaffner had one camera show a close-up of Juror 4 holding up the murder weapon and placing it on the table, and then shifted to the second camera as Juror 8 slams down the second knife. For the motion picture, Sidney Lumet broke the sequence into several different setups: a closeup of Juror 4 holding the murder weapon, then looking over Juror 4's shoulder at Juror 8, back to Juror 4 now joined by Juror 3, and back again to Juror 8, at first seated, then standing up, reaching into his pocket, bringing out a knife and thrusting it on the table, the camera now closing in on the two knives, next to each other for all to see. The result was an unforgettable sequence, tiles of a mosaic telling a powerful story.

THE RAW FOOTAGE, CALLED RUSHES, were reviewed at the end of each day. Fonda confessed to Lumet: "Sidney, what am I going to do? I can't stand seeing myself on the screen. I never go to rushes and sometimes wait two years to see a finished film I've made."[30] Lumet recalled that at one of the early rushes, Fonda took a seat behind the director: "He watched for a while, and then he put his hand on the back of my neck and squeezed so hard I thought my eyes would pop out. He leaned forward and said quietly, 'Sidney, it's magnificent.' Then he dashed out and never came to the rushes again."[31] From then on, as Fonda later said: "I ceased being a producer, having put the thing together that far. I became strictly an actor, and not even an actor in my own company. I became one of twelve actors working for Mr. Lumet."[32]

As production supervisor, George Justin was responsible for making sure that filming stayed on time and on budget. The task was to knock off the scenes, one by one, with metronomic regularity. His mantra: *Tick Tock.* Justin began every day by posting or reading aloud a message to the cast and crew. Valerie Justin remembers her husband getting up at five o'clock every morning to write his memos to the crew, which were sometimes funny, frequently irreverent, and always encouraging. (Moviegoers may remember George Justin for his brief role in *Chinatown* [1974] as Barney, the barber who tells a bawdy joke to Jack Nicholson.)

The thrust of Justin's memos never varied: get the movie done and keep the costs low. His message on June 28 was typical: "Remember, men, we are not doing GONE WITH THE WIND! We are doing a very fine, sensitive, beautiful, highly dramatic, VERY LOW BUDGET picture. Let's get in there and knock off lots of scenes today." The second week began on July 2 with Justin's memo: "The management wishes to take this opportunity to thank both the cast and crew members (some of whom are very fine actors in their own right) for a brilliant performance this past week. CONGRATU-LATIONS AND KEEP UP THE GOOD WORK MEN!!!" The following day, he stayed on message: "Let us stand behind our leader Mr. Lumet! Let us help him carry the ball onward to a brilliant, artistic, LOW BUDGET victory!" Bob Markell exaggerated only slightly: "George wanted to bring it in for nothing."[33]

Reginald Rose spent much of the summer with his family on Fire Island but visited the set on a few occasions. Present during the first week of shooting, he was asked by a reporter about the growing number of television dramas being made into motion pictures. Rose credited the quality of live television: "The characters are much more mature and we find the plot coming out of the characters rather than out of incidents."[34] Rose had recently sold the rights to "Dino" prompting the reporter to ask whether Rose planned to shift to motion pictures. The answer was an emphatic no: "I'm in TV now and always will be." Yet given the disparity in pay, he could understand why writers found Hollywood so attractive. Although Rose preferred to work in New York, who could blame a writer who moved to Hollywood? The solution was to boost the pay for television writers. Rose asked rhetorically: "On a show that is budgeted as high as $200,000, why shouldn't the writer get 10% or 15% for the script?"[35] Looking ahead, Rose said that he planned to make a movie of "Tragedy in a Temporary Town." Several studios had expressed interest, but Rose said that he and Lumet intended to produce it on their own, filming at a real work site the following year.[36] In fact, nothing came of this idea. After *12 Angry Men*, Lumet was in great demand and never looked back.

THE FOUR-WEEK SHOOT WENT very smoothly, in part because there were so few uncertainties—no location shots, no worries about weather, no elaborate sets. As Lumet later said: "It was not one where we had to 'cue the battleship.' We could concentrate on performance and camera."[37] Extensive rehearsals helped, too, so that most scenes needed at most a few takes. Lumet recalled: "If you've prepared it properly, staged it properly, and then you work with the actors properly, you don't go 18 takes."[38]

It was the kind of set, said assistant director Don Kranze, "where everybody expected everybody else to know what they were supposed to do, and respected one another for that. That's why Fonda cast them in the first place. They were pros with theater backgrounds." He added: "You didn't screw around on a Hank Fonda set even when he was just there as only an actor. When he was also the producer, forget it."[39] Fonda, in turn, gave credit to Lumet: "I hired Sidney because he had the reputation of being wonderful with actors. We got a bonus that nobody counted on. He also had incredible organization and awareness of the problem of shooting and not wasting time."[40]

Unlike most movies, where an actor might go days between a scene, a jury room drama meant that all twelve jurors had to be present every day. When not needed on camera, they passed the time conversing or playing cards. Bob Markell commented: "We were a family. We all knew each other. It was just a little group of actors who seemed to agree with one another."[41] That feeling of camaraderie is evident in the many photos taken by Menyhért Munkácsi, a Hungarian-born photographer known to all as Muky, who captured the actors in relaxed moments. As Don Kranze recalled in 2019: "It was a good set of actors, mostly stage actors, coming together to do their professional work professionally. It was a good combination."[42] "It had a great pleasure about it," said Lumet, "because there was this burst of creativity that was just fabulous. Everybody knew that they were doing good work."[43] At some point during the filming, George Justin gathered the cast and crew for a group photo on the set. The featurette of Henry Fonda, speaking to the camera about jury service, was never filmed.

THE THIRD WEEK OF FILMING began on July 9 with George Justin's memo to the crew: "GENTLEMEN! This marks the half-way point in our glorious adventure together. Although I have scolded you, on occasion, you have, all of you, come through with flying colors. Let us carry on from here to the battle's glorious end with a team spirit that will bring us high honor and LOW BUDGET."

By Wednesday, July 11, filming in daylight was complete, and the camera now went around the room a second time in transition lighting. Justin advised: "We are about to begin our RAIN sequence. Let's all put on our galoshes and heavy duty storm gear and into our dogsleds and away we go. Neither wind nor rain nor icy skies shall keep our 12 ANGRY POSTMEN from their LOW BUDGET goal." To create a rainstorm on the sound stage, a member of the crew sat on a stool with a garden hose and kept the water trained on the window, collected in pans below.

"At long last, we approach the end," George Justin wrote at the start of the final week. Lumet and Kaufman went around the room a third time with the overhead lights turned on. The setups were shorter as the pace quickened, with fifty-two scenes completed on a single day, Wednesday July 18. By then the camera was often positioned below eye level, looking upward at the subject with lenses that collapsed space. Said Lumet: "The sense of increasing claustrophobia did a lot to raise the tension of the last part of the movie."[44]

The shooting script was followed exactly with only one exception. In the final moments, when Juror 12 shifts his vote from not guilty back to guilty, the shooting script has Juror 3 gesture derisively toward the ad man: "Batten, Barton, Durstine, and Osborn up there is bouncin' backwards and forwards like a tennis ball," referring to a well-known New York advertising agency. During filming, Lee J. Cobb said something else: "The boy in the gray flannel suit here is bouncing backwards and forwards like a tennis ball," a nod to the movie, *The Man in the Gray Flannel Suit*, released in May 1956, in which Cobb and Joseph Sweeney had prominent roles. Whether the line was ad-libbed by Cobb or suggested by Lumet or Rose is not known, a small mystery in a production that otherwise followed the script to a tee.

ON SATURDAY, JULY 21, cast and crew traveled to Lower Manhattan, taking advantage of a weekend day when court was not in session and city streets would be quiet. After four weeks in close quarters, they were ready for a change of scenery. Bob Markell recalled, "We all loved, in a funny way, getting out of the studio."[45]

Only four setups remained, the two at the start of the movie and the two at the end. Lumet wanted the last shot to release emotions that had been bottled up. He explained: "On the final shot, an exterior that showed the jurors leaving the courthouse, I used a wide angle lens, wider than any lens that had been used in the entire picture. I also raised the camera to the highest above-eye-level position. The intention was literally to give us all air, to finally let us breathe, after two increasingly confined hours."[46] From scaffolding erected to provide that vantage point, the jurors are seen walking down the courthouse steps and flowing back into the city. The last one seen is Lee J. Cobb as Juror 3, walking slowly and holding the bannister for support, a lonely figure profoundly moved by his experience. "It was a beautiful ending, I thought, walking down the stairs," said Bob Markell. The final setup was completed in a single take.

With that last shot, the filming was done. It had taken twenty-two days, four full workweeks plus one day on either end. In March 1954, Reginald Rose had walked up those steps to report for jury duty. Two years and four months later, the movie inspired by his day in court was complete.

12

∷∷

Release and Reviews
(Fall 1956 to Spring 1958)

AFTER THE LAST SCENE of *12 Angry Men*, cast and crew moved on to new projects.

Ed Begley continued to star each night on Broadway in *Inherit the Wind* and on August 19 appeared in "The Big Vote" on *The Alcoa Hour*. Robert Webber still performed in *No Time for Sergeants* and in October acted in "One Bright Day" on NBC's *Robert Montgomery Presents*. By August, E. G. Marshall and Jack Warden were back in front of the cameras for Paddy Chayefsky's *The Bachelor Party*, filmed on location in Greenwich Village and Stuyvesant Town near the East Village.[1] In September, Lee J. Cobb agreed to play the lead role in *The Garment Jungle*, a Columbia Pictures movie about labor practices in the needle trade.[2] The following month, Warden and Jack Klugman appeared on stage in *A Very Special Baby* at the Locust Street Theater in Philadelphia, written by Robert Alan Aurthur and directed by Martin Ritt.[3] Also in October, George Voskovec began a five-month run in the London production of *The Diary of Anne Frank*, in the role of Mr. Frank.

With filming complete, *12 Angry Men* moved into postproduction. Compared to most Hollywood movies, which printed about ten feet of film for every foot in the final cut, this one had been a marvel of efficiency. "We printed less than twice the amount of footage that we eventually used," said Lumet. "From a motion picture point of view, this is insanely economical."[4]

With each setup carefully defined and relatively few shots printed, the task of editing was not especially complex, although the presence of so many actors in such a tight space at times made continuity a challenge. Editing was handled by Carl Lerner, a New Yorker who most recently worked on *Patterns*, with Lumet also taking an active role.

In October, Kenyon Hopkins was hired to provide the film score.[5] A noted jazz composer and arranger, who had recently scored Elia Kazan's *Baby Doll*, Hopkins added music at just three points. At the beginning, when the jurors file out of the courtroom and the camera pans on the defendant, looking forlorn, a wistful melody is played on a single woodwind. The theme returns during the tabulation of the secret ballots, again with a minimal arrangement. Finally, as the jurors walk down the courthouse steps, the theme returns again, this time played by a larger ensemble, the music swelling to a peak. Hopkins's score was discreet but effective, very much in keeping with the overall production.

Titles and credits were added using a simple font without serifs or other ornamentation. When the job was complete, George Justin called Bob Markell with a bit of embarrassing news: the art director's name had been misspelled as *Markel*; the second *l*, Justin confessed, had been misplaced during the montage process. (In 2016, Markell spoke warmly of his friend, who had passed away in 2008. "If you see George," he said, "tell him I want the other L.")[6]

Once in final form, *12 Angry Men* was submitted to the Production Code Administration for approval. Among other requirements, the producers had to complete a checklist about the movie's content and characterizations. For *Races and Nationals*, all were listed as American other than one unidentified European, Juror 11 (George Voskovec), whose portrayal was listed as sympathetic. As for professions there was one, judge, whose portrayal was listed as neither sympathetic nor unsympathetic but as indifferent. For liquor, there was none, and as for crime, they wrote: "Murder before opening scene." The PCA wanted to know the fate of the criminal: Killed, Captured, or Something else? The producers checked the No Punishment box, adding: "Real criminal unknown." Officially, at least, the defendant was innocent and the murderer was still at large.

FOR UNITED ARTISTS, 1956 marked the fifth consecutive year of strong performance since Arthur Krim and Robert Benjamin had taken over.[7] United Artists had released forty-eight movies, taking in $65 million at the box office, up from $55 million in 1955, with solid profits too. Thanks to these excellent results, in early 1957 Krim and Benjamin consolidated their ownership of United Artists, buying Charlie Chaplin's stake for $1.1

million, and then acquiring Mary Pickford's stake for $3 million.[8] From there, they planned a public share offering to raise more capital and expand further.

Looking ahead to 1957, United Artists planned to release fifty-five movies, roughly one per week. Most were the usual fare of popular entertainment: some westerns (*Tomahawk Trail* and *Revolt at Fort Laramie*), a few crime capers (Errol Flynn in *The Big Boodle*), and the occasional horror movie (*Pharaoh's Curse* and *Voodoo Island*). A handful of movies had been given larger budgets and were slated for a major promotional push. *Sweet Smell of Success*, the latest Hecht-Lancaster movie starring Burt Lancaster and Tony Curtis, cost $2.6 million and was scheduled for May. Two months later would see the release of Stanley Kramer's first blockbuster, *The Pride and the Passion*, a Napoleonic War epic starring Cary Grant, Frank Sinatra, and Sophia Loren, with a budget of more than $4 million. Compared with United Artists' other releases, *12 Angry Men* was somewhere in the middle of the pack. It had a bona fide star in Henry Fonda and was a cut above the standard fare in terms of quality, yet few expected it to be a hit.

Years later, Henry Fonda said that he had wanted the same distribution strategy that worked so well for *Marty*: a low-key opening in a small theater, allowing word-of-mouth to build over time.[9] United Artists had other ideas. In early 1957, Arthur Krim called Fonda with an urgent plea: "'What are you doing? We want you. Get down here as fast as you can." Arriving at the company's offices, Fonda found Krim and Benjamin huddling with senior executives of Loew's, one of the largest chains of movie theaters. Loew's top brass had screened *12 Angry Men* and wanted to book it into their flagship theaters across the country.

Fonda recalled that he expressed reservations, but Krim retorted: "Are you out of your ever-loving mind? All you'll have to do is sit back and hire people to take the wheelbarrows of money to the bank." Since United Artists had financed the movie and was responsible for distribution, Fonda felt he had no choice but to agree. At least that's what Fonda said with the benefit of hindsight. In fact, most producers would have been thrilled with a national release, and if Loew's was ready to put the movie in first-run theaters, it's unlikely a producer would have offered much resistance.

For the New York opening, Loew's offered its most luxurious theater, the Capitol. Located a few blocks north of Times Square at Broadway and Fifty-First Street, it was among the most opulent of all Manhattan movie theaters. Built in 1919, the Capitol was better described as a movie palace, decorated in the Italian Renaissance style, with majestic staircases and rock-crystal chandeliers. The theater could seat up to 4,800 patrons and had been the site of Metro-Goldwyn-Mayer's most lavish premieres, including the New York opening of *Gone with the Wind* in 1939 and the New York premiere of Henry Fonda's recent *War and Peace* in August 1956.[10]

To promote the movie, United Artists hired Arthur P. Jacobs Co., a publicity firm with offices in New York and Beverly Hills. A March 2 memo listed a range of proposed initiatives: Getting articles into prominent magazines such as *Life, Saturday Review, Glamour*, and *Esquire*; running an article about the technical challenges of making the movie under Boris Kaufman's byline in *American Cinematographer*; and offering special showings to newspaper and magazine critics, plus private screenings for "Hollywood opinion-makers" such as Louella Parsons, Hedda Hopper, and Erskine Johnson. The memo also mentioned arranging commercial tie-ins with Brookfield Clothes, Van Heusen Shirts, Magnavox, and Contour Chairs. One proposed tie-in, rejected by Fonda, was with Rheingold Beer.[11] (One can only wonder at the possible advertising angle: "Rheingold Beer—Have a few the next time *you're* on a jury!")

Although Arthur P. Jacobs made still photographs available to magazines, there were relatively few takers. The movie offered little of visual interest, no grand vistas or exotic locales, no sizzling romance or fancy costumes. The best that United Artists could come up with was a tagline for the movie poster: *Life Is In Their Hands—Death Is On Their Minds. It Explodes Like 12 Sticks Of Dynamite!*

AS UNITED ARTISTS READIED 12 *Angry Men* for release, Reginald Rose was busy with his next original drama. The idea had come about the previous summer, while chatting on the beach at Fire Island with a friend, Jerome Leitner. "He told me that every lawyer show he'd ever seen, like *Perry Mason*, got everything wrong," Rose recalled. "He started telling me how it really was in a courtroom. I thought this would be another good *Studio One* drama."[12]

"The Defender" told the story of a delivery boy accused of strangling a wealthy woman in her home. The evidence points to his guilt, with one witness able to identify the defendant at the scene of the crime and another who saw him as he fled. In many ways a conventional courtroom drama, Rose added another dimension: The defense attorneys are father and son, the older man believing the defendant is guilty and interested only in providing a conventional defense, while the younger man is willing to resort to questionable tactics in order to acquit his client.

"The Defender" was written as a two-part program with a cliff-hanger at the end of the first hour, and broadcast on successive weeks, February 25 and March 4, 1957. It was produced by Herb Brodkin, who had joined *Studio One* in late 1956, with the lead roles played by Ralph Bellamy as the courtly father and William Shatner, age twenty-six, as the brash son. Other cast members included the then little-known twenty-seven-year-old Steve McQueen as the defendant, and two actors from *12 Angry Men*: Martin Balsam as the prosecutor and Rudy Bond as a shop owner. The *New York Times* featured "The Defender" in an article that described its author as "good-humored and modest" and "one of the medium's more seasoned, gifted, and forceful dramatic writers." The *Times* focused on Rose's television writing, with not a single word about the movie he had coproduced with Henry Fonda that would be released in just six weeks.[13]

ALMOST TWO YEARS after Henry Fonda had watched a kinescope of the *Studio One* performance, the movie version of *12 Angry Men* opened at the Capitol on Friday, April 12, 1957. United Artists mounted the sort of campaign that producers dream of: opening in New York, Boston, Chicago, Portland, Los Angeles, and Fonda's hometown of Omaha, followed one week later by Philadelphia, Baltimore, St. Louis, Indianapolis, Kansas City, and Denver, and then in Cleveland, Louisville, Cincinnati, Buffalo, and Toronto. It was much more ambitious than United Artists' roll-out of Paddy Chayefsky's *The Bachelor Party*, which opened the same week.

The first newspaper review appeared on Sunday, April 14, with Frank Quinn of the *New York Daily Mirror* writing: "*12 Angry Men* is a superior, thought-provoking film. It combines superior writing, directing and performing for a thrilling dramatic impact. . . . Fonda as the focal point is a monument of acting skill. His fellow jurors have been selected with care and perform with realism. Lee J. Cobb is the leading opponent and last to yield. Cobb rages with bitterness, born of an estrangement with his son."[14] It would have been hard to ask for a better review.

More favorable notices appeared on Monday, April 15. The *New York Journal-American* wrote: "Immensely absorbing and exciting is the picture that came to the Capitol over the week-end under the title of *12 Angry Men*. On every count, writing, acting and direction, it qualifies as one of the year's best."[15] A. H. Weiler of the *New York Times* praised the movie for its "taut, absorbing and compelling drama that reaches far beyond the close confines of its jury room setting." He credited Sidney Lumet and Boris Kaufman for a movie that was "ingeniously photographed" and said that "Henry Fonda gives his most forceful portrayal in years."[16]

A further boost came from the April 20 issue of the *Saturday Review* which featured Henry Fonda on its cover. "*12 Angry Men* is remarkably successful at establishing its atmosphere," wrote Hollis Alpert, "from the sultriness of the room on a hot summer day to the tension created by the clash of overheated minds. Reginald Rose's screenplay is considerably improved and developed over its original version seen a few seasons ago on TV; Sidney Lumet's direction (his first in the movie medium) is expert enough to qualify him as an important new talent; and it looks as though Henry Fonda, in his first time out as a producer, has come up with a winner."[17]

First week box office revenues reached $28,000, an encouraging start given that audiences had been "buying a blind item over the weekend." Elsewhere, however, the reception was modest. In Boston it earned just $16,000, described by *Variety* as "slow." In Chicago, revenues of $14,500 were "disappointing." In Omaha, $8,000 was "neat," but at the Fox Wilshire in Los Angeles, revenues of $7,000 were "slow," and takings in Portland were "slim."

Unfortunately, strong reviews in New York newspapers did not translate into box office success. Over the Easter weekend, while movie goers flocked to New York City's movie theaters, not many came to the Capitol. The big winners were *Funny Face* at $215,000, followed by *Boy on a Dolphin* at $135,000 and two enduring hits, *The Ten Commandments* and *Around the World in 80 Days* at $60,000 and $57,300, respectively. *12 Angry Men* was far down the list at $27,000. *Variety* had written that "biz is expected to build." It did not.

Elsewhere the news was no better. In Boston, after a slow first week, *12 Angry Men* was pulled. In Chicago, second week revenues dropped to $13,000 ("mild"); there would be no third week. In Philadelphia, solid first week receipts of $13,000 ("lusty") fell to $9,000 ("fair"), and the movie was yanked. In Los Angeles, second week revenues edged up slightly to $7,300, then fell to $4,500 ("dull").

When *12 Angry Men* earned only $13,000 in its third week at the Capitol ("very sluggish") it was replaced by *The Little Hut*. There would be no chance to build word of mouth, as *Marty* had done at the Sutton.

In city after city, the story was the same. Despite strong critical reviews, *12 Angry Men* was "light" in Louisville, "weak" in Minneapolis, and "didn't catch the public's fancy" in Indianapolis. It lasted one week in Kansas City ("dull") and Denver ("thin"). In Cincinnati, it earned $5,500 for one week and was gone. By the middle of May, just five weeks after its release, *12 Angry Men* had all but disappeared from first-run theaters across the country.

The fate of any single film scarcely mattered to United Artists. In May, it released six new movies including *Sweet Smell of Success*, which became a hit. It brought out three more in June, then seven in July. Each would have its moment in the sun before attention shifted to the next in line. If any given movie didn't find a market, well, that wasn't United Artists' problem.[18]

12 ANGRY MEN MIGHT HAVE disappeared entirely if not for the European film festivals, held in late spring. The most prominent one, the Cannes Film Festival, had been the site of *Marty*'s triumph in 1955. For 1957, the Motion Picture Export Association nominated three movies for Cannes: Paramount's hit musical, *Funny Face*; Allied Artists' epic about Quakers in the Civil War, *Friendly Persuasion*, starring Gary Cooper; and Paddy Chayefsky's *The Bachelor Party*. In something of a surprise, the *Palme d'Or* went to *Friendly Persuasion*, perhaps because its pacifist message appealed to a European audience.[19]

One week after Cannes, the Motion Picture Export Association made its selections for the Berlin International Film Festival, to be held in late June.[20] The American entrants included MGM's *Teahouse of the August Moon* with Marlon Brando and Glenn Ford, the Walt Disney documentary *Secrets of Life*, and, thanks to the efforts of United Artists' Arnold Picker, *12 Angry Men*.[21]

Over eleven days, the Berlin festival screened more than one hundred movies from forty-four countries. *12 Angry Men* was shown on June 27 to general acclaim, and a week later, at the end of the festival, was awarded top honors, the Golden Bear, praised by the jury as "a portrayal of intellect and conscience." One account read: "Judging from the applause when the picture first was shown and the ovation that greeted the award, critical opinion coincided with popular feeling."[22] Henry Fonda, in town for the end of the festival, was presented the Golden Bear by the mayor of West Berlin, Willy Brandt. Not only the festival jury was impressed. A leading German newspaper, the *Frankfurt Allgemeine Zeitung*, wrote: "Nobody doubted that the American feature film 'Twelve Angry Men' would win the Berlin Film Festival Grand Prix, so far was its distance from the level of the entire festival selection. This Henry Fonda production is exemplary. Contrary to all the rules of movie making, the classical units of time, place, and action are meticulous, so accurate that the camera barely allows a view out the window that connects the twelve men in the jury room with the outside world."[23]

Although good reviews had not translated into box office success in the United States, the story was different in Europe. *Variety* wrote: "The Berlin Festival award, exceptionally excellent reviews, and substantial word-of-mouth have helped to make this film the most talked-about one here in some time."[24] When *12 Angry Men* reached Paris cinemas in September 1957, critics hailed it as a "masterpiece." They also registered astonishment: Henry Fonda was well known, of course, but neither director Sidney Lumet nor screenwriter Reginald Rose were known at all, making the movie nothing short of a sensation.[25]

BY THE END OF 1957, two very different narratives about *12 Angry Men* were developing. The critical response had been excellent, with the movie on the Ten Best Film List of the *New York Times*,[26] *New York World-Telegram & Sun*, *New York Journal-American*, *Daily Mirror*, *Daily News*, *Time Magazine*, the *Saturday Review*, and several more publications.[27] Rose won Best Screenplay from *Film Daily*, and Fonda and Lumet were listed among the best actors and directors of the year by the New York Film Critics. Abroad, it took top honors at the Locarno Film Festival, from the Belgian Union of Film Critics, and from the International Catholic Film Office.

Yet revenues had barely reached $1 million, placing *12 Angry Men* in a tie for ninety-first among US movies released in 1957.[28] While Chayefsky's *The Bachelor Party* earned $1.5 million, good for sixtieth place, *12 Angry Men* was barely ahead of such forgettable entries as *Four Girls in Town*, *Gun for a Coward*, and a Dean Martin vehicle called *10,000 Bedrooms*. (He played a hotel executive, should anyone wonder.)

Given this mixed reception, no one could predict how the movie would fare during the major awards season. The big favorite was David Lean's *The Bridge on the River Kwai*, released toward the end of 1957 to great acclaim, but the producers of *12 Angry Men* hoped that a good showing might prompt a box office revival.

First, in February, came the Golden Globes, where *12 Angry Men* gained four nominations—Best Picture, Best Director (Lumet), Best Actor (Fonda), and Best Supporting Actor (Lee J. Cobb)—but received no awards. Next were the British Academy of Film Awards, where *12 Angry Men* earned a nomination for Best Picture, and Henry Fonda took the prize for Best Foreign Actor. As an American citizen, he did not have to compete against Alec Guinness, whose performance in *The Bridge on the River Kwai* earned him the award for Best British Actor.

In early March, the Academy of Motion Picture Arts and Sciences announced its nominations. To the delight of its producers and distributor, *12 Angry Men* received three: Best Picture, Best Director (Lumet), and Best Adapted Screenplay (Rose). The other nominees for Best Picture were all commercial hits: *The Bridge on the River Kwai, Witness for the Prosecution, Sayonara*, and *Peyton Place*. Only *12 Angry Men* had managed a nomination for Best Picture despite weak box office revenues.

The Academy Award ceremonies took place at the Pantages Theater on March 26, 1958. As expected, it was a night of triumph for *The Bridge on the River Kwai*, which took seven Oscars, including Best Picture, Best Director, Best Actor, Best Adapted Screenplay, Best Cinematography, Best Editing, and Best Music. *12 Angry Men* and its three nominations received little attention, much less any carryover at the box office.[29] As Lumet later said: "Even when we got Academy nominations for Best Picture, Best Script, and Best Director, we never did any business in the United States."[30]

After the awards, Reginald Rose's jury movie faded from view.

PART IV

THE DEFENDERS

13

···

New Directions (1957 to 1960)

THE LEGENDARY MOVIE DIRECTOR John Huston once wrote: "There is no doubt about the meaning of the word 'failure' in the motion picture industry. The industry operates for profit, and a failure is a film that doesn't make money."[1] By this definition, *12 Angry Men* was a failure.

For its director, however, the experience had been a great success. Sidney Lumet impressed many in his debut and soon signed a two-movie deal with RKO. His next picture, filmed in early 1957, was *Stage Struck*, the story of a young actress, played by Susan Strasberg, navigating her way in New York.[2] This time, he would have an ample budget and would film in Technicolor.

For Henry Fonda, *12 Angry Men* had been a mixed experience. He had been pleased with the ensemble acting and was proud of the finished product. Yet he had not enjoyed his first experience as a movie producer and had no plans for more. Even before the end of July 1956, Fonda had agreed to appear in *The Tin Star*, a western by Paramount, with filming scheduled for fall, and then signed on for Lumet's *Stage Struck*. Fonda resumed his career as an actor; the deal for six movies with United Artists was quietly shelved.

For Reginald Rose, coproducing *12 Angry Men* had not led to much in the way of financial rewards, but weak box office receipts had been offset by strong critical reviews and an Academy Award nomination. His venture into movie production was not, however, his most pressing concern. From

1953 to 1957, Rose had written fifteen original television dramas, twelve of them performed on *Westinghouse Studio One* and three on other programs. Live anthologies had not only provided him with a good living, they had also been a source of pride. "During an average week," he wrote in *Six Television Plays*, "a viewer can see perhaps fourteen live one-hour plays, at least several of which will offer skillfully written, expertly staged dramas with an intelligent and mature point of view."[3]

Yet even as Rose wrote those words, live anthologies were in decline. In 1951 there had been more than one dozen, all based in New York; by 1956 only a few remained, as networks increasingly favored series and shifted to filmed programs, many of them produced in Hollywood.

To breathe new life into its flagging lineup, and as a response to NBC's *Producers' Showcase*, CBS launched *Playhouse 90*, a weekly ninety-minute anthology broadcast live from Hollywood.[4] Its second episode, aired October 11, 1956, was Rod Serling's "Requiem for a Heavyweight," immediately acclaimed as one of the finest examples of live television drama. *Studio One*, CBS's flagship anthology since 1948, had been eclipsed. After three years at the helm, Felix Jackson was signed to a new contract that called for him to produce only twenty episodes a year, with Herb Brodkin, who joined from NBC, and Gordon Duff, handling the rest.[5] Long-time director Franklin Schaffner departed, leaving Paul Nickell to alternate with new directors. In mid-1957, CBS announced that *Studio One* would move to Hollywood as of January 1958, and by September of that year it was off the air for good; its demise warranted only passing mention: "*Studio One* came to the end of its run last night, only one month short of ten consecutive years on the air."[6]

Writers who had flourished during the Golden Age of Television responded to the decline of live anthologies in different ways. Paddy Chayefsky had already moved on to stage plays and movies, writing screenplays for *The Goddess* (1958) and *Middle of the Night* (1959). Horton Foote, one of the mainstays of *The Goodyear-Philco Playhouse*, wrote for *Playhouse 90* before shifting to movies, winning the Academy Award for his adaptation of *To Kill a Mockingbird* (1962). Rod Serling had several more successes with *Playhouse 90*, including "The Comedian" in February 1957, but unhappy with constraints imposed by the networks, created his own weekly series, *The Twilight Zone*, a brilliantly original program that ran with great success from 1959 to 1964.

For Reginald Rose, the end of *Studio One* was an opportunity as much as a problem. His last contract with CBS, for twelve original outlines, had expired in early 1956. "The Defender," his two-part program that aired in

February and March 1957, turned out to be his last drama for *Studio One*. At age thirty-six, he was ready to move on.

IN THE FLOW OF ROSE'S CAREER, the years from 1953 to 1957 constitute an important period when he established himself as a leading television writer. With guidance and support from Felix Jackson and Florence Britton, he developed his skills and emerged as a unique voice, known for addressing topics of social justice. The years from 1961 to 1965 constitute another distinct period, when Rose was absorbed with his weekly television drama, *The Defenders*—a topic to be covered in the following chapters.

The years in between, from early 1957 through 1960, represent an interregnum, a time when Rose tried his hand at new formats, ventured into new topics, sometimes successfully, and waded into controversies. He explored new aspects of social justice even as the public discussion of those topics was shifting beneath him. Rose's output during this period is not as well known as his works from the first period—"Thunder on Sycamore Street," "Twelve Angry Men," and "Tragedy in a Temporary Town"—or from the third—*The Defenders*—but he was at least as active, as creative, and as ambitious.

Two of Rose's first projects were movie screenplays for producer Walter Mirisch. By early 1957, as "The Defender" aired on *Studio One* and *12 Angry Men* was being readied for release, Rose was adapting a western novel, *The Border Jumpers*, intended as vehicle for Gary Cooper. Rose submitted his first draft in May, and the next month received a detailed seven-page response, very likely from Mirisch's story editor, Eve Ettinger. It was not positive: "I had hoped that Mr. Rose would use the book as a springboard to write a story for Gary that would have an important moral point, with excitement and drama; that would be the equal if not an improvement on *High Noon*. I must say I am disappointed."[7] The memo concluded: "I think he can do much, much better, as he proved in *Twelve Angry Men*." Rose made substantial revisions and his next screenplay was accepted. Along the way the movie's title was changed to *Man of the West*. Mirisch was pleased, describing it as "a challenging script about a complex ex-outlaw thrown back into the world he had fought so hard to escape."[8] Released in 1958, *Man of the West*, in color and CinemaScope, fared very well at the box office, ranking thirty-first among movies that year. It also inspired Clint Eastwood, who made a movie based on the same premise, *Unforgiven*, which won the Academy Award for Best Picture of 1992.

In early 1958, Mirisch asked Rose to adapt *The Man in the Net*, a novel about an artist who is accused of the murder of his alcoholic wife;

eventually he manages to identify the killer and exonerate himself.[9] Rose submitted his screenplay with a letter that suggested an actor for the role of the local policeman: "I don't think you could find anyone more perfect than Jack Warden. He can produce a really terrifying menace from beneath a seemingly simple, shrewdly humorous front better than any actor I've ever seen in my life. . . . Get him if you can. He's just great."[10] *The Man in the Net* was directed by Michael Curtiz and starred Alan Ladd and Carolyn Jones, with the role of the policeman going to Charles McGraw, a frequent movie tough guy. The *New York Times* offered a mixed review but had praise for the writer: "The melodramatic aspects of the tale are old stuff. More interesting is the dialogue by Mr. Rose and his preoccupation with injustice."[11]

Writing screenplays for Walter Mirisch paid well, but Rose did not find the process enjoyable. In an interview the following year, he was blunt: "I hate working for the movies. I'm very bitter about the whole experience I had making movies. I'd only make another if it were my own script or if I were co-producer."[12] A few years later he said: "I'd prefer movie work if I had control of what I write. Otherwise, no. Besides *12 Angry Men*, I have done four other pictures, and they changed my stories so much that I was unhappy with the results."[13] (Those four included the two for Mirisch; *Crime in the Streets*, whose story had been altered by Don Siegel; and *Dino*, released in February 1957, which made the main character less troubled, the poster featuring a cheerful Sal Mineo.) Unhappy with his experience writing screenplays, Rose would wait several years before he tried his hand at another.

ALTHOUGH *STUDIO ONE* WAS CANCELED in 1958, Reginald Rose still contributed to CBS thanks to one of his most ardent supporters.

Herb Brodkin was a native New Yorker, born in 1912. He had studied theater at the University of Michigan and Yale in the 1930s, and produced stage shows in the Army during World War II. After the war, Brodkin worked briefly as a set designer on Broadway before joining CBS. His first job was for *Charlie Wild, Private Detective*, where he worked at the desk next to another designer, Bob Markell. Rather than stay in art direction, Brodkin moved to ABC's *The Elgin Hour*, where he produced "Crime in the Streets." After shifting to NBC he produced two more of Rose's dramas, "The Expendable House" and "Tragedy in a Temporary Town," on *The Alcoa Hour*. Next, after he joined *Studio One*, Brodkin produced Rose's two-part episode, "The Defender."

When *Studio One* folded, CBS moved Brodkin to *Playhouse 90* where he quickly made his presence felt. Six feet tall and with a shock of red hair,

Brodkin was described in a CBS press release as "refreshingly outspoken," a qualitiy that others called blunt and abrasive. By his own admission, he could be very difficult to his higher-ups, as he often demanded, and usually received, artistic freedom. One of his first programs at *Playhouse 90*, broadcast in January 1959, was "The Velvet Alley," Rod Serling's searing tale about an ambitious television writer who spurns the agent responsible for his success. A tale that closely mirrored Serling's treatment of Blanche Gaines, it starred Art Carney as the writer, Jack Klugman as the rejected agent, and George Voskovec as the writer's father. A week later, Brodkin produced his first *Playhouse 90* drama by Rose, "A Quiet Game of Cards," about a group of respectable businessmen who plan a perfect murder for the thrill of it. "We got a reaction, all right," Rose later commented. "Some people thought it was one of the best TV plays they'd seen, others vehemently complained that it was immoral."[14] Two months later, Brodkin produced Rose's domestic tale, "A Marriage of Strangers," adapted from "Three Empty Rooms." Among the many other notable teleplays that Brodkin produced for *Playhouse 90* was "Judgment at Nuremberg," written by Abby Mann, and subsequently made into an Oscar-winning motion picture directed by Stanley Kramer and starring Spencer Tracy and Maximilian Schell.

ALTHOUGH ROSE CONTRIBUTED TELEPLAYS to *Playhouse 90*, which was based in Los Angeles, he continued to live in New York. Many contemporaries, including Rod Serling, were drawn to the sunshine and open spaces of Southern California. Not Rose. "I hate working in Hollywood," he said in 1961. "You never see a dirty kid in Beverly Hills. They don't sit on the curb and talk to one another. They're not allowed." Rose preferred the city of his birth: "I like working in New York, living in New York. I like it where I live on the West side of town. It's restless. Always something going on. You can go out anytime of night, buy a paper or go to the delicatessen."[15] (Sidney Lumet felt the same way and lived in New York for his entire life. He was skeptical of a city whose main industry was . . . entertainment itself. Where was the source of inspiration?)

Life in New York suited Reginald and Barbara Rose. In 1955, expecting the arrival of twins, they had moved to a larger apartment at 151 West Eighty-Sixth Street. Now, in 1958, they moved to an even more spacious apartment next door, at 161 West Eighty-Sixth Street, both buildings owned and managed by the real estate company of Edward Sulzberger. The new home had an office for Rose, a combination study room and playroom for the four boys, who ranged in age from eight to two, and a room for a live-in housekeeper. Jonathan Rose remembers his father in those days as an early riser who ate breakfast with his older sons before walking them to the school bus. Returning to the apartment, he would write for much of the day in his office off the main hallway, and often take a nap before the boys returned from school. In the evenings, Reginald and Barbara would sometimes dine out, see a movie, or entertain friends. He also hosted poker games, as often as once a week, with friends that included writers JP Miller and Paddy Chayefsky, playwright Neil Simon, publicist Johnny Friedkin, and producer Howard Gottfried.[16] Rose enjoyed Broadway shows, including *The Music Man* (whose star, Robert Preston, was a friend since appearing in "Crime in the Streets" on *The Elgin Hour*), and particularly liked the music of Rodgers and Hammerstein, notably *The King and I* and *Flower Drum Song*. For hobbies, Rose enjoyed electronics and built a few high-fidelity sets. And like so many of his generation, Rose smoked cigarettes, for many years consuming two packs of Pall Malls a day. With his wife and young children, a wide circle of friends, and a blossoming writing career, Reginald Rose was very content living in New York.

Perhaps the only people paying any attention to *12 Angry Men* were the accountants, charged with keeping track of revenues and costs. Through August 1958, domestic revenue stood at $680,141. After United Artists took its 30 percent cut and deducted the costs of production and advertising, net domestic income came to $170,326. With revenue from Europe and Canada boosting net income to $420,968, the loan from Bankers Trust could be repaid in full, leaving a net profit of $57,142. At last there were funds to begin paying deferred salaries, with $43,859 going to Henry Fonda, $11,277 to Reginald Rose, and $1,253 to Sidney Lumet. Accountant Charles Renthal was optimistic: "The results look most encouraging, and it is possible that everybody will be paid their deferments and maybe a profit besides."[17] The following year brought further payments, but only in October 1960, three and a half years after the movie was released, did Fonda, Rose, and Lumet receive the entirety of their deferred fees.

NO LONGER UNDER ANY CONTRACT, and not keen to write more screenplays, Rose spent 1959 and 1960 on several projects. At the request of producer David Susskind, he wrote the script for a television tribute to Eleanor Roosevelt on her seventy-fifth birthday, which aired October 11, 1959. The show featured many figures from politics—including former president Harry S. Truman and the current vice president, Richard M. Nixon—as well as prominent names in entertainment such as Lauren Bacall, Henry Fonda, and Sidney Poitier. Rose wrote their lines, creating a warm tribute to a revered human rights activist.

With the struggle for civil rights gaining attention, Rose was inspired to write "Black Monday," a drama that looked at the first day of integration at a junior high school in a Southern town. Rose hoped to make it into a movie to be directed by Sidney Lumet, telling the *New York Post*: "We had done a picture for United Artists—*12 Angry Men*. We thought of doing something on integration." Rose prepared a movie treatment but, finding no interest from studios, converted it into a stage play.[18] He completed the script in September 1959 and showed it to several theater producers but got a cool reception: "They all had various reasons for not doing it, which I think were actually the same. It's a terribly big and expensive play to produce and also it is not exactly what you'd call escapist material. I didn't show it to anyone after that. I figured it was the kind of play that would have to wait until I got a hit on Broadway."[19] The project stalled until Rose eventually took it to television, where "Black Monday" was performed on CBS's *Play of the Week* on January 16, 1961.[20] In March 1962, it was performed off-Broadway at the Vandam Theater in New York but did not earn strong reviews. Rose had been ahead of his time in 1954 with "Thunder on Sycamore Street," but by the early 1960s civil rights protests were on the nightly news, and audiences did not flock to the theater for a retelling of current events.

With his next project, Rose addressed a topic that would soon be pertinent to an American audience. Beginning in 1954, the Algerian *Front de Libération Nationale* (FLN) had mounted sporadic uprisings against French rule, first in the countryside and then in the capital. The struggle for Algiers was one of the first instances of urban terrorism, with FLN members engaging in bombings that killed indiscriminately. The French military made a concerted effort to break the insurgents and reports soon began to circulate about the use of torture. A September 1957 article in the *New York Times* told of detainees subjected to beatings, burning, and electric shocks, and commented that for a country that had suffered at the hands of the Gestapo, "the debate on the use of torture as a weapon of 'pacification' in Algeria has become acutely embarrassing." *Times* reporter Thomas Brady wrote: "Officially there is no such thing as torture. But speaking unofficially, soldiers and civil servants explain that torture is the only effective weapon against underground terrorism."[21]

For Rose, these reports raised familiar concerns about rule of law, protection of civil liberties, and whether the ends can justify the means. To dramatize these issues, he devised the story of a French army captain, newly in command of a garrison, who seeks to uphold correct norms of conduct, while his lieutenant, a veteran of the bloody conflict, favors extreme measures. When the captain is appalled at an instance of torture, the lieutenant tells him: "I've been in Algeria for a long time. The kind of thing you saw this morning used to shrivel my guts. It doesn't anymore. I've seen them with their tongues torn out and I've seen them with their hands and feet sawn off . . . you wouldn't believe what they can do to a man. I don't question the politics of it because that's not my job."[22]

Their opposing positions come to a head when a fifteen-year-old messenger for the FLN is arrested. The lieutenant wants to force him to talk by any means including torture; the captain demurs, forcing a sharp confrontation. Rose recognized the argument for pragmatism, but his sympathies clearly rested with the captain, who sought to maintain proper respect for law. The conflict is eventually resolved when the lieutenant sees an FLN sniper gathering the captain in his sights but does not intervene, allowing the captain to be killed and removing any obstacle to the use of torture.

"The Cruel Day" was broadcast on *Playhouse 90* on February 24, 1960. It was directed by Franklin Schaffner, with Van Heflin as the captain and Cliff Robertson as the lieutenant. For the original work, Rose earned ten thousand dollars. *The Hollywood Reporter*'s Harvey Karman wrote: "Reginald Rose has never hesitated to tackle the controversial or deal with the dilemmas or personal decisions that must destroy either important interpersonal relationships or the individual's own self-respect." To Sid Bakal of the *Herald Tribune*, "The Cruel Day" was "the best *Playhouse 90* that has been seen in some time . . . a timely and provocative play that managed to maintain a high level of interest."[23]

IN PARALLEL WITH THESE PROJECTS, Rose was at work on one of the most ambitious endeavors of his career, a dramatization of the case of Nicola Sacco and Bartolomeo Vanzetti, Italian immigrants convicted in 1921 of murder during a payroll robbery in Massachusetts and executed in 1927 after lengthy appeals that gained worldwide attention. Social historian Edmund Wilson wrote that the case of Sacco and Vanzetti "revealed the whole anatomy of American life, with all its classes, professions, and points of view, and raised every fundamental question of our political and social system."[24] It inspired murals by Diego Rivera, poems by Carl Sandburg and Edna St. Vincent Millay, songs by Woody Guthrie, and books by Upton Sinclair and Howard Fast.

Until Rose's drama, the story of Sacco and Vanzetti had never been brought to television. (It would surely have been too provocative for *You Are There*. A story from ancient Greece or the American Revolution was one thing; an episode about anarchists put to death in 1927 was a different matter.) "The Sacco-Vanzetti Story" consumed Rose for many months and was, he later said, "the most difficult assignment I've ever undertaken." He explained: "I wanted to be absolutely fair and factual. So I read countless books, magazine articles and newspaper stories, in addition to the actual transcript of the trial. You may be sure that the facts and the characterizations are truthfully presented."[25] As to their guilt or innocence: "Many will attack me for this, but after weighing all of the facts, I believe they were innocent"[26]—a conclusion that was reached by numerous historians in subsequent years.[27]

In an interview with the *New York Herald Tribune*, Rose spoke candidly:

> I didn't know very much about the case when I began the research. I didn't even know who had been murdered. Now I think Sacco and Vanzetti were not guilty. But I hope I am not biased. There was no attempt to make editorial comment. The viewer will decide for himself. . . .
>
> They were intelligent, lovely, gentle people. I agreed to do the show because of what it has to say in terms of history is boiled down into one quote from Albert Einstein we've used in the play: "Everything should be done to keep alive the tragic affair of Sacco and Vanzetti in the conscience of mankind. They remind us of the fact that even the most perfectly planned democratic institutions are no better than the people whose instruments they are." It is not until years later that reason begins to prevail. Sacco and Vanzetti were killed in 1927. Now we can look back on it with some detachment. It is valuable to be able to look back in history and say, "Here we went wrong and here we were right."[28]

"The Sacco-Vanzetti Story" was performed as a two-part series on NBC's *Sunday Showcase* on successive weeks, June 3 and 10, 1960, with the first hour about their conviction in 1921, and the second hour about the events leading to their execution in 1927. Directed by Sidney Lumet, it starred one of Rose's mainstays, Martin Balsam, as Nicola Sacco, and Steven Hill as Bartolomeo Vanzetti, with E. G. Marshall as defense attorney William G. Thompson. The *New York Times*'s Jack Gould wrote: "From his play's opening moment, Mr. Rose's position was clear. At every moment he protested against a miscarriage of justice; his choice of material from the voluminous trial record underscored the prejudiced testimony against the defendants and the belief they were convicted as foreign radicals, not as payroll hold-up men and murderers."[29]

Reviews in the national press were favorable, but there were adverse reactions in New England, where the case still elicited strong feelings. Several Boston newspapers denounced Rose and accused NBC of bias. New Hampshire Senator Styles Bridges, one of Senator Joseph McCarthy's most vocal allies in the 1950s, took to the floor of the Senate and protested that "the institutions of our country are constantly open to question and attack" by "Communist propagandists who are trying to undermine us."[30] Mentioning Reginald Rose and NBC by name, Bridges read into the Congressional Record six articles from Boston newspapers. Two *Boston Herald* articles, written by Arthur E. Fetridge, mocked Rose's comment that Sacco and Vanzetti were "intelligent, lovely, gentle people." "What utter rot," Fetridge wrote. "They were admitted draft dodgers, they admitted they carried loaded guns, and there is little doubt they were anarchists."[31] The *Boston Globe* complained that "the script was guilty of shameless distortions and omissions that make it highly suspect as a documentary,"[32] and an article from the *Boston Traveler* concluded: "The TV industry needs a sharp warning, though. It has lost face in allowing itself to be the stooge for the false rantings of author Rose. His is the sort of hokum that turns an audience away in disgust."[33]

By 1960 the worst of the blacklist had subsided, and the network, NBC, and sponsor, Purex, stood behind the program, leading Rose to say he was "amazed and delighted."[34] The critical reception was excellent, too, leading to four Emmy nominations: Program of the Year, Outstanding Drama, Outstanding Drama Direction (Lumet), and Outstanding Drama Writing (Rose). It did not win any, the first three losing to a performance of "Macbeth" on NBC's *Hallmark Hall of Fame*, and Rose losing to Rod Serling for *The Twilight Zone*.[35]

"The Sacco-Vanzetti Story" was especially appreciated by some who had devoted their lives to the fight for civil liberties. Along with many grateful letters, Rose received a telegram from Michael Musmanno, an eminent jurist and legal scholar who had helped to defend Sacco and Vanzetti in the 1920s, and later served as a judge at the Nuremburg war crimes trials before he was named to the Supreme Court of Pennsylvania. Musmanno had long sought to expose the injustices of the trial and wished to focus attention on a "verdict which has cried out for shame ever since it was rendered."[36] After watching Rose's play in June 1960, the aging jurist wrote to express his thanks: "My heart melts in gratitude and my soul exalts in pride and happiness for your beautiful script which masterfully pleads not only for long delayed justice to the martyred shoe maker and fish peddler but for all mankind bleeding outside the gates of tolerance, fair play, and true brotherhood. Michael A Musmanno."[37]

14

⋮⋮⋮

The Defenders
(1960 to Spring 1962)

BY MANY STANDARDS, the greatest achievement of Reginald Rose's career was not *12 Angry Men*, a one-hour teleplay that he wrote in a few days and later expanded into a movie screenplay, but *The Defenders*, a weekly dramatic series that aired from 1961 to 1965. With 132 episodes, each one hour long, *The Defenders* provided Rose with the largest canvas, let him address the widest set of issues, brought him the most accolades, and earned him the most money. It was also the most demanding project he undertook, imposing a relentless schedule that required a new script every seven workdays, ten months a year, year after year.

The Defenders came about from Rose's collaboration with Herb Brodkin. While working on *Playhouse 90*, Brodkin founded Plautus Productions with the aim of making television programs in New York. Its first show was a thirty-minute police drama, *Brenner*, starring Ed Binns as an NYPD detective. The show ran for fourteen episodes on CBS as a summer replacement in 1959.

Rose and Brodkin, both wishing to work in New York, joined forces and submitted two ideas for a new television series to CBS. One was called *Flanagan*, about the life and loves of a young female lawyer, a show that anticipated the feel of *The Mary Tyler Moore Show* by about a decade. Brodkin drafted the concept, and Rose wrote the outline and first script. CBS was not interested. The other was based on Rose's last teleplay for *Studio One*, "The Defender," the two-part episode broadcast in early 1957. In his treatment for a full series, Rose described the lead roles: "Lawrence

Preston, an eminent trial lawyer in his mid-fifties, and his son Kenneth, twenty-four years of age, a fledgling lawyer just out of law school, and his father's junior partner." Unlike most legal dramas, which focused on the clash between prosecution and defense, this one would offer a second dimension. "The relationship between father and son is part of the hard core of this series," Rose explained. "The old and experienced on one hand, and the new and enthusiastic on the other often enter combat not only with the prosecution but with each other. And of course there is right on both sides. Each learns from the other, the youth from the shrewdness and experience of the father, and the father from the freshness and passion of the youth."[1]

The outline was sent to Michael Dann, CBS's head of programming in New York, who approved the pilot because, as he later put it, "there was so little being done in New York."[2] With a green light to make a one-hour program, Brodkin and Rose brought aboard a pair of old hands: George Justin to produce the episode and Bob Markell for art direction. As for the lead roles, Lawrence Preston was played by E. G. Marshall, with a newcomer, Robert Reed, as his son. (Marshall's sober demeanor had recently landed him two roles as lawyers, playing the defense attorney in "The Sacco-Vanzetti Story" and the stern Army prosecutor in *Town Without Pity* [1961].)

Rose's pilot, "Death Across the Counter," was about a murder case where all the evidence points to the defendant's guilt. Even the defendant, who had briefly blacked out and has no memory of the crime, assumes that he must have committed it. Lawrence Preston believes the defendant is culpable and asks the district attorney to allow a guilty plea to the reduced charge of second-degree murder. Kenneth Preston thinks something is amiss with the prosecution's case and, after a brief investigation, uncovers evidence to show that a different man fired the fatal shot. The pilot was filmed in Los Angeles in February 1960, at the same time "The Cruel Day" was made for *Playhouse 90*; Herb Brodkin recalled going from one Reginald Rose drama in the morning to another in the afternoon.[3]

The pilot was screened for James Aubrey, president of CBS television, in early 1960. Aubrey, who preferred shows aimed at a lower common denominator—he would come to be known for *The Beverly Hillbillies* and *Gilligan's Island*—wasn't impressed, and the series was set aside. None of those involved—neither Brodkin nor Rose nor any of the cast and crew—expected it to go any further. It was rescued months later by a lucky break, when top CBS brass, including chairman William S. Paley, convened to decide upon the fall 1961 season, now one year away. Aubrey wanted a new program called *Mr. Broadway*, about the life of a theatrical agent, but Paley didn't like it. Dann recalled: "Paley said to me, 'Don't *you* have anything?' The only thing I had was *The Defenders*."[4] Paley asked to see the pilot and thought it was excellent, and over Aubrey's reservations gave *The Defenders* a primetime slot in CBS's 1961 season.[5] After months of silence, the decision came as a total surprise. E. G. Marshall was working on a movie in Los Angeles when Reginald Rose called with exciting news: "They picked it up!"[6]

Plautus Productions now geared up to film twenty-six episodes of *The Defenders*. Brodkin was listed as producer, and Rose was creator and story supervisor. Rose would write some of the stories himself, and for the rest would draw upon some of the best writers in television, including Max Ehrlich, David Shaw, Ernest Kinoy, and David Davidson, who had worked with Brodkin on *Studio One* and *Playhouse 90*. When Brodkin and Rose proposed that writers be paid $5,000 per episode, CBS countered with $3,500, the amount it paid for its hit legal show, *Perry Mason*. Rose's agent, Ashley-Steiner, replied in a dismissive tone. It might be possible to hire writers for that rate, but "they are not the writers that Herb and Reggie are using or intend to use on *The Defenders*. . . . Suffice it to say that if we had the opportunity to buy the *Perry Mason* writer staff intact at $3,500 per script, we would not be at all interested." For the caliber that Brodkin and Rose had in mind, "I don't see how we can do with anything less than the $5,000 average fee."[7]

In December, CBS and Plautus Productions agreed on a total budget of close to $3 million for the first twenty-six episodes, with each episode allocated $109,000. Of that sum, $11,250 would go to Defender Productions, Inc., a company to be formed by Rose with responsibility for supplying original scripts. For each episode, Rose's company would receive a $3,000 production fee, plus $6,000 for the script, of which up to $5,000 would go to the writer. Other costs included a small administrative staff, office rent and mimeographing, plus $175 per episode to Jerome Leitner, Rose's friend from Fire Island (and later dean of Brooklyn Law School) who served as technical adviser.

The creation of Defender Productions marked a major change in Rose's personal fortunes. In the nine years since he began writing for television, Rose had been paid by the script, at first getting a few hundred dollars for an episode of *Danger* or an adaptation for *Studio One*, later signing a contract to submit outlines to *Studio One*, with additional payments for each one produced. In recent years he had earned more, getting four thousand dollars for "Tragedy in a Temporary Town" in 1956 and ten thousand dollars for "The Cruel Day" in 1960, but nothing was guaranteed, and for every sale he endured many rejections. Now, as creator and story supervisor for a weekly series, Rose was in a very different league. He would earn a substantial fee for every episode of *The Defenders*, plus keep the writer's fee for each story he penned. For 1961 alone, he could look forward to earning upward of one hundred thousand dollars, a very large income at the time.

PRODUCTION OF *THE DEFENDERS* began on January 12, 1961. For the next seven months, the show followed a demanding schedule: seven workdays per episode, one for rehearsal, and six for shooting, Monday to Friday, week after week after week, with no break between episodes. Production took place at Filmways Studios on 246 East 127th Street in East Harlem, two blocks from the Harlem River, with additional location shots around New York City to impart a realistic urban feel. The opening shot, which introduced the stars while the credits rolled, was an exterior view of the courthouse at Foley Square, the same massive structure seen at the start of *12 Angry Men*, and before that, where Reginald Rose had reported for jury duty in 1954. The production schedule called for the first eighteen episodes to be completed by the end of July, followed by a four-week summer break, and eight more to be filmed in the fall. If the response was good, CBS would pay for six more episodes, for a total of thirty-two in the first season.

Joining Brodkin and Rose were Bob Markell as associate producer, and Kenneth Utt, a veteran of *Studio One* who had starred in "Thunder on Sycamore Street," as production manager. Cast members for the first year included many familiar faces: in addition to E. G. Marshall, *The Defenders* featured Martin Balsam and Jack Klugman in several episodes, plus Ed Binns, Joseph Sweeney, and Robert Webber. The series offered roles to many up-and-coming actors, including Robert Duvall, Dustin Hoffman, James Earl Jones, and Martin Sheen.

In March 1961, when five episodes were complete, CBS screened *The Defenders* for potential sponsors. *Variety* reported that "CBS brass are convinced it's the hottest series to come down the pike in some time."[8] A prospectus described *The Defenders* as "the culmination of two years of painstaking planning and development" and claimed that it "combines the appeals of mature, full-dimensional drama and exciting, suspense-laden stories with the basic attraction of week-to-week continuity in characters . . . THE DEFENDERS promises to set new standards—in production, direction and writing—for a weekly series."[9] To underscore its confidence in the series, CBS gave it a prominent time slot: 8:30 PM on Saturday night. In April, consumer products giant Kimberly-Clark agreed to sponsor alternate weeks and was joined by Lever Brothers and Brown & Williamson.[10]

AT THE START OF AUGUST, after working without a pause since January, the cast and crew of *The Defenders* took a month-long break. With the fall season to begin in September, CBS stepped up its publicity campaign. Rose gave numerous interviews to promote the series. In one, he said that he wanted to match the quality of *Studio One* and *Playhouse 90*: "For us, it's a chance to prove you can do a mature series on TV and be successful. We're trying as best we can to take on adult topics and handle them in an adult manner and still be entertaining."[11] *The Defenders* would be nothing like *Perry Mason*, whose star almost always won his cases: "We've already finished 18 shows so far, and they've already lost four or five times."[12] Rather, it aimed to give a realistic depiction of the legal profession: "We hired my lawyer, who has been a trial attorney for 14 years, as a technical [adviser]. Sometimes he writes the courtroom scenes with the writers so that things are technically right." Jerome Leitner "refuses to allow anything said on the show to be incorrect legally."[13] Rose wanted the series "to deal with the real problems of people—the people rather than the gimmicks. Our D.A.s are not villains and the judges are human beings; we meet all of them outside the courtroom."[14] Most of all, Rose wanted to examine serious issues, some of them highly controversial. He was pleased with the support he had received from the network: "CBS has gone along with us on some pretty tough topics. Not one of our ideas has been turned down. Some of them are subjects that TV doesn't usually deal with: abortion, religious sects that don't allow surgery, the rape of a small child."[15]

Developing scripts for a weekly legal series posed several challenges. Unlike an anthology, where each episode was a self-contained story, a series had to maintain consistency of characters across episodes. Moreover, the legal angle was new for many writers. "When we started to line up contributors," said Rose, "we spent weeks explaining in detail to every prospective writer exactly what we wanted. While they may be seasoned dramatists, they haven't all had experience writing courtroom scenes and dialogue." *The Defenders* would pay well, but "this doesn't mean the author turns in sixty pages, picks up his paycheck, and runs. I demand a great deal from a writer."[16]

Rose described how his personal life had been transformed. Before *The Defenders* he had led what he called an uncomplicated life, writing for part of each day in his apartment at 161 West Eighty-Sixth Street, with ample time for family. Now he went each morning to 221 East Fifty-First Street, where Defender Productions and Plautus Productions shared offices, and worked a full day, guiding, editing, and rewriting the many scripts at various stages of development.[17] The first season had not yet begun, but already he dreamed of returning to freelance writing: "I'm kind of lazy," he told a reporter, "and this series is terribly wearing."[18]

IN AUGUST, BRODKIN AND ROSE wrote to James Aubrey with a suggestion for the series opener. Reviewing the episodes completed so far, they noted that one might not be serious enough, one was too much of a whodunnit, one did not provide the right balance between father and son, and so forth. Their choice: "The Quality of Mercy," written by Rose, about a doctor who administers a fatal dose of morphine to a newborn with Down Syndrome and is charged with murder. The program allowed a thoughtful discussion of legal and ethical issues related to so-called mercy killings and, in the view of Brodkin and Rose, "best sets the tone of the program, and at the same time establishes the law as the third important character."[19]

Broadcast on September 16, 1961, "The Quality of Mercy" introduced E. G. Marshall as Lawrence Preston and Robert Reed as Kenneth Preston, with Jack Klugman as the district attorney who insists on prosecuting to the full extent of the law. (The baby's father was played by Gene Hackman, then a little-known actor.) The story followed events from the fatal injection to the Prestons taking the case to the trial of the doctor, with the DA seeking the death penalty. At the last minute, rather than let the case go to the jury, the lawyers reach a compromise and allow the defendant to plead guilty to first-degree manslaughter. The program conveyed the desired tone: lawyers as honorable men, doing their best as advocates in an adversarial system, with society benefitting when justice is dispensed fairly.

THE FIRST SEASON OF THE DEFENDERS featured seven scripts by Rose, including the series opener, the pilot (which was broadcast as an episode in week 3), and five more.[20] A few are worthy of note. "The Accident" could have been a simple story about a drunk driver and vehicular homicide, but in Rose's hands became an exploration of religious freedom, as the parents of the injured boy refuse treatment and contribute to his death. "The Trial of Jenny Scott" had similarities to *12 Angry Men*—a dead body found in an apartment and a suspect at the scene of the crime with plenty of incriminating evidence and no alibi. This time Rose followed the trial into court, with examination and cross-examination of witnesses yielding the truth.

Rose's most remarkable script was "The Search," which aired in January 1962. A man has confessed to a murder committed six years earlier, for which a client of Lawrence Preston had been convicted and executed.

Stunned to learn that his client was innocent, Preston sets out to discover what happened. He meets with the district attorney, played by Jack Klugman, and the judge. How did the system fail? Are the lawyers and judge to blame, or did they properly do their jobs? Preston visits two of the jurors at their homes, one of whom admits that she had concluded the defendant was guilty even before hearing the defense's case, and the other who initially voted not guilty but, turning the dynamics of *12 Angry Men* on its head, gave in to group pressure and voted to convict. ("You know what you feel like, alone? You feel like a little stubborn kid. . . . Eleven of them, one of me. So, I say they're right and I'm wrong, and I switch.") It was a moving story about the fallibility of human beings, and the inherent flaw of a system that cannot correct an error once the death penalty is imposed. Yet instead of exploring the full implications of capital punishment Rose opted for a contrived ending: Preston determines that the man who has just confessed indeed fired a shot with intent to kill, but that the victim died only after Preston's defendant arrived on the scene and, finding him wounded but still alive, strangled him to death. It was an easy way out, letting Preston conclude that his client had been a murderer after all, and therefore that his execution had not been unfair. A year later, Rose would revisit the question of capital punishment and deal with it in a more satisfying way.

Of the other episodes in *The Defenders'* first season, some were excellent and some less so, as the series was finding its voice.[21] They touched on a wide range of topics: "The Iron Man," by David Davidson, about the right to free speech of a neo-Nazi student group. "The Point Shaver," by Mann Rubin, about a basketball player charged with accepting money from gamblers, raising questions about the corrupting influence of money in collegiate athletics. "The Man with the Concrete Thumb," by Ernest Kinoy, about an imperious commissioner of projects, parks and roads, based on Robert Moses, who tries to intimidate citizens who want to save a park from demolition. A dozen years before Robert Caro wrote *The Power Broker*, Rose and Kinoy had taken on New York's most powerful public official.

AS THE SERIES HIT ITS STRIDE, Rose and his team of writers searched for interesting topics. The starting point might be an informal conversation. Ernest Kinoy recalled: "You would come in and say, 'Listen, I got a great idea for a show, here's this thing that's happening legally, why don't we do a story about something like this.' And that would be written up in a small outline form."[22] Rose was now in the role of Florence Britton, responding to outlines and shaping stories. If an idea seemed promising, the writer would submit a first draft. Further drafts would incorporate comments from Rose, from story editor William Woolfolk, and from legal expert Jerome Leitner. A final draft would also reflect suggestions from the director and actors at their first reading.[23]

The demands of story supervision brought about big changes to Rose's daily life. His son Jonathan recalled: "All of a sudden, he was in high gear. Goodness knows he was up for it. He was energized and he plunged into it. He worked a lot of hours, six days a week. I didn't see him Saturdays."[24] There was at least one compensation: Saturday night became *Defenders Night* in the Rose household, with friends and relatives coming to the apartment to watch the show.

By March 1962, *The Defenders* had established itself as a successful program. More than twenty-one million viewers tuned in each Saturday night, far fewer than the number who watched the leading comedies and variety shows, but very impressive for a drama. In a cover story for *TV Guide*, Edith Efron wrote that not for many years had there been "so much television-inspired discussion going on in the American home as there is today," and the cause of this discussion was attributed to *The Defenders*. Credit went to one person above all: "The man behind *The Defenders* is script editor Reginald Rose." Efron quoted Herb Brodkin: "*The Defenders* is Reggie. He dreamed it up. He created it. He lives with it. He provides the consistent point of view."[25] Robert Reed added: "It's Reggie's mind that dominates the show. He has a total grasp of every play that is unusual. You can feel in the writing his concern with ethics, with issues of right and wrong. You can feel it when you're *acting*."

Efron also spoke with writers on the show, who described Rose's close involvement in story development. "He sends you back and back and back for re-writing," said Peter Stone. "My first draft never has human beings in it. He is always telling me, 'Go back and put the *conflicts* in.'" Another writer, John Vlahos, had the opposite experience: "In my case, I get so involved with the people, I have practically no story. He's always sending me back to put the *story* in."[26] After such an intensive process, final scripts often looked very different from the first draft. The result, said Efron, was "a script with the Reginald Rose hallmark—no matter whose by-line is on it: a logically constructed drama built around a severe ethical conflict, intelligently complicated by a few more brain-cracking ethical conflicts, and building to a sharp climax."[27]

GIVEN THE SUCCESS OF *The Defenders*, CBS was quick to renew it for a second season. In March 1962, when the thirty-two episodes for its first season were complete, production began for episodes that would be broadcast beginning September 1962. The pace never let up.

In April, Edith Efron wrote another *TV Guide* article, "Can a TV Writer Keep His Integrity?,"[28] presented as a debate between Reginald Rose, taking the affirmative, and Rod Serling, arguing the negative. Serling was still unhappy at the treatment of his June 1958 *Playhouse 90* drama, "A Town Has Turned to Dust," originally based on the murder of Emmitt Till in 1955 Mississippi but altered to be about a killing in the Southwest in the nineteenth century. To Serling, his unpleasant experience was evidence that network television would not allow honest portrayals of sensitive topics. Rose would have none of it: "I do social plays, controversial plays, all the time. Nobody's forcing me to produce junk." He went on: "All these accusations that commercialism, sponsor or network interference prevent good drama—I don't agree with any of that. My experience as a writer absolutely belies the complaints that there are constant taboos imposed on what can be said on television." When Serling reminded Rose that he had been forced to change a Black family into an ex-convict on "Thunder on Sycamore Street," Rose replied: "I did not compromise on the principle in the least. I was obliged to say it differently, but I *said* it. The proof that the moral issue was unchanged is that 'Thunder on Sycamore Street' was *fully* understood. Actually, making the victim a white man made the play more universal. People knew the play referred to *all* outsiders." Efron gave the last word to Rose: "In all my work, my main purpose has always been to project my own view of good and evil—and this is the *essence* of controversy."[29]

AT THE VERY MOMENT that Rose publicly voiced satisfaction with the network, *The Defenders* was experiencing its first major challenge. One episode, "The Benefactor" by Peter Stone, concerned a doctor who performs illegal abortions. Rose later explained that in the first season, as the program was getting established, he sometimes had to stack the deck, and "The Benefactor" was a prime example. How to make such a doctor appear sympathetic—not a murderer but indeed a *benefactor*? The doctor would not charge for his services. He would not perform an abortion for a woman who was married or who had the financial means to raise the child. He would perform free abortions only for the young, the frightened, and the poor, precisely those whom society should seek to protect. The doctor had once counseled a woman to carry her pregnancy to term and give birth, advice for which she was grateful. Part way through the episode the doctor's motivation was revealed: a decade earlier, his eighteen-year-old daughter had died from a botched abortion, and he wanted to make sure no one else would die needlessly.

"The Benefactor" had been filmed in September 1961 and normally would have been shown a few months later, but the regular advertisers—Kimberly-Clark, Lever Brothers, and Brown & Williamson—refused to sponsor it, forcing CBS to delay the broadcast. When the flap became public in April 1962, CBS president Frank Stanton came out in support of the show, stating that it was "a very fine, realistic and honest dramatization."[30] If need be, he said, the episode would be televised without sponsors. CBS recognized the right of each station to determine what to broadcast in its community but stood behind the program: "We believe 'The Benefactor' fully maintains the high standards of integrity, sensitivity and taste. In our view the program represents another step in television's continuing march toward maturity."[31]

To the rescue came Speidel, maker of watch bands, which had already signed up to sponsor *The Defenders* beginning in September 1962.[32] A print of the program was rushed to Speidel executives, who deemed it acceptable, and the "The Benefactor" was aired on April 28, 1962, with Speidel the sole sponsor. Out of 150 CBS affiliates nationwide, only 10 did not show the program—Binghamton, Buffalo, and Rochester in New York; Green Bay, La Crosse, and Milwaukee in Wisconsin; plus Boston, New Orleans, Providence, and Rockford, Illinois. (*Variety* couldn't resist the headline: "10 CBS Affils Abort 'Defenders.'"[33])

CBS reported that public reaction was overwhelmingly positive, with more than 90 percent of calls voicing approval.[34] Support also came from an unexpected corner, as the National Council of Churches bestowed an award on *The Defenders*, commenting, "[It is] an exemplary attempt to speak provocatively and articulately to contemporary issues, treats difficult subjects with integrity and good taste, and consistently shows a deep respect for the dignity of the individual."[35] Of course, speaking provocatively had been the whole point. The *New York Times* saw the program as an overt plea to change the law, titling its article, "The Benefactor Asks Shifts in Abortion Laws." No other prime-time program in 1962 was willing to make an argument in favor of legalizing abortion; *The Defenders* did so more than ten years before the US Supreme Court's 1973 ruling in *Roe v. Wade*.

Such controversies did nothing to harm the reputation of *The Defenders*, and on May 22, at the Hollywood Palladium, it won four Emmy Awards: Outstanding Program Achievement in the Field of Drama, E. G. Marshall for Outstanding Continued Performance by an Actor in a Series (Lead), Franklin Schaffner for Outstanding Directorial Achievement in Drama

(Schaffner directed six episodes, the award not for any one in particular), and Reginald Rose for Outstanding Writing Achievement in Drama.

With an unqualified hit, Herb Brodkin could look back with pride: "We just went out and did it. . . . And to our surprise it was a big success."[36] Rose, meanwhile, was ready to take *The Defenders* to the next level.

15

The Defenders
(Fall 1962 to 1965)

THE SECOND SEASON OF *The Defenders* opened on September 15, 1962, still in the coveted 8:30 slot on Saturday night. Bob Markell was now listed as producer, as Herb Brodkin focused on Plautus Productions' new series, *The Nurses* (later *The Doctors and The Nurses*). Reginald Rose remained very much in charge as the creator, lead writer, and story supervisor.

The season began with a pair of strong programs that showed a series in full stride and brimming with confidence.[1] The opener was Rose's "Voices of Death," an unusual drama in which the lawyers and the judge express their thoughts and feelings as voice-overs. The case, about a woman who killed her abusive husband and faces capital punishment, is replete with expressions of doubt—the lawyers wondering if the claims they make are based on solid evidence, and the judge worrying that jurors will be swayed by questionable arguments. The jury brings in a guilty verdict, and the program ends with the Prestons needing to inform two young children, ages ten and twelve, of the death sentence imposed on their mother. Such an offense would not normally lead to a charge of first-degree murder, much less a death sentence, yet it was an effective drama at revealing the unspoken doubts and frailties of participants in the most serious of cases.

Next came an episode by Ernest Kinoy called "Blood County," intended to showcase a tactic used to move civil rights cases from the South, where state judges were likely to rule against plaintiffs, to federal courts, where judges might rule more favorably. When CBS executives objected that it cast Southern states in a negative light, the details were changed. Now the story was about two men from New York City, hunting in the backwoods of Pennsylvania, who are arrested and charged with the murder of a local man. From the direction of the fatal shots and other clues, it becomes clear that the killing was committed by another local man, but the hunters are charged with murder and seem headed for conviction. The Prestons are hired to represent the hunters but make little headway, constantly intimidated by the sheriff and his cronies. After Lawrence Preston is the victim of a brutal beating—the only such instance in four years of *The Defenders*—the episode ends with the intervention of federal marshals and the promise that justice will prevail when the case is heard at a higher jurisdiction. In this episode, as in "Thunder on Sycamore Street," Rose was willing to modify details in order to make a larger point.

The most powerful program of the second season took up the question of insanity. The topic had been raised in the first season with "The Hundred Lives of Harry Simms," starring Frank Gorshin as a defendant with multiple personalities, but reviewers had not been impressed.[2] Now Rose returned to the topics of insanity and criminal responsibility. In the script by Robert Thom, a deranged man commits a brutal murder. When Lawrence Preston advises him to plead insanity, he reacts angrily and insists there is nothing wrong with him. Preston puts him on the witness stand where his mental state is revealed for all to see, leading Preston to ask for a directed verdict of not guilty by reason of insanity, and the judge agrees.

Rather than produce Thom's story, Rose expanded it into a two-part drama that raised deeper and more troubling issues. Program files show that Rose essentially took over the script and rewrote it himself, with multiple drafts in his distinctive cursive handwriting. The final version was credited to Robert Thom and Reginald Rose, but Thom, annoyed that he had been pushed aside, asked that his credit be changed to Robert Pendlebury, his mother's maiden name. In response, Rose used the pseudonym Ed Tashley, a play on the name of Rose's agent, Ted Ashley.[3]

"Madman" was broadcast on successive Saturdays, October 20 and 27, 1962. The first hour, "Madman, Part One," credited to Robert Pendlebury, developed the issue of insanity in greater depth, and provided a sharper depiction of the defendant's family in the days leading up to the trial. In "Madman, Part Two," credited to Ed Tashley, the jury convicts the defendant—obviously mad but legally responsible according to the prevailing definition, the so-called McNaughton Rules—and sentences him to death, with the story following events through appeals and eventually his execution. Much more powerful than the original version, "Madman" examined the questionable logic of laws regarding insanity as well as the grim realities of capital punishment, spread over two excruciating weeks.

The broadcast of "Madman" was widely praised, one critic calling it "the best, most effective TV drama of the year. In fact, I can't remember anything better since TV began here." Television columnist John Miles added: "It exposed the horse-and-buggy thinking that still executes mentally ill people in the name of a society which in some ways is advanced enough to send satellites around the moon. It was a powerful argument against all capital punishment. This is the kind of television that makes you cheer, and makes you realize it is all worthwhile."[4]

PRODUCTION OF *THE DEFENDERS* continued on the same relentless schedule through fall 1962. Bob Markell recalled working on an episode titled "Ordeal" in October 1962, when the discovery of Soviet missiles led President John F. Kennedy to announce a naval quarantine of Cuba. With the prospect of nuclear confrontation looming, one of the actors, Robert Webber—Juror 12 in *12 Angry Men*—at one point turned to Markell and said in a sardonic tone: "Imagine, this could be our last day on earth, and I'm spending it with you!"[5]

In November, Rose's role as story supervisor became a topic of public controversy when David Davidson, a writer for the program and chairman of the Writers Guild of America, charged that "television is burying its writers in a formula coffin." He had sharp words for "writers-turned-producers," naming *The Defenders* as a prime offender, alleging that "writers die like flies" because Reginald Rose "imposes his own style and notions on the scripts and the writers resent his rewriting."[6] Davidson pointed out that Robert Thom had asked for a pseudonym on "Madman," just as Davidson had done for a first-season episode, "The Iron Man," to protest interference with his script. Credited to "Albert Sanders," it won the Silver Gavel Award of the American Bar Association, yet Davidson complained that he received no word of congratulations from the producer.[7]

Reginald Rose was not one to start a public argument, but when singled out in a national publication he wasted no time in responding. The next week, *Variety* published his open letter:

Dear David:
    I'm surprised at you, saying all those mean and nasty things in VARIETY. Why would you want to do a thing like that?

It might also interest you to know that there are fifty-three THE DEFENDERS shows already produced, and seven more scripts ready to be filmed, making a total of sixty. We have had requests from writers to remove their names from the credits exactly twice. One was yours and the other was Robert Thom's. From time to time, once say in thirty shows, this kind of thing seems bound to happen, if only because personalities sometimes clash.

Now, as for the writers who *haven't* "died like flies" under my iron fist and malevolent red pencil, let me list a few pretty good ones. We could start with Ernest Kinoy, David Karp, James Lee, David Shaw, A. J. Russell, and Robert Crean, all of whom have written for THE DEFENDERS before, are currently writing for us, and who will, I expect, continue to write for us . . .

Since you're forced to write for these tedious, infantile "formula" shows, for the love of God give us something decent, something which will lift us above what you decry as mediocrity. Don't descend to our despicable level. Lift us up to yours. Try to improve what exists instead of dripping tears all over everything about what doesn't. Write something beautiful! I'll buy it.

Sincerely, Reginald Rose

If David Davidson and Robert Thom were unhappy with Rose's hands-on approach, others were content. After the initial season, *The Defenders* began to rely more and more on a handful of excellent writers. Aside from Rose, who wrote eleven episodes, the major contributors were David Karp (eleven episodes), William Woolfolk (ten), Ernest Kinoy (nine), Stanley Greenberg (eight) and Robert Crean (six). Woolfolk, a close friend of Rose, also edited many episodes without receiving credit.

By now established as television's leading dramatic series, *The Defenders* elicited many letters from appreciative viewers. One letter from September 1962 began: "Dear Mr. Rose, First, let me say that your program is one of the few really valuable programs, valuable for literary excellence, for enlightenment about the processes and mentality of the legal profession; for thoughtful, mature, yet dramatic grappling with serious yet widespread social and personal issues." One from October 1962 read: "Dear Sirs: For some time my wife and I have viewed only one television program each week—The Defenders. The mixture of brilliant social concepts, psychological understanding, and sense for dramatic verity constantly manifest in these programs render them persistently as valuable as they are fascinating. The last two programs entitled 'The Madman' absolutely stunned us.

Please accept our deepest congratulations on the courage you have shown in presenting this program to the public." Several letters came from appreciative organizations, including the National Lawyers Guild, the National Society for Medical Research, the Center for the Study of Democratic Institutions, many church groups, and at least one member of Congress. Rose kept dozens of such letters in his files, and answered many of them personally.[8]

The Defenders also had its share of detractors. After the March 1963 broadcast of "The Heathen," about a school teacher threatened with dismissal, the *Boston Herald*'s Arthur E. Fetridge—the same columnist whose criticism of "The Sacco-Vanzetti Story" made its way into the Congressional Record—wrote: "Once again Reginald Rose, executive producer of *The Defenders*, has managed to outrage a large number of people when he made the teaching of atheism in public schools perfectly all right."

Rose's reply did not mince words:

To Arthur Fetridge:

It would be refreshing if at least once in a while, you were accurate in your comments on my work. Your bias doesn't bother me in the least, but your incredible succession of errors does.

How did you manage in nine lines of print to make three errors such as these:

1. I am not executive producer of *The Defenders*. You merely have to look at your television set more carefully to ascertain the simple fact.

2. In the play you refer to, nobody "made the teaching of atheism in public schools perfectly all right." The teaching of atheism was not the issue, nor was atheism taught. The man in question taught English Literature, and, as a matter of fact, when one of his students turned in an unsolicited piece on atheism, he referred the student to St. Thomas Aquinas, Spinoza, and Descartes so that he might learn something from the world's great teachers of religious philosophy. *The Defenders* defended this teacher's right to his own religious belief or lack of religious belief, a right which also was eloquently defended by Bishop Pike recently.

3. It was not a public school we were dealing with, but a private school. Perhaps if you had listened you might have heard that, too. And then again, it might have occurred to you that public schools don't have Boards of Trustees.

> We attempt to do our show without distorting the truth. It might
> help you in your work if you did the same.
>   Reginald Rose[9]

IN MAY 1963, *THE DEFENDERS* won its second consecutive Emmy for
Outstanding Program Achievement in the Field of Drama, and E. G.
Marshall won again for Outstanding Continued Performance by an Actor
in a Series. "Madman" earned three Emmy nominations: Program of the
Year, Outstanding Directorial Achievement in Drama, and Outstanding
Writing Achievement in Drama. It won for the latter two, with Emmys go-
ing to director Stuart Rosenberg and to writers Robert Thom and Reginald
Rose, now using their proper names.[10] Accepting his second Emmy, E. G.
Marshall paid tribute to the show's guiding force: "As Gertrude Stein might
have said, a Rose is a Rose when it's Reginald Rose." He added: "Reggie *is*
the program. He *is The Defenders*. Yes, he's glad to accept ideas from other
writers, but without Reginald Rose there is no *Defenders*."[11]

Marshall may not have known it, but Rose's central role in *The Defenders* was about to change.

After close to twenty years of marriage, Reginald and Barbara Rose
agreed to divorce. According to Jonathan Rose, his parents had been unhappy for some time. "My mother was very unfulfilled, my father was on
to a career, and he was striving to try to help her be happy. Things were
not working as well as they should. They took vacations, he was successful, they were moving up in the world, they had a burgeoning social life,
but something still was not working." On a cold day in February 1963,
Jonathan remembers his father taking him aside and telling him that they
would be living apart. Many couples of that generation, including some
close friends, were going through divorces, so it was not unheard of. Even
so, it was a time of emotional pain for all members of the family. Neither
party had wronged the other, Jonathan said, but agreed to a mutual part-
ing: "They married very young, in the depths of World War II, and for both
it was a ticket out of where they had been. Both were only children, and
they compensated by having four. They struggled mightily to make a life of
it, but just weren't compatible enough to sustain it."[12]

Rose sublet an apartment nearby on Riverside Drive to stay close to
his sons. Not long after, he was briefly hospitalized for what was said to
be an intestinal ailment. Whether the illness was due to the accumulated
stress from his work, compounded by the breakdown of his marriage, or
due to other factors is impossible to ascertain; the intense pace of Rose's

life was not sustainable. Some months earlier, he had asked David Shaw to take over as story supervisor, but Shaw had said no, he was busy with a Broadway show. Now, as Shaw recalled, "Reggie called from the hospital, and I couldn't say no."[13] From then on, Shaw became story supervisor of *The Defenders* and Rose stepped back from his daily role.

Rose also stopped writing new scripts, completing his last one in spring 1963. Initially titled "The Cool Rebellion" and eventually called "The Star Spangled Ghetto," it was an extraordinary script that examined an emerging concern: the attitudes and values of "today's young people." The story was about a young couple, John and Theresa, from honest and hard-working families, who commit a robbery. They had never been in trouble and can offer no explanation other than to say they wanted to get married and needed money. Utterly untroubled by the implications of their crime, they typified what was seen as a growing trend: young people, disaffected by the affluent society and apparently unconcerned about breaking its laws, staging a "cool rebellion."

In Rose's outline, the couple are charged with armed robbery and, facing a substantial jail term, take the witness stand where they convey "the feelings of emptiness, of cynicism, of hopelessness, of despair, felt by hundreds of thousands, even millions, of young people today." Lawrence Preston would then offer what Rose called "the longest closing statement he has made in this series. He will attempt to show the jury how society has nurtured antisocial feelings within the two defendants, and within millions of other young people." The District Attorney denounces the couple "for their immorality," but the jury comes in with a verdict of not guilty, leaving the DA furious and the judge displeased but with no choice but to accept the jury's verdict. Rose's outline concluded: "Yet Lawrence is satisfied. . . . [H]e has saved the future for what he believes are two good people who deserve one more chance, a chance that the system which has nurtured their discontent would deny them." Rose's outline ended with a statement of the episode's purpose: "What is important is that the courts have allowed a critique of the morals of our society in general, and that two first offenders have been shown mercy, if not by the administrators of the law, then at least by their peers."[14]

"The Star Spangled Ghetto" was a startling departure from most episodes of *The Defenders*, offering an indictment of the broader social order—"the system." It was not easy to imagine that Lawrence Preston, a straight-laced middle-aged lawyer, would make such an argument, and even less plausible that a jury would accept it. At some point, perhaps after discussions with colleagues or the network, Rose backed away from his

proposed ending. In the revised script, Preston still offers a critique of contemporary values: "We live in a materialistic society where the ownership of
things is what rules our lives, and if we can't own what we are told we must
own, we then become miserable, unhappy, envious, bitter wretches. And
some of us retaliate by committing crimes against the society which has
imprisoned us in its own peculiar ghetto, a ghetto reserved for people who
are unable to own the proper resources. John and Theresa are residents of
that ghetto." This time, however, the jury is unable to reach a verdict, and
the judge declares a mistrial. No longer does the jury acquit a couple who
had, quite clearly, committed a crime. The episode ends with Lawrence
Preston expressing his hope that the DA will either drop the case or reduce
the charges, a victory of sorts, but not a complete exoneration.

Filmed in August 1963, "The Star Spangled Ghetto" was broadcast in
November, early in the third season. It would be Rose's final writing credit
on *The Defenders*.

BY EARLY SUMMER HIS HEALTH had recovered, and Rose told his sons
at their beach house on Fire Island that he planned to remarry. His new
wife was Ellen McLaughlin, a secretary at Defender Productions. Not yet
twenty-nine, she was raised in Queens, her father an Irishman from County
Donegal and her mother from the South. Ellen had graduated from Con-
verse College in South Carolina, the latest in a long line of women in the
family to do so, and retained some of the grace and charm of her Southern
roots. Ellen was, Jonathan recalled, beautiful and stylish, and very smart;
she had studied at the Sorbonne after college. Jonathan and his brother
Richard, the two older sons, were pleased for their father.

By the following year, Reginald and Ellen Rose moved into a townhouse at 156 East Sixty-Second Street, and under custodial terms, the
four boys—Jonathan, thirteen, Richard, eleven, and Andrew and Steven,
eight—spent weekends with their father and stepmother. Rose had grown
up without siblings and without a strong relationship with his father, and
had wanted to do better for his sons. There was, said Jonathan Rose, an
"honest striving for a happy family." No longer carrying the burden of story
supervision, Rose managed to spend more time with his family.

AFTER JUNE 1963, with David Shaw taking the reins as story supervisor,
production files no longer show Rose's distinctive cursive writing, with
copious comments in pencil on lined yellow paper. Yet he remained involved with *The Defenders* and was particularly committed to exploring
an important subject that had not yet been examined on television: the

blacklist. It was an audacious idea, using a television program to expose the complicity of television networks in a practice that had harmed so many, a topic that was still raw and had not been discussed openly. It would have been impossible to get such an episode on the air during the program's first season, but by the third season, after so many awards and strong ratings, the time was right.

Rose said that he got CBS to agree to the episode by means of a diversionary ruse. Among the stories he had proposed was one about a Black district attorney who turned out to be crooked. CBS executives had rejected it: a dishonest DA was bad enough, but making him Black was too much. Rose had countered: "What the hell, anybody can be a bad guy." When CBS would not relent, he offered a deal: "I'll drop this if you'll let me do a show on the blacklist." The CBS executive thought for a moment and replied: "O.K. If you do it with taste." Rose retorted: "You mean the way you did the actual blacklisting with taste?"[15]

Rose broached the idea over lunch with Ernest Kinoy, who recalled: "Somewhere along with the coffee he asked me if I could write a script about the Blacklist in the Entertainment Industry." Kinoy agreed on one condition: they would do it "the hard way," meaning that the victim would not have been mistakenly accused, which could suggest that the practice of blacklisting was not wrong, only unfair in this instance. "Write it any way you want," Rose told him. "We'll get it on."[16]

Kinoy's script, initially titled "What's the Matter with Harry Larch?," told the story of an actor (later renamed Joe Larch) who suddenly finds himself unable to get work. Almost overnight he is "too old, too young, too hard, or too soft," a change of fortune that coincides with the publication of a list revealing his past support of leftist causes—precisely what led to the blacklisting of Martin Ritt, Walter Bernstein, and so many others. His luck seems to change when he is hired by a small town in upstate New York to make a documentary film, but the offer is withdrawn when town officials learn of his past. Larch contacts the Prestons, whose inquiry strongly suggests that Larch has been blacklisted, although they cannot establish definitive proof that would be needed to win in court. The outline explains the problem: the "hazy Kafka-like world of blacklisting, where nothing is 'said' and everything is 'understood' is against them. . . . Even though you know it is true in your soul . . . you can't prove it is true in court."[17]

Recognizing that a lawsuit would be very costly and probably lead nowhere, Larch declines to sue. "I don't have the money for a grand gesture that doesn't have much chance of working," he tells his lawyer. Then, in a heartfelt statement, he sums up the episode:

You know, Mr. Preston, this whole thing, blacklisting, throwing people out of their jobs because of their political beliefs, it grows out of an atmosphere. People are afraid, afraid of communists, socialists, of folksingers. They're not sure who anybody is. Of course, ten years ago it was worse, even five. It's still going on. It's not in the headlines, but there are actors like myself who can't work, newspaper men who can't work, and teachers who can't work. I guess it'll get better when people start believing in what they say they're defending. When they believe in the Constitution. Well good night. Thanks anyway.[18]

Rose's first choice to play Joe Larch was Zero Mostel, a victim of the blacklist, but CBS said no and the role went to Jack Klugman.[19] (CBS had insisted on one other change: Larch had to have been blacklisted from movies, not television.) Renamed simply "Blacklist," the program aired on January 18, 1964.[20] It was widely acclaimed and received four Emmy nominations: Kinoy for Best Writing Achievement in Drama, Klugman for Best Actor in a Single Performance, Stuart Rosenberg for Outstanding Directorial Achievement in Drama, and a nomination for Program of the Year. At the Hollywood Palladium, on May 25, it won two of the four, for Kinoy and Klugman. For good measure, *The Defenders* won Outstanding Program Achievement in the Field of Drama for the third year in a row.

With "Blacklist," Rose demonstrated once again that he was ahead of his time. Twelve years would pass before a feature film examined the blacklist: *The Front* (1976) was written by Walter Bernstein, directed by Martin Ritt, and starred Zero Mostel and Herschel Bernardi, all victims of the blacklist. Of course, by then the blacklist was long since over and could be the subject of a bittersweet comedy, the title role played by Woody Allen. When Rose took up the topic in 1963, the wounds were still fresh. There was nothing humorous, only pain and anguish, in the story of Joe Larch.

ALMOST ALL OF REGINALD ROSE'S written output took the form of scripts, whether for screen or stage. His ideas and principles were most often expressed through the words and actions of his characters. Yet Rose also thought deeply about broader questions of drama and society, and on one occasion found an opportunity to express his views in an extended essay.

In 1964, *Television Quarterly*, published by the National Academy of Television Arts and Sciences, ran a pair of articles about law on television. The first, "The High Cost of Television's Courtroom," was written by Edward Bennett Williams, one of the most prominent Washington, DC, attorneys. Williams was critical of the way television portrayed the law and concerned that one-hour shows sacrificed reality for dramatic interest. The worst offender was *Perry Mason*, whose titular character won his cases thanks to his brilliance as "a courtroom magician—an attorney who wins consistently by springing an overlooked piece of evidence or by forcing a seemingly innocent witness to confess on the witness stand that he committed the crime." Williams had kinder words for *The Defenders*, noting that it dealt with real issues and made an effort to introduce substantive topics, adding: "I admire Lawrence Preston's persistent campaign against capital punishment." On balance, however, he remained skeptical of the way that television often distorted reality in its depiction of the law.

The second article, "Law, Criticism and Drama," was a three-thousand-word essay in which Rose offered his most eloquent statement about drama in a free society. After reviewing the origins and intentions of *The Defenders*, Rose responded at length to Williams's concerns:

> Drama is an art which results, like all art, from selection and arrangement in creating expressions of human experience and activity. It "distorts" because it is designed to do so. Its purpose is to distill what is meaningful out of human interaction. It can certainly be judged upon the basis of whether it does this well or badly, but not upon the doing itself. Its concern is not with literal detail, but with an essence (or truth) inherent among those details. . . .
>
> . . .
>
> Each week we want to put before the audience a story that is entertaining, that is adult, that poses a moral, intellectual or social problem in which people can become involved, and that carries a point of view provocative enough to stimulate them into discussing its implications. We have tried to do that. If we have stimulated both the intellectual and the "average" man into serious thought about these issues, then we have accomplished something in service of our own creative motivations, the audience-building problems of the network, and—above all—the society in which both law and drama are engaged in finding answers to the human dilemma. Criticism, then, ought to be made from this perspective. It must ask how well we deal with the same conflicts the law must resolve within our own form and purpose.
>
> . . .
>
> In our four years with *The Defenders* we have reached untold millions in terms that grip and hold them, which cause them to think about and discuss our work. There is no other possible way in which

they could get the information we give, acquire some feeling about the morality and ethics of the law, and be exposed to explanations of the law's processes. Most people simply do not go into the courtroom each day to discover more about this precious heritage. They learn about law through newspaper headlines of lurid crime trials, when they are called for jury duty, or when they are on trial. So long as we go to great lengths to understand the law and interpret it in honest dramatic terms, I am convinced that we are doing good.[21]

Rose's essay in *Television Quarterly* is a remarkable statement, written by a man at full maturity as a dramatist and as a citizen. It is, as well, one of the few times we hear Rose speaking with clarity about his medium, and about the higher purpose of his craft.

BY 1964, CHANGES IN SOCIETY brought about changes on television. *The Defenders* had been a breakthrough program in 1961, but now a new crop of programs began to address social issues in a more forthright manner. One of them, *East Side/West Side*, produced by David Susskind, premiered in September 1963 with George C. Scott and Cicely Tyson as social workers. Its racially diverse cast and gritty street-level view made *The Defenders* look staid by comparison.

An opposite trend was at work, too. Under James Aubrey, CBS had dominated the ratings with a lineup of comedies and light fare. *The Defenders* was a notable exception and often mentioned by William S. Paley when responding to criticism that CBS catered to lowbrow tastes. When ABC, the perennial laggard among the networks, stirred to life with hit shows like *Bewitched, The Addams Family*, and *Voyage to the Bottom of the Sea*, CBS felt compelled to respond. Its new programs for 1964 included *The Munsters* and *Gilligan's Island*, the latter a silly sitcom that was given a slot on Saturday night, bumping *The Defenders* to a much less desirable time, Wednesdays at 10 PM.

The Defenders opened its fourth season with another two-part program, "The Seven Hundred Year Old Gang," a wryly comical story about a group of elderly Jewish men who make wine for the high holidays without a license. The Prestons urge them to plead diminished capacity, given their advanced age, but they refuse, leading to a meditation about the letter and the spirit of the law, and about the problems of the elderly. Subsequent programs addressed topics ranging from extortion to free speech to the use of LSD. There was no sense that *The Defenders* was reaching its end. Ratings remained strong, and as Rose had said in his *Television Quarterly* article, he expected there to be a fifth season. Herb Brodkin's Plautus Productions had just launched a third series, *For the People*, starring William Shatner as a district attorney, which premiered as a mid-season replacement in January 1965.

All of that changed in February 1965, when James Aubrey was abruptly fired. His replacement, Jack Schneider, moved quickly to revamp the network's offerings, and announced in March that all three of Brodkin's programs—*The Defenders*, *The Doctors and The Nurses*, and *For the People*—would not return for a new season.[22] CBS's fall 1965 lineup featured one comedy after another: *Lucy*, *Andy Griffith*, *Petticoat Junction*, *Green Acres*, *The Beverly Hillbillies*, *Hogan's Heroes*, and *Gomer Pyle USMC*.

With the news that *The Defenders* would go off the air, Rose received an outpouring of letters from loyal viewers. A youth counselor in Georgia wrote: "Without question, *The Defenders* has been since its inception the best program on television. Thank you for the improvement." A minister in Maine wrote to CBS executives: "It was with a great deal of disappointment that I learned of the removal of *The Defenders* from your programming. This was the most profound and well-written series—with above-average acting and casting—being telecast today." Scores of such letters, warm and appreciative, made their way to Rose, who kept several dozen in his files.[23]

The final episode of *The Defenders* was filmed in April and broadcast on May 13, 1965. The series had achieved what Rose intended: it was a serious program on thoughtful themes, a show that educated as well as entertained, and was recognized as the finest dramatic series of its era. William Woolfolk put it best: "It was Reggie's series. You could do it without E. G. [Marshall]. You could do it without Brodkin. You couldn't do it without Reggie."[24]

16

After *The Defenders*

THE DEFENDERS WAS THE HIGH-WATER mark of Reginald Rose's career, a commercial and critical success that was perfectly suited to its time. Production began one week before the inauguration of President John F. Kennedy, continued through Kennedy's New Frontier, and extended into the first eighteen months of Lyndon B. Johnson's presidency. During those years, the federal government advanced a progressive agenda, with Congress enacting civil rights legislation, while the US Supreme Court, led by Chief Justice Earl Warren, expanded civil liberties. The values that undergirded *The Defenders*—a commitment to a more just society and a belief that our institutions could help achieve that aim—were widely shared. It was an earnest program in an era when such efforts were admired.

The month that *The Defenders* was canceled, March 1965, Marines came ashore at Danang, marking the beginning of America's military escalation in Vietnam. Five months later, the Los Angeles district of Watts exploded in violence, the first of several riots that would convulse Detroit, Newark, and other cities. Very soon, a program like *The Defenders* would feel obsolete. Clean-cut Kenneth Preston, happy to be his father's junior partner, no longer represented a younger generation caught up in student protests and anti-war demonstrations. Rose had sensed generational discontent in "The Star Spangled Ghetto," but the disaffected couple he portrayed was tame compared to what was to come. Had *The Defenders* continued much longer it would have seemed dated; but for those four years it was very much in step with the times.

EVEN BEFORE THE DEFENDERS's last season, Rose had turned his creative energies elsewhere. For the first time, he was writing a stage play. Its title was The Porcelain Year, a reference to the traditional gift after eighteen years of marriage, roughly the length of Rose's marriage when it broke up.

Rose wrote a first draft in 1964 and completed the revision in 1965. In its final form, the play was about a married couple with two teenage children, living in Los Angeles. The husband's boss arrives unexpectedly from New York and is invited for dinner; after the meal, the father and son leave to attend a function while the daughter goes out with friends, leaving the wife and boss together. An affair follows, discovered by the daughter when she comes home early. She tells the father on his return, forcing the couple to address, in the play's final act, the crumbling foundations of their marriage.

His eye on a Broadway run, Rose formed a joint venture with Gabriel Katzka and Gus Berne, who had recently produced Neil Simon's first hit, Barefoot in the Park.[1] Katzka-Berne Productions would seek limited partners to invest a total of $115,000 to go along with $10,000 from Rose's Defender Productions. The budget of $125,000 would underwrite casting, rehearsals, and initial staging needed to get the play ready for New York. Profits would be shared among the limited partners (46 percent), Katzka-Berne Productions (33 1/3 percent) and Defender Productions (20 2/3 percent). Although a hit play could be lucrative, the prospectus did not downplay the risks: "Of the plays produced for the stage in the 1963–1964 season 80% resulted in loss to investors."[2]

As the production took shape, veteran stage actress Barbara Bel Geddes (known to future generations as Miss Ellie on the television series Dallas) and Arthur Hill were cast as the married couple. Martin Balsam played the boss, the latest in his long string of roles written by Rose.

In June 1965, Rose wrote to Elia Kazan in the hope he would direct. ("I've been told that you're holed up writing a novel, and although I hesitate to interrupt your work, you are so right for the play, and the play is so right for you that I must send it to you to read. Can I?")[3] Kazan said no, but another prominent director agreed: Ulu Grosbard, recently nominated for a Tony Award for The Subject Was Roses. In late August, Grosbard quit amid reports of disagreements with Rose about the script and was replaced by Alex Segal, who had directed two of Rose's teleplays for Playhouse 90.[4]

In a typical pattern for a Broadway-bound play, *The Porcelain Year* was scheduled to open in Philadelphia in mid-October, then go to Washington, DC, for a week, followed by brief stops in Wilmington, Delaware, and New Haven, Connecticut. The aim was to work out any bugs and create a buzz of publicity before arriving at the Longacre Theatre on West Forty-Eighth Street in mid-November.

From the beginning, however, the play was in trouble. Rose, so sure-handed in stories about the law and justice, seemed out of his element when writing about love and marriage. The opening in Philadelphia got a harsh review: "Rose's intention in the play at the New Locust Theater is to peel the overlay of sham from an average marriage, to ask questions like why do people get married and why do they stay married. These are questions most people know the answers to but Rose doesn't seem so sure." Strong acting gave the play "a veneer of good china but underneath is five-and-dime crockery."[5] The most egregious error was to depict the illicit affair: "A situation which at best is unbelievable is made ludicrous by specifically showing it to us."[6]

A week later, the *Washington Post* was scathing: "If the respected author of TV's 'The Defenders' was in the house, he must have had a gruesome time, for audiences have several kinds of laughter. One is the honest laughter of agreement. Another is a nervous snicker of embarrassment. Quite the worst, to a playwright's ears, must be the horselaugh, recognizing the false and jeering at it. Mr. Rose was fed enough of these to last a lifetime."[7] The *Washington Daily News* was equally tough: "Mr. Rose has nothing new to say about infidelity in the suburbs, the corrosive effects of marriage, or any of the banal themes he has unaccountably selected for airing in his first Broadway play. The writing and pacing are maladroit; the audience laughed with relief at lines obviously meant to be humorous, and tittered at lines inadvertently funny. When a playwright has them laughing at him as much as with him, he's in ba-a-a-a-d trouble."[8]

Rose hurriedly attempted rewrites but nothing could help. The premise was too far-fetched, the staging too clumsy. After Wilmington, the play limped into New Haven but went no further. "The play just kept getting worse and worse," Rose later recalled. "We finally said, 'Close the damn thing.'"[9] Producer Katzka made the official announcement, saying "it would have been unrealistic to continue," and estimated a loss in excess of one hundred thousand dollars.[10] The direct financial damage to Rose was limited but the effect was sobering. *The Porcelain Year* was Rose's first major failure, and came at a time when he was trying to branch out, to move beyond television to the stage, and away from legal dramas to

more personal themes. As Rose would later say: "It was a very, very difficult experience."[11]

HIS FORAY INTO THEATER unsuccessful, Rose tried to return to what he
knew best. With dramatic anthologies all but dead, he tried to create another weekly series, although very likely expecting to entrust the task of
story supervision to others. In 1965, Rose and his friend, JP Miller, pitched
an idea for a television series, *The Avenger*, about an urban activist in the
mould of Bruce Wayne. They devised an outline and produced a full script
for a pilot but had no success taking the idea further. A year later, Rose and
Robert Crean had the idea for a series called *The New Yorkers*, about four
young men who share an apartment on the Upper West Side. They wrote
a pilot script but elicited no interest from networks. In 1967, Rose developed *The Carroll Files*, about a father-daughter detective team. He spent
considerable time and effort on the project, devising a lengthy treatment
with detailed character profiles and a full pilot script. Like the two ideas
that preceded it, *The Carroll Files* went nowhere.

An opportunity presented itself in 1966 when Herb Brodkin, whose
three programs had been abruptly canceled in 1965, was named producer
of *CBS Playhouse*, a new program that would present original plays, up
to two hours in length, a few times a year. Among the first writers he
signed was Reginald Rose, whose services were rewarded with the hefty
fee of twenty-five thousand dollars. Speaking to a reporter, Rose sounded
relieved: "It's like old times. And I'm told by CBS that I have absolute
freedom in writing what I want."[12]

The resulting play, "Dear Friends," was broadcast in December 1967.
Once again Rose addressed the theme of marriage, this time with a story
about four couples, probing below the surface of seemingly solid relationships. The cast featured leading stage actors, including Anne Jackson and
Eli Wallach. "It's the best time I've had in years," Rose said. "It was like old-
time TV. The writer, producer and director get together and work on the
cast and then we had 2½ weeks of rehearsal. Of course, it wasn't live, but it
felt the same on tape."[13] Reactions to "Dear Friends" were generally very
favorable, called "a smashing triumph" by the *St Louis Globe-Democrat*,
and the *Chicago Tribune* writing that it "was not only beautifully acted
but had something to say." One viewer from Berkeley, California, wrote
to express thanks: "May you continue to write as you always have written
(from the good old live TV dramas), concisely, superbly, and truthfully,
about life."[14] Another letter came from Karl E. Weick, a thirty-one-year-old
associate professor at the University of Minnesota and later a prominent

organizational psychologist. Weick's letter read in part: "I can say without qualification that the drama was the most insightful piece of work on interpersonal relations that has ever come to my attention. . . . I would like to secure a copy of the script of this play for use in my advanced graduate seminars in organizational behavior."[15]

After Rose's failure with *The Porcelain Year* and his inability to get a new series produced, "Dear Friends" was a welcome success, but it did not make him optimistic about the current state of television. In an opinion piece published to coincide with "Dear Friends," Rose expressed his disappointment at the lack of intelligent drama on television and the dearth of opportunities for young writers. "The *CBS Playhouse* does attempt to light one candle, but in the main it is still necessary to curse the darkness."[16] The title of the article, "TV's Age of Innocence—What Happened to It?," suggested that Rose, although just forty-seven, was beginning to sound like a relic from a bygone era.

A year later, Rose and Brodkin tried to parlay "Dear Friends" into a weekly series, with each episode to be about one or another of the four couples. Again, they prepared outlines and treatments. Again, nothing came of the idea. Times had changed and television networks were looking for fresh ideas from new talent.

THE LATE 1960S BROUGHT several changes to Reginald Rose's personal life. In the first years of their marriage, Rose and his wife, Ellen, lived on East Sixty-Second Street. Financially secure thanks to *The Defenders*, and no longer absorbed with the demands of a weekly series, they decided to look for a country retreat. Shown a large home in a wooded area in North Stamford, Connecticut, the Roses acquired the property and turned it into their primary residence, keeping a smaller apartment in New York only for occasional visits. Rose's sons continued to visit on weekends, now taking the train from Grand Central Station after school on Friday or Saturday morning, and returning to New York on Sunday.

Within a year, Reginald and Ellen Rose had a son of their own, Thomas, born October 1966. Rose was a life-long New Yorker, but the center of his life was beginning to shift. In early 1967, invited to a meeting in New York, Rose begged off: "I now live in Connecticut and don't get into New York very often."[17] Another son, Christopher, was born in November 1968, bringing to six the number of Rose's sons.

After four years in Connecticut, and without a new television series to keep him tied to the US, Rose was ready for a new chapter in his life. Jonathan Rose recalled that his father and stepmother had long wanted to live in England, and in January 1970 they moved to London. At first they rented a townhouse near Marble Arch, and then bought a flat at 30 Kingston House North in Knightsbridge, across from Hyde Park and close to the Royal Albert Hall. "They were so happy in London," said Jonathan. "They went to shows, they went to museums, they ate out. There were trips to the South of France."[18] Rose remained active with a few writing projects, including a screenplay based on the book, *The Boy Who Could Disappear*, eventually released as *Baxter!* (1973), that earned him fifty-thousand dollars,[19] plus a series for British television about former World War II resistance fighters who team up to fight crime, titled *The Zoo Gang*. Years later, Rose would describe his time in England as "absolutely the best years of my life."[20]

In July 1974, mostly for family reasons, the Roses moved back to the United States and settled in Westport, Connecticut. By then, Ted Ashley had sold his agency to become chief executive of Warner Bros., and Rose was represented by the Sy Fischer Company.

Now in his early fifties, Rose tried to return to familiar territory with a weekly television series about the law. His 1976 outline for *The Adversaries* began:

> Times have changed since Lawrence and Kenneth Preston brought the realities of our adversary system to the television screens all over the world. People have changed. Attitudes have changed. Values are no longer the same. And the American public is faced with new and constantly shifting issues which are difficult to define and which produce vast and sometimes violent disagreement between next-door neighbors on every Main Street in the country. The world is not the same world we lived in from 1961 to 1965.[21]

Rose wanted *The Adversaries* to deal with "today's people and today's issues, problems and attitudes," looking at both sides of the law through the eyes of Americus Adams, a blue-blood WASP defense lawyer, and Mario Kelly, a street-smart prosecutor, the son of Italian and Irish immigrants.[22] He wrote an extensive treatment, with each of several main characters given a detailed profile in the thirty-seven-page outline. There were no takers. Television was looking to a younger generation of producers, typified a few years later by Steven Bochco, whose 1981 cop show, *Hill Street Blues*, signaled a new style for a weekly series with a large ensemble cast, intersecting stories that stretched across episodes, and witty dialogue.[23] In 1984, Bochco launched *LA Law*, a hit legal show with the same fast-paced and irreverent style. There would be no second legal series for the man who had blazed the trail in the 1960s.

Through the 1970s, while unsuccessful at launching a new television series, Rose worked on several more movie screenplays. He developed a comedy intended for Woody Allen that eventually became *Somebody Killed Her Husband* (1978), a lightweight romance starring Farrah Fawcett and Jeff Bridges. "Lines that were supposed to be funny just weren't," said Rose, reminded again that a writer had little influence once a screenplay was sold.[24] He adapted a screenplay for British producer Euan Lloyd, *The Wild Geese* (1978), based on the story of mercenary "Mad Mike" Hoare, starring Richard Burton, Roger Moore, and Richard Harris. It earned mixed reviews, with Burton giving an especially uninspired performance, although Rose was praised by critic Janet Maslin as "an old-fashioned scenarist mindful of such old-fashioned niceties as pacing, clarity, and economy."[25] A second screenplay for Lloyd, *The Sea Wolves* (1980), was a tepid war movie with aging stars, Gregory Peck, David Niven, and Roger Moore.[26] None of these projects brought much satisfaction. Recalling those years, Jonathan Rose said: "I don't think he was as fulfilled. He needed, and might not have found, something to really spark him."[27] One project that briefly captured his interest was *Hermanos*, a 1969 novel about the Spanish Civil War by William Herrick, an American who had served in the Abraham Lincoln Battalion. Rose wrote a script treatment and had initial discussions to make it into a movie, hoping to interest famed French-Greek director Costa-Gavras. It never came to fruition.

FORTUNATELY, A PROJECT EVENTUALLY came along that fully engaged Rose's creative energies. In 1976, Lorimar Productions, a leading television production company (famous in the 1970s for *The Waltons* and in the 1980s for *Dallas* and *Knots Landing*), decided to make a miniseries based on James T. Farrell's *Studs Lonigan*, the trilogy about Irish Catholics in South Side Chicago that had captivated Rose as a youth. A movie version had been made in 1960, an attempt to shoehorn an eight-hundred-page epic into one hour and thirty-five minutes, with predictably poor results.[28] During filming, director Irving Lerner said that in his version "Studs Lonigan will not die, he will marry the girl he made pregnant, thereby making the film a bit more cheerful and moral than the book."[29] Author Farrell issued a swift rebuke: "The entire point of the work is obviously missed when the death is described as immoral and is therefore eliminated. It is quite obvious that those who are connected with the making of the film do not understand the Irish and do not know what life was like in the Nineteen Twenties . . . I want no connection with the film now being made."[30] The finished movie was a mish-mash of scenes that scarcely made sense, and that conveyed none of the depth or anguish of Farrell's classic.

Sixteen years later, in a very different era, Lorimar's Chuck McLain wanted to develop *Studs Lonigan* as a miniseries. McLain pitched the idea to Lorimar boss Lee Rich: "I cannot remember when I read something that I consider so universal in appeal. There are things that everyone, both young and old, will identify with and I think that's the key to this as a miniseries."[31] This version would be true to the original in both structure and tone.

Reginald Rose later described the events that followed: "A phone call. A question. 'Would you like to adapt 'Studs Lonigan' for television?' An instant yes. A race to find the book and an astonishing weekend of reading that which I remembered reading when I was sixteen . . . and had not remembered at all."[32]

As a youth, Rose had revelled in the language and the characters of *Studs Lonigan*, in its unvarnished depictions of urban life, but had not been able to grasp the power of Farrell's work. "Studs Lonigan was a tough Chicago kid. I knew that. But tormented? No. Reeling with false dreams and hopeless hopes? Not at all. In love? Yes. But with whom, and why, and how, and what became of that love? No. Was he a hero, a failure, a leader, a cypher, a powerful force? Did he wage a hopeless or a triumphant struggle against life? I had no idea."[33] Reading the trilogy again was a deeply moving experience. At sixteen, Rose had been "far too immature to understand the joy and sadness of all of it, the monumental statement it made about those people in that situation in those times."[34] Now in his fifties, Rose could understand the characters and their conflicts. (Rose did not comment on the anger and bitterness expressed by Irish Catholics at Blacks moving into their South Side neighborhoods; these were the same people who, two decades later, would react violently when a Black family moved into the nearby suburb of Cicero, the event that inspired "Thunder on Sycamore Street.")

Soon a contract was in place, with Rose to be paid sixty-five thousand dollars for the adaptation.[35] Distilling the essence of a massive work was a major challenge, described as "extracting a film from a vast and thunderous book."[36] Just as daunting was to convey the inner thoughts of its characters. The title character, Studs Lonigan, had been "so despairingly inarticulate, so unable to express emotions, dreams, fears, love." That was not a problem for the novelist, who could express what characters were thinking with interior monologues. For a television audience to understand Studs, Rose needed a way for the main character to express himself, to "illuminate the violent shades of light and darkness within him."[37] A relatively minor character in the novel, Danny O'Neill, based on Farrell himself, became "the receptable into which Studs pours his most secret thoughts. A device, perhaps, but a method which allows us to *know* Studs Lonigan rather than simply observe him."[38]

In January 1977, Rose turned in a complete outline. NBC's Department of Broadcast Standards noted that the outline followed the book faithfully, but would need substantial changes: "the cumulative effect of the verbal barrage of profanity and crude language, repeated racial slurs and the visual depictions of violence and sexual excesses which will assault the eyes and the ears, raises grave concerns of acceptability for this project." NBC went on to provide seven pages of comments, single spaced, under five headings: "Profane Language," "Crude Gutter Language," "Violence," "Racial and Ethnic Slurs," and "On the Subject of Sex."[39]

In years past, Rose had tussled with television networks about depictions of racial discrimination, abortion, and the blacklist. NBC's concerns about the language in Studs Lonigan seemed minor by contrast. Rose made the required modifications, tempering the language and altering a few scenes. Lorimar's Chuck McLain later expressed his thanks: "You were so much better than I was in terms of what we had to cut; I want you to know that working with you has been probably the best experience I've ever had with anyone."[40]

Rose's screenplay was true to Farrell's epic, closely following the story line and including most important scenes. Rose added a final touch: after Studs's death, Danny O'Neill and Catherine, Studs's pregnant fiancée, are seen strolling in the Washington Park Arboretum, while Danny offers a touching coda in a voice-over: "Ah, Studs, what's sad about it is that all you ever wanted to be was a hero. You made it once, but you were a little kid and you got stuck inside your dream, and you never could make it real. How many dreams do fit reality? A handful in all history. So you dreamed and suffered and died, and you never understood that you were loved, and that love needs no heroes, and that life is its own excuse. Your dreams never allowed you peace. Now there are no more dreams. Rest in peace, Studs."[41]

As the script neared completion, Rose sent a draft to William Woolfolk, his long-time friend and collaborator on *The Defenders*. Woolfolk answered: "I think this has the potential to rank with your very best work. There's such an abundance of scene and incident and characters, and it's all very well controlled."[42]

Lorimar assembled an excellent cast, with Harry Hamlin in one of his first major roles as Studs Lonigan, Charles Durning as his gruff father, Colleen Dewhurst as his devout and strict mother, and Brad Dourif as

Danny O'Neill. When Rose viewed the finished production, he expressed his appreciation to Lorimar: "I couldn't be happier with what I've seen."[43]

Studs Lonigan was broadcast on three successive Wednesdays in March 1979, two hours for each volume of the trilogy.[44] NBC felt the need to begin each week with an advisory note: "*Studs Lonigan* is an American literary classic. Its characters are raw reflections of their ethnic backgrounds and the triumphant, tragic times in which they lived . . . proud, bigoted, often profane—a passionate and realistic echo of urban America as it used to be." To John O'Connor of the *New York Times*, Rose's *Studs Lonigan* was "a brilliant portrait of a certain kind of Irish-American environment— lower middle class, urban, first-generation, church-going, close-knit. It is at once curiously exhilarating and devastating." The sharp edges of Farrell's epic had been softened, but what remained was "extraordinarily good." O'Connor concluded: "*Studs Lonigan* is the kind of production that usually wins praise and awards for public television. It is a pleasure to find it on commercial network."[45]

Reginald Rose had been proud to adapt a beloved book for a new generation. His teleplay for *Studs Lonigan* was "dearest to me of all the work I've done, save some of my own originals. It belongs to James Farrell, yet I feel it peculiarly mine. . . . We have never met, Farrell and I, nor spoken to each other, but I have immense respect for him and I pray that I have done him justice."[46]

AS THE 1970S CAME to an end, Reginald Rose was approaching sixty years of age. In 1980, he adapted a Broadway hit, *Whose Life Is It, Anyway?*, for a movie starring Richard Dreyfuss.[47] A year later, he wrote a miniseries for CBS, "The Rules of Marriage," starring Elizabeth Montgomery and Elliott Gould as a couple whose "perfect marriage" begins to disintegrate. Rose explained: "It opens with their 15th anniversary and the drama tells us why it fell apart and why it manages to get back together." The acrimony of *The Porcelain Year* had given way to themes of reconciliation and understanding. The final scene "has to do with what's going to make a marriage work." The key lesson, said Rose, was that relationships work when people feel safe, even if they sometimes fight or disagree: "When a marriage is not safe, it doesn't work."[48]

To help publicize the miniseries, Rose was interviewed by veteran entertainment reporter Rex Polier at his home in Westport. His writing studio featured mementos from his career: Emmys for "Twelve Angry Men" and *The Defenders*, an autographed picture of Eleanor Roosevelt, a print of Sacco and Vanzetti by artist Ben Shahn, and posters from his various movies.[49] Looking back on three decades in television, Rose said that many of his early works had been protests against social injustice: "So many of the things I wrote about in those days were burning issues. Injustices and outrages that I saw bothered me. I saw them and I wanted to fight against them. I wanted to get them out of my system."[50] More recently he had gravitated toward human relationships, which called for more subtle and nuanced writing, with characters who were not so obviously right or wrong. Rose had evolved in the opposite direction from his contemporary and friend, Paddy Chayefsky: "He went from little things like *Marty* and *The Bachelor Party* to such highly dramatic, adventurous things like *Network* and *[The] Hospital*. It was the other way with me, and it's funny because I never thought of it until this moment. . . . Over the years, we gradually changed."[51]

Rose's final project brought him back to the concerns of his early years. When his agent sent a copy of Richard Rashke's *Escape from Sobibor: The Heroic Story of the Jews Who Escaped from a Nazi Death Camp*, Rose quickly agreed to write the screenplay: "It was so compelling, so horrifying. I knew I wanted to adapt it."[52] Rose talked about the project with words that echoed from the beginning of his career: "The most important thing to write about, for me, is injustice. Sobibor was an extreme example, yet it's an historical footnote. That to me is incomprehensible, if for no other reason than the human drama it presents."[53] *Escape from Sobibor*, a three-hour CBS docudrama starring Alan Arkin and Rutger Hauer, aired in April 1987. It would be his last major work.

While Rose willingly publicized his motion pictures and miniseries, and often responded graciously when contacted for telephone interviews, he was less and less in the public eye. In 1985, Ron Simon, director of the Museum of Television and Radio in New York (now the Paley Center for Media), invited Rose to take part in a panel discussion about *The Defenders* with Herb Brodkin, Ernest Kinoy, and Michael Dann; he declined. Two years later, the museum produced a video history series on *Studio One* and interviewed many actors and directors, but again, Rose did not participate. Simon recalled: "Rose was sort of reluctant. He called himself a recluse. He didn't really want to travel. He didn't care that much for the rhythm of Manhattan in the late 20th century, and preferred just to live alone."[54] Nor did Rose take part in the Television Academy Interviews in the late 1990s, unlike his friends and colleagues Sidney Lumet, Bob Markell, E. G. Marshall, and David Shaw, each of whom sat for extensive interviews and shared their recollections. (Markell was aware that Rose did not take part, at one point telling his interviewer: "It's too bad you're not talking to Reggie, because Reggie knows the story better than I do, but . . ."[55]) Jonathan Rose said about those years: "He was rather self-contained in Connecticut. I just think he was of a mind that his works spoke for themselves."[56]

Yet as Reginald Rose receded from view, something remarkable was happening. One of his original dramas had taken on a life of its own.

PART V

THE JOURNEY OF
12 ANGRY MEN

17

***

A Life on Stage

THE REGINALD ROSE PAPERS, housed at the Wisconsin Center for Film and Theater Research, hold more than thirty years of the writer's output, stored in sixty-eight large boxes. Included are dozens of outlines for television dramas, some of them very compelling, like "The Unborn" and "The Joiner," that never made it past that initial stage. Many other outlines were developed into teleplays for leading anthologies, such as "An Almanac of Liberty" on *Westinghouse Studio One* and "The Cruel Day" on *Playhouse 90*, that were praised at the time but are not well-remembered today. There are also several treatments for weekly series, some of them with full-length scripts for pilots, like *The Carroll Files* and *The Adversaries*, that never made it into production. Included, too, are screenplays for movies like *Man of the West*, successful in their day but no longer familiar. Close to half the collection is devoted to the 132 episodes of *The Defenders*, the finest dramatic series of its era, but never widely syndicated and long since superseded.

Of Reginald Rose's extensive body of output, by far the most attention has been paid to a single work: *12 Angry Men*.[1]

It would be logical to infer that Rose's jury room drama, often hailed as his masterpiece, must somehow stand out from the rest of his work in terms of quality or craftsmanship, but that's not the case.[2] In fact, it was not at all inevitable that of all his works, *12 Angry Men* should be the one to achieve such fame. The teleplay was only Rose's fourth original one-hour play, written early in his career and long before he reached full maturity as a dramatist. It wasn't even Rose's favorite among his early works; that was "The Remarkable Incident at Carson Corners." The first teleplay made into a feature film, thought to be the best candidate for success on the big screen, was "Crime in the Streets." The one that received the most laurels was "Tragedy in a Temporary Town," which earned multiple Emmy nominations plus awards from the Ford Foundation's Fund for the Republic and the Anti-Defamation League of B'nai B'rith. The teleplay that required the most research was "The Sacco-Vanzetti Story"; and in terms of length and scale, no single work came close to *Studs Lonigan*, an epic trilogy adapted into six hours of drama. As for sheer effort and volume of output, nothing could match *The Defenders*, which absorbed Rose's energy, week after week, for years.

Any of these teleplays or adaptations could have grown in reputation, but none of them did. The one that achieved greatness had the unlikeliest of origins: inspired by a chance event and written in a matter of days. It scarcely had the ingredients of a hit, featuring little more than a dozen nameless men arguing in a single room. Yet from that inauspicious beginning, *12 Angry Men* has achieved the status of an American classic.

Today, *12 Angry Men* stands in elite company, ranking with two other mid-century American works of moral importance, Arthur Miller's *Death of a Salesman* and Harper Lee's *To Kill a Mockingbird*. Yet the road it followed was very different.

When *Death of a Salesman* opened on Broadway in 1948, it was immediately hailed as a monumental achievement. Even in rehearsals, Lee J. Cobb, the original Willy Loman, remarked to Miller: "This play is a watershed. American theater will never be the same."[3] The public response was overwhelming; for many, *Death of a Salesman* was "the best play ever written."[4] "I dare repeat it," Miller wrote in his memoirs, *Timebends*, "because it would be said often in the next months and would begin to change my life."[5] A movie version followed, with Fredric March as Willy Loman and Mildred Dunnock reprising her stage role as Linda Loman, earning five Academy Award nominations and four Golden Globes. *Death of a Salesman* remains revered primarily as a stage play, the role of Willy Loman a supreme challenge for great actors from Cobb and March to George C. Scott, Dustin Hoffman, Brian Dennehy, and Philip Seymour Hoffman. Miller produced a work of universal resonance, its themes of ambition and disappointment, of expectation and disillusion, speaking to audiences around the world. When the Beijing People's Theater decided, in 1983, for the first time to stage a Western play, it chose *Death of a Salesman*.[6]

Harper Lee's *To Kill a Mockingbird* was published to great acclaim in

1960, a debut novel that won the Pulitzer Prize for fiction. (It also won the Brotherhood Award of the National Conference of Christians and Jews, the same organization that praised "Thunder on Sycamore Street" in 1954). Within a year it was made into a movie starring Gregory Peck and with a screenplay by Horton Foote, both of whom would win Academy Awards. For decades the novel has been taught to high school students for its exploration of justice and mercy.[7] In recent years, *To Kill a Mockingbird* has been adapted into a hit Broadway play by Aaron Sorkin, yet remains best known as a book of great depth and empathy.

12 Angry Men matches these works in acclaim and importance, but its journey was much slower and more complex.

ANY ATTEMPT TO EXPLAIN the enduring success of *12 Angry Men* must begin with the 1957 movie. Of course, it was a true gem: Sidney Lumet's direction was crisp and energetic, and Boris Kaufman's cinematography captured intensity and emotion. Henry Fonda led a superb ensemble cast that included no fewer than three actors who would go on to win Academy Awards—Fonda, Ed Begley, and Martin Balsam—and four who played lead roles in Arthur Miller's greatest plays— Begley in *All My Sons*, Lee J. Cobb in *Death of Salesman*, E. G. Marshall in *The Crucible*, and Jack Warden in *A View from the Bridge*.

But in fairness, there were many excellent black-and-white movies in the late 1950s. Consider just a handful: *The Night of the Hunter* (1955), directed by Charles Laughton with Robert Mitchum and Shelley Winters; *A Face in the Crowd* (1957) directed by Elia Kazan with Andy Griffith; *Paths of Glory* (1957), directed by Stanley Kubrick and starring Kirk Douglas; *The Defiant Ones* (1958), directed by Stanley Kramer with Sidney Poitier and Tony Curtis; and Tennessee Williams's *Suddenly, Last Summer* (1959) with Elizabeth Taylor and Montgomery Clift. Placed within the company of these fine movies, why did *12 Angry Men* achieve such great acclaim?

The long climb of *12 Angry Men* is evident in the American Film Institute's list of the one hundred greatest American movies. When the AFI held its first such poll in 1997, the list was headed by *Citizen Kane* (1941), *Casablanca* (1942), and *The Godfather* (1972). Twenty movies from the 1950s were on the list, but *12 Angry Men* was not among them. Ten years later, when the AFI ran another poll, the same three were at the top, while several recent releases were added and some older ones dropped off. The number of movies from the 1950s fell to sixteen, yet *12 Angry Men* was now *on* the list, ranked 87. Remarkably, the movie gained in stature between 1997, forty years after its release, and 2007, when it turned fifty.

The journey of *12 Angry Men* has been the result of several factors in addition to its brilliance as a motion picture. These factors, some of them improbable, have combined and reinforced one another.[8] There's no way to determine exactly how much was contributed by each one, but we can detect several distinct strands.

First is *12 Angry Men*'s success as a stage play, performed by amateurs and professionals alike for decades. The brilliance of the movie has contributed to the popularity of the play, and the success of the play has helped maintain interest in the movie.

WITHIN DAYS OF ITS BROADCAST in September 1954, CBS received several requests for copies of the script. Theater groups across the country recognized that Reginald Rose's teleplay had the makings of a superb ensemble piece. Not only was it a riveting drama, but the jury room was a natural stage. The play could be easily performed, requiring nothing more than a single set with a long table and a dozen chairs.

Soon after the *Studio One* broadcast, Ashley-Steiner sold the stage rights to "Twelve Angry Men" to Dramatic Publishing Company, a Chicago-based publisher owned by the Sergel family.[9] Dramatic had already bought the rights to Rose's first three plays, with adaptation for the stage written by Kristin Sergel. For "The Remarkable Incident at Carson Corners," she closely followed the structure of Rose's teleplay but added a few more schoolchildren and suggested that flashbacks could be illuminated by spotlights on far corners of the stage. For "Thunder on Sycamore Street," she added a few more neighbors, and introduced a subplot by turning the young children of the Morrison and Blake families into teenagers who know each other from school.[10] Kristin Sergel also adapted Rose's third teleplay, "The Death and Life of Larry Benson" and two years later would adapt "Dino." In all of these, she hewed closely to Rose's original works, making adjustments as needed for a stage production.

Twelve Angry Men was adapted by the Sergel's thirty-one year old son, Sherman L. Sergel. He included a stage chart that showed a long table with seven chairs upstage, facing the audience, one chair at either end, and three downstage. Sergel noted: "This arrangement of the chairs will enable most of the action to be directed toward the audience, with a minority of characters placed with their backs toward the audience."[11]

Sergel's adaptation began with the judge's instructions spoken over a darkened set. When the lights come on, the twelve are already in the jury room. From there, Sergel made numerous changes to Rose's play. He expanded the opening scene, with much more initial banter among jurors.

Elsewhere, too, he added to the dialogue, often in ways that weakened the play. As professor Steven Price has noted: "points made relatively succinctly in Rose's dialogue are attenuated in needlessly lengthy exchanges."[12] What had been implicit now became explicit; subtlety was replaced with excessive explanation.

Rose's teleplay had been structured around *Studio One*'s two commercial breaks. Although a stage play had no such requirement, Sherman L. Sergel kept the three-act structure, which had the effect of slowing the pace. He also made important changes to act 3. With the vote deadlocked at six to six, Juror 3 proposes that they are a hung jury, leading to debate—and eventually a vote—about whether they should quit deliberations. Moments later, Juror 4 conducts a reenactment of the crime which suggests that the killer must have taken longer to run out of the apartment and down the stairs, and therefore *could* have been identified by the man downstairs even if he had moved only slowly to his door. Juror 2 and Juror 5 are persuaded to change their vote back to guilty, although they later shift back. These additions, too, made the drama slower and more cumbersome.

Although the Dramatic adaptation was weaker than Rose's original teleplay, at the time it did not seem to matter. *Twelve Angry Men* became very popular among drama groups, a notable achievement in an era when amateur productions tended to favor light comedy.[13] The Dramatic adaptation sold so well that, after the 1957 movie fizzled at the box office, *Variety* noted a "unique show biz twist" where the play "stands a chance of outgrossing the picture," the opposite of the usual pattern.[14]

AFTER *12 ANGRY MEN* won top honors at the 1957 Berlin International Film Festival and did well at cinemas across Europe, it caught the eye of Lars Schmidt, the Swedish-born artistic director of Paris's Théâtre de la Gaîté-Montparnasse (and for a time, husband of Ingrid Bergman). Schmidt had recently produced a French version of Tennessee Williams's *Cat on a Hot Tin Roof* (*La Chatte sur un Toit Brûlant*), and wanted to bring *12 Angry Men* to the Parisian stage.

Not bound by the Dramatic Publishing version, Schmidt looked to André Obey, a prominent playwright and administrator of the *Comédie Française*, who had translated *Cat on a Hot Tin Roof*. Obey translated Rose's movie screenplay almost exactly, turning it into a one-act play without any breaks. Even American slang expressions were retained: Juror 12's ad-man phrase—"Let's run it up the flagpole and see if anyone salutes" became "*Faisons-la flotter au mât et voyons si quelqu'un la salue,*" a literal translation that means nothing in French but signals that these are

Americans speaking informally.[15] The final scene, too, followed the movie exactly, but without the close-up of Juror 3 tearing the photo of his son, which could not have been easily seen by a theater audience. As in the movie, Juror 8 helps Juror 3 with his coat as the others file out, a moment of reconciliation after a long and bitter argument.

Douze Hommes en Colère, with authorship credited to André Obey-Réginald Rose, opened in October 1958. It was directed by Michel Vitold, who also played Juror 8, known for his role in Jean-Paul Sartre's *Huis Clos* (*No Exit*) in 1944. Staged on a proscenium, the table was arranged so that most jurors faced the audience, as in the Dramatic version, with a back-drop of skyscrapers visible through the windows of the jury room.

Reviews from the Parisian press were superb, prompting Rose to express his thanks to Schmidt: "You must know the fondness I feel for '12 Angry Men' and the deep personal involvement I have in it. I must say that it was a difficult thing to let this piece of work out of my hands without re-taining some measure of artistic control over it. However, judging from the enthusiastic press notices your obviously fine production has received in Paris, it would seem my work has fallen into exceedingly capable hands."[16]

Very soon, stage versions were performed elsewhere in Europe. A German version, *Die Zwölf Geschworenen* (*The 12 Jurors*) was performed in Munich and Frankfurt, and was said to be the second most frequently produced play in Germany in 1959.[17] A Slovenian version, *Dvanajst Porot-nikov* (*12 Jurors*), premiered October 22, 1959, at the Slovenian National Theater in Ljubljana, Yugoslavia. Other productions were planned for Italy, Spain, the Netherlands, and Scandinavia.

OVER THE NEXT FEW YEARS, while writing screenplays for Walter Mirisch and television dramas for *Playhouse 90*, Rose kept a strong interest in the stage version of his jury room drama. It had been popular among amateurs in the United States and professionals in Europe, and Rose hoped one day to bring it to Broadway.

In 1961, *Twelve Angry Men* was staged by an excellent regional theater, the Bucks County Playhouse in New Hope, Pennsylvania. Next, it was per-formed at the Arena Stage in Washington, DC, in January 1963. (The cast included Roy Scheider, age thirty and not yet a movie actor, as Juror 12.) One critic described it as "Reginald Rose's modern classic about the perils and glory of the jury system. Though familiar since 1954 as a TV drama, movie, and stage play (in that order) it still has the power to make a first night audience burst into partisan applause at a point well scored."[18] Both productions used the Dramatic Publishing version, which held exclusive rights in the United States.

The Capitol, an opulent movie palace at Broadway and Fifty-First Street, in the summer of 1954. *12 Angry Men* opened on April 12, 1957, and closed after three weeks of modest attendance. (Merlis / oldNYCphotos.com)

Left: How to promote a drama about a dozen men talking in a dingy room? United Artists' efforts did not lead to box office success. (Photofest)

Right: *12 Angry Men* took top honors at the Berlin International Film Festival, June 1957. Henry Fonda received the Golden Bear from Berlin Mayor Willy Brandt, later Chancellor of West Germany and winner of the Nobel Peace Prize. (Alamy)

Cast and crew of *12 Angry Men*, Fox Movietone Studios, Tenth Avenue and Fifty-Fourth Street, New York City, July 1956. (*In front, at right*): Faith Hubley (script), Muky (with glasses, photographer Menyhért Munkácsi). (*Seated, from left*): Boris Kaufman, Jack Warden (in hat), Jim Gartland (grips) in dark shirt. (*Seated, at right*): Martin Balsam, Herman Buchman (makeup, with hands on Balsam). (*Standing, from left*): Henry Fonda, Robert Webber, E. G. Marshall (partly obscured), Jack Klugman, Sidney Lumet. (*Standing, at right*): George Voskovec (with moustache), Bob Markell (with glasses)

(*In front*): Muky (with glasses, photographer Menyhért Munkácsi), Don Kranze, James
Kelly (with tie). (*Seated, at left*): Martin Balsam, Herman Buchman (makeup, with
hands on Balsam's shoulder). (*Seated, from right*): Ed Begley, Lee J. Cobb (without
hairpiece), Joseph Sweeney. (*Standing, from right*): George Justin, Reginald Rose,
unidentified, John Fiedler (in shadow). (*Standing, at rear*): Ed Binns (in dark shirt)
(The George Justin Collection, Museum of Modern Art, New York)

Left: Herb Brodkin and Reginald Rose collaborated on *The Defenders*, the most acclaimed television drama of the early 1960s. (1963 publicity photo, author's collection)

Right: Rose with E. G. Marshall (*seated*) and Robert Reed, stars of *The Defenders*. (Photofest)

Photo accompanying a 1962 *TV Guide* interview with Reginald Rose and Rod Serling: "Can a TV writer keep his integrity?" (Everett Collection)

Staging *Douze Hommes en Colère* at Théâtre de la Gaîté-Montparnasse, Paris, in October 1958. (Getty Images)

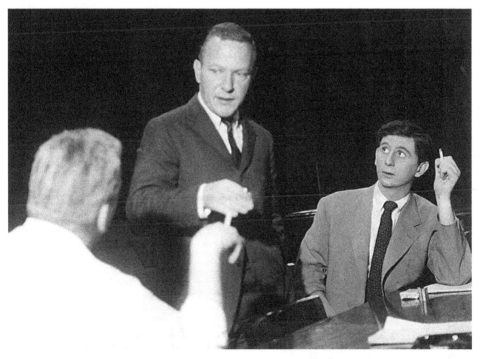

Reginald Rose, with actors Harry Bergman and René Auberjonois, during rehearsals at the Arena Theatre, Washington, D.C., January 22, 1963 (Alamy)

Jurors glance at the defendant after hearing the judge's instructions: "If there is a reasonable doubt in your minds as to the guilt of the accused—a reasonable doubt—then you must bring me a verdict of not guilty." (Photofest)

Judith S. Kaye, Chief Judge of the New York Court of Appeals, 1993–2008. "*12 Angry Men* will continue to excite audiences because, whatever the latest challenges of a new world . . . the quest for justice is timeless." (Fred R. Conrad / The New York Times / Redux)

U.S. Supreme Court Justice Sonia Sotomayor at Fordham Law School, 2010. "It was a very important film in terms of developing me both as a lawyer and subsequently as a judge." (Bruce Gilbert)

Although Reginald Rose had no formal training in social psychology, he possessed a keen understanding of group dynamics and peer pressure. (Alamy)

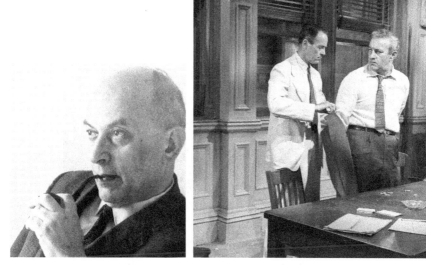

Left: Solomon Asch, whose landmark studies about social conformity in the early 1950s are vividly depicted in *12 Angry Men*.

Right: At the end of the deliberations, a moment of reconciliation between Juror 3 (Lee J. Cobb) and Juror 8 (Henry Fonda). (Courtesy of MGM Media Licensing, 12 ANGRY MEN © 1957 The Estate of Henry Fonda and Defender Productions, Inc. All Rights Reserved.)

Clockwise from top left: *12*, directed by Nikita Mikhalkov, Russia, 2007; Zeina Deccache's *12 Angry Lebanese*, staged by inmates at Beirut's Roumieh Prison, 2009; *Douze Hommes en Colère*, at the Théâtre Hébertot, Paris, winner of the *Globes de Cristal* for *Best Play*, 2019; *Twelve Citizens* (十二公民, Shi Er Gong Min), directed by Xu Ang, China, 2014.

Twelve Angry Men also continued to be performed with success by amateur groups. In 1961, the director of a production in West Virginia wrote for advice: "Any background material or Mr. Rose's specific recommendations as to treatment of this material would be appreciated." Rose responded graciously and wished the production well, but commented that he was not a director and couldn't "honestly offer advice on how to handle the play." After that disclaimer, Rose went on to offer suggestions that showed a keen understanding of his work as a stage play:

> The main problems of course, are first characterizations, and second, movement. It is important to cast this thing with twelve different looking men so that the audience can sort them out immediately. And it's important to bring out as fully as possible the characters of each of them so that they become separate and distinct human beings.
>
> And second, it is vital in what is basically a static situation, to keep the actors moving. I don't know what kind of stage you have, but TWELVE ANGRY MEN works quite well either in a proscenium or in the round. Whichever it is, just remember that there must be movement.
>
> Hope this has been helpful. Good luck and regards,
> Reginald Rose[19]

Rose could respond very differently when his economic interests were involved. In 1961, he learned that the Brooklyn Theater Arts Company was planning to perform *Twelve Angry Men*. The production was generating considerable publicity in New York City, and Rose worried it could make a Broadway production unlikely. He expressed his displeasure to Clark Sergel, head of Dramatic Publishing: "I don't like the idea of having so much publicity connected with an amateur performance in New York City. . . . I would appreciate it if you could confine this play to groups which are not seeking national publicity."[20]

The matter remained there until January 1962, when the Brooklyn producer contacted Rose with a further request. The New York State Council on the Arts was funding a tour in upstate New York. Would Rose allow the Brooklyn Theatre Arts Company to perform *Twelve Angry Men*? When Rose's secretary relayed his answer—No—the director appealed to Rose's sense of pride. Another prestigious theater group, Joseph Papp's Public Theater, was taking part. "Joe Papp wants to send out 'Julius Caesar' and 'Antony and Cleopatra' and we would like 'Twelve Angry Men' to be our number one choice for this project."[21] Would Rose allow his play to be included along with the works of Shakespeare?

Rose answered the next day:

It's fairly obvious William Shakespeare no longer has ownership in "Julius Caesar" and "Antony and Cleopatra" whereas I do have ownership in Twelve Angry Men.

I cannot seem to convince you that this is a most valuable property which I am not about to dissipate by allowing it to tour with your group.

The answer is as before, no.

Yours truly,

Reginald Rose[22]

A year later, Rose responded warmly to the request from an old friend. Ashley-Steiner had initially declined to authorize a Czech translation of *Twelve Angry Men*, prompting George Voskovec to write to Henry Fonda. After noting that their movie had enjoyed a "tremendously successful run in one of Prague's top cinemas" and received "regular standing ovations and rounds of applause during each showing," the actor who had spoken so eloquently about democracy as Juror 11 added a heartfelt note: "I personally consider this a most valuable contribution to cultural contacts across the Iron Curtain. TWELVE ANGRY MEN is a wonderful testimony to American freedom of expression and our high artistic standards in independent film-making. The more of such stuff that we can show East of Berlin the less effective the old Red chestnut about the 'Coca-Cola culture' will be."[23]

Fonda forwarded the letter to Rose, with a handwritten note at the bottom: "Dear Reggie—I don't think this needs my permission—I certainly have no objection though. All My Best, Hank." Rose agreed, and a Czech translation, *Dvanáct Rozhněvanych Mužů*, was published in Prague the following year. The foreword was by Václav Havel, then a twenty-five-year-old playwright just beginning to gain attention for his satirical plays about Communist society. Havel wrote that *Twelve Angry Men* was a remarkable play that forced the audience to reflect on the nature of reality: "Along with truths and lies, there are probabilities and possibilities. The world does not consist of eternal and given magnitudes—truth can take on various shapes." Havel also found *Twelve Angry Men* to be a wonderful play for actors. Unusually, all of the actors are on stage for the entire play, with no entrances or exits. He wrote: "Is it possible to imagine more ideal conditions for developing a truly real, intrinsic and fully human modern form of acting?"[24]

ALTHOUGH *TWELVE ANGRY MEN* remained popular among amateur groups in the United States, it did not reach Broadway in the 1960s, which some believed was due to the poor quality of the Dramatic Publishing version. An opportunity to get around the Dramatic adaptation arose in 1964, when a classically trained British actor, Leo Genn sought to stage a production in London. Genn, known for his portrayal of Horatio in Laurence Olivier's *Hamlet* (1944) and Starbuck in John Huston's *Moby Dick* (1956), had appeared in a 1963 episode of *The Defenders*. He expressed an interest in playing Juror 8 in a London production, leading to a joint venture with Rose that granted to Genn "the right to perform on the professional theatre stage the play entitled *Twelve Angry Men*."[25]

Not bound to use the Dramatic version outside the United States, Rose prepared a script that closely followed his 1957 screenplay, and licensed it to Samuel French Ltd., a London-based theatrical publisher.

In the new version, Rose added two passages that he had written for the first complete screenplay but omitted for the movie, one where the jurors ask who other than the defendant could have committed the crime and the other regarding testimony of a psychiatrist. Rose also made a small but crucial change to the climactic scene. The movie had shown Juror 3 tearing up the photograph of his son, but a close-up would not be possible on stage. How to make clear that his desire to punish the defendant was based on anger toward his estranged son? Now, after Juror 3 summarized the evidence against the defendant, he railed: "That goddam rotten kid. I know him. I know what they're like. What they do to you. How they kill you every day. My God, don't you see? How come I'm the only one who sees? Jeez, I can feel that knife going in." Juror 8 responds quietly: "It's not your boy. He's somebody else." Juror 4 adds: "Let him live." With that, Juror 3 gives up. As in the movie, Juror 8 helps the distraught man put on his coat while the others file out.

In June 1964, Rose traveled to London to attend rehearsals with director Margaret Webster. He brought his wife, Ellen, and oldest sons for a vacation and stayed for the first week of performance. On July 10, *Twelve Angry Men* opened at the Queen's Theatre on Shaftsbury Avenue in London's West End. Most reviews were excellent, with *Punch* writing that *Twelve Angry Men* "has now turned into a stage play continuously exciting even if you do remember how the story ends."[26] One review was not as kind, with Julian Holland of the *Daily Mail* observing: "Something has evaporated in putting *Twelve Angry Men* on the stage." Whereas the movie had been tense, showing "each sweating face as it wrestled in the heat of a New York summer," the stage could not offer close-ups. "The camera was inside the jury room: we are outside it."[27]

Rose's reply to the *Daily Mail* was less the complaint of a wounded author, and more a thoughtful reflection about the nature of stage and screen performances:

> This business of pitting one medium against another seems arbitrary and pointless. What has actually "evaporated" is the motion picture camera, which, as Mr. Holland points out, followed each sweating face as it wrestled with the problem. It would seem then, taking Mr. Holland's point of view, that there is no such thing as a play which cannot be more effectively reproduced on film.
>
> This is just not so. I have seen a dozen plays in London during the past month, some good, some bad, but not once did I feel the need of a camera poking its lens into the face of each actor to tell me what he was really thinking. The plays were good or bad in their own right, which is as it should be. As films they would simply be something else.
>
> Film is one art; the stage is another. When we sit before the proscenium we see an ensemble performance. We see all of the actors all of the time, and we make our own selection of which one deserves our concentration at any given moment. We are not bound by the choice a film editor makes for us in the cutting room.
>
> Theatre is not meant for the "sweaty close-up" but rather the experience of being moved by a group of living, breathing actors in what is hoped to be a living, breathing play.
>
> The film camera projects the actor but in the theatre the actor projects himself.
>
> Yours faithfully,
> Reginald Rose[28]

Performances at the Queen's Theatre continued through August, and then shifted to the Lyric Theatre for the remainder of a respectable four-month run.[29] Success in London led to a request to license the play in South Africa at financial terms similar to the British production. London producer Kenneth Wagg wrote to Rose in late September: "Leo and I have assumed your approval and are going right ahead," leading to a production at the Alexander Theatre in Johannesburg, with renowned South African actor, Patrick Mynhardt, as Juror 8.[30]

Upon learning of the South African production, Rose was very unhappy, since the performance ran counter to a petition recently signed by leading British and American playwrights, including John Osborne, Harold Pinter, Lillian Hellman, and Arthur Miller. The decision could not be reversed, but when a new request came from a theater in the South African province of Natal, Rose's office was quick to reply: "Reggie asked me to tell you he would certainly not want his plays to be performed before segregated audiences."[31] There was no way the author of "Thunder on Sycamore Street" and "Black Monday" was going to abide by South African apartheid laws.

THROUGHOUT THE 1970S AND 1980S, as *Twelve Angry Men* remained popular among amateur groups across the United States, Rose was periodically asked to revise the script to include parts for women. He declined, explaining: "I just felt that would change the whole dynamic. It would have to be completely rewritten because not only do women not talk like men, but men don't talk the same way if there are women in the room. So I said no. I resisted it."[32] He once described the dramatic setup as "twelve men in a box," with tension arising from so many men, locked in close quarters, and forced to reach a unanimous verdict.[33] All of that, he felt, would be undercut with a mixed gender cast.

Dramatic Publishing felt differently, and in 1983 issued a new version called *Twelve Angry Women*. Oddly, Dramatic made almost no changes to the text. The characters are described in the exact same words, merely substituting *she* for *he*, *ladies* for *gentlemen*, and *Madame Foreman* for *Mister Foreman*. No attempt was made to explore how women might express agreement and disagreement, or how they might bond and argue, or confront one another, directly or indirectly. Juror 3 remained an overtly aggressive person, although now, incongruously, she was busy with crochet, like a modern-day Madame Defarge. In the movie, Juror 3 and Juror 12 distract themselves by playing tic-tac-toe; when Juror 8 reprimands them—"This isn't a game!"—Juror 3 responds fiercely: "I've got a good mind to walk around this table and belt him one." In *Twelve Angry Women*, Juror 3 leans over to Juror 12: "Want to see the pattern of a crocheted skirt my daughter sent me?"; when Juror 8 intervenes—"This isn't a sewing circle"—Juror 3 counters: "I've got a good mind to walk around this table and slap her." Possible, perhaps, but not very probable. Nor was any change made to the confrontation at the end of act 2, when Juror 3 charges at Juror 8 and is physically restrained by the others, now shouting "I'll kill her! I'll kill her!"

No matter. Whether *Twelve Angry Men* or *Twelve Angry Women*, the play was popular with school groups, who were also allowed to mix and match parts for a show they could call *Twelve Angry Jurors*.[34] Any role could be played by any actor, said Dramatic, although it had a suggestion for Juror 3 and Juror 8: "These should probably be played by men, if you have them available—though any combination of men and women you have available will work."[35]

SOME THEATER PRODUCERS BEGAN to find ways to get around the Dramatic version. Jack Marshall was a young lawyer in the Washington, DC, area who had grown up watching *The Defenders* and was enraptured when he first saw *12 Angry Men* broadcast on late-night television. In the late 1980s, he staged an amateur production at his alma mater, the Georgetown Law School. Marshall paid Dramatic Publishing its fee, but devised his own version by renting a home projector and painstakingly transcribing the dialogue of the movie.

A few years later, Marshall staged another amateur production for the Association of Trial Lawyers of America, earning rave reviews and impressing its audience both for the gripping story and for the important legal questions it raised. One member of the cast remarked that *12 Angry Men* was an overlooked gem that deserved wider attention. Marshall agreed, and was inspired to found the American Century Theater, a company whose mission was "to rediscover classic works of American theater, particularly those first produced during what *Time* publisher Henry Luce called 'The American Century.'"[36] Its inaugural production was never in doubt: *Twelve Angry Men*.

Now that he was planning a professional production, Marshall felt he should seek Reginald Rose's approval to use the screenplay, even if the fee was paid to Dramatic. His dramaturg contacted Rose in Connecticut, who expressed his pleasure at the news. The Dramatic version, Rose agreed, had been "an embarrassment."[37]

The American Century Theater production opened in July 1995 at the Lanier Theater in Fairfax City, Virginia. Rather than seat most of the jurors facing the audience, Marshall arrayed the jurors so they faced one another around a table, as they had in the movie. About one hundred seats were placed in a tight circle around the jury table and chairs, making for an intimate setting that allowed actors to speak and gesture in a natural way. Bob Mondello, theater reporter for *Washington City Paper*, wrote that "*Twelve Angry Men* remains a gripping cautionary tale about the vagaries of American justice." The staging was particularly effective: "When tempers finally flare and various members of the jury resort to threatening postures and general carousing, the tight quarters markedly increase the tension level. Picture being trapped on a subway car as a minor disagreement develops into a fistfight, and you've about got the picture."[38]

The next year, in 1996, Harold Pinter directed *Twelve Angry Men* in

Great Britain, opening at the Bristol Theatre Royal and moving to London's Comedy Theatre for a successful run. He used the Samuel French version, to which Rose made a few small adjustments. (The judge's instructions, heard off-stage at the beginning of the play, had been recorded by E. G. Marshall.) *The Daily Telegraph* reported: "Who would have thought that Harold Pinter, the modern master of enigma and menace, would have chosen to direct a trusty old war horse like this? We should, however, be glad that he did."[39] The play, as Pinter showed, could still captivate an audience.

REGINALD ROSE SPENT HIS later years in Connecticut. In June 2000, he published *Undelivered Mail*, the memoirs from his youth in New York, set in 1937, the cover showing a vintage photograph of the Central Savings Bank building at Broadway and Seventy-Third Street. By then Rose's health had declined, and complications from a sudden infection took him in April 2002, at age eighty-one. Regrettably, he did not live to see the fulfilment of a dream: a Broadway production of *Twelve Angry Men*.

Not long after Rose's death, director Scott Ellis of the Roundabout Theater in New York was visiting Nicky Martin, artistic director of the Huntington Theater Company in Boston. Martin had recently attended a reading of *Twelve Angry Men* by a college group, and had been struck by how well the play held up. Ellis knew the movie but had never seen the play performed, although he had heard of its recent success with Harold Pinter in London and was keen to learn more.

When Ellis got a copy of the Dramatic script, he was surprised: "I started reading it, and I thought, this is not very good. Surely this isn't the script that the London production used." He contacted Ellen Rose, who confirmed that Pinter had used the Samuel French version and sent a copy to Ellis. This one was excellent: "We did a reading of it, a one-night reading, and you could tell it worked."[40]

Roundabout's artistic director, Todd Haines, was equally impressed, and on October 28, 2004, fifty years and one month after it was first performed on *Studio One*, *Twelve Angry Men* opened on Broadway. The cast included Boyd Gaines as Juror 8 and Philip Bosco as Juror 3. Ellis staged the play as one continuous act. The jury doesn't get a break, he explained, and neither should the audience. From the moment the jury room door is locked, until the unanimous verdict is reached, no one is allowed to leave. The jurors must confront one another and work out their differences, and the audience must feel that tension as fully as possible.

Reginald Rose's family, including wife Ellen and three of his sons, gathered for the opening. "I don't think Reggie thought this would ever happen," said Ellen Rose. "There are so many stops and starts in this business." It was a special thrill to watch the play with family and friends, she added: "Most of them have never seen the play—only the movie and TV show."[41] Jonathan Rose recalled: "They did a brilliant job. I thought it went over with great tautness, and electricity, and feeling. It drew you in. I thought, this is a wonderful example of how theater can be great."[42] Adam Liptak of the *New York Times* noted the "legal and social anachronisms"— no longer would juries be all male or all white, nor would jurors be allowed to smoke, nor would the death penalty be mandatory—but it didn't matter: "Despite all this, the play remains fresh, engaging and powerful."[43]

After a very successful eight-month run, the Roundabout production toured nationally from 2006 to 2008, now with Richard Thomas as Juror 8 and George Wendt as Juror 1. Audiences across the country found the drama compelling and the issues relevant. Following the 2004 Broadway triumph, Samuel French Ltd. acquired the US professional rights, leading to many more excellent productions. It is, said one reviewer of a recent production, a play that "still manages to grip an audience as though it were ripped from today's headlines."[44]

MORE THAN SIXTY YEARS after it was first performed on stage, *Twelve Angry Men* shows no signs of diminishing. It remains one of the most popular plays in the United States for amateur groups—Dramatic Publishing confirmed in 2020 that it "has continually been one of our top selling plays for the past decade"[45]—and ranked the sixth-most popular high school play in the United States in 2020.[46] Several factors explain its appeal to school groups. It's an ensemble piece with many speaking parts. It's easy to stage, requiring a single set and little in the way of props, costumes, or makeup. There is no profanity, no sexual content, and no violence, making it acceptable to school administrators. It's also well known, giving it a marketing appeal. Very few plays tick all those boxes, which makes *Twelve Angry Men*—or *Twelve Angry Women* or *Twelve Angry Jurors*—such an enduring favorite.[47]

Perhaps even more impressive is the admiration from professionals. To Jack Marshall, *Twelve Angry Men* is "a near perfect stage drama, *sui generis*, and brilliant in concept and execution" and "the best ensemble drama there is."[48] To Scott Ellis, *Twelve Angry Men* is unusual for having so many actors together on stage for such an extended period of time. The movie was superb, but the viewer only sees what Sidney Lumet and Boris Kaufman wanted them to see. The stage experience is different: the audience can watch any actor, at any time, for as long as they wish. As Rose had noted in his letter to the *Daily Mail*, the result is not better or worse, but a different medium that offers a different experience.

For both its excellence as an ensemble drama and the importance of the ideas it raises, *Twelve Angry Men* has come to be considered a classic play. Scott Ellis said: "I think it's as important today as it was in the Fifties, and to be honest, it will be important 50 years from now. *Twelve Angry Men* will be around for a very long time."[49]

Some excellent stage plays become fine movies. Less common are great movies that become outstanding stage plays. *12 Angry Men* is one of the very few dramas that is both.

But there's more. *12 Angry Men* has also been embraced by experts in two other very different fields.

18

A Lesson in the Law

AMONG THE LETTERS TO CBS following the *Westinghouse Studio One* broadcast in September 1954 came one from Wichita, Kansas. It read in part: "Twelve Angry Men made a tremendous impression in this area and the Wichita Bar Association feels it would be highly worthwhile to produce it locally with a cast of lawyers. The general public and the legal profession can both learn a lot from it."[1]

This note was the first indication that Reginald Rose's teleplay had struck a chord with lawyers. There had been countless courtroom dramas, of course, but this one was different, as it followed the jurors through their deliberations and offered a fresh perspective on the criminal justice system. There was, as the Wichita Lawyer's Drama Group noted, a lot to learn from it.

By 1957, the special appeal of *12 Angry Men* to the legal community was well understood. Although Reginald Rose's featurette, with Henry Fonda speaking from the movie set, had not been filmed, publicist Arthur P. Jacobs listed several other ways to promote the movie using a legal angle. It suggested that members of local bar associations could give talks at high schools with titles such as "The Law as a Profession" and "The Duty of Every Citizen as a Potential Jury Member." It proposed that "Judge Leibowitz and Morris Ernst or some prominent legal authority" be asked to write letters to newspaper editors, explaining why the movie should be seen.[2] The choices were most appropriate: Samuel Leibowitz had defended the Scottsboro Boys, nine Black teenagers convicted by an all-white jury of raping a white woman in Alabama in 1931, and Morris Ernst was general counsel of the American Civil Liberties Union. Both could speak with authority about a movie that addressed racial prejudice and the law. (There's no evidence that either man helped to publicize the movie, although it seems that Judge Leibowitz was at least contacted. Long after his death, his family came across a kinescope of the *Studio One* broadcast of "Twelve Angry Men," very likely received as part of the publicity effort. Donated to the Paley Center in 2003, it is the only complete version that exists.)

"IN FORM, *12 ANGRY MEN* is a courtroom drama," wrote film critic Roger Ebert. "In purpose, it's a crash course in those passages of the Constitution that promise defendants a fair trial and the presumption of innocence."[3]

As a short course about criminal justice, *12 Angry Men* offers a few important lessons, the first of which is implicit in the title: Article III, Section 2 of the Constitution guarantees to defendants of criminal cases the right to trial by jury. The Sixth Amendment goes further: "the accused shall enjoy the right to a speedy and public trial, by an impartial jury of the State and district wherein the crime shall have been committed."[4] The twelve are meant to be that impartial jury.

How a jury of twelve white men came to be empaneled raises other questions. Such a jury might have been unusual in 1950s New York, but not impossible. In describing his time at the Central Jury Room in March 1954, Rose recalled that the pool of potential jurors was "98 percent" white men, a figure of speech perhaps, but suggesting that the vast majority were indeed white men. The 1954 trial of William Viragh, which likely inspired Rose, had a jury of ten men and two women, the exact ethnic composition not clear but likely most or all were white; and another famous trial that took place at 60 Centre Street, the 1951 trial of Julius and Ethel Rosenberg, had a jury of ten white men, one Black man, and one white woman.

Reginald Rose said that he composed his jury for dramatic purposes, but even so, a jury of twelve white men compels us to ask about the broader pool. If the pool was *not* more diverse, we should ask why. And if it *was* more diverse, how did these twelve get selected?

Regarding race, if a jury pool in 1950s New York was overwhelmingly white, we should want to know if there had been bias in selection. In his defense of the Scottsboro Boys, Samuel Leibowitz argued that the state of Alabama had prevented many Blacks from registering to vote, which had the effect of keeping them off juries. The US Supreme Court agreed, reversing the conviction of one defendant, Clarence Norris, and ruling that although Alabama had no laws prohibiting Blacks from serving on juries, its voting practices had that effect, in violation of the Equal Protection Clause of the Fourteenth Amendment.[5]

If the pool of prospective jurors *had* been racially mixed, we should ask how a jury composed only of whites was empaneled. Had prosecutors used peremptory challenges—that is, rejecting potential jurors without having to give any reasons, but perhaps doing so based on race? In 1986, the US Supreme Court ruled that peremptory challenges could not be used to exclude jurors based solely on their race, which again would violate the Equal Protection Clause of the Fourteenth Amendment.[6]

The all-male jury raises other issues. In most states, women became eligible to serve on juries shortly after the ratification of the Nineteenth Amendment in 1920, which gave women the right to vote. In New York, women became eligible for jury service in 1927. They did not have to serve, however, because women were assumed to have a primary role of homemaker and could ask to be excused much like doctors, health care workers, undertakers, and a range of other service employees.[7] The largely male jury pool that included Rose was at least in part the result of women asking to be excused.

Allowing so many citizens to be excused from jury service meant that others were called with much greater frequency and had to shoulder a disproportionate burden. The resulting lack of diversity in the jury pool—not only in terms of gender but also occupation—was also potentially unfair to defendants. These inequities in jury selection, as well as the frustrating experience of those who were more often summoned for service—with long and tedious questioning during *voir dire*, rejection for service without explanation, plus crowded and often uncomfortable surroundings—led New York State Chief Judge Judith S. Kaye in the 1990s to undertake a series of reforms. At that time, there were close to ten thousand jury trials in New York each year, with upwards of 650,000 citizens called for jury service. Judge Kaye saw that the jury system was not only central to the delivery of justice but was the only link that many citizens had to the judicial system. The best way to ensure public trust in the judicial system, she maintained, was with a more inclusive and effective approach to jury service.[8]

Under Judge Kaye's reforms, automatic exemptions for women and for many occupations were ended. Sources used to identify potential jurors were expanded to include unemployment and public assistance rosters. She later wrote: "These reforms sent a strong message: no person, no group is more privileged, or less important, when it comes to jury service, and no one gets excused automatically."[9] Judge Kaye also sought to improve the experience of those called for jury duty by making the selection process more efficient and transparent, by letting jurors take notes during trials, and by improving the facilities. The chance of an overwhelmingly male jury, and the level of discomfort experienced by the jurors in Rose's drama, were less likely in the state of New York after Judge Kaye's reforms.

A SECOND LESSON SPEAKS to a core principle of criminal justice: a defendant is presumed to be innocent until proven guilty. The burden of proof rests with the prosecution.

Presumption of innocence goes back many centuries, to Talmudic law, which declares that "every man is innocent until proved guilty," and to the sixth-century Roman Law Code, which asserts that "proof lies on him who asserts, not on him who denies." The concept was already well established in the 1760s, when William Blackstone, in *Commentaries on the Laws of England*, set out what is known as Blackstone's Formulation: "Better that ten guilty persons escape than that one innocent suffer."

In *12 Angry Men*, the topic comes up early in the deliberations, when Juror 2 is asked to explain his vote. He stammers: "I just think he's guilty. I thought it was obvious from the word go. I mean, nobody proved otherwise." Juror 8 speaks up: "Nobody *has* to prove otherwise. The burden of proof is on the prosecution. The defendant doesn't even have to open his mouth. That's in the Constitution."[10] In fact, the words "presumption of innocence" never appear in the Constitution, although the Constitution *has* been interpreted to mean that a defendant is presumed innocent until proven guilty. In 1895, the US Supreme Court declared: "The principle that there is a presumption of innocence in favor of the accused is the undoubted law, axiomatic and elementary, and its enforcement lies at the foundation of the administration of our criminal law."[11]

Presumption of innocence is crucial in *12 Angry Men*, since it means that those voting guilty must persuade Juror 8, not the other way around. A few moments after the exchange with Juror 2, described above, Juror 1, the foreman, addresses Juror 8: "Your turn down there. Let's go." Juror 8 replies: "I didn't expect a turn. I thought you are all going to try to convince me. Wasn't that the idea?" Juror 8 knows that although he is the only one to vote not guilty, his position is strong, and he makes sure that everyone else understands, as well.

A THIRD LEGAL CONCEPT IN *12 Angry Men*, and the most important one in Rose's drama, is the doctrine of reasonable doubt. It provides the dramatic arc of the story: At first, only Juror 8 has a reasonable doubt about the defendant's guilt; over the course of their deliberation, the other eleven come to share that doubt.[12]

The importance of reasonable doubt was immediately recognized by reviewers. In the *Saturday Evening Post*, Hollis Alpert described *12 Angry Men* as "a primer in the definition of those important words, 'a reasonable doubt.' The entire action is concerned with establishing it."[13] *New York Times* film critic A. H. Weiler wrote that Rose's basic idea was that "'beyond a reasonable doubt' should not be regarded as just a flat phrase casually coined by the law-makers" but was something real.[14] In her syndicated newspaper column, *My Day*, Eleanor Roosevelt paid tribute to *12 Angry Men*, commenting that the movie "makes vivid what 'reasonable doubt' means when a murder trial jury makes up its mind on circumstantial evidence."[15]

Rose had the doctrine of reasonable doubt clearly in mind when he wrote the outline, mentioning the phrase no fewer than ten times. When he developed the outline into a full script, however, he used the phrase sparingly, having it spoken only a few times and rarely more than once by the same person. A skilled dramatist, Rose knew that the phrase would be more powerful if it was used rarely. (By contrast, Sherman L. Sergel's adaptation used the phrase many times, with jurors repeatedly discussing whether some concern about evidence amounted to reasonable doubt, an obvious device that weakened the play.)

In Rose's screenplay the phrase is first heard in the opening scene, when the judge mentions it explicitly and repeats it for emphasis: "If there is a reasonable doubt in your minds as to the guilt of the accused—a *reasonable* doubt—then you must bring me a verdict of not guilty. If, however, there is no reasonable doubt, then you must in good conscience find the accused guilty."[16] After that, almost an hour passes before the term is heard again, yet without question it is on the jurors' minds. As they consider various points of evidence, they are thinking: How good is the evidence, really? Are we sure of the defendant's guilt, or is there reason for doubt?

The words are next heard when Juror 11 shifts his vote and is confronted by Juror 3. Juror 11 replies: "I don't have to defend my decision to you. There is a reasonable doubt in my mind." Juror 3 counters: "What reasonable doubt? That's nothing but words." The exchange draws a sharp contrast between a juror who understands that reasonable doubt is the ultimate criterion for deciding guilt or innocence, and another juror who cannot, or will not, take the concept seriously. Minutes later, with the tide turning toward acquittal, Juror 5 says to Juror 7: "You still don't think there's room for reasonable doubt?" When Juror 7 says he does not, Juror 11 is prompted to say: "Pardon me. Maybe you don't fully understand the term 'reasonable doubt.'"

Much later, when only three guilty votes remain, Juror 8 appeals to those jurors directly, the only time that he uses the phrase: "We have a reasonable doubt, and that's something that's very valuable in our system. No jury can declare a man guilty unless it's sure. We nine can't understand how you three are still so sure. Maybe you can tell us." Although Juror 8 has deftly guided the others over the previous hour, he has waited until now to utter the crucial phrase, saving it for a moment when he wishes to persuade the last holdouts.

Moments later, when Juror 4 realizes that the woman across the street could not have been wearing glasses at the moment she said she saw the killing, he changes his vote, explaining: "I have a reasonable doubt now"—a simple comment but utterly definitive. Only Juror 3 is left, a man whose insistence on conviction has been based all along on emotion, not reason.

Not only was Rose smart not to overuse the term, he was also wise not to try to define it precisely. The judge offered no definition of reasonable doubt, nor did the jurors attempt to parse its meaning. Had they done so, the screenplay might have become bogged down, for the precise meaning of reasonable doubt has been a topic of much debate. In 1993, Chief Judge of the United States Court of Appeals Jon O. Newman wrote that phrase had become a "mere incantation," recited to juries without any practical guidance, and therefore "ambiguous and open to widely disparate interpretations." Judge Newman called for "renewed consideration as to what reasonable doubt means and how it should be applied as a rule of law, so that the standard might serve as a more precise divider of the guilty from the innocent."[17]

One reason for the confusion is that the original purpose of the doctrine of reasonable doubt is not well understood. Contrary to common belief, it was not intended to set a *higher* standard for conviction, but precisely the opposite. In medieval times, jurors worried that convicting an innocent person was a mortal sin, and felt that if they had any doubt at all, they should not vote to convict. The doctrine of reasonable doubt came about, says Yale Law School professor James Q. Whitman, to allow juries to convict even when they were *not* absolutely certain of guilt, but only certain beyond a reasonable doubt. The effect was not to raise the standard for conviction but to *lower* it.[18] This common misperception is repeated by Juror 8 toward the end of deliberations when he says that "No jury can declare a man guilty unless it's sure." In fact, the doctrine of reasonable doubt was intended to let a jury convict a defendant even if it was *not* entirely sure.

Discussions about the religious origins of reasonable doubt notwithstanding, in recent years most states have tried, as suggested by Judge Newman, to provide more useful guidance than what was offered by the judge in *12 Angry Men*. For example, as of 2020, the New York State Unified Court System asks judges to instruct the jury with these words:

> A reasonable doubt is an honest doubt of the defendant's guilt for which a reason exists based upon the nature and quality of the evidence. It is an actual doubt, not an imaginary doubt. It is a doubt that a reasonable person, acting in a matter of this importance, would be likely to entertain because of the evidence that was presented or because of the lack of convincing evidence. Proof of guilt beyond a reasonable doubt is proof that leaves you so firmly convinced of the defendant's guilt that you have no reasonable doubt of the existence of any element of the crime or of the defendant's identity as the person who committed the crime.[19]

Thankfully, Reginald Rose did not attempt to define the term, which would have taken considerable time without advancing the drama, nor did he have the jurors spend much time trying to apply the standard to various points of evidence. The phrase was sufficiently understood without needing to be defined in more detail.

The more important question is: Did the jurors in *12 Angry Men* do a good job of applying the doctrine of reasonable doubt as it is commonly understood? To that question, the answer is yes. The jurors applied their critical faculties to many points of evidence and raised enough doubts about the evidence to warrant acquittal. By this standard, the eventual verdict of not guilty is just.[20]

ASIDE FROM TRIAL BY JURY, presumption of innocence, and the doctrine of reasonable doubt, *12 Angry Men* can also help illustrate rules about the admissibility of evidence, capital punishment, and more. As Jack Marshall of the American Century Theater discovered, it can even be used to discuss important points of Talmudic law.

In 1995, as Marshall was preparing to stage *12 Angry Men*, a professor at Georgetown Law School told him that Rose's script illuminates two tenets of Talmudic law. One holds that if the first vote among Sanhedrin judges—the elders who sat in tribunals and passed judgment in ancient Israel—was unanimous for a guilty verdict, the defendant should be set free. At first glance counterintuitive and perhaps even nonsensical, this tenet has been explained as reflecting a concern about the possibility of judicial collusion. Since the function of the Sanhedrin was to search for evidence of innocence as well as of guilt, a first vote that was unanimous for guilt would suggest that something was amiss, and should therefore result in acquittal.[21] Since the judges would be aware of this rule, they would be sure to deliberate fully before reaching the most serious of verdicts, guilt in a capital case. Juror 8's vote of not guilty, which ensured a full debate rather than a quick verdict, is thus entirely consistent with Talmudic law—indeed, when all others vote guilty, it becomes a duty to cast a vote for not guilty no matter what one's personal opinion might be. A second tenet is the rule of *halanat hadin*, which holds that a guilty verdict cannot be reached in a single day, again to avoid a rush to judgment. When Juror 7 complains about lengthy deliberations ("You know, we could be here all night"), Juror 9 replies, "It's only one night. A boy may die." This comment, too, is in keeping with Talmudic law, ensuring that jurors spend more than one day in deliberation before convicting a defendant in a capital case.

Marshall recalled that when these observations were relayed to Reginald Rose, the author's reaction—"Really?"—was one of complete surprise. Although of Jewish heritage, Rose had not been educated in the Jewish tradition; and although his father was a lawyer, they had not had a close relationship. Yet somehow, perhaps because he had absorbed the fundamental values of his culture, two tenets of Talmudic law were reflected in Rose's best-known work.

YET FOR ALL ITS LESSONS ABOUT criminal law and for all its references to the Constitution, *12 Angry Men* is adored by legal professionals for something else. Rose's great insight was to look beyond the legal experts—the judges in black robes and the eloquent lawyers—and to focus on the jury. As law professor Michael Asimow notes: "*12 Angry Men* is considered the iconic jury film, and it has done more than any movie, television show, or other cultural work to enshrine the jury as the central and indispensable element of the American judicial system."[22]

That said, Rose's depiction of a jury's deliberations is far from realistic. It would be exceedingly unlikely for jurors in a murder case to reach a verdict in just over an hour, and almost unheard of for an initial vote of eleven to one for conviction to turn into a unanimous vote for acquittal.

("How often does one holdout juror turn the other eleven around?," asks Asimow. "Well, almost never, according to studies of the jury system."[23])

Even more troubling, Rose's jurors engage in several instances of improper conduct. Jurors in criminal cases are instructed to consider the evidence admitted in court, but must not conduct their own analyses, as they did when simulating the old man's walk to his apartment door. They are admonished not to visit the scene of the crime, which Juror 8 did when he walked through the defendant's neighborhood. They certainly must not bring new evidence into court, as Juror 8 did with the switchblade knife. As one scholar put it: "We may admire *12 Angry Men* as a movie. It is terrific theater. But we should not praise the jury in the film."[24]

The enduring appeal of *12 Angry Men* comes from a deeper truth: that in a democracy, a system of justice is only as good as its citizens. *Time* magazine grasped this notion in its 1957 review: "the onlooker learns better than he could from any law-school course that the law is no better than the people who enforce it, and that the people who enforce it are all too human."[25] The judge in the movie, played by Rudy Bond, is bored and disinterested; in the play, the judge is not seen at all. Nor is there a valiant or principled lawyer, an Atticus Finch or a Clarence Darrow, to provide insight or moral guidance; to the contrary, we learn that the defendant's lawyer overlooked important points and failed to mount an effective defense. If justice is to prevail in *12 Angry Men*, it is not because of the legal professionals, but in spite of them.

Rather, we are shown ordinary citizens who are entrusted with the most important of tasks—to pass judgment on a fellow citizen—and who, despite disagreements and conflict, carry out that task in a competent manner. Their solemn duty is described by Juror 11: "to come down to this place to decide on the guilt or innocence of a man we have never heard of before. We have nothing to gain or lose by our verdict. This is one of the reasons why we are strong." Although they have no legal training, and are given no guidance on how to conduct their deliberations, they are expected to take their responsibility seriously, to wrestle with conflicting evidence, to overcome personal biases, to fight indifference and apathy, and to do their duty no matter how unpleasant or difficult. According to Nancy Gertner, district court judge of the District of Massachusetts, the brilliance of the drama rests on its portrayal of "twelve lay people, struggling with questions of guilt or innocence, bias and fairness, or racism and rationality."[26] It speaks to our wish that everyday people, through their honest efforts, can make the system work. As the movie ends, Juror 8 is shown on the courthouse steps, walking among the immense pillars. "It is a most fitting image," one writer noted, "for the 'pillars' our justice system really relies upon are not stone, but the human pillars of a civilized society."[27]

WITH ITS STIRRING BELIEF that the efforts of ordinary people can bring about a just outcome, *12 Angry Men* has inspired countless young people.

Alex Kozinski was a fourteen-year-old immigrant from Romania, living in Baltimore and trying to learn about his new country by watching television. One evening, flipping channels, he chanced upon an image that captured his attention: "The scene was a small room filled with a bunch of guys sitting around a conference table arguing about the fate of someone who wasn't there to stand up for himself. I almost changed channels when the vote was eleven to one to convict, but there was something in the quiet determination of the lone dissenter that kept me from turning the knob."

Enthralled, he watched the rest of the movie and was profoundly moved:

> My whole adolescent conception of certainty, of knowledge itself, was shaken. The case against the defendant sounded so airtight; the reasons offered by the eleven sounded so irrefutable. I couldn't imagine how (or why) anyone could reach a different conclusion. Then, as one reason after another started to come apart, as inconsistencies crept into the picture, as jurors began changing their votes, I came to understand that truth does not spring into the courtroom full-blown, like Athena from the head of Zeus. Rather, facts have to be examined carefully and skeptically, moved around and twisted like pieces of a puzzle, before they will yield a complete picture.[28]

That boy went on to pursue a legal career, and in 1985, Kozinski was appointed to the United States Court of Appeals for the Ninth Circuit, where he served with distinction for more than thirty years.

Another young person inspired by the movie now sits on the US Supreme Court. In 2010, Fordham University Law School invited Justice Sonia Sotomayor to choose a movie for a public screening and discussion. She picked *12 Angry Men*, explaining: "I saw this movie at the very end of high school or the very beginning of college. I had been thinking about becoming a lawyer, but I really never thought about juries until I saw this movie." The moment that made the greatest impression came from Juror 11, the immigrant watchmaker: "That scene when he talked about the greatness of democracy being the jury system, he sold me. He sold me that I was on the right path, that my choice of profession was a noble one. I was inspired by the sense that decision makers like this jury would take their work so seriously. So it was a very important film in terms of developing me both as a lawyer and subsequently as a judge."[29]

Justice Sotomayor recognized that the movie was far from realistic. As a prosecutor, she had cautioned prospective jurors not to be misled by the movie, which she knew that many of them had seen. Yet *12 Angry Men* conveyed an important truth: "We expect that same attention to detail and that same passion about doing what's right."[30]

FOR EVERY STORY OF A distinguished jurist, an Alex Kozinski or a Sonia Sotomayor, there have been thousands of others who were attracted to the legal profession by the depiction of people finding a way to set aside differences and work together in the cause of justice.[31] Many more have watched the movie in high school civics classes or in law school.[32] John Fiedler, who played Juror 2, remarked late in life that he was frequently recognized by lawyers, adding that many told him they had seen the film in law school.[33]

One of the movie's many admirers is Professor Nancy Marder of the Chicago-Kent College of Law, who shows it in her course "Juries, Judges and Trials." "I never tire of watching it," she said. "This movie has withstood the test of time, not only because of the great ensemble cast, but also because it portrays the jury as a group of twelve ordinary men who learn in the course of their deliberations what it means to be a jury."[34]

In 2007, to commemorate the fiftieth anniversary of the movie's release, Professor Marder organized an academic panel at the Association of American Law Schools annual meeting in Washington, DC, and at the Law and Society Association annual meeting held in Berlin. The response was so positive that she organized a symposium on *12 Angry Men* for the *Chicago-Kent Law Review*. Professor Marder found an extraordinary level of interest: "Just about everyone I invited responded immediately and said that they would love to participate. Some people invited additional people to write with them. Other people who heard about the project asked if they could be part of it."[35] The issue eventually included eighteen articles by twenty-three authors, in fields from jurisprudence to political science to religion, and showed the extent to which *12 Angry Men* is "a favorite of legal academics, judges, lawyers, and those who study law and popular culture."[36]

One of the contributors was Chief Judge Judith S. Kaye, whose article, "Why Every Chief Judge Should See *12 Angry Men*," revisited some of the themes that had prompted her to undertake jury reforms in the 1990s. The jury of all white men, she wrote, underscored the need for broad participation on juries, both in gender and ethnicity: "Today, we know that diversity matters in so many things, including juries. Imagine if the rich diversity of life experience of the twelve angry white men had been enlarged by the life experience of women and minorities!"[37] The uncomfortable conditions that the jurors in *12 Angry Men* endured—a hot and stuffy room, cramped seating, and a token payment of three dollars a day—could very likely have contributed to an ill-considered verdict. Surely citizens who perform such a crucial role in our society are deserving of more appropriate surroundings.

But above all, Judge Kaye articulated what is most compelling about Reginald Rose's drama: "Many times over the past fifty years—as a college student, a law student, a lawyer, and a judge—I have seen, and loved, the American classic *12 Angry Men*. . . . I know no more powerful depiction of the genius of the American jury system than *12 Angry Men*, starting with its stark simplicity, dramatically escalating story and outstanding cast, especially Juror #8, my hero Henry Fonda." Her article concluded with words that speak for legal professionals everywhere: "So much has changed, but the essence of the film has not. I have little doubt that even at its centennial, *12 Angry Men* will continue to excite audiences because, whatever the latest challenges of a new world for Chief Judges and others, the quest for justice is timeless."[38]

19

░░░

A Masterclass in Human Behavior

BY THE EARLY 1960S, Henry Fonda was in his late fifties and increasingly cast in the role of an authority figure. In 1962, he played a nominee for secretary of state in Otto Preminger's *Advise & Consent*, and Brigadier General Theodore Roosevelt Jr. in the D-Day epic, *The Longest Day*. Fonda's tall frame and dignified bearing also made him a natural for the Oval Office. In 1964, he played a presidential candidate in Gore Vidal's *The Best Man* and the president of the United States in *Fail Safe*, Sidney Lumet's tense drama about nuclear confrontation.

In late 1965, Fonda returned to Broadway to star in *Generation* at the Morosco Theater. ("I played a confused father," he later quipped. "I was a living authority on the subject."[1]) One evening, at a party, he met Dr. Guy Robbins, a prominent surgeon at Memorial Sloan Kettering Cancer Center, who told him that *12 Angry Men* was widely used in management training classes. Intrigued, Fonda said he'd like to know more.

Robbins contacted Dr. Clovis R. Shepherd, Program Director at the National Training Laboratories in Washington, DC, who wrote to Fonda: "*12 Angry Men* is almost a classic in the management and human relations training field. We utilize it a great deal and it always proves to be highly entertaining and very evocative of the kinds of discussions and interaction which leads participants to learn a great deal about the psychology of interpersonal relations."[2] The low-budget movie that Fonda had produced several years earlier had somehow developed a strong following among academics and clinicians.

THE STORY OF *12 ANGRY MEN*'S use in the field of human relations begins with Kurt Lewin, a prominent social psychologist and director of MIT's Research Center for Group Dynamics. In 1946, Lewin founded the National Training Laboratory (NTL), aimed at improving self-awareness and interpersonal effectiveness. After Lewin's death, his colleagues carried on his work, and NTL soon became highly regarded for its research about human behavior, as well as for seminars at its training center in Bethel, Maine.

Among the topics of interest at NTL was group decision making, and whether groups make better decisions than individuals. Around 1960, three psychologists—Robert Blake, Jane Mouton, and Ernest J. Hall— devised an experiment using *12 Angry Men*. Subjects watched the first third of the movie, until the moment when Juror 8 calls for a secret ballot. Told that the rest of the jurors would eventually vote not guilty, they were asked to predict the order in which the eleven would change their votes, marking their answers on a seating chart. Next, the subjects were placed in small groups of six to eight, and asked to arrive at a group consensus. Researchers could compare individual and group predictions to determine which was more accurate.

The results, published in the *Journal of Social Psychology* in 1963, found that groups tended to do significantly better than the average of individuals.[3] The authors couldn't say *why* most groups did better—they hadn't monitored what went on in the group discussions—but surmised it was "a function of social interaction."[4] Something in the way people shared information and exchanged ideas made groups more effective than the average of their parts. From there, one of the psychologists, Ernest J. Hall, working with Martha Williams, compared two kinds of groups: established groups, made up of people who had already worked together, and ad hoc groups, newly composed for the experiment. Employing what they called "the *12 Angry Men* group exercise," Hall and Williams found that established groups generally did better than ad hoc groups, and reasoned that familiarity among members let them deal more constructively with conflict.[5]

By the mid-1960s, these experiments were frequently replicated at NTL seminars. As Clovis Shepherd summarized in his letter to Fonda: "The film is unique in that the script is faithful to psychological theory and research, the acting is superb, and the change of vote from guilty to not guilty takes place person by person, thus providing a training exercise with a criterion against which to assess one's ability to predict human behavior. I hope this gives you some inkling of the usefulness the film has been to use as an educational device."[6]

Dr. Shepherd's enthusiasm notwithstanding, using *12 Angry Men* to study group decisions had an obvious flaw: it could not really "assess one's ability to predict human behavior," but at best could assess the ability to match the voting sequence that Reginald Rose had devised in what was, after all, a work of fiction. To remedy this problem, Hall created a new exercise called *Desert Survival*, where subjects were put in the role of passengers who had survived an airplane crash in the desert. Finding in the wreckage fifteen items—a flashlight, a map, matches, salt tablets, a tarp, a pistol, and more—their task was to rank the items based on their importance for survival. For this exercise, there was a "correct" answer that reflected the expert judgment of people trained in survival skills. As before, groups usually did somewhat better than the average of individuals. Today, more than fifty years later, *Desert Survival* remains in use and continues to spark useful discussions about how and why groups can perform effectively.

ALTHOUGH *12 ANGRY MEN* was superseded as a way to teach group decision making, it didn't disappear from NTL. Thanks to its exposure at Bethel, Maine, where during the 1960s it was often shown on Wednesday night "free evenings,"[7] many psychologists and management theorists came to see it as a rich source of material. The order in which jurors changed their votes was not the only topic worth discussing. On closer inspection, Reginald Rose's script was studded with examples of group dynamics and interpersonal behavior that could impart useful lessons.

Many participants at NTL seminars were college professors, who began to show the movie in their courses. By the mid-1960s, *12 Angry Men* was used in Harvard Business School's MBA program, one of the top programs in the world. A required first-year course, *Human Behavior in Organizations*, relied mostly on written case studies but also showed five movies over the semester. *12 Angry Men* was used to explore group dynamics, power, and influence.[8]

In time, *12 Angry Men* became part of the curriculum at many business schools. By 1976, it was used in *Individual and Group Behavior*, a graduate course at the Yale School of Management led by professors Victor Vroom and Clayton Alderfer.[9] In fall 1978, when I was a first-year MBA student at UCLA, *12 Angry Men* was used in an introductory management course taught by Professor Eric G. Flamholtz. A projector was wheeled into class, the lights were dimmed, and for the next ninety minutes we watched the entire movie, afterwards discussing what we had seen. To this day, I vividly remember lessons about formal and informal power, about shifts in group participation, and about tactics used by Juror 8 to influence other jurors.

Students went on to become teachers, and in time *12 Angry Men* became a staple in business schools around the world. For many years, my colleagues and I at the International Institute for Management Development (IMD), a business school in Lausanne, Switzerland, have used it in programs with executives from many countries. Now more than sixty years since it was released, the movie has lost none of its ability to illustrate human behavior; its lessons are as powerful today as when Sidney Lumet directed his actors on the Fox Movietone Studios sound stage.

12 ANGRY MEN HAS PROVEN to be an excellent way to observe the dynamics of behavior in small groups, defined as large enough to have subgroups and coalitions, but small enough so that all members can interact directly.[10] A jury is a unique setting to examine group behavior, and not just because of its size, twelve members who can sit around a table. In a very real sense, a jury is a "pure" group. Its members have been assembled at random, with no prior relationships or knowledge of one another. No one is a long-standing member or a newcomer. They are all equal; no one is in a higher or lower position. With these elements held constant, the behavior we observe is more likely to arise purely from the dynamics among group members.

Yet the jury in *12 Angry Men* also finds itself in an unusually difficult situation. The jurors have been given only the most general instructions, told to deliberate until they reach a unanimous verdict, with no time limit, no rules to follow, and no processes to observe. Moreover, their decision has enormous consequences, the judge stating that a guilty verdict will result in a mandatory death sentence. To this, Rose added physical discomfort. The jury room is small and cramped, the weather is oppressive—"This is the hottest day of the year" says Juror 7—and the fan doesn't work. The single door is locked with a guard stationed outside. The jurors have been placed in an extremely stressful setting from which they cannot escape.

Given these circumstances, Rose's decision to compose a jury of white men is especially important. Many of the twelve would have looked around the room, and, seeing other white men, assumed that they had much in common and should be able to reach a verdict without difficulty. As they deliberate, however, fault lines begin to appear—by age, by education, by national origin, by socioeconomic level, by values, and by temperament. Rose's outline made this point clearly: as the drama progresses, "there are tensions developing, tensions which may well explode later on."[11] These tensions are all the more powerful when they emerge in a group that had seemed, at the outset, to be composed of similar people.

Having devised a setting that crackles with pressure, Rose went on to write a script that, as Clovis Shepherd said, was faithful to psychological theory. The many concepts from social psychology are never stated explicitly—there is no equivalent to the judge's reference to reasonable doubt, nor is there any amendment of the Constitution to cite—but are revealed through the behavior of the characters. As a skillful dramatist, Rose does not tell us but shows us. The script is so rich with concepts from social psychology that we could imagine it had been written for that purpose—and indeed, on at least one occasion in the 1980s, a graduate course at Yale used *12 Angry Men* as its final exam, with students asked to watch the movie and identify as many concepts as they could spot.

The list is a long one. Very early, there are instances of avoidance behavior, as several jurors seek to escape a difficult situation by finishing quickly, or by telling stories, or by playing games—anything but focusing on the task at hand. We observe how patterns of participation shift, the conversation at first dominated by jurors who appear to be the most confident and self-assured (Jurors 3, 4, 7, and 10), while little is said by those who are less confident or feel marginal (Jurors 2, 5, 9, and 11); as the deliberations progress, the marginal jurors gain in confidence and begin to take a more active role, while others recede.

The jurors exhibit instances of affiliation and repulsion, seeking either to bond with an admirable character (when Jurors 11 and 2 join sides with Juror 8), or to reject an unpleasant person (when Jurors 5 and 6 recoil from Jurors 3 and 10). We observe displacement, when Juror 3 takes his frustration out on the meekest member, Juror 2. Finally, the movie's climax is an illustration of transference, as Juror 3 understands that anger toward his estranged son has been transferred onto the defendant, with potentially tragic consequences.

OF ALL THE PSYCHOLOGICAL CONCEPTS in *12 Angry Men*, the most important one is conformity, the pressure felt by individuals to comply with a majority. Although the word is never uttered, it is a thread that runs through the entire drama.

Rose's concern with conformity was very much in keeping with the times. In the years after World War II, revelations about genocide, brought to light during war crime trials, raised many troubling questions. Why do people follow orders? Under what conditions do they go along, and when are they able to resist group pressure? Such questions were relevant not only to Nazi Germany in the 1940s but also to the United States in the 1950s, as ordinary men and women came under pressure to name alleged Communist sympathizers, or to sign loyalty oaths, a theme Rose had explored in *The Challenge*.

In 1951, Solomon Asch, a psychologist at Swarthmore College, conducted a landmark series of experiments to study how individuals respond to group pressure.[12] In his most famous experiment, Asch placed subjects in a setting where their judgments would be in conflict with the expressed views of other people. He found that even for a relatively easy task, such as describing the lengths of lines clearly visible from a few feet away, many subjects, faced with a strong consensus of contrary opinion, did not report what their eyes told them to be true. Interviewed afterward, subjects said they had gone along with the majority out of fear of being ridiculed. They had preferred to give an incorrect answer than to be singled out for criticism.

In subsequent experiments, Asch modified a few variables. He found that when subjects did not have to state their judgments aloud, but could simply write down their answers, the rate of conformity declined. He also found that when one member of the group had *already* resisted majority pressure, the likelihood that another person would also refuse to conform went up significantly. It was much easier to be the second person to buck the majority than to be the first.

Today, Asch's research is usually cited as evidence that people often conform to group pressure.[13] Indeed, a large majority of subjects in his experiments yielded to group opinion at least some of the time, and many did so several times. Often overlooked, however, is that most subjects gave correct answers most of the time, and many subjects conformed only rarely or not at all.[14] Asch himself took a balanced view, writing in a 1955 *Scientific American* article that despite a strong tendency to conform to group opinion, "the capacities for independence are not to be underestimated."[15]

There is no evidence that Reginald Rose was aware of Asch's research, which by 1954 had been reported in scientific journals but not yet widely publicized beyond the academic world. Even so, Rose was an astute observer of human behavior, and it is uncanny how closely the jurors in his script hew to the findings of Asch's research. The first instance of pressure for conformity is evident early on, when Juror 1, the foreman, asks for all those voting guilty to raise their hands. Rose's script for *Studio One* said: "Seven or eight hands go up immediately. Several others go up more slowly. Everyone looks around the table. There are two hands not raised, No. 9's and No. 8's. No. 9's hand goes up slowly now as the foreman counts."[16] As directed by Sidney Lumet in the movie, the foreman is immediately joined by five others: Jurors 3, 4, 7, 10, and 12. An instant later, Juror 2, who has been watching the others, raises his hand, and is joined a half-beat later by Jurors 5 and 6. A moment later Juror 11 lifts his arm, and finally Juror 9's hand goes up, slowly and hesitantly.[17] The entire process takes barely five seconds. Although eleven hands are raised when the voting is complete, several jurors had waited to see what others did before making their vote.

Several minutes later, when Juror 8 makes his offer to abide by a second vote, he asks that jurors vote by secret ballot. He sensed, consistent with Asch's research, that it would be more likely for another juror to join him if it were not necessary to raise a hand in public. The secret ballot brings about the first conversion, Juror 9, which makes it easier for Juror 5 and Juror 11 to follow. As a coalition for not guilty emerges, the pressure to vote guilty has effectively vanished. As momentum continues to shift and a majority now favors acquittal, Juror 8 uses a public vote to put pressure on the remaining holdouts. Those voting guilty no longer feel the safety of the majority; they must now find reasons to justify their positions. That vote reveals that Jurors 1, 7, and 12 have converted, leaving only three votes for guilty.

After Juror 10 unleashes his racist diatribe and is shunned by the others, and after Juror 4 changes his vote based on doubts about the eyewitness, pressure to conform eventually swings to the other extreme, with Juror 3 now the only vote for conviction. Members of the majority are not shy about using their new-found power. Juror 9 remarks aloud: "Eleven to one." With the rain pelting violently against the windows, Juror 8 looks directly at Juror 3: "You're alone." At the outset, Juror 8 held out courageously against a majority of eleven; now Juror 8 uses the power of conformity to put pressure on the final holdout.

AS A LESSON IN INTERPERSONAL behavior, the actions of Juror 8 are highly instructive. In the original outline, and in Rose's first full script for *Studio One*, Juror 8 had been the person who challenged almost all the key points of evidence. Over time, Rose scaled back Juror 8's role, transforming him into a skilled facilitator who shapes the behavior of the group without needing to dominate the proceedings. He works indirectly as well as directly, giving confidence to others, particularly those who feel marginalized, and enabling them to contribute, knowing that the group will perform better when all can put forward their ideas. Juror 8 plays this role skillfully, attuned to all members of the group, knowing when to engage one person, draw out another, and (on one occasion) provoke still another.

Remarkably, Juror 8 achieves this turnaround without the benefit of any formal power. Juror 1, the foreman, as *primus inter pares*, has a chance to establish his authority, but rather than consolidate his power he squanders it at the outset, telling the others: "You fellows can handle this any way you want to. I mean, I'm not going to make any rules." With Juror 1 having fumbled away any chance to exercise power, others try to step into the vacuum. The person who does so most effectively, of course, is Juror 8.

In the 1970s, researchers began to study the phenomenon of "minority influence," in which members of a minority can get the majority to reconsider their views.[18] Although the ideas had not been formalized when Reginald Rose crafted 12 *Angry Men*, it is remarkable to see how many points he anticipated. Early on, Juror 8 is effective at setting the terms of the discussion. He doesn't attempt to prove the defendant is innocent but merely says that there is reason to find him not guilty. He does not feel the need to explain with certainty what happened, often saying: "It's *possible*." Juror 8 also establishes his informal power by demonstrating expertise. By citing the Constitution and insisting that the burden of proof is on the prosecution, Juror 8 shows himself to be credible and authoritative.

Juror 8 is also adept at using different media, relying on more than just words to make his points. Producing a knife identical to the murder weapon is not only a moment of high drama, but signals that he is one step ahead of the rest. (The other jurors must wonder: If Juror 8 had the knife in his pocket all along but only revealed it now, what other surprises might he have? What else does he know that we do not?) Recreating the walk by the old man who lived downstairs, marking off the approximate distance and timing the seconds it would take for a crippled man to get to his door, is effective and vivid. Both of these scenes have a dramatic purpose, injecting movement into what could otherwise be a static play, but are also effective as ways to challenge majority thinking. Finally, Juror 8 is a master at tailoring his approach to different jurors. He is able to size up the different men and adapt his behavior, sensing who needs support and encouragement (Jurors 2 and 9), who should be challenged on rational grounds (Juror 4), and who must be challenged on emotional grounds (Juror 3).

Equally striking is what Juror 8 does *not* do. He does not try to explain his vote. After the first vote, when he raises the only hand for acquittal,

Juror 8 does not feel the need to list his reasons or justify himself. He does not fall into the trap of feeling he must persuade others, but reminds them that *they* must persuade *him*. He is not afraid to say: "I don't know." (Indeed, even when Henry Fonda says he does not know, his tone and manner suggest that he may know a great deal.)

Juror 8 is also careful not to overstate his case, never making bold claims that he later must withdraw. He does not insist on having the final word, and has the good sense not to keep arguing when doing so would only weaken his case. On two occasions, Juror 4 makes a good point: when he says that the defendant may have reached a breaking point after receiving one slap too many, and when he says that for someone else to have killed the father with a similar knife was possible but highly improbable. In each instance, Juror 8 is wise not to reply. Finally, he does not celebrate or gloat as votes change, taking care not to alienate those whom he still needs to persuade.

Scott Ellis, who directed the 2004 Broadway play, commented on the challenge of playing Juror 8: "You have to be active without being too active. And you have to be interesting, saying, 'All I want to do is discuss.' It takes a really good actor to make that interesting."[19] It is a role of subtlety and nuance, being active but not domineering, guiding the group while creating space for others, caring deeply but not allowing emotions to get the better of him. As written by Reginald Rose and played by Henry Fonda, Juror 8 offers a masterclass on interpersonal behavior.

12 ANGRY MEN IS OFTEN SAID to be the story of ordinary citizens, summoned to serve on a jury, who use their powers of reasoning to reach a just verdict. That was the view of the *New York Times* when it described how Juror 8's "logical reasoning implants facts and doubts into the minds of his colleagues so that they finally change their vote to not guilty." As we've seen, that's a standard interpretation among members of the legal community.[20]

An alternate view conceives of the drama less in terms of legal issues and more about group dynamics and interpersonal behavior. In fact, on closer inspection, there is only one juror who changes his vote solely on the basis of evidence: Juror 4, who realizes that the eyewitness could not have been wearing glasses at the moment of the murder. The others shift their votes for a variety of reasons, some of which, as Sidney Lumet once remarked, are "brought about by personal feelings that may or may not have anything to do with the case."[21]

The first to change his vote is Juror 9, who wished to support Juror 8, a man whom he admires for his courage and whose motives he respects. Next comes Juror 5, who had been offended by Juror 10's contempt for people who grew up in slums, and was wrongly accused by Juror 3 of changing his vote; he votes not guilty to reject these repugnant men. Juror 11 is the third to shift, partly based on doubts that the defendant would have returned to the apartment if he had killed his father, but also for personal reasons; after changing his vote, he glances toward Juror 8 with a smile that says: *We're on the same side now*. Juror 2 switches in large part to reject those who bullied and demeaned him, and to affiliate with Juror 8, who has been supportive and kind. Juror 6, the house painter, changes in part based on the accumulation of doubts and also to join with the growing number of decent people.

By now, two subgroups are taking shape: a growing coalition voting not guilty, depicted as thoughtful and righteous, and a small set of hardliners voting guilty, some of them downright nasty. Three others—Jurors 1, 7, and 12—constitute a third subgroup, men who sided with the majority at the start but are not as adamant in their position and susceptible to the shifting dynamics. These three, effectively swing voters, are the next to shift, doing so as much to join the emerging majority as because of any single piece of evidence. Their shift, revealed when Juror 8 calls for a public vote, transforms the six-to-six deadlock to a nine-to-three vote for acquittal, and places mounting pressure to conform on the last holdouts. Of the final trio, Juror 10 reveals himself to have been motivated by bigotry all along; and after Juror 4 shifts his vote for reasons of logic, Juror 3 crumbles when he comes to understand that his vote has been based on anger toward his son.

Reviewing these votes allows us to ask: Is *12 Angry Men* the story of a jury grappling with points of evidence that happens to exhibit some characteristics of group behavior? Or is *12 Angry Men* the story of human behavior in a group that just happens to be a jury? If we look at the decision of each juror, and consider the shifting forces for conformity, support for the latter view is at least as strong as support for the former.

Yet there is really no reason why we must accept one and dismiss the other, to favor either the legal or the behavioral view, any more than we need to prefer either screen or stage as a dramatic medium. To paraphrase Reginald Rose's letter to the *Daily Mail*, pitting one field against another seems arbitrary and pointless.

The greater truth is that both views are entirely valid, which explains why *12 Angry Men* has gained such devoted followings in two very different fields.

20

New Versions, New Meanings

A REVERED MOVIE, ADMIRED BY critics and beloved by the public. A classic stage play, popular with amateurs and hailed by professionals. An inspiration for countless lawyers and judges. A powerful way to teach group dynamics and interpersonal behavior.

Several strands, each one reinforcing the others. Seeing the movie inspires an amateur performance, which leads to a professional staging. A production of the play is accompanied by a panel discussion among legal experts, leading to its use in a classroom. Watching the movie in class leads to attending a performance of the play. After six decades, the whole is greater than any of its component parts.

THE JOURNEY OF *12 ANGRY MEN* began with a moment of insight, Reginald Rose's vision of "one man holding out against the others and beginning to convince them."[1] A simple idea, perhaps, but one that has become very well known, the figure of Henry Fonda raising his hand instantly recognizable.

When an image becomes so familiar, one outcome is parody, not to be confused with mockery or ridicule, but exaggeration for comedic effect. Already in 1962, *The Dick Van Dyke Show*, a game-changing sitcom, had an episode titled "One Angry Man," in which Van Dyke's character is called for jury service. Smitten with the attractive defendant, Rob is the only vote for not guilty. As deliberations drag on into the night, one juror grouses:

"Hey, we're not making a movie here, Mr. Henry Fonda."[2] The jury is unable to reach a verdict, but the defendant is later shown to be innocent, vindicating Rob, with laughs all around.

As *12 Angry Men* grew in renown, the parodies continued. In 1970, the first season of *The Odd Couple*, starring Jack Klugman and Tony Randall, had an episode called "The Jury Story," with a flashback to Oscar and Felix meeting while on a jury, their basic characters revealed during deliberations.[3] A year later, the most popular comedy of its time, *All in the Family*, had an episode titled "Edith Has Jury Duty," with Edith Bunker, played by Jean Stapleton, as the lone holdout for not guilty. Some of the dialogue echoes Rose's screenplay: when one man, based on Juror 10, says that three witnesses couldn't be mistaken and moments later says that "all those people are born liars," Edith counters with Juror 8's line: "Well, if they was all born liars, how can you believe the neighbors?" Spoken by Henry Fonda the line had an edge; coming from Edith Bunker, not known for her sharp mind but blessed with common sense, it's clever and earns a laugh. The trial ends when another man confesses to the crime, freeing the defendant and making a hero of Edith.[4]

And so on and so on, with parodies on *Happy Days*, *Matlock*, *Second City TV*, *The Simpsons*, *Malcolm in the Middle*, *Family Guy*, and *Monk*. There were a few serious treatments, too, such as a 2000 episode of *7th Heaven*, "Twelve Angry People," with the Reverend Eric Camden the only juror voting guilty and needing to persuade the others to convict. The most elaborate tribute was surely a 2015 episode on Comedy Central's "Inside Amy Schumer," a parody faithful to the movie in many respects, with a carefully recreated set and jurors dressed as characters in the movie, shot in stark black and white, and several verbatim passages of dialogue, as twelve male jurors debate whether Schumer is "hot enough to be on TV." Called the best sketch of the year by *TV Guide*, it was a humorous look at a serious topic, how some men talk about female bodies, and how women are often depicted on television. Said Amy Schumer: "I'm more proud of it than anything I've ever done."[5] A brilliant mash-up of past and present, it was only the latest in a long line of parodies, taking a distinctive work and bending it for comedic purposes.

12 Angry Men has also shown itself capable of new interpretations, a classic drama used to address current issues.

In the aftermath of the 1995 O. J. Simpson murder trial, which saw the jury vote for acquittal despite seemingly overwhelming evidence of guilt, William Friedkin, director of *The French Connection* (1971) and *The*

Exorcist (1973), used Rose's drama to explore the concept of reasonable doubt. His aim was to show how "a jury that lets a guilty man go can still be performing its duty properly, by adhering closely to the rules of evidence, no matter how emotionally difficult that may prove."[6]

The result was a 1997 movie for television, broadcast on Showtime, with an all-male jury of mixed ethnic groups: seven white men, four Black men, and one Hispanic man. (The judge was female, played by Mary McDonnell.) Friedkin assembled an eminent cast, with Jack Lemmon as Juror 8 and George C. Scott as Juror 3, plus Ossie Davis as Juror 2 and Hume Cronyn as Juror 9. The Black men played Jurors 1, 2, 5, and, most unusually, Juror 10, with Mykelti Williamson as a member of the Nation of Islam, exhibiting prejudice against a Hispanic defendant. It was, said one reviewer, an odd choice: "When the Williamson character yells about him, 'They're different from us,' what can he possibly mean by 'us' in this diverse group that includes blacks and whites of all social classes?"[7] (There were other weaknesses in Friedkin's remake. Jack Lemmon, at seventy-one, was not a convincing choice for Juror 8. Early on, when Juror 3 asks pointedly: "You really think he's innocent?," Juror 8 replies, "I don't know." From Robert Cummings, the phrase was spoken in a matter-of-fact tone; from Henry Fonda, it hinted that he knew more than he was willing to say; from Jack Lemmon, it sounded like a confused comment from a befuddled old man.)

Some years later, another event inspired a very different interpretation. In 2013, George Zimmerman, a neighborhood watch volunteer in Sanford, Florida, was acquitted in the death of Trayvon Martin, an unarmed seventeen-year-old Black high school student, shot while walking in a residential area while holding a soft drink and a bag of candy. The verdict sparked outrage, prompting President Barack Obama to speak in moving terms: "When Trayvon Martin was first shot I said that this could have been my son. Another way of saying that is Trayvon Martin could have been me 35 years ago."[8] To many, the death of Trayvon Martin and acquittal of his killer was one more instance of racial injustice.

With a desire to contribute to the national conversation, Sheldon Epps, artistic director of the Pasadena Playhouse, decided to stage a production of *Twelve Angry Men*.[9] Epps knew the 1957 movie and had seen the 2004 Roundabout production on Broadway, which had reminded him how well the play works on stage.[10] Rather than the standard all-white jury, or Friedkin's mixed jury that downplayed the aspect of race, Epps addressed it head on. "Racial issues have always been at the heart of the material," he said. "When you go back to the original production, it was a bunch of white men deciding the fate of someone of color."[11]

In Epps's casting, not only would Juror 8 be Black but so would be the next five men to vote not guilty—Jurors 9, 5, 11, 2, and 6. Moreover, some of the Black jurors would be educated and well-off, and resented by less affluent white jurors. The casting worked on several levels. As a Black man, the life experience of Juror 9 became even more powerful. Said Epps: "When that older Black man discusses being nobody, being ignored, it has a richer subtext. You know what that man has been through in a deeply resonant way."[12] Juror 11 was now an immigrant from an African country without strong democratic institutions, who could speak with great conviction about the right to participate in a democracy and the obligation to search for the truth.

As Epps had intended, the vote that reveals a deadlock at six to six became "a seismic moment in the play."[13] Yet after that stark division becomes clear, the jurors still have to find a way to break the impasse and reach agreement. The director said: "Almost everyone in the room is eventually doing the right thing, working through the issues, and working past skin color and listening to [one another] and getting out of their own way to let justice prevail."[14]

In the subsequent years, after more Black men and women died at the hands of law enforcement officers, Epps was asked to reprise his play at Ford's Theater in Washington, DC. He agreed, and the play enjoyed a run in early 2019, with 12 Angry Men again helping to raise awareness about issues of race and justice.[15] An enduring lesson of the play, said Sheldon Epps, is that in order to overcome differences, we must first acknowledge that they exist: "Then we can move forward, just as the characters do in the play."[16]

Although much attention was paid to his novel approach to casting, Epps took pains to emphasize the quality of the underlying material: "It's a damn good play, well structured, a roller coaster ride for an audience." He said: "12 Angry Men ranks among the classic American plays, along with Tennessee Williams's A Streetcar Named Desire and August Wilson's Fences. It holds up in the same way. The real test of a great play is that it remains great over a number of decades, and 12 Angry Men does that. There have been thousands of productions, and that doesn't happen unless the source material is incredibly strong and touches souls."[17]

THE SUCCESS OF 12 ANGRY MEN around the world has been no less impressive. Its international appeal was clear from the moment it earned the top prize at the Berlin International Film Festival in June 1957. This was not the sort of movie that European audiences had come to expect from Hollywood, not a flashy movie but one with great emotional depth. The first success on the professional stage, as we've seen, was in France, where *Douze Hommes en Colère* impressed audiences in 1958, followed by successful runs in Germany, Slovenia, and elsewhere. Over the next years, Rose's drama was also remade on television as *Die Zwölf Geschworenen* (Germany, 1963), *Kaksitoista Valamiestä* (Finland, 1963), *Twaalf Gezworenen* (The Netherlands, 1966), *Doce Hombres sin Piedad* (Spain, 1970 and 1973), *Douze Hommes en Colère* (France, 1971), *Doze Homens em Conflito* (Portugal, 1973), *Oi Dodoka Enorkoi* (Greece, 1976), and *Tolv Edsvorne Menn* (Norway, 1982).

The global appeal of *12 Angry Men* has little do with the specifics of the American criminal justice system, but more about human behavior as it is found in any society. People everywhere understand the courage required to raise one's hand and to stand alone, and to resist the pressure to conform. Rose's characters are recognizable everywhere. Almost any group will have some people who are overbearing and some who are timid, some who are outspoken, narrow, generous, serious, or flippant. Any society will have members who are diligent and take their responsibilities seriously, and others who can't be troubled to expend the effort. Any group will have some who are quick to impose their ideas, and others who take the time to provide support and safety for those less able to speak out.

So compelling are these characterizations, so universal are the group dynamics, that it was probably inevitable that Sidney Lumet's movie would inspire full-length remakes in other languages and cultures. One of the first was a 1986 version in Hindi, *Ek Ruka Hua Faisla (A Pending Decision)*, directed by Basu Chatterjee, which was virtually identical to the original. In recent years, there have been several more translations of very high quality, showing that, much like its climb in the American Film Institute's list of the 100 Greatest American Films of All Time, *12 Angry Men* may be more popular around the world today than ever before.

In 2007, one of Russia's leading directors, Nikita Mikhalkov, made a version titled *12*. While acknowledging "the great movie of Sidney Lumet," Mikhalkov said that his work was not simply a remake: "Copying an American movie would be no more interesting than an American copy of *Anna Karenina*. Even if technically accurate, it would add nothing." Mikhalkov adapted elements of the story to a Russian context: twelve Muscovites must pass judgment on a Chechen teenager accused of killing his adoptive father, a Russian army officer. "I made *12* to make every viewer think—and above all those in Russia."[18] The result was "a film for Russia and about Russia." The accused was meant to represent any defenseless person: "a

Chechen boy, an orphan, a beggar who is not needed by anyone, whose guilt is taken for granted." Mikhalkov said the movie's greatest lesson was about democracy—not political democracy, which is declared from the outside, but the kind of democracy that lives inside every person, the ability to think freely. *12* was highly regarded in Russia, winning Golden Eagle awards for Best Feature Film, Best Director, and Best Actor, and received an Academy Award nomination for Best Foreign Language movie.

In 2009, *12 Angry Men* was brought to life in a very different setting. Lebanese dramatist Zeina Daccache went to Roumieh, Beirut's most crowded and dangerous prison, to help inmates develop their artistic talents and learn to work together. The play she suggested was *12 Angry Men*, in part for its large cast and simple staging, but also for the topics it addressed. The twelve jurors are ordinary people whom the inmates can readily understand. Many can also identify with the defendant—the product of a broken home, raised in difficult circumstances, who fell into a life of crime—whose fate is in their hands. The response was enthusiastic, the prisoners saying: "We've been judged by the society, now we're playing it; it's a role reversal, we are playing the role of the society that is judging us." The play offered an enduring lesson: "Mercy is more important than justice." Daccache's project was the subject of a remarkable documentary, *12 Angry Lebanese*, which garnered numerous awards and honors.[19] As Václav Havel had observed in a different country many years earlier, the play speaks about the nature of truth and the search for justice, themes that are relevant in Lebanon and everywhere else.

Perhaps the most impressive recent adaptation has been *12 Citizens* (十二公民, Shi Er Gong Min), a 2014 film by Xu Ang, a thirty-five-year-old Chinese director. Since China does not have jury trials for criminal cases, Xu turned the story into a deliberation among parents and friends of law students who were conducting a mock jury trial to learn about Western criminal justice.[20] Yet his aim was not to compare or contrast legal systems, but to use the drama to examine issues in his native land. As Xu explained, *12 Angry Men* "very accurately describes an insoluble problem—prejudice. In any society, as long as there are people there will be prejudice." That problem has special relevance in modern China, prompting him to use the drama as a way to bring twelve citizens of diverse backgrounds together around a table: "I wanted to portray my beloved Chinese people, as I see them in my everyday life, who, like me, can never entirely rid themselves of their prejudices."[21]

The crime of patricide is especially heinous in Confucian society, where filial piety remains a deeply held value. To this, Xu probed several fault lines in Chinese society: rural and urban, traditional and newly successful, young and old, ideological and pragmatic. The accused was the adopted son of a rich man, charged with killing his birth father, a poor peasant from the central province of Henan. The adoptive father was also from Henan but had become a millionaire in the pharmaceuticals industry. Several jurors are suspicious: surely the father is a profiteer who became rich by cheating and scheming.

Under Xu Ang's direction, the jury deliberation becomes an encounter that lays bare tensions and prejudices in contemporary China. Juror 9 is an old man who had been persecuted in the 1950s, his family denounced as "rightists" and subjected to torture. Only one neighbor had the courage to stand up for his family, and Juror 9 will repay that debt by helping the defendant in this case. Juror 5 had been falsely convicted of a crime and sentenced to eight years in prison, only to be released after one and a half years. The stigma still hurts: "No one cares that you were innocent, you are branded as someone who served time."

Juror 10 is a bitter man who despises the "rich kid from the provinces" and rails at China's hypercompetitive system: "Why didn't *my* son get to go to college? He studied so hard that it broke my heart, but he has to be a laborer . . . Who wants his son to be a laborer?" Juror 7 runs a noodle stand at the school and resents the wealthy students he must serve. Juror 11 is a young man who failed his entrance exam and works as a security guard at the school, reminded every day of his inferior social position. As for the final holdout, Juror 3 has a son who chafed at the discipline of a traditional Chinese family and ran away from home, a source of deep humiliation. The last to give up, he cries: "I felt that rich boy stab me."

As powerful and effective as any rendering of Reginald Rose's drama, Xu Ang's *12 Citizens* won more than a dozen awards, including six at the 2015 Shanghai International Film Festival, plus a Golden Rooster from the China Film Association for Best Adapted Screenplay, as well as several nominations for acting and directing.

AT ONE LEVEL, IT'S TEMPTING to say that Xu Ang took a story set in 1954 New York and adapted it to 2014 Beijing, just as Nikita Mikhalkov took a story from 1954 New York and placed it in 2007 Russia. Yet the Chinese and Russian versions are no less valid than the original. It's every bit as reasonable to say that *12 Angry Men* is a drama about issues found in any society—about prejudice and conformity, courage and empathy, and the need for mercy and reconciliation. Reginald Rose brought that idea to life in the context he knew best, New York of the 1950s; others did so in the times and places they understood, creating versions that are just as authentic and every bit as satisfying as the original.

To this day, Rose's drama continues to be performed on stages around the world. A few recent productions give a sense of the sheer diversity of productions: In Singapore, an all-Chinese cast performed a Mandarin translation, *12 Angry Chinese* (十二 怒 汉, Shi Er Nu Han), where a guilty verdict would lead to death by hanging, the form of capital punishment in that country. The performance offered "a burning reminder that more than fifty years later, the figures who populate the judicial system are not just righteous and angry. They are tired, frustrated and flawed—and also deeply and powerfully human."[22] In Mexico City, the Foro Cultural Chapultepec staged a successful production of *Doce Hombres en Pugna (Twelve Men in Conflict)*. One of the actors, Héctor Suárez, described why the play is as powerful in Mexico as anywhere else: "This work will never lose its relevance because it's about human passions, how people can make mistakes, and how they can behave well or badly by the way they think and the passions they unleash."[23] In India, a Kolkata-based theater group staged *12 Angry Men*, set in Bengal of the 1950s, and infused it with elements of classical Indian dance to shed light on communal tensions, economic disparities, and class systems.[24] "My intention was to explore the content beyond the thriller," said director Tathagata Chowdhury. "It's not just another whodunnit or murder mystery. It's an intense philosophical take on our pride and prejudices arising from our origin."[25]

The enduring appeal of Rose's drama was made clear to me on a recent visit to Paris, where I attended a stage performance of *Douze Hommes en Colère*. Sixty years after its success at the Théâtre de la Gaîté-Montparnasse, the play was revived at the Théâtre Hébertot in the 17th arrondissement, where it ran for several months to critical acclaim, winning the *Globe Cristal* for the Best Play of 2018.

Francis Lombrail, the theater's owner, told me that staging *12 Angry Men* was the fulfillment of a lifelong dream. As a youngster in the 1960s, he had seen the movie and was transfixed. In subsequent years he saw it several times on French television, and with each viewing, he told me, "I was astonished at its beauty, at its extraordinary depth, and at every one of its fascinating characters." He had a passion for cinema and for theater, and wanted to become an actor, and vowed that one day he would perform the drama.[26] Years later, after taking ownership of a Parisian theater, Lombrail acquired the French rights and set about writing an adaptation that would be true to the original but create a more contemporary feel. "The play," he explained, "captures the range of human nature—weakness, vulnerability, incompetence, and even brings a smile, despite the serious subject. In human nature we find not only deep feelings but also humor." Lombrail also cast himself as Juror 3.

To direct, Lombrail chose Charles Tordjman, a veteran of the French theater. Tordjman told me that he loved the play for its simplicity and power, and deliberately designed a set with nothing more than a single bench. With a minimalist stage and characters stripped to their essentials, *12 Angry Men* had the power of a Greek drama. As for the lead role, Tordjman commented: "I was interested in the way that Juror 8 insisted that each of the jurors confront their own humanity, by which I mean the values we have in common, like generosity, forgiveness, acceptance."[27] When I asked about the playwright, Tordjman said that although Reginald Rose did not display a mastery of language to rival Tennessee Williams or write with the poetry of Eugene O'Neill, his power came from an authentic portrayal of ordinary people, expressed in a language that was direct and unadorned.

Francis Lombrail and Charles Tordjman, producer and director, agreed that *12 Angry Men* is a masterpiece of modern theater. Neither one knew much about the author. They knew that Rose had been primarily a television writer, but beyond that could say little. Neither one could name any of his other works. It didn't matter. This one was enough.

Outside the Théâtre Hébertot, on the boulevard des Batignolles, the marquee showed the name of the play in large letters, DOUZE HOMMES EN COLÈRE. In Paris, as in so many cities around the world, audiences know and love *12 Angry Men*, a drama that continues to speak to us about individual courage and social justice.

Above that was the name of the playwright, REGINALD ROSE, a man whose passion for justice and whose skills as a dramatist gave rise to a work that has touched many more lives, and made a far greater impact, than a young man answering a summons for jury duty in 1954 could ever have imagined.

Epilogue

THE CAST OF *12 ANGRY MEN* had expected a six-week gig, two weeks to rehearse and four to film. None of the actors imagined that a low-budget movie, shot in black and white, would produce some of the best-known performances of their careers. "I don't think anyone said, fifty years later we will be talking about *12 Angry Men*," Don Kranze told me in 2019. "These are professional actors, getting together to do their best, and you hope for the best."[1]

In 1956, Jack Warden acted in two plays (*A View from the Bridge* and *A Very Special Baby*), two television dramas ("Tragedy in a Temporary Town" and an episode of *Climax!*) and three movies (*Edge of the City*, *12 Angry Men*, and *The Bachelor Party*.) Had he been asked, at year end, which performance would be remembered several decades later, it's doubtful he would have singled out his appearance as Juror 7. Ed Begley considered his starring role in *Inherit the Wind* to be the high point of his career, with more than eight hundred shows between April 1955 to June 1957. Apart from a few still photos, not much remains of his performance as Matthew Harrison Brady, while his brief turn as Juror 10 left an indelible mark. Begley later said: "It's strange, but before the movie *12 Angry Men*, people just took me for granted, thinking I was the person I was portraying. They finally sat up after that movie."[2]

For Henry Fonda, already a famous actor, the movie had little effect on his career, although in time he became proud of his performance. Perhaps better than any other role, Juror 8 captured his qualities of honesty, decency, and integrity. When Jane and Peter Fonda produced a documentary about their father, *Fonda on Fonda* (1992), the opening image, the one they chose to convey their father's screen presence, was of Juror 8, reaching into his pocket and slamming a switchblade onto the table, a moment of brilliance.

For Sidney Lumet, *12 Angry Men* opened the way to a marvelous career as a movie director, leading to a succession of great films in the 1950s and 1960s (among them *The Fugitive Kind, Fail Safe,* and *The Pawnbroker*) before reaching a peak in the 1970s (with *Serpico, Dog Day Afternoon, Murder on the Orient Express,* and *Network*) and beyond (with *The Verdict, Prince of the City,* and *The Morning After*). Many of these projects offered larger casts, more elaborate sets, and far bigger budgets; but as for movie direction none was better.

For Reginald Rose, in time *12 Angry Men* proved to be a transformational work. "It established his confidence in himself as a writer of substance, as a writer who had something to say to the public at large," said his son Jonathan.[3] In 1997, at the time of William Friedkin's remake for Showtime, Denis Hamill of the *Daily News* interviewed Rose. He recalled their conversation: "He wasn't full of himself for having written it, but I think he was proud as hell of *12 Angry Men*. Who wouldn't be? It was one of those happy coincidences where a story finds you like a fastball in the hitting zone and you just belt it out of the park."[4]

AT THE END OF 1987, *New York* magazine devoted a special issue, *You Must Remember This,* to a look back at the changing city. One article, by Pete Hamill, older brother of Denis, was titled "The New York We've Lost." It began: "Once there was another city here, and now it is gone. There are almost no traces of it anymore, but millions of us know it existed, because we lived in it: the Lost City of New York."[5] The New York of Hamill's younger days was big and loud and bustling, yet somehow more intimate than today, with shops that kept doors unlocked, cab drivers who helped with luggage, and waitresses who called you Honey. "That New York is gone now," he wrote, "hammered into dust by time, progress, accident, and greed."[6]

By 1987, much about New York City had changed in the thirty years since *12 Angry Men* was released as a movie. The last elevated train was torn down, Hamill wrote, "vanishing into the Lost City, to be replaced with still another bland arroyo of steel and glass."[7] The grand Pennsylvania Station was demolished in 1964, giving way to a grim warren of underground tracks with none of the grace and splendor of its predecessor. Next door, at Seventh Avenue and Thirty-Fourth Street, a vast new Madison Square Garden opened in 1968, replacing the more intimate arena at Eighth Avenue and Fiftieth Street. The Stork Club on East Fifty-Third Street, where Henry Fonda's character in *The Wrong Man* worked as a musician, closed in 1965 and was soon razed, the land turned into a pocket park named after CBS boss William S. Paley. The Fifty-Second Street jazz joints that Reggie Rose visited, The Hickory House and Kelly's Stables, had long since closed, and gone too were the favorite haunts of his youth, the Tip Toe Inn at Broadway and Eighty-Sixth Street, Schulte's cigar store, and Perla's pharmacy.

The Hotel Astor, on Broadway at Forty-Fourth Street, from whose roof NBC television cameras broadcast VE Day celebrations in 1945, and the Astor Theater next door, where *On the Waterfront* premiered in 1954, were leveled in 1967, replaced by a fifty-four-story office tower, One Astor Plaza. A few blocks to the north, the Capitol, the opulent palace where *12 Angry Men* played for three weeks in April 1957, was bulldozed in 1968, the space now occupied by Paramount Plaza, with forty-eight stories of glass and steel at 1633 Broadway.[8] No movie theater is likely to survive where a high-rise can stand.

Several of the principals were gone by 1987: Ed Begley had died in 1970, followed by Lee J. Cobb in 1976. Boris Kaufman passed away in 1980 and Henry Fonda in 1982, a few months after winning the Academy Award for Best Actor for his performance in *On Golden Pond*. Some of Rose's peers, too, vanished at tragically young ages: Rod Serling at fifty in 1975, and Paddy Chayefsky at fifty-eight in 1981.

The medium of television changed, as well. In the 1950s, Worthington Miner had believed that television could be a force for good, and for several years he produced intelligent drama on *Studio One* before trying to launch *The Challenge* with backing from the Ford Foundation and the ACLU. His aim of elevating the national dialogue was shared by organizations like the National Conference of Christians and Jews, which praised "Thunder on Sycamore Street" in 1954, and the Anti-Defamation League of B'nai B'rith, which bestowed its Television Award to Reginald Rose for "An Almanac of Liberty" and again for "Tragedy in a Temporary Town."[9] In time those awards would be discontinued, reflecting a sense that network programming could not, or would not, do much to inform public thinking. Already by the mid-1950s, deep-pocket sponsors were demanding ever more viewers, which led to more and more programs aimed at a lower common denominator, a trend that only accelerated over the next decades.

Pete Hamill offered a word of caution: "Nostalgia is a treacherous emotion, at once a curse against the present and an admission of permanent resentment, never to be wholly trusted."[10] From his vantage point in 1987, he looked ahead: "I suppose that thirty years from now (as close to us as we are to 1958), when I've been safely tucked into the turf at the Green-Wood, someone will write in these pages about a Lost New York that includes Area and the Mudd Club and Nell's, David's Cookies and Aca Joe and Steve's Ice Cream. Someone might mourn Lever House or Trump Tower or the current version of Madison Square Garden. Anything is possible."[11] Well, maybe not everything.

Those thirty years have now passed, and many more of the people and places that contributed to the journey of 12 Angry Men are gone.

The Fox Movietone Studios, on Tenth Avenue and Fifty-Third Street, where Sidney Lumet and Boris Kaufman worked over four weeks in the summer of 1956, was bought by Sony Pictures and for a time used to make music videos, until it outlived even that purpose. It was sold in 2007 and soon torn down; a residential complex now stands in its place. The dockyards at Twelfth Avenue and Thirty-Third Street, where Edge of the City was filmed, are long gone; the adjacent blocks are still called Hudson Yards although now home to fifty-story skyscrapers and swanky shops. Filmways Studios, at Second Avenue and 127th Street in East Harlem, where The Defenders was produced—and later used for great movies like Klute (1971), The Godfather (1972), and Annie Hall (1977)—closed in the early 1980s and was later reduced to rubble, the site now a parking lot.[12] The Sutton, the beloved art house on East Fifty-Seventh Street where Marty packed the house for months on end, is gone, too, replaced by a forty-story residential tower, its fate sealed by the same economic forces that doomed the Capitol.

Other landmarks remain. Franklin Towers, where Reginald Rose lived as a youth, still stands at 333 West 86th Street, now a care home for the elderly. The townhouse where he was born, on West 113th Street, appears from the outside to have changed very little, the block looking much as it did one hundred years ago although no longer a neighborhood of prosperous Jewish families.

To the south, about seven miles or 120 city blocks, the New York State Supreme Court Building, formerly the New York County Courthouse, stands prominently at 60 Centre Street on Foley Square. Large letters atop four-story Corinthian columns declare a solemn purpose: "The True Administration of Justice Is the Firmest Pillar of Good Government," a quote from George Washington in 1789. After walking up the broad front steps, visitors pass through metal detectors—Juror 8 could not enter with a knife today—into the central rotunda. Had Boris Kaufman's camera panned upward, it would have shown a circular band of twelve murals that represent the evolution of law, six pairs of paintings each with a portrait between them. The sequence begins with the most ancient of legal codes, from Assyria and Egypt, flanking a portrait of Hammurabi; then Persian and Hebraic law, with a portrait of Moses; Greek and Roman law, and Solon; Frankish and Byzantine law, and Justinian; English and Colonial law, and William Blackstone; and a final pair for the United States of America, with portraits of George Washington and Abraham Lincoln on either side of John Marshall, the first Chief Justice of the US Supreme Court. This was America's view of itself in the 1930s, as the most advanced nation on earth, its legal system the culmination of humankind's long pursuit of justice, one that forever strives toward a more perfect union, but that can never be better than the efforts of its citizens.

By now, all who contributed to the 1957 movie are gone. Sidney Lumet passed away in New York City, age eighty-six, in 2011. Three of the jurors survived into the twenty-first century, with Jack Klugman living the longest. In late 2011, at eighty-nine, his voice reduced to a rasp after surgery for throat cancer, he agreed to appear in a production of *12 Angry Men* at the George Street Playhouse in New Brunswick, New Jersey, for a three-week run in early 2012. Klugman had played a young man, Juror 5, in the movie, and now would take the role of Juror 9, the old man played so memorably by Joseph Sweeney. He recalled: "Sweeney showed me, as an actor, what it took to play a low-key rebel that Juror 9 became." The movie held very fond memories: "Working with Fonda and Sidney Lumet was like a dream for me. It'll be an honor to appear in the play—I'll be thinking of all those guys from the film."[13] Weeks before the opening, Klugman had to withdraw for health reasons, and in December 2012 he passed away, the very last of the twelve angry men.[14] Even Pete Hamill, who may have surprised himself by living more than another thirty years, died in August 2020 at age eighty-five, and was laid to rest at the Green-Wood in a plot he had chosen, near that most New Yorker of politicians, Boss Tweed.[15]

Over the course of this research I was able to speak with two important contributors, but they too are now gone: assistant director Don Kranze left us in August 2019 and art director Bob Markell in January 2020. Markell, in particular, enjoyed talking at length about his collaboration with Sidney Lumet on *Danger* and *You Are There* and about his work on *The Defenders* with Reginald Rose, whom he regarded as a dear friend. Always gracious, he spoke with me several times by telephone and welcomed me to the home on Shelter Island that he and his wife shared for more than fifty years. Markell remembered with clarity many details about the making of 12 *Angry Men*, telling stories about George Justin and Jack Warden and George Voskovec, and recalling his problems with Boris Kaufman about backdrops, and about ten-foot walls with nine-foot lights.

He summoned up, too, his feelings when the movie was first released, before it embarked on a journey that began with the spark of an idea in the mind of a young writer, and went on to earn a place in the hearts of people around the world:

> When it didn't make any money at the Capitol, everybody felt we had a flop. I said, "I can't believe it."
>
> About six months later, we realized we were all wrong. We had done something absolutely special. And I'm really very proud of it.
>
> I'm so pleased now that it's become such a classic.
>
> Because it *is*.

❚❚❚

"Twelve Angry Men"
(TV Featurette)

AS REGINALD ROSE COMPLETED the shooting script in spring 1956, he wrote a short "TV Featurette" intended to promote the movie at its release, as described in Chapter 11. Although a stirring statement, with Henry Fonda not only speaking about the importance of jury service but also conveying some of the most important elements of the drama, the "TV Featurette" does not appear to have been produced. No evidence of a finished version has been found; production supervisor George Justin does not mention it in his daily memos to the crew; and set designer Bob Markell did not recall it in our conversations. (The script is part of the Reginald Rose Papers, U.S. Mss 94AN, box 3, folder 7, Wisconsin Center for Film and Theater Research, University of Wisconsin–Madison.)

1. LONG SHOT   THE JURY ROOM

We see the Jury Room set, with one wall broken away. The jury table is littered with paper, ash trays, etc. The twelve chairs around it are empty. We see enough of the lights and electrical equipment to make this look like a typical working movie set. Camera moves in very slowly on jury table as we hear voice over.

VOICE

If you've ever served on a jury, this room will probably look familiar to you. But if you've never been called for jury duty

before, take a good long look at it, because one day your turn
will come, and in a room like this one, you'll spend what may
be the most exciting and dramatic hours of your life—and the
most important hours in the life of someone you've never met
before.

Henry Fonda enters set, walks to head of table. He carries an envelope.
Camera continues to move in on him as he opens the envelope.

VOICE

As you can see, this is actually a motion picture set. A movie
called TWELVE ANGRY MEN is being filmed here, in New
York City. TWELVE ANGRY MEN tells the story of 12
jurors locked in this room to deliberate a murder trial while a
human life hangs on the threads of their arguments.

Camera is on medium shot of Fonda now. He takes a slip of paper out
of the envelope.

VOICE

Henry Fonda plays the part of one of those jurors . . .

Fonda looks into the camera.

FONDA
(referring to envelope)

Ever gotten one of these? It's a notice for jury duty. If you're
over twenty-one you're eligible to receive one.

2. INSET   JURY NOTICE

FONDA

Here's what it looks like. It's just another official form.
(reading) Joe Doe will report to such and such an address at
such and such a time, and so on.

3. MEDIUM SHOT   FONDA

FONDA

(number) million of these things are mailed every year in
America. If anyone ever did any research on this I'd bet he'd
find that just about (number) million reactions to receiving
them would go something like this: "Oh, no! Jury duty? Are
they kidding? I haven't got time to waste on that stuff. Let
somebody else do it."

Fonda walks down alongside the jury table, camera panning with him.   We
see the table, and the papers, pencils, ash-trays, etc., on it.

FONDA

Well, I suppose that reaction is normal. But maybe if more
people understood what an experience such as serving on a
jury could mean to them, they'd think differently about it.

Camera moves into close-up during following lines.

FONDA

There's something that's pretty difficult to describe about jury
duty. As much as you resent being called, when you finally
enter the courtroom for the first time and you see the person
on trial sitting there, and you realize what your own personal
decision can mean to that person and to your community, your
attitude changes suddenly, and drastically. You hear the quiet
voice of the judge, the hushed whispers of the attendants,
and you can feel the tension hanging in the air. You sense the
weight of a new responsibility, and you know, all in a moment,
how important this thing you're doing is.

DISSOLVE TO . . .

4. FILM CLIP   [TRACKING SHOT] OF THE JURY

We hear the voice of the judge charging the jury, and over it, Fonda's voice.

FONDA

You look at your neighbor, and you can feel that he too has
undergone a change. It's as if you've suddenly grown up. And
if you're dealing with a human life . . .

5. FILM CLIP   SHOT OF JUDGE

We hear the last half-minute or so of the judge's charge to the jury. Then we see the clerk rise, excuse the alternate jurors, and then finally tell the jury to retire. As the jury begins to file out we

DISSOLVE TO . . .

6. MEDIUM SHOT   FONDA

Standing outside jury room door.

FONDA

When your time comes to serve on a jury you'll learn that this door is the threshold to a strange exciting new battle you'll find yourself waging—a battle with your own conscience. Until you reach this point, the entrance of the jury room, you've merely listened. You've heard the prosecuting attorney, the defense attorney, witnesses, and finally the judge. You've tried to digest many complex facts. Each side feels that right and justice is with them. Now, you are one of twelve who must finally decide what the truth is. That's not an easy thing to do sometimes, but it must be done. It all begins in here.

He points to the door. Camera moves in on words "Jury Room."

7. FILM CLIP   JURY ENTERING JURY ROOM

There is silence for perhaps twenty seconds. Then, as clip keeps running, we hear Fonda's voice over

FONDA

Twelve strangers. One of them is you. What have you decided about the case in question? Is the accused Guilty? Innocent? Or don't you know? What are you going to say when they ask your opinion? And what if they disagree with you? Supposing you think the defendant is not guilty, and suddenly you find that you're the only one. The other eleven vote guilty. Will you battle with all your capabilities to change their minds? Or will you let them change yours? Maybe they're right and you're wrong. But how do you know? How does anyone know?

At this point we should reach the moment in the film clip which just precedes the first line of dialogue.

DISSOLVE TO . . .

8. MEDIUM SHOT   FONDA

STILL outside jury door.

FONDA

Still, it just may happen that your intellect and your conscience tells you that you must pit yourself against all the others. You must fight for what you think is right. And suddenly you find yourself, a plain, ordinary peaceful citizen, battling tooth and nail for justice ... battling a person you've never met before, for the life of a person you'll never know.

DISSOLVE TO . . .

9. FILM CLIP

This is the scene in which Fonda baits Lee Cobb into shouting "I'll kill him." After Fonda's line, "You don't really mean you'll kill me, do you?"

DISSOLVE TO . . .

10. FILM CLIP   EMPTY JURY ROOM

The Jury has filed out. After a long pause we hear Fonda's voice over.

FONDA

Well—that's how it happens in our picture, "12 ANGRY MEN." I star in the film which I produced with Reginald Rose—You may have recognized some of the other stars who appear with me—Lee J. Cobb, Ed Begley, E.G. Marshall, Jack Warden and other fine actors in our cast—as I said—that's how it happens in "12 ANGRY MEN."

And that's how it may happen, in a room like this, when you get the call to serve your community in the name of justice.

DISSOLVE TO . . .

11. MEDIUM SHOT   FONDA IN JURY ROOM

He stands at head of table holding jury notice. He holds up notice, looks at it.

FONDA

    Yours may be in the mail right now . . . if you're lucky.

He smiles. Camera dollies back. He puts the jury notice in his pocket.

FADE OUT

ACKNOWLEDGMENTS

Some years back, I had the idea of writing a monograph that would examine *12 Angry Men* from three perspectives: a legal perspective, a behavioral perspective, and a decision perspective. The first would explain the jury's deliberations through the lens of burden of proof and reasonable doubt, the second would draw on concepts from social psychology, and the third would use conjunctive probability and conditional probability to argue that, given the evidence, it is almost certain the defendant in fact committed the murder. To this short work, which I thought might be about sixty pages long, I envisioned a brief introduction about the making of the movie.

As I began to learn how the movie was made, I found myself immersed in several interesting topics: the early days of live television, the blacklist in Hollywood and in television, New York in the 1950s, the rise of United Artists, and more. Soon the proverbial tail was wagging the dog, and my initial idea morphed into a project about the making of *12 Angry Men*. To this, I expected to add a brief introduction about the screenwriter, Reginald Rose.

Yet as I read about Rose, I began to have the sense that his life and work was a worthy story in its own right, every bit as important as *12 Angry Men* but much less well known. Once again the project changed shape, this time into a volume that examines not just Rose's most famous drama but the broader trajectory of his career, including teleplays for *Westinghouse Studio One* and *Playhouse 90*, his dramatic series, *The Defenders*, plus a number of lesser-known works for stage and screen. Some of the original ideas about a legal perspective and a behavioral perspective can be found in chapters 18 and 19, respectively, while the third idea, about probability and decision analysis, largely fell by the wayside.

To conduct research about people and events from the 1950s and 1960s, I relied heavily on library collections and archives. I am indebted to:

The Wisconsin Center for Film and Theater Research at the University of Wisconsin–Madison, which houses the Reginald Rose Papers as well as those of Rod Serling and David Susskind. I wish to thank Mary K. Huelsbeck, assistant director, and the staff of the center, including Amanda Smith, film archivist, for assisting me during my visits to Madison in June 2018 and October 2019.

The Beinecke Rare Book and Manuscript Library, Yale University, which houses the Herbert Brodkin archives, with complete scripts and production files from *The Defenders* and other teleplays. Thanks to the staff that helped me during my visit in April 2019.

The New York Public Library for the Performing Arts, at Lincoln Center Plaza, which houses the Worthington Miner *Studio One* collection, as well as back issues of *Cue*, and many clip files. My thanks to John Calhoun, chief reference librarian, and other staff during my visits in March 2017, October 2018, and October 2019.

The New York City Department of Records, Municipal Archives, where I consulted the New York District Attorney homicide docket for the Borough of Manhattan, 1950 to 1953, during my visit in March 2017, and subsequently for the file on the trial of William Viragh. My thanks to Rossy Mendez and Dwight Johnson.

The Film Study Center at the Museum of Modern Art in New York for access to the George Justin Collection, with articles and photographs. Thank you to Ashley Swinnerton.

The Paley Center for Media in New York, which makes available for viewing television programs not easily found elsewhere, including "Crime in the Streets" and "Thunder on Sycamore Street." Thanks to Ron Simon, curator, and to Mark Ekman, manager of visitor services.

The Columbia University Rare Book and Manuscript Library, which has the transcripts of interviews with Sidney Lumet, March 1959, and Henry Fonda, April 1959. Thanks to archivist David A. Olson.

The Academy of Motion Pictures, Arts and Sciences, Beverly Hills, California, which I visited in May 2016.

I was able to interview several people who were involved in the making of *12 Angry Men*, or who had been involved in television and film in the 1950s and 1960s. I am grateful to: Bob Markell, art director of *12 Angry Men* and producer of *The Defenders*; Don Kranze, assistant director of *12 Angry Men*; Loring Mandel, television writer who started with CBS's *Westinghouse Studio One*; Valerie Justin, wife of production supervisor George Justin; Jerome Hellman, in 1955 an agent at Ashley-Steiner; and Chiz Shultz, at the time a young production assistant for *Studio One*.

Special thanks to Jonathan Rose, eldest son of Reginald Rose, who generously spent more than five hours with me over four interviews, sharing his personal memories and filling in many gaps in the public record. Jonathan also read the entire manuscript and offered comments. This book is much the better for his contributions, and I am sincerely grateful for his kindness and support.

I wish to thank two long-time friends and fraternity brothers from undergraduate days: Jeff Burbank, writer and cinephile, who offered initial guidance, reviewed the completed manuscript, and provided encouragement throughout; and Alan Yochelson of the Los Angeles district attorney's office for his expertise about judges' instructions regarding reasonable doubt.

At an early stage of this research, I was fortunate to come across Stephen Bowie's Classic TV History Blog (www.classictvhistory.wordpress.com) and its excellent sections about Sidney Lumet, *The Defenders*, and Herb Brodkin. From the Lumet section I contacted Loring Mandel, who put me in touch with Bob Markell, Valerie Justin, and Jerome Hellman. Stephen later connected me to Don Kranze. His contributions to this book, both direct and indirect, are significant and much appreciated.

Over the months, I contacted many people who very kindly replied to email inquiries or took part in telephone interviews: Tino Balio, professor emeritus at the University of Wisconsin, about United Artists in the 1950s; David Berg, professor at Yale University, about classroom use in the 1970s; Dexter Dunphy, professor emeritus at the University of New South Wales, who taught the first-year course, *Human Behavior in Organizations*, at Harvard Business School in the 1960s; Scott Ellis, about directing *12 Angry Men* on Broadway; Sheldon Epps, artistic director emeritus, Pasadena Playhouse, and as of 2020, senior artistic advisor, Ford's Theater; Denis Hamill, journalist who interviewed Reginald Rose for the *Daily News* in 1997; Dave Itzkoff of the *New York Times*, about Paddy Chayefsky and *Marty*; Sam Kim, whose radio program, "American Icons: 12 Angry Men," broadcast in January 2020, led me to Jonathan Rose; Jeff Kisseloff, author of *The Box*; Selma Kuurtra at the NTL Institute for Applied Behavioral Science, regarding *12 Angry Men* at Bethel, Maine, in the 1960s; Francis Lombrail of the *Théâtre Hébertot* in Paris; Nancy Marder, professor at Chicago-Kent College of Law; Jack Marshall, founder and artistic director of the American Century Theater, Washington, DC; Keith A. Minoff and Fran Minoff, son and widow of Phil Minoff; Paul F. Occhiogrosso at City University of New York and Olga Dais, Registrar of Baruch College, for information about Reginald Rose's university experience; Ron Simon, curator of the Paley Center who met with me and shared his recollections; Maura Spiegel, professor at Columbia and author of *Sidney Lumet: A Life*; Tom Stempel, author of *Storytellers to the Nation*, who generously shared his notes of interviews with Reginald Rose and William Woolfolk; Charles Tordjman, director of *Douze Hommes en Colère*; and Rachel Wise, for information about the course curricula at Harvard Business School in the 1960s.

My thanks also to Zane Dille for his research assistance at UCLA regarding the manuscript of Charlie Russell; to my cousin, Geoff Hayden, for the genealogical research about Reginald Rose; to my nephew, Greg Washburn, for going through the case file on the trial of William Viragh and for accompanying me on walks through the East Village; and to Greg's wife, Sabrina Jacob Washburn, for her expertise about *Twelve Angry Men* as an amateur play. Throughout the entire project, my wife Laura, as always, provided her love and encouragement.

Several people read the entire manuscript and offered comments: thanks to Stephen Bowie, Jeff Burbank, Tom Stempel, Tino Balio, Jonathan Rose, Eric Newman, and Laura Rosenzweig. As well, some colleagues read chapters that touched on their expertise and provided comments: UCLA law professor Paul Bergman (chapter 18) and my IMD colleagues Ben Bryant, Anand Narasimhan, and Ginka Toegel (chapter 19).

I'm grateful for the support of the International Institute for Management Development (IMD), in Lausanne, Switzerland, where I have taught since 1996. The original idea about group behavior and decision analysis was related to my professional work, and I asked for and received some initial research funding. As the book shifted focus and became the biography of a writer and story of his most famous drama, I stopped asking for financial support; trips to New York, to Wisconsin, and to Yale, were funded on my own. Yet even as this project diverged from its initial topic and no longer had direct relevance to business administration, it was warmly encouraged by our director of research, Anand Narasimhan, who would occasionally ask with genuine interest about the progress of my project on Reginald Rose and at times offer ideas and suggest sources.

Being based at IMD has been useful to get translations of articles and foreign language versions of *12 Angry Men*. I thank several colleagues, former students, and friends for their help: from German, Albrecht Enders and Ralf Seifert; from Russian, Ilona Beklenishcheva; from Czech, Petr Bilek and Wolfgang Luber; from Slovenian, Miha Bobic; from Chinese, Wang Xiaohui, Ira Belkin, and Catherine Lin; and from Hindi, Anand Narasimhan. Wang Xiaohui also mediated my correspondence with Xu Ang, passing along my questions and the director's answers through a common friend.

Thanks to the team at Fordham University Press, including Fred Nachbaur, Eric Newman, Mark Lerner, Kate O'Brien-Nicholson, and Will Cerbone. Special thanks to Michael Koch for his excellent editing. For the cover design, thanks to Antonio Alcalá.

Not least, I am grateful to Eric G. Flamholtz, professor at UCLA, who showed *12 Angry Men* to a class of first-year MBA students in fall 1978. For at least one of them, twenty-three years old at the time, it made a lasting impression.

As a novice biographer, I found inspiration and guidance from three works: Robert A. Caro's memoir, *Working: Researching, Interviewing, and Writing*, which includes the admonition to "Turn every page," a phrase that sent me back to the University of Wisconsin for a second visit, determined to leave nothing unread; Alice Kaplan's *Looking for* The Stranger: *Albert Camus and the Life of a Literary Classic*, a similar project about an author and his best-known work which served as an example of what could be achieved; and James Atlas's *The Shadow in the Garden: A Biographer's Tale*, which offered many useful ideas about the craft of biography.

Atlas shared his view that "the key to writing biography is the capacity to be empathetic," and cited Robert Holmes's image of the biographer as extending a handshake toward the subject. I hope that this volume meets that test, an empathetic hand extended to Reginald Rose.

NOTES

Introduction

1. *The Ten Commandments* was shot in VistaVision and *Around the World in 80 Days* in Todd-AO.

2. "Of Local Origin," *New York Times*, April 8, 1957.

3. "Twelve Angry Men, Publicity and Promotion Report," The Arthur P. Jacobs Company, March 2, 1957, Reginald Rose Papers, U.S. Mss 94AN, box 3, folder 7, Wisconsin Center for Film and Theater Research, University of Wisconsin–Madison.

4. Henry Fonda, *My Life: As Told to Howard Teichmann* (New York: New American Library, 1981), 249–250.

5. Distributed by MGM, it grossed $2 million in 1957 and eventually earned close to $3.6 million.

6. *Variety*, February 27, 1957.

7. *Variety*, January 23, 1958.

8. IMDb Top Rated Movies list, June 14, 2021, https://www.imdb.com/chart/top /?ref_=nv_mv_250.

9. "On Reginald Rose," special feature, *12 Angry Men* (1957; Criterion Collection, 2011), DVD.

10. Reginald Rose, "Law, Drama, and Criticism," *Television Quarterly* 3, no. 4 (Fall 1964): 21–27.

11. Robert Crean, "On the (Left) Side of the Angels," *Today: National Catholic Magazine*, January 1964, 3–5.

12. Bob Markell, interview, Television Academy Foundation, April 18, 1998, https:// interviews.televisionacademy.com/interviews/bob-markell.

13. Tina Kelley, "Reginald Rose, 81, TV Writer Noted for 'Twelve Angry Men,' Dies," *New York Times*, April 21, 2002.

14. "Beyond Reasonable Doubt: Making *12 Angry Men*," featurette, *12 Angry Men* (1957; Metro-Goldwyn-Mayer Studios, 2007), DVD.

15. "If Men were angels, no government would be necessary. If angels were to govern men, neither external nor internal controls on government would be necessary." The Federalist, No. 51, at 322 (James Madison) in *The Federalist Papers*, ed. Clinton Rossiter (New York: Penguin, 1961).

16. David Frum, "In Defense of Liberalism," review of *A Thousand Small Sanities: The Moral Adventure of Liberalism* by Adam Gopnik, *New York Times*, May 16, 2019.

17. Jeff Kisseloff, *The Box: An Oral History of Television, 1920–1961* (New York: Viking, 1995), 248.

1. Dreams of a Writer

1. Irving Howe, *World of Our Fathers* (New York: New York University Press, 1976), 69.

2. Howe, 131.

3. Howe, 131.

4. Howe, 131.

5. Howe, 131.

6. Jonathan Rose, interview with the author, June 2020.

7. Reginald Rose, *Undelivered Mail: A Memoir* (Bloomington, IN: Xlibris Corporation, 2000), 265.

8. Rose, 90.

9. Rose, 90.

10. Rose, 109.

11. J. Rose interview.

12. "On Adapting 'Studs Lonigan' for Television," unpublished essay intended for *New York Times*, dated January 31, 1979, Reginald Rose Papers, U.S. Mss 94AN, box 61, folder 1. Wisconsin Center for Film and Theater Research, University of Wisconsin–Madison.

13. Phyllis Battelle, "Odyssey of a TV Writer," *New York Journal-American*, August 15, 1961, 11.

14. Townsend Harris High School was closed in 1942, and the site is now occupied by Baruch College. The school was reopened in 1984 and is now located in Queens.

15. Rose, *Undelivered Mail*, 12.

16. Rose, 12 and 13.

17. Rose, 12.

18. Rose, 13.

19. Rose, 170.

20. Rose, 203 and 205.

21. J. Rose interview.

22. Rose, *Undelivered Mail*, 273-274.

23. Rose, 287.

24. Rose, 109.

25. Rose, 285.

26. Rose, 10.

27. Rose, 10.

28. Rose, 55.

29. Rose, 135.

30. Rose, 135.

31. Rose, 137.

32. Rose, 134.

33. Rose, 137.

34. Olga Dais, registrar of Baruch College, the successor to CCNY's business college, wrote to me on January 5, 2018: "He attended Baruch from fall 1937 through spring 1938. According to his transcript it was his intention to major in business. Since he was only here for one academic year, he enrolled in courses that we consider to be prerequisites for the business majors, i.e., economics and math."

35. Dan Ross, "Playwright Best 'When I'm Angry,'" *New York Herald Tribune*, March 4, 1962.

36. Vince Leonard, "Reggie's a Regular Sort of Guy," *Pittsburgh Press*, November 29, 1967.

37. J. Rose, interview.

38. In *Undelivered Mail*, Rose omits any mention of his year at CCNY but says that immediately after high school he went to work at S. Leibovitz and Sons.

39. Rose, *Undelivered Mail*, 160.

40. Rose, 160.

41. Rose, 162.

42. Rose, 159.

43. Rose, 141.

44. Rose, 168.

45. Rose, 168.

46. Rose, 213.

47. Rose, 160.

48. J. Rose interview.

49. Ross, "Playwright Best 'When I'm Angry.'"

50. Ross.

51. Richard F. Shepard, "Man with a Script: Reginald Rose Thinks All T.V., Even Sponsors, Gain from Controversy," *New York Times*, February 24, 1957.

52. J. Rose interview.

53. Reginald Rose, *Six Television Plays* (New York: Simon and Schuster, 1956), xi–xii.

54. Battelle, "Odyssey of a TV Writer," 11.

55. Jeff Kisseloff, *The Box: An Oral History of Television, 1920–1961* (New York: Viking, 1995), 239. Also: "I wrote at night at home. God knows how many short stories and the halves of three novels. And then my then-wife was pregnant, and we didn't have money to pay the doctor." Pierre Bowman, "He's Reginald Rose, the Legendary TV Dramatist," *Honolulu Star-Advertiser*, July 30, 1980

56. Kisseloff, *The Box*, 239.

57. Rose, *Six Television Plays*, ix.

58. Reginald Rose, "TV's Age of Innocence—What Became of It?" *New York Times*, December 3, 1967. Rose recalled: "My introduction to Sidney Lumet consisted of one brief phone call to him by a man named Phil Minoff who was then television editor of Cue magazine and a friend of mine." While it's clear that Rose and Minoff became friends, it's far from certain that they were already friends in December 1951. In 2018, I spoke with Minoff's widow, Fran, and his son, Keith, both of whom remembered a warm friendship, but neither could say

when it began or how they first met. Phil Minoff was two years older than Rose and had been editor-in-chief of the CCNY student newspaper, *The Campus*, before graduating in February 1939; Rose spent just one year at CCNY's School of Business, far from the main campus in Upper Manhattan. It's possible their paths crossed before December 1951, but given that Rose contacted Minoff immediately after reading the article about *Out There* in *Cue*, it's also possible that Rose, eager to break into television writing, simply cold-called him.

59. Rose.

60. Rose.

61. Kisseloff, *The Box*, 239.

62. Philip Minoff, "For No Earthly Reason," *Cue*, December 8, 1951, 13, 34–35.

63. Murray Martin, "Drama of an Adolescent Boy, '12:32 A.M.,' by Reginald Rose," CBS press release, December 3, 1954.

64. Kisseloff, *The Box*, 239.

2. Getting Started (1952 to Summer 1953)

1. "Empire of the Air: The Men Who Made Radio," *American Experience*, PBS, January 29, 1992.

2. "Empire of the Air."

3. William S. Paley, *As It Happened: A Memoir* (Garden City, NY: Doubleday, 1979), 182.

4. Paley, 277.

5. "Rod Serling: Submitted for Your Approval," *American Masters*, PBS, October 1, 1997.

6. Tad Mosel, interview, Television Academy Foundation, October 18, 1997, https://interviews.televisionacademy.com/interviews/tad-mosel.

7. Delbert Mann, *Looking Back . . . at Live Television and Other Matters* (Los Angeles: Directors Guild of America, 1998), 17.

8. Mann, 2.

9. Mann, 7.

10. In a speech at the end of August 1939, Miner delivered a blistering critique: "When we speak of the theater, we speak of one city—New York. Yet even within the confines of that one city, the theater isn't democratic. It is a Park Avenue nightclub, a luxury for a selective few with the price of admission. It is for the rich in the richest city of this country, and I believe this situation is deplored by every author, actor and manager in the business." Robert S. Bird, "Theatre Is Called Monopoly of Rich," *New York Times*, September 1, 1939.

11. Paley, *As It Happened*, 239–240.

12. Paley, 217.

13. Mann, *Looking Back*, 20.

14. Worthington Miner, *Worthington Miner: Interviewed by Franklin J. Schaffner* (Metuchen, NJ: Directors Guild of America and the Scarecrow Press, 1985), 196.

15. Harry Castleman and Walter J. Podrazik, *Watching TV: Six Decades of American Television*, 2nd ed. (Syracuse, NY: Syracuse University Press, 2010), 41.

16. Paley, *As It Happened*, 239–240.

17. David Halberstam, *The Fifties* (New York: Random House, 1993), 497.

18. William Hawes, *Live Television Drama, 1946–1951* (Jefferson, NC: McFarland, 2001), 98. Hawes writes that Miner's departure for NBC was due to a salary dispute, CBS never having paid him more than $750 per week and balking at any raise despite years of success.

19. Miner, *Worthington Miner*, 197.

20. Jeff Kisseloff, *The Box: An Oral History of Television, 1920–1961* (New York: Viking, 1995), 245.

21. Steven H. Scheuer, "Meet Mr. Reginald Rose—Outstanding TV Author," *Brooklyn Daily Eagle*, May 30, 1954.

22. Two of Gallico's books were made into well-known—and entirely different—movies, thirty years apart: *Pride of the Yankees* (1942) and *The Poseidon Adventure* (1972).

23. Jonathan Rose, interview with the author, June 2020.

24. See also the entry on Martin Ritt in Britannica, https://www.britannica.com/biography /Martin-Ritt.

25. Charles K. Russell, *In the Worst of Times It Was the Best of Times* (Beverly Hills, CA: CKR Productions), 1982

26. Jack Gould, "Radio and TV in Review," *New York Times*, September 20, 1950.

27. Walter Bernstein, *Inside Out: A Memoir of the Blacklist* (New York: Da Capo Press, 1996), 152.

28. Patrick McGilligan, *Backstory 3: Interviews with Screenwriters of the 60s* (Berkeley: University of California Press, 1997).

29. Russell, *In the Worst of Times*, 9.

30. *By Sidney Lumet*, directed by Nancy Buirski (2015; Augusta Films and American Masters). For Lumet's early life, see his biography by Maura Spiegel, *Sidney Lumet: A Life* (New York: St. Martin's Press, 2019).

31. Maura Spiegel, *Sidney Lumet: A Life* (New York: St. Martin's Press, 2019), 142.

32. Stephen Bowie, "Angry Man," Classic TV History Blog, December 23, 2011, https:// classictvhistory.wordpress.com/2011/17/18/sidney-lumet-memories-from-the-early-years.

33. Frank R. Cunningham, *Sidney Lumet: Film and Literary Visionary* (Lexington, KY: University Press of Kentucky, 1991), 17.

34. Bowie, "Angry Man."

35. Bowie.

36. Sidney Lumet, interview, Television Academy Foundation, October 28, 1999, https:// interviews.televisionacademy.com/interviews/sidney-lumet.

37. Bob Markell, interview with the author, April 2016.

38. Larry Ceplair and Steven Englund, *The Inquisition in Hollywood: Politics in the Film Community, 1930–60* (Urbana: University of Illinois Press, 2003), 386.

39. Kisseloff, *The Box*, 414.

40. Ronald Davis, "A Conversation with Martin Ritt," in *Martin Ritt: Interviews*, ed. Gabriel Miller (Jackson: University of Mississippi Press, 2002), 159.

41. Russell, *In the Worst of Times*, 10.

42. Walter Bernstein, *Inside Out: A Memoir of the Blacklist* (New York: Da Capo Press, 1996), 22.

43. Bernstein, *Inside Out*, 152–153.

44. Born Emanuel Cohen in New York City, John Randolph (1915–2004) was an original member of Actors Studio and active in social causes in the 1930s and 1940s. He was able to resume his movie career only in the 1960s.

45. Russell, *In the Worst of Times*, 21.

46. Russell, 22.

47. Russell, 17–18.

48. Russell, 40.

49. Russell, 40.

50. Sidney Lumet, "Notes on TV," *Cue*, July 19, 1952, 6.

51. Russell, *In the Worst of Times*, 37.

52. Russell refers to this episode as "The Christmas Present."

53. Russell, *In the Worst of Times*, 37.

54. "Radio and Television," *New York Herald Tribune*, February 26, 1952.

55. Kisseloff, *The Box*, 239.

3. Two Programs, Two Movies (1952 to 1954)

1. Harry Castleman and Walter J. Podrazik, *Watching TV: Six Decades of American Television*, 2nd ed. (Syracuse, NY: Syracuse University Press, 2010), 41.

2. Charles K. Russell, *In the Worst of Times It Was the Best of Times* (Beverly Hills, CA: CKR Productions, 1982) 32.

3. Philco and Goodyear alternated weeks, with Fred Coe's anthology called *The Philco Television Playhouse* one week and *The Goodyear Theatre* the next. Essentially a single show, it is often called *The Goodyear-Philco Playhouse*.

4. Paddy Chayefsky, *Television Plays* (New York: Simon and Schuster, 1955), 178.

5. Delbert Mann, *Looking Back . . . at Live Television and Other Matters* (Los Angeles: Directors Guild of America, 1998), 59.

6. Mann, 59.

7. Shaun Considine, *Mad as Hell: The Life and Work of Paddy Chayefsky* (New York: Random House, 1994), 51. Also recounted in Tom Stempel, *Storytellers to the Nation: A History of American Television Writing* (New York: Continuum, 1992), 49.

8. Mann, *Looking Back*, 60.

9. Chayefsky, *Television Plays*, 173–174.

10. Mann, *Looking Back*, 62.

11. Philip Minoff, "Notes on TV: One Misplaced Actor and One Fast-Rising Star," *Cue*, June 6, 1953.

12. Tom Mackin, "Rose Finds Plot in Life," *Newark Evening Star*, December 3, 1967.

13. "Special Citations," *Variety*, April 21, 1954, 29.

14. Philip Minoff, "The Finest Writing in the Entire Medium," *Cue*, January 8, 1955, 35.

15. Mann, *Looking Back*, 52.

16. One of New York's most elegant hotels, affordable for a CBS producer with an expense account who could treat his blacklisted writers. Now the Peninsula New York, part of the Hong Kong–based Peninsula Group.

17. Russell, *In the Worst of Times*, 1-1A.

18. Walter Bernstein, *Inside Out: A Memoir of the Blacklist* (New York: Da Capo Press, 1996), 216.

19. Abraham Polonsky, *You Are There Teleplays, The Critical Edition* (Northridge, CA: Center for Telecommunication Studies, California State University, Northridge, 1997), 12.

20. Aljean Harmetz, *Round up the Usual Suspects: The Making of Casablanca—Bogart, Bergman, and World War II* (New York: Hyperion, 1992), 43.

21. Larry Ceplair and Steven Englund, *The Inquisition in Hollywood: Politics in the Film Community, 1930–60* (Urbana: University of Illinois Press, 2003), 404.

22. Jeff Kisseloff, *The Box: An Oral History of Television, 1920–1961* (New York: Viking, 1995), 419.

23. Polonsky, *Teleplays*, 8

24. Polonsky, 9.

25. Polonsky, 9.

26. "Director Participation: Sidney Lumet Kisses, Fights, Dies, Running Two Top TV Shows a Week," *Life*, June 8, 1953, 103–104.

27. "Director Participation," 103–104.

28. *By Sidney Lumet*, directed by Nancy Buirski (2015; Augusta Films and American Masters), DVD.

29. IMDb, although not necessarily complete, lists Edward Binns (7 episodes), E. G. Marshall (3), Martin Balsam (2), Jack Warden (2), George Voskovec (2), Ed Begley (1).

30. For a thumbnail history, see Richard Alleman, *New York: The Movie Lover's Guide* (New York: Harper and Row, 1988).

31. Cited in Elia Kazan, *Kazan, A Life* (London: Pan Books, 1989), 552.

32. Thomas M. Pryor, "Brando Will Star in Local Pier Film," *New York Times*, November 7, 1953.

33. "On Boris Kaufman," special feature, *12 Angry Men* (1957; Criterion Collection, 2011), DVD.

34. "On Boris Kaufman," special feature.

35. Boris Kaufman, mini bio on IMDb, by Jon C. Hopwood, https://www.imdb.com/name/nm0442100/bio?ref_=nm_ov_bio_sm.

36. Valerie Justin, interview with the author, December 2016.

37. Howard Thompson, "George Justin: Local Movie Man on Our Town," *New York Times*, November 26, 1961, X7.

38. "Stock to be sold by United Artists," *New York Times*, March 20, 1957.

39. "Robert Benjamin & Arthur Krim," *New York Herald Tribune*, September 13, 1964.

40. Jesse Kornbluth, "The Little Studio That Could," *New York Magazine*, April 6, 1987.

41. Howard Thompson, "Random Observations on Pictures and People," *New York Times*, September 20, 1953.

42. Shaun Considine, *Mad as Hell: The Life and Work of Paddy Chayefsky* (New York: Random House, 1994), 70.

43. "Philco TV 'Marty' Set for Theatres; Del Mann Debuting as Director," *Variety*, April 14, 1954, 7.

44. Considine, *Mad as Hell*, 71.

45. Mann, *Looking Back*, 62.w

46. Adamantine (*adjective*): Utterly unyielding, extremely hard, and unwilling to change. A word used by Chayefsky in *Network* (1976): Walter C. Amundsen (played by Jerome Dempsey): "You would describe Mr. Jensen's position on Beale as inflexible?" Frank Hackett (played by Robert Duvall): "Intractable and adamantine."

47. Mann, *Looking Back*, 62.

48. Considine, *Mad as Hell*, 71.

4. Original Dramas for *Studio One* (Summer 1953 to Spring 1954)

1. "Television News," *New York Times*, May 12, 1953.

2. Val Adams, "The Pessimistic Television Drama: Felix Jackson Says Life Cannot Be as Bad as Video Portrays It," *New York Times*, October 11, 1953.

3. Jack Gould, "Schlitz Playhouse Presents 'Haunted Heart,' Specially Staged TV Musical Comedy," *New York Times*, March 14, 1952.

4. Adams, "Pessimistic Television Drama."

5. Jack Gould, "Television in Review: Orwell's '1984,'" *New York Times*, September 23, 1953.

6. Gould.

7. "From the Production Centres," *Variety*, June 24, 1953.

8. Stephen Bowie, "Voices from the Studio," Classic TV History Blog, January 27, 2009, https://classictvhistory.wordpress.com/tag/paul-nickell.

9. "Rod Serling: Submitted for Your Approval," *American Masters*, PBS, Broadcast October 1, 1997.

10. George F. Sander, *Serling: The Rise and Twilight of Television's Last Angry Man* (New York: Dutton, 1992), 74.

11. "Rod Serling: Submitted for Your Approval."

12. Reginald Rose, *Six Television Plays* (New York: Simon and Schuster, 1956), x.

13. Rose, 53.

14. Rose, 55.

15. Rose, 53.

16. "The Remarkable Incident at Carson Corners," outline for *Studio One*, Reginald Rose Papers, U.S. Mss 94AN, box 15, folder 6, Wisconsin Center for Film and Theater Research, University of Wisconsin–Madison.

17. Tom Stempel notes of interview with Reginald Rose, March 9, 1991.

18. Rose, *Six Television Plays*, 55.

19. Philip Minoff, "Community Tragedy Makes a Superb 'Studio One,'" Notes on TV, *Cue*, January 30, 1954.

20. Rose, *Six Television Plays*, 54–55.

21. Rose, 105–106.

22. Jeff Kisseloff, *The Box: An Oral History of Television, 1920–1961* (New York: Viking, 1995), 516–517.

23. Rose, *Six Television Plays*, 105.

24. Tom Stempel notes of interview with Reginald Rose, March 9, 1991.

25. Rose, *Six Television Plays*, 106.

26. Kisseloff, *The Box*, 516–517.

27. Kisseloff, 517.

28. Rose, *Six Television Plays*, 107.

29. "Thunder on Sycamore Street," outline for *Studio One*, Reginald Rose Papers, U.S. Mss 94AN, box 17, folder 9.

30. Kenneth Utt worked in television as producer on *The Defenders* and *NYPD* and in motion pictures as associate producer on *Midnight Cowboy* (1969), *The French Connection* (1971), and *All That Jazz* (1979). He won an Academy Award as coproducer of *Silence of the Lambs* (1991).

31. Rose, *Six Television Plays*, 109.

32. Rose, 108.

33. Gould, "Television in Review."

34. Gould.

35. Steven H. Scheuer, "Meet Mr. Reginald Rose—Outstanding TV Author," *Brooklyn Daily Eagle*, May 30, 1954, 23. The following year, Rose's contract with *Studio One* called for twelve outlines. With the going rate for a *Studio One* teleplay at about $1,250, the contract may

have called for twelve outlines for a salary of $12,000, with more paid for each outline that was produced.

5. A Visit to Foley Square (Spring 1954)

1. Reginald Rose, *Six Television Plays* (New York: Simon and Schuster, 1956), 155.

2. Rose, 156.

3. Denis Hamill, "Time to Get 'Angry' Again," *Daily News*, August 17, 1997.

4. Hamill.

5. Rose, *Six Television Plays*, 155.

6. Hamill, "Time to Get 'Angry' Again."

7. Jeff Kisseloff, *The Box: An Oral History of Television*, 1920–1961 (New York: Viking, 1995), 259.

8. Kisseloff, 259.

9. Hamill, "Time to Get 'Angry' Again."

10. Of the 713 homicides in Manhattan between 1950 and 1953, 87 did not identify a defendant and 626 led to a defendant; of those 626, charges were pressed in 323 cases—for the others, charges dropped. Of those 323 cases, there were 105 for first-degree murder, 131 for second-degree murder, 71 for first-degree manslaughter, 9 for second-degree manslaughter, 2 for assault, and 6 for vehicular homicide. Of the 71 charges of first-degree manslaughter, 51 resulted in a guilty plea to a lower charge and 20 went to trial, with six defendants guilty as charged, three convicted of the lesser charge of second-degree manslaughter, four listed as "DOR" (probably dismissed on review, or a directed verdict of acquittal), one found to be insane, and six acquitted. Not one was convicted of assault. Of the eight second-degree manslaughter charges, only one went to trial, resulting in a conviction for assault—the trial of William Viragh.

11. Program of the 1996 London performance, quoted by Steven Price in Reginald Rose, *Twelve Angry Men*, ed. Steven Price (London: Bloomsbury, 2017), 27.

12. Rose, *Six Television Plays*, 156.

13. Kisseloff, *The Box*, 259.

14. Hamill, "Time to Get 'Angry' Again."

15. Tina Kelley, "Reginald Rose, 81, TV Writer Noted for 'Twelve Angry Men Dies,'" *New York Times*, April 21, 2002.

16. In 1956, Rose recalled it ran twenty-seven pages. Rose, *Six Television Plays*, 156.

17. Reginald Rose, "12 Angry Men," undated outline for *Studio One*, 1, Reginald Rose Papers, U.S. Mss 94AN, box 19, folder 3, Wisconsin Center for Film and Theater Research, University of Wisconsin–Madison.

18. Rose, "12 Angry Men," undated outline for *Studio One*, 6. Elsewhere Rose elaborated: "Since I felt that a dozen names would be quite meaningless to a viewing audience (members of a jury seldom address each other by name), I omitted the sometimes annoying chore of selecting names for my characters." Rose, *Six Television Plays*, 155.

19. Rose, "12 Angry Men," undated outline for *Studio One*, 4–6.

20. Rose, 4.

21. Rose, 7.

22. Rose, 10.

23. Rose, 16.

24. Rose, 24.

25. Hamill, "Time to Get 'Angry' Again."

26. Hamill. In a 1995 interview, Rose varied the timing slightly: "I wrote "Twelve Angry Men" in four days, and that first draft with very, very minor changes was what was done." Kisseloff, *The Box*, 259.

27. Rose, *Six Television Plays*, 156.

28. Thomas M. Pryor, "Dizzy Dean to Try Hand as an Actor," *New York Times*, July 8, 1954.

29. Rose, *Twelve Angry Men*, 19.

30. As an example: "Clearly, *Twelve Angry Men* was born straight out of the Spring 1954 McCarthy hearings." Ross Munyan, "Reginald Rose: A Biography," in *Readings on Twelve Angry Men* (San Diego, CA: Greenhaven Press, 2000), 24.

31. Steven H. Scheuer, "Meet Mr. Reginald Rose—Outstanding TV Author," *Brooklyn Daily Eagle*, May 30, 1954, 23.

32. Scheuer, 23.

33. Scheuer, 23.

6. "Twelve Angry Men" (Summer 1954)

1. "The Unborn," unpublished outline, Reginald Rose Papers, U.S. Mss 94AN, box 53, folder 21, Wisconsin Center for Film and Theater Research, University of Wisconsin–Madison.

2. "The Silent City," unpublished outline, Reginald Rose Papers, U.S. Mss 94AN, box 53, folder 19.

3. "Of local origin," *New York Times*, July 28, 1954.

4. Elia Kazan, *A Life* (Boston: Da Capo Press, 1997), 529.

5. Bosley Crowther, "'On the Waterfront' Bids Strongly to Be the Season's Top Film," *New York Times*, August 8, 1954.

6. A. H. Weiler, "'On the Waterfront' Is an Arresting Use of the Motion Picture Medium," *New York Times*, August 1, 1954.

7. Oscar Godbout, "'Marty' Hits Jackpot," *New York Times*, September 11, 1955, X7.

8. Press Release, September 9, 1954. Worthington Miner Studio One Scripts, Billy Rose Theater Collection, New York Public Library, Series III, Publicity Materials, Press Releases (1954).

9. "Edward Arnold, Actor, Dies at 66," *New York Times*, April 27, 1956.

10. Ethan Mordden, *The Hollywood Studios: House Style in the Golden Age of the Movies* (New York: Knopf, 1988), 368.

11. Murray Martin, "Westinghouse Studio One Returns to the Air for Seventh Year with Outstanding Drama, 'Twelve Angry Men,' September 20, CBS-TV," September 9, 1954, *Studio One*, Worthington Miner Collection, New York Public Library.

12. *Studio One*, undated, "Twelve Angry Men" without handwritten changes, Reginald Rose Papers, box 19, folder 3.

13. Reginald Rose, *Six Television Plays* (New York: Simon and Schuster, 1956), 157.

14. Rose, *Six Television Plays*, 157.

15. Rose, 158.

16. Trau, "Television Reviews: Studio One (Twelve Angry Men)," *Variety*, September 22, 1954, 31.

17. Val Adams, "Television in Review: Montgomery Show—'Studio One' Conflict on Mondays Poses Dilemma for Viewer," *New York Times*, September 22, 1954.

18. David Bordwell, "Endurance: Survival Lessons from Lumet," Observations on Film Art (blog), April 21, 2011, http://www.davidbordwell.net/blog/2011/04/21/endurance-survival-lessons-from-lumet/: "Early live TV drama, confined by the home screen's 21-inch format and weak resolution and hamstrung by punishing shooting schedules, pushed directors to rely on flatly staged mid-range shots, goosed up with close-ups, fast cutting, and meaningless camera movements."

19. "Hewell," Naval History and Heritage Command, https://www.history.navy.mil/content /history/nhhc/research/histories/ship-histories/danfs/h/hewell.html. See also *Mister Roberts* (1955 film)," Wikipedia, https://en.wikipedia.org/wiki/Mister_Roberts_(1955_film).

7. Gaining Momentum (Fall 1954 to Spring 1955)

1. "One for All, or Rose in Bloom: A Leading 'Studio One' Playwright's Works Draw Institutional Attention," *Variety*, November 3, 1954, 23.

2. Reginald Rose, interview with Tom Stempel, March 9, 1991.

3. Murray Martin's press release of December 3, 1954, refers to "12:32 A.M.," which matches the title of Rose's script in the University of Wisconsin archives. The December 13 listing in the *New York Times*, gave the title as "12:30 A.M.," which was also the title in the broadcast. I have used "12:30 A.M." throughout for purposes of consistency. Murray Martin, Letter to TV Editors, December 3, 1954, Studio One Worthington Miner Collection, New York Public Library.

4. Martin, Letter to TV Editors.

5. Martin, Letter to TV Editors.

6. Martin, Letter to TV Editors.

7. Jack Gould, "Television in Review," *New York Times*, December 17, 1954.

8. Television Follow-up Comment, *Variety*, December 15, 1954, 34.

9. Val Adams, "Filmed 'You Are There' for Schools," *New York Times*, November 21, 1954.

10. Abraham Polonsky, You Are There *Teleplays: The Critical Edition* (Northridge, CA: Center for Telecommunication Studies, 2003), 16.

11. Charles K. Russell, *In the Worst of Times It Was the Best of Times* (Beverly Hills, CA: CKR Productions, 1982), 149.

12. Bob Markell, interview with the author, October 2016.

13. "Lumet's Freelance (TV-Legit) Status," *Variety*, December 1, 1954, 25.

14. Gilbert Millstein, "Rod Serling, Patterns of a Television Playwright," *New York Times Magazine*, December 2, 1956.

15. "Rod Serling: Submitted for Your Approval," *American Masters*, PBS, Broadcast October 1, 1997.

16. "Rod Serling: Submitted for Your Approval."

17. Jack Gould, "Television in Review: 'Patterns' Is Hailed as a Notable Triumph," *New York Times*, January 17, 1955.

18. Letter to Ben Gettler, March 24, 1955, Rod Serling Papers, U.S. Mss 43AN, box 6, folder 3, Wisconsin Center for Film and Theater Research, University of Wisconsin—Madison.

19. "Rod Serling: Submitted for Your Approval."

20. Reginald Rose Papers, U.S. Mss 94AN, box 6, folder 3, Wisconsin Center for Film and Theater Research, University of Wisconsin–Madison.

21. "Rod Serling: Submitted for Your Approval."

22. Reginald Rose Papers, U.S. Mss 94AN, box 53, folder 4.

23. Reginald Rose, *Six Television Plays* (New York: Simon and Schuster, 1956), 249.

24. Rose, 249.

25. Budget and title information from Herbert Brodkin Television Production Files, box 14, Beinecke Rare Book and Manuscript Library, Yale University.

26. Rose, *Six Television Plays*, 252.

27. Jack Gould, "Television: Social Drama; Teen-Age Gang Seen in 'Crime on Streets,'" *New York Times*, March 11, 1955, 33.

28. Gould, 33.

29. Gould, 33.

30. Rose, *Six Television Plays*, 252.

31. Rose, 252.

32. Rose, 158.

33. Thomas M. Pryor, "Columbia to Film Poems by Jeffers," *New York Times*, March 17, 1955.

34. Tom Stempel, *Storytellers to the Nation: A History of American Television Writing* (New York: Continuum Publishing Company, 1992), 53. See also, "AA Reuniting TV 'Crime' Participants in Pic," *Variety*, April 20, 1955.

35. "Top TV Writers Able to Call Directorial Shots in Selling H'wood Their Videoperas," *Variety*, June 2, 1955, 11.

36. "AA Reuniting TV 'Crime' Participants in Pic," *Variety*, April 20, 1955.

37. *By Sidney Lumet*, directed by Nancy Buirski (2015; Augusta Films and American Masters), DVD.

38. Peter Bogdanovich, *Who the Devil Made It: Conversations with Legendary Film Directors* (New York: Ballantine Books, 1997), 743.

39. Bogdanovich, 744.

40. Kate Cameron, "Bronx Style Romance on Sutton's Screen," *New York Daily News*, April 12, 1955.

41. *Variety*, April 22, 1955, 3; and *Variety*, May 6, 1955, 2.

42. Oscar Godbout, "'Marty' Hits Jackpot," *New York Times*, September 11, 1955, X7.

43. Godbout; see also "The Top Box-Office Hits of 1955," *Variety Weekly*, January 25, 1956.

44. Cameron, "Bronx Style Romance on Sutton's Screen."

45. "Worthington Miner Productions has three new series blueprinted for early production, all with NBC. Frontier, Medic, and Challenge, being produced with cooperation of the Fund for the Republic, under a grant from Ford Foundation. Series all are repped by Ashley-Steiner Agency." "Miner, Atop 'Medic,' to 'Briefcase' Lawyers, Plans Other Telepix," *Variety*, March 3, 1955, 20.

46. "Accepts 'Challenge,'" *Variety*, April 22, 1955, 3.

47. Steven H. Scheuer, "Reginald Rose Offers More Good TV Drama," *Lansing State Journal*, May 12, 1959, 24.

48. Worthington Miner, *Worthington Miner: Interviewed by Franklin J. Schaffner* (Metuchen, NJ: Directors Guild of America and Scarecrow Press, 1985), 250.

49. Miner, 250.

50. Serling was paid one thousand dollars and Rose likely received the same amount. In September 1955, Miner wrote to Serling's agent, Blanche Gaines, claiming that her client had not lived up to his agreement. Gaines responded that the agreement was unclear and not valid; a next letter suggested that Miner agreed to release Serling from any obligations. Even so, Serling

retained a writing credit. Letters from Blanche Gaines to Worthington Miner, September 1, 1955, and September 8, 1955, Rod Serling Papers, U.S. Mss 43AN, box 21, folder 1.

51. *Variety*, April 22, 1955, 3.

52. "Fund for Republic Sets Sept 15 'Screening' for Tony Miner's 'Challenge,'" *Variety*, August 24, 1955.

8. Henry Fonda and the Deal for *12 Angry Men* (Spring and Summer 1955)

1. Henry Fonda, *My Life: As Told to Howard Teichman* (New York: New American Library, 1981), 102.

2. Fonda, 127.

3. Peter B. Flint, "Henry Fonda Dies on Coast at 77; Played 100 Stage and Screen Roles," *New York Times*, August 13, 1982.

4. Fonda, *My Life*, 179.

5. Flint, "Henry Fonda Dies on Coast at 77."

6. The Alvin Theater, now the Neil Simon Theater, is at 250 West Fifty-Second Street.

7. The cast of the national tour included Henry Fonda and Jack Klugman, plus Lee Van Cleef and Rance Howard, among others.

8. "Great Talent Makes Great Pictures!" Warner Brothers advertisement, *Variety*, July 6 and October 21, 1954.

9. Tino Balio, *United Artists: The Company That Changed the Film Industry* (Madison: University of Wisconsin Press, 1987), 82.

10. "Fonda Will Produce Six Pix for UA, Star in 3 in Next 3 Years," *Variety*, February 11, 1955, 1.

11. Delbert Mann, *Looking Back . . . at Live Television and Other Matters* (Los Angeles: Directors Guild of America, 1998), 82.

12. Mann, 82

13. Helm, Television Reviews, *Variety*, May 31, 1955, 9.

14. Fonda, *My Life*, 236.

15. Thomas M. Pryor, "Fonda and Rose to Film TV Play: Actor and Author of 'Twelve Angry Men' Team for First of Star's Productions," *New York Times*, July 18, 1955.

16. Fonda, *My Life*, 248.

17. As an example, film historian Robert Osborne said in a 2007 interview: "Henry Fonda had seen the television show, and then he went around to studios with his name attached. Nobody was interested. They couldn't care less about it. Number one, it had been on television for free. It was nothing they thought would pull people to the box office. And because of his name, he did get United Artists somewhat involved, but he put a lot of the money up himself." "Beyond Reasonable Doubt: Making *12 Angry Men*," special feature, *12 Angry Men* (1957; Metro-Goldwyn-Mayer Studios, 2007), DVD.

18. Henry Fonda, Popular Arts Project, 2nd series, vol. 3, Motion Pictures, Oral History Research Office, Columbia University, 1959, recorded April 1, 1959.

19. Fonda, Popular Arts Project.

20. Fonda, Popular Arts Project.

21. Pryor, "Fonda and Rose to Film TV Play."

22. Reginald Rose Papers, U.S. Mss 94AN, box 3, folder 5, Wisconsin Center for Film and Theater Research, University of Wisconsin–Madison.

23. Pryor, "Fonda and Rose to Film TV Play."

24. William Goldman, *Adventures in the Screen Trade* (New York: Grand Central Publishing, 1983).

25. Letter from Leon Kaplan to Reginald Rose, August 17, 1955, 2. Reginald Rose Papers, U.S. Mss 94AN, box 3, folder 5.

26. As an example, if box office revenues came to $2 million and cinemas kept 25 percent, United Artists' gross revenues would come to $1.5 million. Next, the company would take 30 percent or $450,000 as its distribution charge, leaving a gross income of $1,050,000. If direct marketing costs amounted to $300,000, net income would be $750,000 of which the company would recoup production outlay of $400,000, leaving $350,000. Henry Fonda would get his fee of $175,000 and Rose his remaining $45,000, plus other small deferrals of $10,000, yielding a net profit of $120,000. That amount would be shared 50/25/25: $60,000 to Fonda, $30,000 to Rose, and $30,000 to United Artists.

27. "Bonanza," *New York Times*, August 21, 1955, 101.

9. Developing the Screenplay (Fall 1955 to Spring 1956)

1. Felix Jackson to Reginald Rose, August 25, 1955, Reginald Rose Papers, U.S. Mss 94AN, box 53, folder 20, Wisconsin Center for Film and Theater Research, University of Wisconsin–Madison.

2. Reginald Rose, *Six Television Plays* (New York: Simon and Schuster, 1956), 158.

3. Herb Brodkin to Mary Shea, December 31, 1955: "The authors' fee shall be $4,000 except that if the program is telecast in color from California the authors fee shall be $5,000." Herbert Brodkin Television Production Files, box 14, Beinecke Rare Book and Manuscript Library, Yale University.

4. Legend has it that during the climactic scene, Lloyd Bridges let slip a profanity. Lumet said: "He got so involved, so intense about it, he stated 'You sons of bitches' . . . with tears coursing down his face. It was terrific acting, but it was disastrous as live television because of the language he was using." *By Sidney Lumet*, directed by Nancy Buirski (2015; Augusta Films and American Masters), DVD. The audio quality of live television was often not very good, and even with repeated listening it is not clear that Bridges said anything other than the scripted words: "You dirty stinkin' pigs." For years Rose would be asked if he had written the offending phrases, or if Bridges had ad-libbed them.

5. Sal Mineo was also nominated for Best Actor for *Dino*. Both lost, Mineo to Jack Palance in Rod Serling's "Requiem for a Heavyweight" on *Playhouse 90* and Rose to Serling.

6. "Fund for the Republic Awards to 2 NBC Shows, Baltimore Documentary," *Variety*, June 25, 1956, 7.

7. "Inside Stuff—Radio-TV," *Variety*, November 21, 1956, 24.

8. Paddy Chayefsky, *Television Plays* (New York: Simon and Schuster, 1955), 179.

9. Reginald Rose, *Six Television Plays* (New York: Simon and Schuster, 1956), ix.

10. Rose, x.

11. Rose, 54.

12. Shaun Considine, *Mad as Hell: The Life and Work of Paddy Chayefsky* (New York: Random House, 1994), 100.

13. "Chayefsky Chides Pix for 'Bad' Ad Policies," *Variety*, August 28, 1957.

14. Jeff Kisseloff, *The Box: An Oral History of Television, 1920–1961* (New York: Viking, 1995), 252.

15. Leonard Traube, "Scorecard on 'TV-To-H'Wood," *Variety*, February 22, 1956, 21.

16. "Dino" was nominated for an Emmy. It became the third Reginald Rose program to be made into a movie, with Sal Mineo retaining the starring role. Thomas Carr directed the movie, which was released July 21, 1957.

17. See Army Archerd, "Just for Variety," *Variety*, April 18, 1956, 2; and "A Show Biz Coealition," *Variety*, May 23, 1956, 54.

10. Assembling the Team (Spring 1956)

1. Jeff Kisseloff, *The Box: An Oral History of Television, 1920–1961* (New York: Viking, 1995), 237.

2. Lumet recalled: "I had a workshop for actors in a loft down on Irving Place in the Village, where I actually began directing. Just thirty of us studying body movement and voice and diction and scenes. At the end of each year, we would try to do a new American play. One of the kids in the play, Joe Gerard, was appearing in *Mr. Roberts* on Broadway. And Fonda was in it, too. So Fonda came down, always being the generous man he was to young people. Two years later, when Reggie proposed my name, Fonda recalled it and said, 'I remember seeing something of his off-Broadway. Very interesting. Let's go with him.' It was that simple. I didn't have to talk with anybody. We didn't have to take breakfast, lunch, drinks or dinner. I didn't have to go in and discuss my ideas. I didn't have to audition for it. It just fell into my lap." Harold Goldberg, "Sidney Lumet: The Director Talks about Shooting in Snowstorms," *Hollywood Reporter*, New York special issue, June 10, 1997, in *Sidney Lumet: Interviews*, ed. Joanna E. Rapf (Jackson: University of Mississippi Press, 2006), 161.

In another interview, Lumet recalled: "One year we did a very interesting play called *Ward Six*, about guys who had been wounded in the war. I directed it, Maury Houghton saw that, and I know Hank Fonda saw it. Two of the kids in *Mister Robert* were in our workshop and brought him down to see it. And when *12 Angry Men* came up, and Hank was coproducer with Reggie Rose, and Reggie said I'd like you do to this. And I said what about Fonda, I've never done a picture before, will he accept me. And he said, 'Oh he saw your production down in the Village and thought you did a marvelous job.' That's how my first picture happened." "Sidney Lumet," interview, Television Academy Foundation, https://interviews.televisionacademy.com/interviews/sidney-lumet.

3. "RKO Pacts Stan Rubin, TV Director Sid Lumet," *Variety*, February 28, 1956, 3.

4. *By Sidney Lumet*, directed by Nancy Buirski (2015; Augusta Films and American Masters), DVD.

5. "Beyond Reasonable Doubt: Making *12 Angry Men*," special feature, *12 Angry Men* (1957; Metro-Goldwyn-Mayer Studios, 2007), DVD.

6. In a 2011 interview, writer Loring Mandel provided a somewhat different account: "Sidney negotiated himself the opportunity to direct the film *12 Angry Men*. I heard about this both from my friend Frank Schaffner, who had directed that property for *Studio One*, and from Jerome Hellman, Frank's agent and mine. Frank very much wanted to direct the film, and felt he had some claim to do so. Sidney (according to Hellman) was reaching the end of his commitment to his agent, and said that if the agent got him the assignment, he would stay with that agency. And so he got the job, pretty much devastating Frank and, I think, rupturing Frank's relationship with Reginald Rose." Stephen Bowie, "Sidney Lumet: Memories from the Early Years," Classic TV History Blog, July 18, 2011, https://classictvhistory.wordpress.com/2011/07/18/sidney-lumet-memories-from-the-early-years/. When I met Loring Mandel in October 2016, he reaffirmed that this explanation came from Jerome Hellman; when I spoke by telephone with

Mr. Hellman a few days later, he said that Rose had preferred Lumet without adding further details. The relationship between Rose and Schaffner may have been strained but did not rupture; Schaffner went on to direct six episodes of *The Defenders*.

7. Charles K. Russell, *In the Worst of Times It Was the Best of Times* (Beverly Hills, CA: CKR Productions, 1982), 146.

8. Russell, 146.

9. "Beyond Reasonable Doubt: Making *12 Angry Men*," special feature.

10. Bob Markell, interview with the author, April 2016.

11. "Writer Released from Ellis Island: Voskovec, a Czech, Had Been Held 10½ months in 'Prison' on Security Charges," *New York Times*, April 3, 1951.

12. George Voskovec, Letters to the *Times*: Security Jitters in the West, Comparison Made Between Our Methods and Those Behind Iron Curtain, *New York Times*, May 12, 1951.

13. "Beyond Reasonable Doubt: Making *12 Angry Men*."

14. Klugman was with the production for many months and played two prominent roles, Doc and chief petty officer Dowdy. In the 1955 movie, William Powell played Doc and Ward Bond played Dowdy.

15. "Beyond Reasonable Doubt: Making *12 Angry Men*."

16. Producer Jerome Hellman, at the time an agent at Ashley-Steiner, told me in 2016 that Cobb was suggested by Marion Dougherty, a well-known independent casting director.

17. "'Angry' Role for Cobb," *Variety*, March 9, 1956, 13.

18. G. S. Bourdain, "Robert Webber, Actor, Dies at 64," *New York Times*, May 20, 1989.

19. Elizabeth Messina, *What's His Name? John Fiedler: The Man, The Face, The Voice* (Bloomington, IN: AuthorHouse, 2012), 42.

20. Rudy Bond appeared in another scene with Brando, visible for less than a second, peeling an apple, at the meeting of the Five Families in *The Godfather*. Somehow, he received a first billing as Cuneo, although mob boss Cuneo, murdered in the baptism sequence, was played by a different actor. In *12 Angry Men*, Bond plays a vital role but received no credit; in *The Godfather*, he got credit for the briefest of glimpses.

21. Wayne Phillips, "Merchants Who Deal with Negroes and Whites Are Hard Hit Caught in the Middle Corner Loses Value," *New York Times*, February 28, 1956.

22. Haley Raines, "On Location in Gotham: Tall Problems Hurdled by Local Crew Filming 'A Man Is Ten Feet Tall,'" *New York Times*, April 15, 1956.

23. Carlton Jackson, *Picking up the Tab: The Life and Movies of Martin Ritt* (Bowling Green, OH: Bowling Green State University Popular Press, 1994), 38.

24. Letter from David Susskind to Arthur Loew, February 14, 1956, David Susskind Papers, U.S. Mss 73AN, box 17, folder 5, Wisconsin Center for Film and Theater Research, University of Wisconsin–Madison. See also Jackson, *Picking up the Tab*, 41.

25. Jonathan Productions Budget, February 16, 1956, David Susskind Papers, box 17, folder 3.

26. "Guilt Trip: Hitchcock and *The Wrong Man*," special feature, *The Wrong Man* (1956; Warner Bros. Entertainment, 2004), DVD.

27. "Fonda's Multiple Yens for Stage, Specs, Own Pix," *Variety*, December 21, 1955, 4.

28. "Guilt Trip" special feature.

29. "Guilt Trip" special feature.

30. "Guilt Trip" special feature.

31. "Guilt Trip" special feature.

32. "Guilt Trip" special feature.

33. "Edward Arnold, Actor, Dies at 66," *New York Times*, April 27, 1956, 27.

34. Gilbert Millstein, "The Long Running Ed Begley," *New York Times*, December 9, 1956, 289.

35. "Ed Begley Inherits Arnold's 'Angry' Role," *Variety*, May 31, 1956, 2.

11. Six Weeks of Work (Summer 1956)

1. "Fonda's Multiple Yens for Stage, Specs, Own Pix," *Variety*, December 21, 1955, 4.

2. Don Ross, "A Dozen Happy Actors Become '12 Angry Men,'" *New York Herald Tribune*, July 15, 1956, D1. See also, A. H. Weiler, "By Way of Report," *New York Times*, June 24, 1956.

3. Henry Fonda, Popular Arts Project, 2nd series, vol. 3, Motion Pictures, Oral History Research Office, Columbia University, 1959, recorded April 1, 1959.

4. Ross, "A Dozen Happy Actors Become '12 Angry Men,'" D1 and D3.

5. Fonda, Popular Arts Project.

6. "Beyond Reasonable Doubt: Making *12 Angry Men*," special feature, *12 Angry Men* (1957; Metro-Goldwyn-Mayer Studios, 2007), DVD.

7. Sidney Lumet, *Making Movies* (New York: Vintage, 1995), 58.

8. Bob Markell, interview with the author, April 2016.

9. Sidney Lumet quoted in Peter Bogdanovich, *Who the Devil Made It: Conversations with Legendary Film Directors* (New York: Ballantine Books, 1997), 802.

10. Lumet, *Making Movies*, 161–162.

11. Lumet, 81.

12. Lumet, 81.

13. "Good Men and True and All Angry," *Life*, April 22, 1957, 137–138.

14. Markell interview, April 2016.

15. Markell interview.

16. Markell interview.

17. Henry Fonda, as told to Howard Teichmann, *Fonda: My Life* (New York: New American Library, 1981), 248.

18. "Beyond Reasonable Doubt," special feature.

19. Markell interview.

20. In my interviews with Bob Markell and Don Kranze, both men, age ninety-two and ninety-four, chose their words carefully when speaking about Boris Kaufman, a European cinematographer with an imposing manner. Markell felt he had been subjected to unwarranted criticism about the backdrops, and Kranze said that the cast was often annoyed by the lengthy delays as Kaufman, a meticulous artist, set up the lighting. Neither man wanted to sound critical, as if they did not wish to incur Kaufman's disfavor in case he was listening from beyond the grave.

21. "Memos to Crew from Film Production Mgr. George Justin: A Collection of Choice Communiques from the Coach." Reginald Rose Papers, U.S. Mss 94AN, box 3, folder 4, Wisconsin Center for Film and Theater Research, University of Wisconsin–Madison.

22. Markell interview.

23. Lumet, *Making Movies*, 124.

24. "Good Men and True and All Angry," 137–138.

25. "Beyond Reasonable Doubt," special feature.

26. Lumet, *Making Movies*, 25.

27. "Good Men and True and All Angry," 137–138.

28. Lumet, *Making Movies*, 26.

29. Lumet, 26.

30. Fonda, *My Life*, 249.

31. Fonda, 249. Lumet told the story on more than one occasion. In *Making Movies*: "Henry Fonda never went to rushes his whole career. In fact, he rarely saw the movie until it had been out for over a year. But on *12 Angry Men*, he was also the producer, so he had to come. After we'd seen the first day's rushes, he leaned forward, squeezed my shoulder, whispered 'It's brilliant,' and fled, never to return" (139). Another version gave essentially the same story: "At the end of every day we'd go and see the rushes, we'd go see the film of the previous day's work. Fonda hated watching himself. He couldn't bear to watch himself on the screen. So he came to the first day's rushes, sat directly behind me. First two shots came up, he watched. Third shot came up, he was in it, he barely sat through it, leaned forward, grabbed me by the shoulder and said, 'It's wonderful,' got up, fled, and never came to rushes again." Lumet interview, "Beyond Reasonable Doubt: Making *12 Angry Men*."

32. Fonda, Popular Arts Project.

33. Markell interview.

34. Hy Hollinger, "Reginald Rose Sees TV-Derived Stories Hit by Broad Condemnation," *Variety*, June 27, 1956, 3.

35. Hollinger, 3.

36. A. H. Weiler, "Of Pictures and People: Prize Television Drama to Be Filmed," *New York Times*, July 1, 1956.

37. "Beyond Reasonable Doubt," special feature.

38. "Beyond Reasonable Doubt," special feature.

39. Dewey, 208.

40. Fonda, *My Life*, 249.

41. Markell interview.

42. Don Kranze, interview with the author, July 2019.

43. "Beyond Reasonable Doubt," special feature.

44. Lumet, *Making Movies*, 81.

45. Markell interview.

46. Lumet, *Making Movies*, 81.

12. Release and Reviews (Fall 1956 to Spring 1958)

1. "Of Local Origin," *New York Times*, August 25, 1956.

2. "Lee Cobb Cast in Col 'Garment Center' Pic," *Variety*, September 19, 1956.

3. *Variety*, October 17, 1956.

4. Sidney Lumet, Popular Arts Project, 2nd series, vol. 3, Motion Pictures, Oral History Research Office, Columbia University, 1959, March 1959.

5. "Hopkins 'Angry' Scorer," *Variety*, Oct. 22, 1956, 7.

6. Bob Markell, interview with the author, April 2016.

7. "Stock to Be Sold by United Artists," *New York Times*, March 20, 1957.

8. "Gross Sets Record for United Artists," *New York Times*, January 9, 1957.

9. Henry Fonda, *Fonda: My Life* (New York: New American Library, 1981), 250.

10. Bosley Crowther, "Old-Time Star-Filler Benefit to Close Capitol Theater Tonight," *New York Times*, September 16, 1968.

11. "Twelve Angry Men, Publicity and Promotion Report," The Arthur P. Jacobs Company, March 2, 1957. Reginald Rose Papers, U.S. Mss 94AN, box 3, folder 7, Wisconsin Center for Film and Theater Research, University of Wisconsin–Madison.

12. Denis Hamill, "Time to Get 'Angry' Again," *New York Daily News*, August 17, 1997, 21.

13. Richard P. Shepard, "Man with a Script: Reginald Rose Thinks All TV, Even Sponsors, Gains from Controversy," *New York Times*, February 24, 1957.

14. Frank Quinn, "12 Angry Men Win Verdict of Superior," *New York Daily Mirror*, April 14, 1957.

15. Rose Pelswick, "The Verdict—Fine Film," *New York Journal American*, April 15, 1957, 15.

16. A. H. Weiler, "Screen: '12 Angry Men'; Jury Room Drama Has Debut at Capitol," *New York Times*, April 15, 1957, 24.

17. Hollis Alpert, "Gentlemen of the Jury," *Saturday Review*, April 20, 1957, 29–30.

18. At least the Orion-Nova production of *12 Angry Men* had stayed on budget, thanks to the efforts of George Justin and Sidney Lumet. *Sweet Smell of Success* went far over budget, leading Burt Lancaster to call it the "greatest failure our company ever made. . . . We lost a fortune on it." *The Bachelor Party* also went over budget, costing three times the amount of *Marty*. In both cases, cost overruns were largely absorbed by Hecht-Hill-Lancaster Productions; United Artists was protected by the terms of its contract. See Tino Balio, *United Artists: The Company that Changed the Film Industry* (Madison: University of Wisconsin Press, 1987), 151.

19. "Yank Festival Films Might Better Be Picked by European Officers; MPEA Closely Studied 1957 Cannes," *Variety*, May 22, 1957, 5, 10; "Quaker 'Persuasion' Win at Cannes Film Festival Amazes Even Yankees," *Variety*, May 22, 1957, 5

20. Anita Gates, "Michèle Morgan, the First 'Best Actress' at Cannes, Dies at 96," *New York Times*, December 22, 2016.

21. "Berlin Selections," *Variety*, May 22, 1957, 4.

22. Harry Gilroy, "Movie Fete Postscript: American Entries Take Top Prizes in Berlin's Seventh Annual Festival," *New York Times*, July 7, 1957; "'12 Angry Men' Best Film; British and Mexican Win Berlin's Personal Awards," *Variety*, July 3, 1957, 3; Harold Myers, "At Berlin Fest. Yankee Showmen & Bureaucrats Not Wholly Compatible," *Variety*, July 10, 1957, 19; "Die Preise," *Frankfurter Allgemeine Zeitung*, July 4, 1957, 10.

23. "Kein Turmbau im Filmbabel," *Frankfurter Allgemeine Zeitung*, July 4, 1957, 10; translation by Albrecht Enders.

24. "Yank Pix Tops in W. Berlin Preem Houses," *Variety*, August 28, 1957, 15.

25. Jacques-G. Perret, "Quand la télévision influence la cinéma et le théâtre," *l'Avant Scène*, Novembre 1958. "Personne, en effet, ne connaissait les auteurs de cet ouvrage : Reginald Rose (scénariste et coproducteur), Sidney Lumet (réalisateur) qui semblait aborder le cinéma pour la première fois. Comme on ne s'improvise pas du jour au lendemain cinéaste et que ce film fut accueilli comme un chef-d'œuvre, l'événement avait de quoi surprendre." ["No one had heard of the movie's creators: Reginald Rose (screenwriter and co-producer) and Sidney Lumet (director) who are making a movie for the first time. Since one does not become a skilled moviemaker overnight, and as this film has been hailed as a masterpiece, this turn of events is remarkable." Translation mine.]

26. Bosely Crowther, "Best Pictures of 1957," *New York Times*, December 29, 1957, 53 and 57.

27. *Variety*, January 23, 1958.

28. "Top Grosses of 1957," *Variety*, 8 January 1958, 30.

29. David Lean's epic was released December 14, 1957, thereby qualifying for the Academy Awards in 1957, but too late for 1957 box office figures. The following year, 1958, it grossed $17.2 million.

30. "Beyond Reasonable Doubt: Making *12 Angry Men*," special feature, *12 Angry Men* (1957; Metro-Goldwyn-Mayer Studios, 2007), DVD.

13. New Directions (1957 to 1960)

1. John Huston, *An Open Book* (New York: Da Capo, 1994), 336.

2. Maura Spiegel, *Sidney Lumet: A Life* (New York: St. Martin's, 2019), 205.

3. Reginald Rose, *Six Television Plays* (New York: Simon and Schuster, 1956), x–xi.

4. "Herbert Brodkin: 'Playhouse 90' Producer of Television Originals," *CBS Television Biography*, October 8, 1958.

5. Val Adams, "Brodkin of N.B.C. Goes to Columbia," *New York Times*, November 21, 1956.

6. Jack Gould, "TV: Rockefeller Campaign Begins," *New York Times*, September 30, 1958, 62.

7. Letter to Reginald Rose, unsigned but likely from Eve Ettinger, Reginald Rose Papers, U.S. Mss 94AN, box 2, folder 2, Wisconsin Center for Film and Theater Research, University of Wisconsin–Madison.

8. Walter Mirisch, *I Thought We Were Making Movies, Not History* (Madison: University of Wisconsin Press, 2008), 95. Cooper was fifty-six when the movie was filmed; playing his uncle was Lee J. Cobb, ten years younger at forty-six.

9. Richard W. Nason, "Screen: Canvas of Goya; Naked Maja, on Bill with 'Man in Net,'" *New York Times*, June 11, 1959.

10. February 5, 1958, Reginald Rose letter to Walter Mirisch, Reginald Rose Papers, U.S. Mss 94AN, box 1, folder 4.

11. Nason, "Screen: Canvas of Goya."

12. John Crosby, "Crosby on TV: The Sacco-Vanzetti Case," *New York Herald Tribune*, June 1, 1960.

13. Ben Gross, "New TV Writers Are Out, Noted Dramatist Reveals," *Sunday News*, June 5, 1960, 17.

14. Steven H. Scheuer, "Reginald Rose Offers More Good TV Drama," *Lansing State Journal*, Lansing Michigan, May 12, 1959, 24.

15. Margaret McManus, "Prolific Playwright Finds Everything's Coming Up Rose's," *New York World-Telegram and Sun*, September 2, 1961.

16. Shaun Considine, *Mad As Hell: The Life and Work of Paddy Chayefsky* (New York: Random House, 1994), 239.

17. Letter from Charles H. Renthal, September 5, 1958, Reginald Rose Papers, U.S. Mss 94AN, box 3, folder 5. Accountant Charles Renthal was paid $752 of the $57,142.

18. Bennett Schiff, "Plays on Integration Are Brought with All Deliberate Speed," *New York Post*, January 17, 1961.

19. Schiff, "Plays on Integration."

20. Schiff, "Plays on Integration."

21. Thomas F. Brady, "Torture Charges Vexing to French," *New York Times*, September 9, 1957, 3.

22. "The Cruel Day," final script, Reginald Rose Papers, U.S. Mss 94AN, box 9, folder 4.

23. From *Playhouse 90 Reviews*, "The Cruel Day," CBS Television Network memo, Herbert Brodkin Television Production Files, box 30, Beinecke Rare Book and Manuscript Library, Yale University.

24. "Massachusetts executed two Italian immigrants 90 years ago: Why the global fallout still matters," Conversation, August 30, 2017, https://theconversation.com/massachusetts-executed -two-italian-immigrants-90-years-ago-why-the-global-fallout-still-matters-82416.

25. Gross, "New TV Writers Are Out," 17.

26. Gross, 17.

27. Subsequent years would see a movie, *Sacco & Vanzetti* (1971), directed by Giuliano Mondaldo, and no shortage of documentaries, including *Sacco and Vanzetti* (2006), a definitive account with new ballistic evidence and eyewitness accounts that cast doubt on the prosecution's case. Directed by Peter Miller, it won the 2007 John E. O'Connor Film Award for the best historical film from the American Historical Association.

28. Crosby, "Crosby on TV: The Sacco-Vanzetti Case."

29. Jack Gould, "TV: Sacco-Vanzetti': First Hour of Documentary Drama by Reginald Rose Given on N.B.C.," *New York Times*, June 4, 1960.

30. *Congressional Record—Senate*, June 22, 1960, 13708.

31. Arthur E. Fetridge, "On Television," *Boston Herald*, June 3, 1960.

32. Percy Shain, "Night Watch—Governor Fuller Vilified as S-V Drama Ends—Sacco-Vanzetti Story, Channel 4," *Boston Globe*, June 11, 1960.

33. "Bias and Distortion," *Boston Traveler*, June 14, 1960; from *Congressional Record— Senate*, June 22, 1960, 13710.

34. Crosby, "Crosby on TV: The Sacco-Vanzetti Case."

35. "CBS Shades NBC in Emmy Nominations," *Variety*, May 2, 1961.

36. Michael A. Musmanno, "The Sacco-Vanzetti Jury," *Villanova Law Review* 5, no. 2 (Winter 1959–60): 169–180.

37. Telegram from Michael Musmanno to Reginald Rose, April 11, 1960, Reginald Rose Papers, U.S. Mss 94AN, box 16, folder 1.

14. *The Defenders* (1960 to Spring 1962)

1. "The Defenders," undated treatment, Reginald Rose Papers, U.S. Mss 94AN, box 22, folder 4, Wisconsin Center for Film and Theater Research, University of Wisconsin–Madison.

2. "Produced by . . . Herb Brodkin, Day 2: Producing 'The Defenders,'" panel discussion with Mike Dann, Ernest Kinoy, and Herbert Brodkin, *Museum of Broadcasting Seminar Series*, March 18, 1985.

3. "Brodkin to Pilot 1 (or 2) for CBS," *Variety*, January 13, 1960, 1 and 10.

4. "Produced by . . . Herb Brodkin, Day 2."

5. "CBS-TV 'Defender' 'Diagnosis' Shows Aiding N.Y. Cause." *Variety*, October 26, 1960, 25.

6. E. G. Marshall, interview, Television Academy Foundation, https://interviews .televisionacademy.com/interviews/e-g-marshall?clip=84700#interview-clips.

7. Letter from Alden Schwimmer to Oscar Katz, November 22, 1960, Reginald Rose Papers, U.S. Mss 94AN, box 22, folder 1.

8. "CBS 'Defenders' As Thurs. Punch," *Variety*, March 8, 1961, 24.

9. *The Defenders*, CBS prospectus, March 1961, Reginald Rose Papers, U.S. Mss 94AN, box 22, folder 7.

10. "Sponsor for 'Defenders,'" *Variety*, April 13, 1961, 3.

11. Doc Quigg, "New 'Type' Courtroom Series," UPI, *New York Herald Tribune*, September 7, 1961, 2.

12. Quigg, 2.

13. Kay Gardella, "Writer Finds New Way in the Same Old Medium," *Daily News*, August 25, 1961, 50.

14. Quigg, "New 'Type' Courtroom Series," 2.

15. Quigg, 2.

16. Kay Gardella, "Writer Finds New Way in Same Old Medium," *Daily News*, August 25, 1961, 50.

17. Margaret McManus, "Prolific Playwright Finds Everything Coming Up Rose's," *New York World Telegraph & Sun*, September 2, 1961.

18. McManus, "Prolific Playwright Finds Everything Coming Up Rose's."

19. Gardella, "Writer Finds New Way," 50.

20. The thirty-two episodes of the first season of *The Defenders* and the 1957 *Studio One* episode of "The Defender" are available on DVD: *The Defenders*, Season One (Shout! Factory, CBS Broadcasting, 2016).

21. Stephen Bowie of the Classic TV History blog writes: *"The Defenders* is one of those shows that didn't hit its stride until its second season. Although there are many strong hours in the first year . . . nearly all of the series' worst duds can be found in [the first year], too." "Defending the Defenders," Classic TV History, July 14, 2016. https://classictvhistory.wordpress .com/2016/07/14/defending-the-defenders/.

22. "Produced by . . . Herb Brodkin, Day 2."

23. "The Show that Dared to Be Controversial," *Viewer* 8, no. 5 (May 1964): 2–3

24. Jonathan Rose, interview with the author, June 2020.

25. Edith Efron, "The Eternal Conflict between Good and Evil . . ." *TV Guide*, March 17–23, 1962, 7.

26. Efron, 8.

27. Efron, 8.

28. Edith Efron, "Can a TV Writer Keep His Integrity?" *TV Guide*, April 21–27, 1962, 8–11.

29. Efron, 8–11.

30. "CBS-TV to Air 'Defenders' Seg Dealing with Abortion Tho All 3 Sponsors Bow Off," April 10, 1962, 9.

31. "10 CBS Affils Abort 'Defenders,'" *Variety*, April 27, 1962, 1.

32. "A Defense of 'Defenders': Speidel Benefactor in More Ways than One," *Variety*, April 25, 1962, 21.

33. "10 CBS Affils Abort 'Defenders,'"1.

34. "CBS Sez Reaction to 'Defenders' Seg 90% Favorable," *Variety*, April 30, 1962.

35. Inside Stuff-Radio-TV, *Variety*, June 27, 1962.

36. "Produced by . . . Herb Brodkin, Day 2."

15. *The Defenders* (Fall 1962 to 1965)

1. Seasons 2, 3, and 4 of *The Defenders* are not available on DVD. I was able to view several episodes at the Wisconsin Center for Film and Theater Research, including "The Voices of

Death," "Blood County," "The Madman (Parts 1 and 2)," "Blacklist," and "The 700 Year Old Gang."

2. "The Defenders," *Variety*, October 30, 1961, 10.

3. Bob Markell, interview, Television Academy Foundation, April 18, 1998. https://interviews.televisionacademy.com/interviews/bob-markell.

4. John Miles, "Defenders Was the Best TV Fare," TV Last Night, newspaper clipping, Reginald Rose Papers, U.S. Mss 94AN, box 22, folder 1, Wisconsin Center for Film and Theater Research. University of Wisconsin–Madison.

5. Bob Markell, interview with the author, April 2016.

6. Murray Horowitz, "TV 'Burying Writers in Formula Coffin' Laments David Davidson," *Variety*, November 7, 1962.

7. Horowitz, "TV 'Burying Writers in Formula Coffin.'"

8. Letters from viewers, Reginald Rose Papers, U.S. Mss 94AN, box 22, folder 1.

9. Letter to Arthur Fetridge, April 2, 1963, Reginald Rose Papers, U.S. Mss 94AN, box 22, folder 1.

10. John P. Shanley, "'Tunnel' Wins TV's Top Emmy," *New York Times*, May 27, 1963.

11. Clifford B. Mandell, "Popular Defender of Unpopular Causes," *St. Louis Post Dispatch*, June 7, 1963.

12. Jonathan Rose, interview with the author, June 2020.

13. David Shaw, interview, Television Academy Foundation, August 31, 2004, https://interviews.televisionacademy.com/interviews/david-shaw.

14. Outline of "The Cool Rebellion," June 5, 1963, Reginald Rose Papers, U.S. Mss 94AN, box 35, folder 2.

15. Tom Stempel notes from interview with Reginald Rose, March 9, 1991. David Shaw tells the same story in his Television Academy interview, part 4 at 20:00, https://interviews.televisionacademy.com/interviews/david-shaw?clip=27087#interview-clips.

16. Val Adams, "Blacklist a Topic for 'Defenders,'" *New York Times*, November 6, 1963.

17. Ernest Kinoy, outline of "Blacklist," June 25, 1963, Reginald Rose Papers, U.S. Mss 94AN, box 37, folder 1.

18. Ernest Kinoy, "What's the Matter with Joe Larch?" (script), October 23, 1963, Herbert Brodkin Television Production Files, box 11, Beinecke Rare Book and Manuscript Library, Yale University.

19. E. G. Marshall, interview, Television Academy Foundation, October 15, 1997, https://interviews.televisionacademy.com/interviews/e-g-marshall.

20. Tom Stempel, notes from interview with Reginald Rose, March 9, 1991.

21. Rose, Reginald. "Law, Drama, and Criticism." *Television Quarterly* 3, no. 4 (Fall 1964): 25–27.

22. Harry Castleman and Walter J. Podrazik, *Watching TV: Six Decades of American Television*, 2nd ed. (Syracuse, NY: University of Syracuse Press, 2010), 176.

23. *The Defenders* correspondence and fan mail, Reginald Rose Papers, U.S. Mss 94AN, box 22, folders 1 and 2.

24. Tom Stempel, notes from interview with William Woolfolk, September 1, 1990.

16. After *The Defenders*

1. "Gabriel Katzka, 59, Producer in Theater, Films, and Television," *New York Times*, February 21, 1990.

2. "Offering circular," Katzka-Berne Productions Inc., May 1965. Reginald Rose Papers, U.S. Mss 94AN, box 5, folder 2, Wisconsin Center for Film and Theater Research. University of Wisconsin–Madison.

3. Reginald Rose to Elia Kazan, June 9, 1965, Reginald Rose Papers, U.S. Mss 94AN, box 5, folder 1.

4. Grosbard "had not seen eye to eye with Mr. Rose on the script." "Alex Segal New Director of Rose's 'Porcelain Year,'" *New York Times*, August 26, 1965.

5. Ernest Schier, "Writer's Zeal in 'The Porcelain Year' Creates One-man Kinsey Report," *Philadelphia Bulletin*, October 12, 1965.

6. "This Marriage Is Doomed before It Hits B'Way," *Washington Post*, October 20, 1965.

7. "This Marriage Is Doomed before It Hits B'Way."

8. Tom Donnelly, "The Decline and Fall of Alice Potter," *Washington Daily News*, October 19, 1965.

9. Pierre Bowman, "He's Reginald Rose, the Legendary TV Dramatist," *Honolulu Star-Advertiser*, July 30, 1980.

10. Louis Calta, "Theater Leaders Back Ticket Plan," *New York Times*, November 11, 1965.

11. Bowman, "He's Reginald Rose."

12. Val Adams, "C.B.S. to Get Play by Reginald Rose," *New York Times*, August 9, 1966.

13. TV News, *New York Daily News*, December 6, 1967.

14. Letter from Eugene Turner, December 7, 1967, Reginald Rose Papers, U.S. Mss 94AN, box 9, folder 5.

15. Letter from Karl E. Weick, December 11, 1967, Reginald Rose Papers, U.S. Mss 94AN, box 9, folder 5.

16. Reginald Rose, "TV's Age of Innocence—What Became of It?" *New York Times*, December 3, 1967, A193.

17. Reginald Rose letter to Tino Balio, January 23, 1967, Reginald Rose donation file, Wisconsin Center for Film and Theater Research.

18. Jonathan Rose, interview with the author, June 2020.

19. Correspondence between Maurice S. Spanbock and Sy Fischer, January and February 1970, Reginald Rose Papers, U.S. Mss 94AN, box 54, folder 15.

20. Rex Polier, "Reflections on TV's Golden Age," *Los Angeles Times*, January 1, 1982.

21. "The Adversaries," concept for a one-hour TV series, July 23, 1976, Reginald Rose Collection, box 54, folder 1.

22. "The Adversaries."

23. Tom Stempel, *Storytellers to the Nation: A History of American Television Writing* (New York: Continuum, 1992), 237.

24. Bowman, "He's Reginald Rose."

25. Janet Maslin, "Burton in 'Wild Geese,' Film about Mercenaries," *New York Times*, November 11, 1978.

26. "Moore Reconsiders, Joins Cast of Lloyd's 'Wolves,'" *Variety*, August 29, 1979.

27. Jonathan Rose, interview with the author, June 2020.

28. Producer Philip Yordan was credited with the adaptation, but in fact it was written by one blacklisted writer, Arnaud d'Usseau, with a voice-over narration intended to fix problems of continuity and motivation by another blacklisted writer, Bernard Gordon. Bernard Gordon, *Hollywood Exile, or, How I Learned to Love the Blacklist: A Memoir* (Austin: University of Texas Press, 1999), 89–90.

29. Murray Schumach, "'Studs Lonigan' Is the Only Feature to Be Filmed during the Strike," *New York Times*, April 3, 1960.

30. James T. Farrell, letter to the editor, *New York Times*, April 10, 1960.

31. Chuck McLain to Lee Rich, Lorimar Productions Memorandum, November 11, 1976. Reginald Rose Papers, U.S. Mss 94AN, box 60, folder 9.

32. Rose, "On Adapting 'Studs Lonigan' for Television," unpublished essay intended for *New York Times*, dated January 31, 1979, Reginald Rose Papers, U.S. Mss 94AN, box 61, folder 1.

33. Rose.

34. Rose.

35. Karl Honeystein, The Sy Fischer Company Inc. Memorandum, December 23, 1976, Reginald Rose Papers, U.S. Mss 94AN, box 60, folder 9.

36. Rose, "On Adapting 'Studs Lonigan' for Television."

37. Rose.

38. Rose.

39. Jane Crowley to Eleanor Timberman, NBC Memorandum, February 17, 1977, Reginald Rose Papers, U.S. Mss 94AN, box 60, folder 9.

40. Chuck McLain to Reginald Rose, Lorimar Productions Inc. Memorandum, September 26, 1977. Reginald Rose Papers, U.S. Mss 94AN, box 60, folder 9.

41. Transcribed from *Studs Lonigan*, James Goldstone director, Harry R. Sherman producer, James T. Farrell (novel) and Reginald Rose (teleplay), Lorimar Productions, 1979. The 1979 Lorimar production of *Studs Lonigan* is not easily available; the author's copy was bought from *Robert's Hard to Find Videos*, http://www.robertsvideos.com/.

42. "Studs," Notes from Bill Woolfolk, undated memo, Reginald Rose Papers, U.S. Mss 94AN, box 60, folder 9.

43. Reginald Rose to Phil Capice, February 22, 1979, Reginald Rose Papers, U.S. Mss 94AN, box 60, folder 9.

44. Rose changed very little of Farrell's story, with one curious exception: Mrs. George Jackson, who invites four men to her apartment to cover a gambling loss, turns out to be Studs's lost love, Lucy Scanlan, a very odd twist that is never explained.

45. John J. O'Connor, "TV: 'Lonigan' on NBC," *New York Times*, March 7, 1979.

46. Rose, "On Adapting 'Studs Lonigan' for Television."

47. Bowman, "He's Reginald Rose."

48. Rex Polier, "Reflections on TV's Golden Age," *Los Angeles Times*, January 1, 1982.

49. Polier.

50. Polier.

51. Polier.

52. Frank Lovece, "Writer Reginald Rose Brings Sobibor to TV," *Newsday*, April 1987.

53. Lovece.

54. "On Reginald Rose," special feature, *12 Angry Men* (1957; Criterion Collection, 2011), DVD.

55. Bob Markell, interview, Television Academy Foundation, April 18, 1998, https://interviews.televisionacademy.com/interviews/bob-markell.

56. J. Rose interview.

17. A Life on Stage

1. For clarity, *12 Angry Men* refers to the drama in general as well as the 1957 movie; the original teleplay is "Twelve Angry Men" and the stage play is *Twelve Angry Men*.

2. One reference to *12 Angry Men* as a "masterpiece" can be found in Jack Marshall's Audience Guide, American Century Theater, 2015, 29.

3. Arthur Miller, *Timebends: A Life* (London: Methuen, 1987), 187.

4. Miller, 191.

5. Miller, 191.

6. Miller, 585.

7. Tom Santopietro, *Why To Kill a Mockingbird Still Matters: What Harper Lee's Book and the Iconic American Film Mean to Us Today* (New York: St. Martin's Press, 2018).

8. In *The Tipping Point*, Malcolm Gladwell describes how the popularity of a product, or the widespread adoption of a habit, is rarely due to a single cause. More often there is an interplay of factors that reinforce one another. Malcolm Gladwell, *The Tipping Point: How Little Things Can Make a Big Difference* (New York: Little, Brown and Company, 2000).

9. Parents Roger and Ruth Sergel, sons Clark F. Sergel, born 1921, Sherman L. Sergel, born 1924.

10. Reginald Rose, *Thunder on Sycamore Street: A Play in Three Acts, Made into a Play by Kristin Sergel* (Woodstock, IL: Dramatic Publishing Company, 1958 and 1986).

11. Reginald Rose, *Twelve Angry Men*, adapted by Sherman L. Sergel (Dramatic Publishing Company, 1955), 9.

12. Steven Price, "Commentary," in Reginald Rose, *Twelve Angry Men* (London: Bloomsbury, 2017), 8.

13. "Rose's '12 Angry Men' Hot with Tyro Thesps," *Variety*, November 14, 1956, 28.

14. Hy Hollinger, "Telecast and Theater Film, Looks As If '12 Angry Men' May Reap Most Dough as Legit Play," *Variety*, December 24, 1958, 5.

15. A French equivalent might be: "Tentons le coup et nous verrons si cela marche."

16. Reginald Rose to Lars Schmidt, October 25, 1958, Reginald Rose Papers, U.S. Mss 94AN, box 6, folder 4, Wisconsin Center for Film and Theater Research, University of Wisconsin Madison.

17. Ben Gross, "New TV Writers Are Out, Noted Dramatist Reveals," *Sunday News*, June 5, 1960, 17.

18. Kathleen Carmody, "Rousing Drama," *Catholic Standard*, January 18, 1963, Reginald Rose Papers, U.S. Mss 94AN, box 6, folder 11.

19. Letter from R. R. Brown, WOAY-Television, to Dave Williams CBS Television, December 8, 1961; Reginald Rose to R. R. Brown, December 18, 1961. Reginald Rose Papers, U.S. Mss 94AN, box 6, folder 4.

20. Reginald Rose to Clark Sergel, April 4, 1961, Reginald Rose Papers, U.S. Mss 94AN, box 6, folder 4.

21. Jay Rosenblatt to Reginald Rose, January 8, 1962, Reginald Rose Papers, U.S. Mss 94AN, box 6, folder 4.

22. Reginald Rose to Jay Rosenblatt, January 9, 1962, Reginald Rose Papers, U.S. Mss 94AN, box 6, folder 4.

23. George Voskovec to Henry Fonda, March 19, 1962, and Reginald Rose to George Voskovec, April 2, 1962, Reginald Rose Papers, U.S. Mss 94AN, box 6, folder 4.

24. Václav Havel, director's remark, method supplement, *Dvanáct rozhněvanych muzu*, (Praha: Divaldlo, 1962); translation by Petr Bilek, July 2018.

25. Contract with Leo Genn and RERO, Reginald Rose Papers, U.S. Mss 94AN, box 6, folder 5.

26. *Punch*, July 15, 1964, Reginald Rose Papers, U.S. Mss 94AN, box 6, folder 11.

27. "The 12 Angry Men lapse into caricature," *Daily Mail*, n.d., Reginald Rose Papers, U.S. Mss 94AN, box 6, folder 11.

28. Reginald Rose to *The Daily Mail*, undated letter, Reginald Rose Papers, U.S. Mss 94AN, box 6, folder 11.

29. "Twelve Angry Men," About the Artists, https://www.abouttheartists.com/productions /128477-twelve-angry-men-at-queens-theatre-and-others-1964.

30. Kenneth Wagg to Reginald Rose, September 24, 1965, Reginald Rose Papers, U.S. Mss 94AN, box 6, folder 4.

31. Annette Littman to Ashley Famous Agency, November 29, 1965, Reginald Rose Papers, U.S. Mss 94AN, box 6, folder 4.

32. Denis Hamill, "Time to Get 'Angry' Again: TV Revival Puts Classic Jury Film's Author Back in Court," *New York Daily News*, August 17, 1997.

33. Jack Marshall, *Audience Guide, Twelve Angry Men by Reginald Rose*, American Century Theater, 2015, 30.

34. Carrie Blomquist, professional leasing director at Dramatic Publishing Company, correspondence with the author, November 2020.

35. Sherman L. Sergel, *Reginald Rose's Twelve Angry Women: A Play in Three Acts* (Woodstock, IL: The Dramatic Publishing Company, 1983), 8.

36. "Twelve Angry Men," American Century Theater (website), http://www.americancentury .org/show_men.php.

37. Jack Marshall, interview with the author, December 2020.

38. Bob Mondello, "Grand Jury," *Washington City Paper*, April 14, 1995, https:// washingtoncitypaper.com/article/294691/grand-jury/.

39. Charles Spencer, *Daily Telegraph*, April 1996, cited on "Twelve Angry Men," Harold Pinter (website), http://www.haroldpinter.org/directing/directing_angry.shtml.

40. Scott Ellis, interview with the author, December 2020.

41. "'Angry' Preem Casts Wistful Note," *Daily Variety*, November 2, 2004, 19.

42. Jonathan Rose, interview with the author, June 2020.

43. Adam Liptak, "Trial by Actors: Judging 'Twelve Angry Men'" *New York Times*, October 17, 2004.

44. Aileen Jacobson, "One More Time, Clawing Their Way to a Verdict," *New York Times*, October 4, 2013.

45. Correspondence with Carrie Blomquist, November 2020.

46. Elissa Nadworny, "The Most Popular High School Plays and Musicals," NPR, July 30, 2020, https://www.npr.org/sections/ed/2019/07/31/427138970/the-most-popular-high-school -plays-and-musicals?t=1604239589663.

47. Sabrina Jacob Washburn, conversation with the author, November 2020.

48. Joel Markowitz, "The American Century Theater's Jack Marshall on 'Broadway Hit Parade' and '12 Angry Men' and Reflections," DC Metro Theater Arts, March 19, 2015 https://dcmetrotheaterarts.com/2015/03/19/tacts-jack-marshall-on-broadway-hit-parade -and-12-angry-men-and-reflections/.

49. "Beyond Reasonable Doubt: Making *12 Angry Men*," special feature, *12 Angry Men*, (1957; Metro-Goldwyn-Mayer Studios, 2007) DVD.

18. A Lesson in the Law

1. "One for All, Or Rose in Bloom: A Leading 'Studio One' Playwright's Works Draw Institutional Attention," *Variety*, November 3, 1954, 23.

2. "Twelve Angry Men, Publicity and Promotion Report," The Arthur P. Jacobs Company,

March 2, 1957. Reginald Rose Papers, U.S. Mss 94AN, box 3, folder 7, Wisconsin Center for Film and Theater Research, University of Wisconsin–Madison.

3. Roger Ebert, "12 Angry Men," RogerEbert.com, September 29, 2002, http://www .rogerebert.com/reviews/great-movie-12-angry-men-1957.

4. The Sixth Amendment reads: "In all criminal prosecutions, the accused shall enjoy the right to a speedy and public trial, by an impartial jury of the State and district wherein the crime shall have been committed, which district shall have been previously ascertained by law, and to be informed of the nature and cause of the accusation; to be confronted with the witnesses against him; to have compulsory process for obtaining witnesses in his favor, and to have the Assistance of Counsel for his defence."

5. *Norris v. Alabama* (1935).

6. *Batson v. Kentucky* (1986).

7. James Barron, "After 45 Years, Manhattan Clerk Is Issuing His Last Call for Jury Duty," *New York Times*, December 10, 2014, A25.

8. Judith S. Kaye, "My Life as Chief Judge: The Chapter on Juries," *New York State Bar Association Journal* 78, no. 8 (October 2006): 10–13.

9. Kaye, "My Life as Chief Judge," 12.

10. As performed on *Studio One*, Robert Cummings says the same lines: "Nobody has to prove otherwise. The burden of proof is on the prosecution. The defendant doesn't have to open his mouth. That's in the Constitution." In Rose's *Six Television Plays*, it is slightly different: "The defendant doesn't have to open his mouth. That's in the Constitution. The Fifth Amendment. You've heard of it." Juror 8 is correct that the Fifth Amendment means the defendant doesn't have to testify, but it does not stipulate that the burden of proof is on the prosecution.

11. *Coffin v. United States* (1895).

12. "Eleven of the jurors move from an initial position of certainty about their verdict to a true appreciation of what it means to speak of a 'reasonable doubt,' as their certainties dissolve in the re-examination of the 'facts.'" Henry F. Nardone, "Using the Film *12 Angry Men* to Teach Critical Thinking," in *Proceedings of the Third Annual Conference on Argumentation*, ed. H. Eemeren, R. Grootenndorst, A. Blair, and C. Willards (Netherlands: International Centre for the Study of Argumentation, 1995), 85. See also Ross Munyan, ed., *Readings on Twelve Angry Men* (San Diego, CA: Greenhaven Press, 2000).

13. Hollis Alpert, "Gentlemen of the Jury," *Saturday Review*, April 20, 1957, 29–30.

14. A. H. Weiler, "Screen: '12 Angry Men'; Jury Room Drama Has Debut at Capitol," *New York Times*, April 15, 1957.

15. Eleanor Roosevelt, *My Day*, vol. 3: *First Lady of the World*, ed. David Emblidge (New York: Da Capo Press, 1991), quoted in Munyan, *Readings on Twelve Angry Men*, 55.

16. In the *Studio One* version, the term is heard again early in the deliberations. After Juror 7 asks Juror 8: "I'd like to ask you something. If the kid didn't kill him, who did?" Juror 8 replies: "We're not concerned with anyone else here. We're supposed to decide whether or not the boy on trial is guilty," and Juror 9 adds: "Guilty beyond a reasonable doubt. Now, that's an important thing to remember." Rose removed that line for the movie screenplay.

17. Jon O. Newman, "Beyond 'Reasonable Doubt,'" *New York University Law Review* 68, no. 5 (November 1993): 979–1002.

18. James Q. Whitman, *The Origins of Reasonable Doubt: Theological Roots of the Criminal Trial* (New Haven, CT: Yale University Press, 2008).

19. "Proof beyond a Reasonable Doubt," Instructions of General Applicability, New York State Unified Court System, https://www.nycourts.gov.

20. To be justified in reaching a verdict of not guilty does not mean that defendant was

innocent. In fact, the evidence as presented suggests strongly that the defendant was guilty. If either the man downstairs or the woman across the street was correct, the defendant is guilty. For him to be not guilty, both would have to be in error, which is possible but not likely. Next, someone would have had to enter unseen and use a knife that was a good match for the defendant's knife—and commit the crime on the same night that the father got into a loud argument with his son. The chance of all those things happening is very small. No wonder Rose knew better than have his jurors speculate who else might have committed the crime. It was not wrong and indeed probably appropriate for the jury to have reached a verdict of not guilty based on various flaws in the evidence, but the overall evidence still suggests strongly that the defendant killed his father.

21. See, for example, Ephraim Glatt, "The Unanimous Verdict According to the Talmud: Ancient Law Providing Insight into Modern Legal Theory," Pace International Law Review Online Companion 316 (2013), http://digitalcommons.pace.edu/pilronline/35/.

22. Michael Asimow, "12 Angry Men: A Revisionist View," Chicago-Kent Law Review 82, no. 2 (2007): 711.

23. Asimow, 711. The 2021 trial of Minneapolis police office Derek Chauvin in the death of George Floyd is more typical: "When the jury foreman tallied the votes that morning, one of the jurors recalled, there were 11 papers with a "G" written on them—guilty. One paper said "U," for unsure." Over the next hours, the sole uncertain juror joined the majority to reach unanimous guilty verdicts on all counts. Nicholas Bogel-Burroughs, "Inside the Chauvin Jury Room: 11 of 12 Jurors Were Ready to Convict Right Away," New York Times, April 29, 2021, https://www.nytimes.com/2021/04/29/us/chauvin-jury-brandon-mitchell.

24. Charles D. Weisselberg, "Good Film, Bad Jury," Chicago-Kent Law Review 82, no. 2 (2007): 717.

25. "New Picture: Twelve Angry Men," Time, April 29, 1957, 94–96.

26. Nancy Gertner, "Twelve Angry Men (and Women) in Federal Court," Chicago-Kent Law Review 82, no. 2 (2007): 613.

27. Jay Boyer, Sidney Lumet (New York: Twayne Publishers, Macmillan Publishing, 1993), 9.

28. Paul Bergman and Michael Asimow, Reel Justice: The Courtroom Goes to the Movies (Kansas City, MO: Andrew McMeel Publishing, 2006), xv–xvi.

29. Sam Kim, "American Icons: '12 Angry Men'" Studio 360, PRI, January 30, 2020, https://www.pri.org/stories/2020-01-30/american-icons-12-angry-men. Kirk Semple, "The Movie That Made a Supreme Court Justice," New York Times, October 17, 2010, https://www.pri.org/stories/2020-01-30/american-icons-12-angry-men.

30. Kim, "American Icons."

31. "Beyond Reasonable Doubt: Making 12 Angry Men," special feature (1957; Metro-Goldwyn-Mayer Studios, 2007), DVD.

32. Valerie P. Hans, "Deliberation and Dissent: 12 Angry Men versus the Empirical Reality of Juries," Chicago-Kent Law Review 82, no. 2 (2007): 579.

33. Elizabeth Messina, What's His Name? John Fiedler: The Man, the Face, the Voice (Bloomington, IN: AuthorHouse, 2012), 42.

34. Nancy S. Marder, "Introduction to the 50th Anniversary of 12 Angry Men," Chicago-Kent Law Review 82, no. 2 (2007): 558.

35. Nancy Marder, correspondence with the author, November 2020.

36. Marder correspondence.

37. Judith S. Kaye, "Why Every Chief Judge Should See 12 Angry Men," Chicago-Kent Law Review 82, no. 2 (2007): 629.

38. Kaye, "Why Every Chief Judge Should See 12 Angry Men," 631.

19. A Masterclass in Human Behavior

1. Henry Fonda, *My Life: As Told to Howard Teichmann* (New York: New American Library, 1981), 289.

2. Clovis R. Shepherd to Henry Fonda, June 8, 1966, Reginald Rose Papers, U.S. Mss 94AN, box 3, folder 4, Wisconsin Center for Film and Theater Research, University of Wisconsin–Madison.

3. Ernest J. Hall, Janes S. Mouton, and Robert R. Blake, "Group Problem Solving Effectiveness Under Conditions of Pooling vs. Interaction," *Journal of Social Psychology* 59, no. 1 (1963): 147–157. The twenty-two groups had *individual* scores that averaged 20.50, and *group consensus* scores that averaged 12.72. Accuracy was calculated by "summing the deviation in rank order from the actual order of prediction," so that a lower number meant a smaller deviation and greater accuracy.

4. One possibility not explored by the researchers is that some subjects might have observed the order in which jurors raised their hands to vote guilty and predicted the sequence of change would be the reverse.

5. A subsequent study went further, comparing groups that had been trained in group dynamics with others that had not received such training. Once again using "the *12 Angry Men* decision making task" as the measure of performance, groups which had undergone training in group dynamics were found to perform better than untrained groups.

6. Published in 1970, the research may or may not have been already in progress in 1966.

7. Clovis R. Shepherd to Henry Fonda, June 8, 1966, Reginald Rose Papers, U.S. Mss 94AN, box 3, folder 4.

8. Reaching out to "NTL old-timers" yielded memories of watching *12 Angry Men* at Bethel on Wednesday "free evenings." I am endebted to Selma Kuurstra of NTL for collecting recollections about the use of *12 Angry Men* at Bethel, Maine.

9. The other movies in the 1966 course were *The Hunters* (1958), about rival American pilots during the Korean War who must learn to cooperate; *Nothing But a Man* (1964), about an African American couple facing racial discrimination; *David and Lisa* (1962), about mental illness and love; and *The Kitchen* (1961), about rush hour at a café. *12 Angry Men* was the oldest of the five, but the only one well-remembered today.

10. David Berg of Yale School of Management, correspondence with the author, September 2017.

11. Clovis R. Shepherd, *Small Groups: Some Sociological Perspectives* (San Francisco: Chandler Publishing Company, 1964), 4–5: "For our purposes in this book an adequate criterion is that a group be large enough for group characteristics to develop and become stable, but small enough so that the members feel a sense of common identity and mutual awareness. In most cases the kind of group discussed in this book will have at least four members and will be small enough to share a common table." That would put an upper limit at "no more than twenty people and usually fewer than fifteen."

12. "12 Angry Men," undated outline for *Studio One*, Reginald Rose Papers, U.S. Mss 94AN, box 19, folder 3.

13. Solomon E. Asch, "Effects of Group Pressure on the Modification and Distortion of Judgments," in *Groups, Leadership and Men*, ed. H. Guetzkow (Pittsburgh, PA: Carnegie Press, 1951), 177–190.

14. Over the next decades, Asch's experiments were replicated more than 130 times around the world with very consistent results. "Asch's findings seem to capture something universal

about humanity. The overall pattern of errors—with people conforming between 20 to 40 percent of the time—does not show huge differences across nations. And though 20 to 40 percent of the time might not seem large, remember that this task was very simple. It is almost as if people can be nudged into identifying a picture of a dog as a cat as long as other people before them have done so." Richard Thaler and Cass Sunstein, *Nudge: Improving Decisions about Health, Wealth, and Happiness* (New Haven, CT: Yale University Press, 2008), 56.

15. Ronald Friend, Yvonne Rafferty, and Dama Bramel, "A Puzzling Misinterpretation of the Asch 'Conformity' Study," *European Journal of Social Psychology* 20, no. 1 (1990): 29–44.

16. Solomon E. Asch, "Opinions and Social Pressure," *Scientific American* 193, no. 5 (November 1955), 34.

17. Reginald Rose, *Six Television Plays* (New York: Simon and Schuster, 1956), 119.

18. The shooting script reads: "Seven or eight hands go up immediately. Several others go up more slowly. Everyone looks around the table as the Foreman begins to count hands. #9's hand goes up now, and all hands are raised, save #8's." The stage version, written some years later, provided more direction: Foreman: "Okay, all those voting guilty raise your hands." [Jurors Three, Seven, Ten, and Twelve put their hands up instantly. The Foreman and Two, Four, Five, and Six follow a second later. Then Eleven raises his hand and a moment later Nine puts his hand up.] This order, of course, is very close to the reverse of the order in which they will shift their votes. The biggest difference between the movie and the later play is Juror 4, who immediately casts a vote for guilty in the movie but not in the play.

19. Antonis Gardikiotis, "Minority Influence," *Social and Personality Psychology Compass* 5, no. 9 (2011): 679–693.

20. "Beyond Reasonable Doubt: Making *12 Angry Men*," special feature (1957; Metro-Goldwyn-Mayer Studios, 2007), DVD.

21. A. H. Weiler, "Screen: '12 Angry Men'; Jury Room Drama Has Debut at Capitol," *New York Times*, April 15, 1957.

22. "Sidney Lumet on *12 Angry Men*," American Film Institute interview, September 29, 2009, https://www.youtube.com/watch?v=OrMXC_X2HU8.

20. New Versions, New Meanings

1. Jeff Kisseloff, *The Box: An Oral History of Television, 1920–1961* (New York: Viking, 1995), 259.

2. *The Dick Van Dyke Show*, season 1, episode 24, "One Angry Man," March 7, 1962.

3. *The Odd Couple*, season 1, episode 4, "The Jury Story," October 22, 1970.

4. *All In the Family*, season 1, episode 9, "Edith Has Jury Duty," March 9, 1971.

5. Sadie Gennis, "Amy Schumer's *12 Angry Men* Parody Is the Best Sketch of the Year," *TV Guide*, May 6, 2015, https://www.tvguide.com/news/amy-schumer-12-angry-men-parody/.

6. James Sterngold, "A Tense Jury Room Revisited, and Racism Is Given a Twist," *New York Times*, August 17, 1997.

7. Caryn James, "For These Angry Jurors, the Judge Is a Woman," *New York Times*, August 16, 1997.

8. Barack Obama, "Remarks by the President on Trayvon Martin," White House press briefing, July 19, 2013, https://obamawhitehouse.archives.gov/the-press-office/2013/07/19/remarks-president-trayvon-martin.

9. Steven Leigh Morris, "Pasadena Playhouse Creates a 12 Angry Men for Trayvon Martin Era," *LA Weekly*, October 31, 2013.

10. "Director Sheldon Epps Discusses His Ford's Theatre 'Twelve Angry Men' Production," Ford's Theater (blog), www.fords.org/blog/post/director-sheldon-epps-discusses-his -ford-s-theatre-twelve-angry-men-production/.

11. Morris, "Pasadena Playhouse Creates a 12 Angry Men."

12. Jonas Schwartz, "Twelve Angry Men Director Sheldon Epps Expounds on His Meditation on Race in the American Justice System," *Theatermania*, November 20, 2013.

13. Lynne Heffley, "Pasadena Playhouse Holds Up a Modern-Day Mirror to 'Twelve Angry Men,'" *Los Angeles Times*, November 12, 2013.

14. Schwartz, "Twelve Angry Men Director Sheldon Epps."

15. "Epps Discusses His Ford's Theatre 'Twelve Angry Men' Production."

16. "Epps Discusses His Ford's Theatre 'Twelve Angry Men' Production."

17. Sheldon Epps, interview with the author, November 2020.

18. Olga Grinkrug, "Mikhalkov: I Made the Film '12' to Make the Audience Think," RIA Novosti, September 7, 2007; translation by Ilona Beklenishcheva.

19. *12 Angry Lebanese: The Documentary* (2009) won the Muhr Arab Documentary First Prize; the People's Choice Award at the Dubai International Film Festival (2009); and first prize audience award at the DOX BOX International Documentary Festival (2010).

20. Julie Makinen, "Chinese Remake of '12 Angry Men' Faced Its Own Legal Drama," *Los Angeles Times*, September 23, 2015.

21. Xu Ang, correspondence with the author, July 2017; translation by Wang Xiaohui, Ira Belkin, and Catherine Lin.

22. Corrie Tan, "Twelve Angry Men is Lyrical and Incisive," *Straits Times*, February 18, 2013, https://www.straitstimes.com/singapore/ theatre-review-twelve-angry-men-is-lyrical-and-incisive.

23. "Regresa 12 hombres en pugna con un gran elenco," El Economista, May 7, 2013, https://www.eleconomista.com.mx/arteseideas/Regresa-12-hombres-en-pugna-con-un-gran-elenco—20130507-0071.html; translation by the author.

24. "Reginald Rose classic 12 Angry Jurors played in town as 12 Angry Men," ETimes, April 28, 2014, https://timesofindia.indiatimes.com/entertainment/hindi/theatre/Reginald-Rose-classic-12-Angry-Jurors-played-in-town-as-12-Angry-Men/articleshow/34337746.cms.

25. Arundhati Chatterjee, "Art in Mumbai: One Angry Courtroom," *Hindustan Times*, May 3, 2014, https://www.hindustantimes.com/art-and-culture/art-in-mumbai-one-angry -courtroom/story-qEpk8fAdmHjGIQEhJyj5uJ.html.

26. Francis Lombrail, interview with the author, December 2018. Translation by the author.

27. Charles Tordjman, interview with the author, November 2018. Translation by the author.

Epilogue

1. Don Kranze, interview with the author, July 2019.

2. From an uncited newspaper article in Ed Begley's scrapbook, consulted at the Margaret Herrick Library, Academy of Motion Pictures Arts and Sciences, Beverly Hills, CA.

3. Jonathan Rose, interview with the author, June 2020.

4. Denis Hamill, correspondence with the author, November 2019.

5. Pete Hamill, "The New York We've Lost," *New York Magazine*, December 21–28, 1987.

6. Hamill.

7. Hamill.

8. Bosley Crowther, "Old-Time Star-Filled Benefit to Close Capitol Theater Tonight," *New York Times*, September 16, 1968.

9. "Inside Stuff—Radio-TV," *Variety*, November 21, 1956, 24.

10. Hamill, "The New York We've Lost."

11. Hamill.

12. Richard Alleman, *New York: The Movie Lover's Guide* (New York: Broadway Books, 2005).

13. Patrick Healy, "Jack Klugman, After Half a Century, Returning to 'Twelve Angry Men,'" *New York Times*, December 21, 2011.

14. Patrick Healy, "Health Reasons Force Klugman's Withdrawal from 'Twelve Angry Men,'" *New York Times*, March 8, 2012; Bruce Weber, "Jack Klugman, Actor of Everyman Integrity, Dies at 90," *New York Times*, December 24, 2012.

15. "Pete Hamill: Brooklynite, Journalist, Friend of 'The Green-Wood,'" Green-Wood, August 12, 2020, https://www.green-wood.com/2020/pete-hamill-brooklynite-journalist-friend-of-the-green-wood/.

SELECTED BIBLIOGRAPHY

Adams, Val. "Blacklist a Topic for 'Defenders.'" *New York Times*, November 6, 1963.

———. "Television in Review: Montgomery Show–'Studio One' Conflict on Mondays Poses Dilemma for Viewer." *New York Times*, September 22, 1954.

Alleman, Richard. *New York: The Movie Lover's Guide*. New York: Broadway Books, 2005.

Alpert, Hollis. "Gentlemen of the Jury." *Saturday Review*, April 20, 1957.

Asch, Solomon E. "Effects of Group Pressure on the Modification and Distortion of Judgments." In *Groups, Leadership and Men*, ed. H. Guetzkow. Pittsburgh, PA: Carnegie Press, 1951.

———. "Opinions and Social Pressure." *Scientific American* 193, no. 5 (November 1955): 31–35.

Asimow, Michael. "*12 Angry Men*: A Revisionist View." *Chicago-Kent Law Review* 82, no. 2 (2007): 711–716.

Balio, Tino. *United Artists: The Company that Changed the Film Industry*. Madison: University of Wisconsin Press, 1987.

Battelle, Phyllis. "Odyssey of a TV Writer." *New York Journal-American*, August 15, 1961.

Bergman, Paul, and Michael Asimow. *Reel Justice: The Courtroom Goes to the Movies*. Kansas City: Andrews McMeel Publishing, 2006.

Bernstein, Walter. *Inside Out: A Memoir of the Blacklist*. New York: Da Capo Press, 1996.

Bogdanovich, Peter. *Who the Devil Made It: Conversations with Legendary Film Directors*. New York: Ballantine Books, 1997.

Bowman, Pierre. "He's Reginald Rose, the Legendary TV Dramatist." *Honolulu Star-Advertiser*, July 30, 1980.

Boyer, Jay. *Sidney Lumet*. Twayne's Filmmaker Series. New York: Twayne, 1993.

Castleman, Harry, and Walter J. Podrazik. *Watching TV: Six Decades of American Television*. 2nd ed. Syracuse: University of Syracuse Press, 2010.

Ceplair, Larry, and Steven Englund. *The Inquisition in Hollywood: Politics in the Film Community, 1930–60*. Urbana-Champaign: University of Illinois Press, 2003.

Chayefsky, Paddy. *Television Plays*. New York: Simon and Schuster, 1955.

Considine, Shaun. *Mad as Hell: The Life and Work of Paddy Chayefsky*. New York: Random House, 1994.

Crean, Robert. "On the (Left) Side of the Angels." *Today: National Catholic Magazine*, January 1964.

Crosby, John. "Crosby on TV: The Sacco-Vanzetti Case." *New York Herald Tribune*, June 1, 1960.

Cunningham, Frank R. *Sidney Lumet: Film and Literary Visionary*. Lexington: University Press of Kentucky, 1991.

Davis, Ronald. "A Conversation with Martin Ritt." In *Martin Ritt: Interviews*, ed. Gabriel Miller, 148–185. Jackson: University of Mississippi Press, 2002.

Dewey, Donald. *Lee J. Cobb: Characters of an Actor*. Plymouth: Rowan and Littlefield, 2014.

Ebert, Roger. "12 Angry Men." RogerEbert.com. September 29, 2002. http://www.rogerebert .com/reviews/great-movie-12-angry-men-1957.

Efron, Edith. "Can a TV Writer Keep His Integrity?" *TV Guide*, April 21–27, 1962.

———. "The Eternal Conflict between Good and Evil . . ." *TV Guide*, March 17–23, 1962.

Flint, Peter B. "Henry Fonda Dies on Coast at 77; Played 100 Stage and Screen Roles." *New York Times*, August 13, 1982.

Fonda, Henry, *My Life: As Told to Howard Teichmann*. New York: New American Library, 1981.

Gardella, Kay. "Writer Finds New Way in the Same Old Medium." *Daily News*, August 25, 1961.

Gardikiotis, Antonis. "Minority Influence," *Social and Personality Psychology Compass* 5, no. 9 (2011): 679–693.

Gertner, Nancy. "Twelve Angry Men (and Women) in Federal Court." *Chicago-Kent Law Review* 82, no. 2 (2007): 613–636.

Glatt, Ephraim. "The Unanimous Verdict According to the Talmud: Ancient Law Providing Insight into Modern Legal Theory." Pace International Law Review Online Companion 316 (2013). http://digitalcommons.pace.edu/pilronline/35/.

Godbout, Oscar. "'Marty' Hits Jackpot." *New York Times*, September 11, 1955, X7.

Goldberg, Harold. "Sidney Lumet: The Director Talks about Shooting in Snowstorms." *The Hollywood Reporter*. New York Special Issue, June 10, 1997.

Goldman, William. *Adventures in the Screen Trade*. New York: Grand Central Publishing, 1983.

Gould, Jack. "Television in Review: Reginald Rose Play on 'Studio One' Protests Credo of Conformity." *New York Times*, March 19, 1954.

———. "Television: Social Drama; Teen-Age Gang Seen in *'Crime on Streets.'*" *New York Times*, March 11, 1955.

———. "TV: Sacco-Vanzetti': First Hour of Documentary Drama by Reginald Rose Given on N.B.C." *New York Times*, June 4, 1960.

Halberstam, David. *The Fifties*. New York: Random House, 1993.

Hall, Ernest J., Janes S. Mouton, and Robert R. Blake. "Group Problem Solving Effectiveness under Conditions of Pooling vs. Interaction." *Journal of Social Psychology* 59 (1963): 147–157.

Hamill, Denis. "Time to Get 'Angry' Again: TV Revival Puts Classic Jury Film's Author Back in Court." *New York Daily News*, August 17, 1997.

Hamill, Pete. "The New York We've Lost." *New York Magazine*, December 21–28, 1987.

Hans, Valerie P. "Deliberation and Dissent: *12 Angry Men* versus the Empirical Reality of Juries." *Chicago-Kent Law Review* 82, no. 2 (2007): 579–590.

Hawes, William. *Live Television Drama, 1946–1951*. Jefferson, NC: McFarland, 2001.

Healy, Patrick. "Health Reasons Force Klugman's Withdrawal From 'Twelve Angry Men.'" *New York Times*, March 8, 2012.

———. "Jack Klugman, After Half a Century, Returning to 'Twelve Angry Men.'" *New York Times*, December 21, 2011.

Hollinger, Hy. "Reginald Rose Sees TV-Derived Stories Hit by Broad Condemnation." *Variety*, June 27, 1956.

———. "Telecast and Theater Film, Looks as If '12 Angry Men' May Reap Most Dough as Legit Play." *Variety*, December 24, 1958.

Horowitz, Murray. "TV 'Burying Writers in Formula Coffin' Laments David Davidson." *Variety*, November 7, 1962.

Howe, Irving. *World of Our Fathers: The Journey of the Eastern European Jews to America and the Life They Found and Made*. New York: New York University Press, 1976.

Huston, John. *An Open Book*. New York: Da Capo, 1994.

Kaye, Judith S. "My Life as Chief Judge: The Chapter on Juries," *New York State Bar Association Journal* 78, no. 8 (October 2006): 10–13.

———. "Why Every Chief Judge Should See *12 Angry Men*." *Chicago-Kent Law Review* 82, no. 2 (2007): 627–632.

Kazan, Elia. *Kazan, A Life*. London: Pan Books, 1989.

Kelley, Tina. "Reginald Rose, 81, TV Writer Noted for 'Twelve Angry Men,' Dies." *New York Times*, April 21, 2002.

Kisseloff, Jeff. *The Box: An Oral History of Television, 1920–1961*. New York: Viking, 1995.

Leonard, Vince. "Reggie's a Regular Sort of Guy." *The Pittsburgh Press*, November 29, 1967.

Life. "Director Participation: Sidney Lumet Kisses, Fights, Dies, Running Two Top TV Shows a Week." June 8, 1953.

Life. "Good Men and True and All Angry." April 22, 1957.

Lumet, Sidney. *Making Movies*. New York: Vintage, 1995.

Mackin, Tom. "Rose Finds Plot in Life." *Newark Evening Star*, December 3, 1967.

Mandell, Clifford B. "Popular Defender of Unpopular Causes." *St. Louis Post Dispatch*, June 7, 1963.

Mann, Delbert. *Looking Back . . . at Live Television and Other Matters*. Los Angeles: Directors Guild of America, 1998.

Marder, Nancy S. "Introduction to the 50th Anniversary of *12 Angry Men*." *Chicago-Kent Law Review* 82, no. 2 (2007): 557–576.

McGilligan, Patrick. *Backstory 3: Interviews with Screenwriters of the 60s*. Backstory Series. Berkeley: University of California Press, 1997.

McKinney, Devin. *The Man Who Saw a Ghost: The Life and Work of Henry Fonda*, New York: St. Martin's, 2012.

McManus, Margaret. "Prolific Playwright Finds Everything's Coming Up Rose's." *New York World-Telegram and Sun*, September 2, 1961.

Messina, Elizabeth. *What's His Name? John Fiedler: The Man, the Face, the Voice*. Bloomington, IN: AuthorHouse, 2012.

Miller, Arthur. *Timebends: A Life*. London: Methuen, 1987.

Millstein, Gilbert. "The Long Running Ed Begley." *New York Times*, December 9, 1956.

———. "Rod Serling, Patterns of a Television Playwright." *New York Times Magazine*, December 2, 1956.

Miner, Worthington. *Worthington Miner: Interviewed by Franklin J. Schaffner*. Metuchen, NJ: Directors Guild of America and Scarecrow Press, 1985.

Minoff, Philip. "Community Tragedy Makes a Superb 'Studio One.'" Notes on TV. *Cue*, January 30, 1954.

———. "For No Earthly Reason." *Cue*. December 8, 1951.

Mirisch, Walter. *I Thought We Were Making Movies, Not History*. Madison: University of Wisconsin Press, 2008.

Mordden, Ethan. *The Hollywood Studios: House Style in the Golden Age of the Movies*. New York: Knopf, 1988.

Munyan, Ross, ed. "Reginald Rose: A Biography." In *Readings on Twelve Angry Men*. San Diego, CA: Greenhaven Press, 2000.

Musmanno, Michael A. "The Sacco-Vanzetti Jury." *Villanova Law Review* 5, no. 2 (Winter 1959–60): 169–180.

Nardone, Henry F. "Using the Film 12 Angry Men to Teach Critical Thinking." In *Readings on Twelve Angry Men*, edited by Ross Munyan, 84–96. San Diego, CA: Greenhaven Press, 2000.

Newman, Jon O. "Beyond 'Reasonable Doubt,'" *New York University Law Review* 68, no. 5 (November 1993): 979–1002.

O'Connor, John J. "TV: 'Lonigan' on NBC." *New York Times*, March 7, 1979.

Paley, William S. *As it Happened: A Memoir*. Garden City, NY: Doubleday, 1979.

Pelswick, Rose. "The Verdict—Fine Film." *New York Journal American*, April 15, 1957.

Polier, Rex. "Reflections on TV's Golden Age." *Los Angeles Times*, January 1, 1982.

Polonsky, Abraham. *You Are There Teleplays: The Critical Edition*. Northridge, CA: Center for Telecommunication Studies, California State University, Northridge, 1997.

Price, Steven. "Commentary." In Reginald Rose, *Twelve Angry Men*. London: Bloomsbury, 2017.

Pryor, Thomas M. "Fonda and Rose to Film TV Play: Actor and Author of 'Twelve Angry Men' Team for First of Star's Productions." *New York Times*, July 18, 1955.

———. "Fonda Joins List of Independents." *New York Times*, February 11, 1955.

Quinn, Frank. "12 Angry Men Win Verdict of Superior." *New York Daily Mirror*, April 14, 1957.

Rose, Reginald. "Law, Drama, and Criticism." *Television Quarterly* 3, no. 4 (Fall 1964): 21–27.

———. *Six Television Plays*. New York: Simon and Schuster, 1956.

———. *Thunder on Sycamore Street: A Play in Three Acts, Made into a Play by Kristin Sergel*. Woodstock, IL: Dramatic Publishing Company, 1958 and 1986.

———. "TV's Age of Innocence—What Became of It?" *New York Times*, December 3, 1967.

———. *Twelve Angry Men*. Adapted by Sherman L. Sergel. Woodstock, IL: Dramatic Publishing Company, 1955.

———. *Twelve Angry Men: Samuel French Version, Commentary*. Edited by Steven Price. London: Bloomsbury, 2017.

———. *Undelivered Mail: A Memoir*. Bloomington, IN: Xlibris Corporation, 2000.

Ross, Dan. "Playwright Best 'When I'm Angry.'" *New York Herald Tribune*, March 4, 1962.

Russell, Charles K. *In the Worst of Times It Was the Best of Times*. Beverly Hills, CA: CKR Productions, 1982.

Scheuer, Steven H. "Meet Mr. Reginald Rose—Outstanding TV Author." *Brooklyn Daily Eagle*, May 30, 1954.

———. "Reginald Rose Offers More Good TV Drama." *Lansing State Journal*, May 12, 1959.

Semple, Kirk. "The Movie That Made a Supreme Court Justice." *New York Times*, October 17, 2010.

Shepard, Richard F. "Man with a Script: Reginald Rose Thinks All T.V., Even Sponsors, Gain from Controversy." *New York Times*, February 24, 1957.

Shepherd, Clovis R. *Small Groups: Some Sociological Perspectives*. San Francisco, CA: Chandler Publishing Company, 1964.

Spiegel, Maura. *Sidney Lumet: A Life*. New York: St. Martin's, 2019.

Stempel, Tom. *Storytellers to the Nation: A History of American Television Writing*. New York: Continuum Publishing Company, 1992.

Thompson, Howard. "George Justin: Local Movie Man on Our Town." *New York Times*, November 26, 1961.

Weiler, A. H. "Screen: '12 Angry Men'; Jury Room Drama Has Debut at Capitol." *New York Times*, April 15, 1957.

Weisselberg, Charles D. "Good Film, Bad Jury." *Chicago-Kent Law Review* 82, no. 2 (2007): 717–734.

Whitman, James Q. *The Origins of Reasonable Doubt: Theological Roots of the Criminal Trial*. New Haven, CT: Yale University Press, 2008.

INDEX

297

Eastwood, Clint, 147
Ebert, Roger, 209
Ed Sullivan Show, The (TV show), 24. See also *Toast of the Town*
Edge of the City (1957 film), 117, 120–121, 239, 242
Edison Laboratories, 40
Edison Studios, 83
Edison, Thomas, 81
Educational Television and Radio Center, 91
Edwards, Douglas, 24
Efron, Edith, 162–163
Ehrlich, Max, 157
Eight Iron Men (1952 film), 69
Einstein, Albert, 153
Ek Ruka Hua Faisla (Hindi), 234
Elgin Hour, The (TV show), 86–87, 104, 148, 150
Ellis Island, 116
Ellis, Scott, 205–207, 228
Emmy Awards, 4–5, 87, 98, 109–111, 113, 154, 164, 171, 175, 188
empathy, 87, 124, 195, 236
Empire State Building, 24
"Endless Night, The" (Rose outline), 86
Engel, Alice Oberdorfer Rose (mother), 13, 15–16, 19
Engel, Leonard David (stepfather), 15–16, 19
Epps, Sheldon, 232–233
Epstein, Julius, 38
Epstein, Philip, 38
Equitable Building, 100
"Ernie Barger is Fifty" (*Philco* episode), 85
Ernst, Morris, 208–209
Escape from Sobibor (Rose CBS docudrama), 189
Escape from Sobibor: The Heroic Story of the Jews Who Escaped from a Nazi Death Camp (Rashke book), 189
Esquire, 136
Ethical Culture Society, 15
Ettinger, Eve, 147
Executive Order 9981, 51
Exorcist, The (1973 film), 231
"Expendable House, The" (Rose *Goodyear-Philco* episode), 105, 148

Face in the Crowd, A (1957 film), 195
Fail Safe (1964 film), 220, 240

Fairbanks, Douglas, 43
Family Guy (TV show), 231
Farrell, James T., 14, 185–188
Fast, Howard, 152
Fawcett, Farrah, 185
Fences (Wilson play), 233
Ferber, Edna, 25
Fetridge, Arthur E., 154, 170
Fiedler, John (Juror 2), 117, 121, 218
Fifties, The (Halberstam book), 27
Film Daily, 140
Filmways Studios, 158, 242
Fire Island, 72, 103–104, 129, 136, 157, 173
Fisk University, 51
Flame and the Arrow, The (1950 film), 44
Flamholtz, Eric G., 223, 255
Flanagan (Rose series proposal), 155
Flower Drum Song (Rodgers and Hammerstein musical), 150
Flynn, Errol, 135
Foley Square, 57–58, 61–62, 69–70, 121, 158, 242
Fonda on Fonda (1992 film), 240
Fonda, Henry (Juror 8), 1, 2, 3, 6, 7, 122, 145, 200, 208, 220, 228, 230, 239–240, 241, 243; deal for *12 Angry Men*, 98–102; early years, 95; filming *Mister Roberts*, 80, 96–97; founding Orion, 98; as Juror 8, 115, 117, 128, 140, 195; military service, 95–96; "The Petrified Forest," 98–99; producer of *12 Angry Men*, 113–114, 116, 121, 124, 126, 130, 135–139, 150; *War and Peace*, 98; *The Wrong Man*, 118–120
Fonda, Jane, 240
Fonda, Peter, 240
Foote, Horton, 34, 146, 195
For the People (TV show), 178
Ford Foundation, 89
Ford, Glen, 139
Ford, John, 88, 95–96
Ford's Theater, Washington, DC, 233
Fordham University Law School, 217
"Formula, The" (Rose *Studio One* episode), 28
Foro Cultural Chapultepec, 237
Forward, 12
Four Girls in Town (1957 film), 140
Fox Movietone Studios, 2, 42, 121, 125–126, 223, 242

Phil Rosenzweig is a professor of business administration at IMD in Lausanne, Switzerland, where he has used *12 Angry Men* for many years to teach executives about interpersonal behavior and group dynamics. He is author of *The Halo Effect . . . and the Eight Other Delusions That Deceive Managers*, an award-winning book translated into fourteen languages. He received his PhD from the Wharton School, University of Pennsylvania.

EMPIRE STATE EDITIONS

SELECT TITLES FROM EMPIRE STATE EDITIONS

Patrick Bunyan, *All Around the Town: Amazing Manhattan Facts and Curiosities*, Second Edition

Salvatore Basile, *Fifth Avenue Famous: The Extraordinary Story of Music at St. Patrick's Cathedral*. Foreword by Most Reverend Timothy M. Dolan, Archbishop of New York

William Seraile, *Angels of Mercy: White Women and the History of New York's Colored Orphan Asylum*

Anthony D. Andreassi, C.O., *Teach Me to Be Generous: The First Century of Regis High School in New York City*. Foreword by Timothy Michael Cardinal Dolan, Archbishop of New York

Daniel Campo, *The Accidental Playground: Brooklyn Waterfront Narratives of the Undesigned and Unplanned*

Gerard R. Wolfe, *The Synagogues of New York's Lower East Side: A Retrospective and Contemporary View, Second Edition*. Photographs by Jo Renée Fine and Norman Borden, Foreword by Joseph Berger

Joseph B. Raskin, *The Routes Not Taken: A Trip Through New York City's Unbuilt Subway System*

Phillip Deery, *Red Apple: Communism and McCarthyism in Cold War New York*

North Brother Island: The Last Unknown Place in New York City. Photographs by Christopher Payne, A History by Randall Mason, Essay by Robert Sullivan

Stephen Miller, *Walking New York: Reflections of American Writers from Walt Whitman to Teju Cole*

R. Scott Hanson, *City of Gods: Religious Freedom, Immigration, and Pluralism in Flushing, Queens*. Foreword by Martin E. Marty

Dorothy Day and the Catholic Worker: The Miracle of Our Continuance. Edited, with an Introduction and Additional Text by Kate Hennessy, Photographs by Vivian Cherry, Text by Dorothy Day

Mark Naison and Bob Gumbs, *Before the Fires: An Oral History of African American Life in the Bronx from the 1930s to the 1960s*

Sharon Egretta Sutton, *When Ivory Towers Were Black: A Story about Race in America's Cities and Universities*

David J. Goodwin, *Left Bank of the Hudson: Jersey City and the Artists of 111 1st Street*. Foreword by DW Gibson

Nandini Bagchee, *Counter Institution: Activist Estates of the Lower East Side*

Susan Celia Greenfield (ed.), *Sacred Shelter: Thirteen Journeys of Homelessness and Healing*

For a complete list, visit www.fordhampress.com/empire-state-editions.

CPSIA information can be obtained
at www.ICGtesting.com
Printed in the USA
JSHW080734270223
38210JS00002BA/4